Monster Musume 5
Technicolor Bathing Beauties

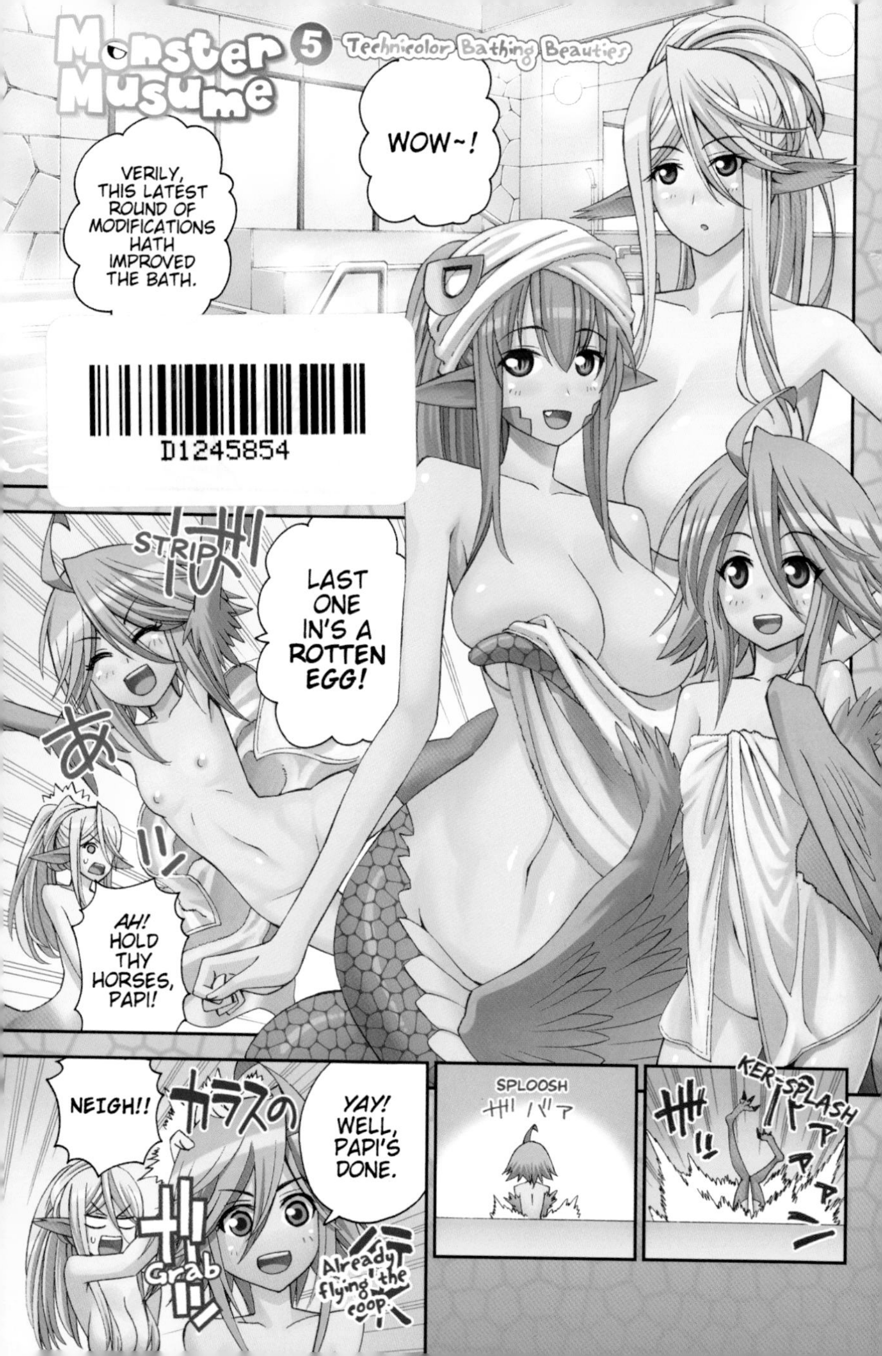
WOW~!
VERILY, THIS LATEST ROUND OF MODIFICATIONS HATH IMPROVED THE BATH.
STRIP
LAST ONE IN'S A ROTTEN EGG!
AH! HOLD THY HORSES, PAPI!
KER-SPLASH
SPLOOSH
YAY! WELL, PAPI'S DONE.
NEIGH!!
カラスの
Grab
Already flying the coop.

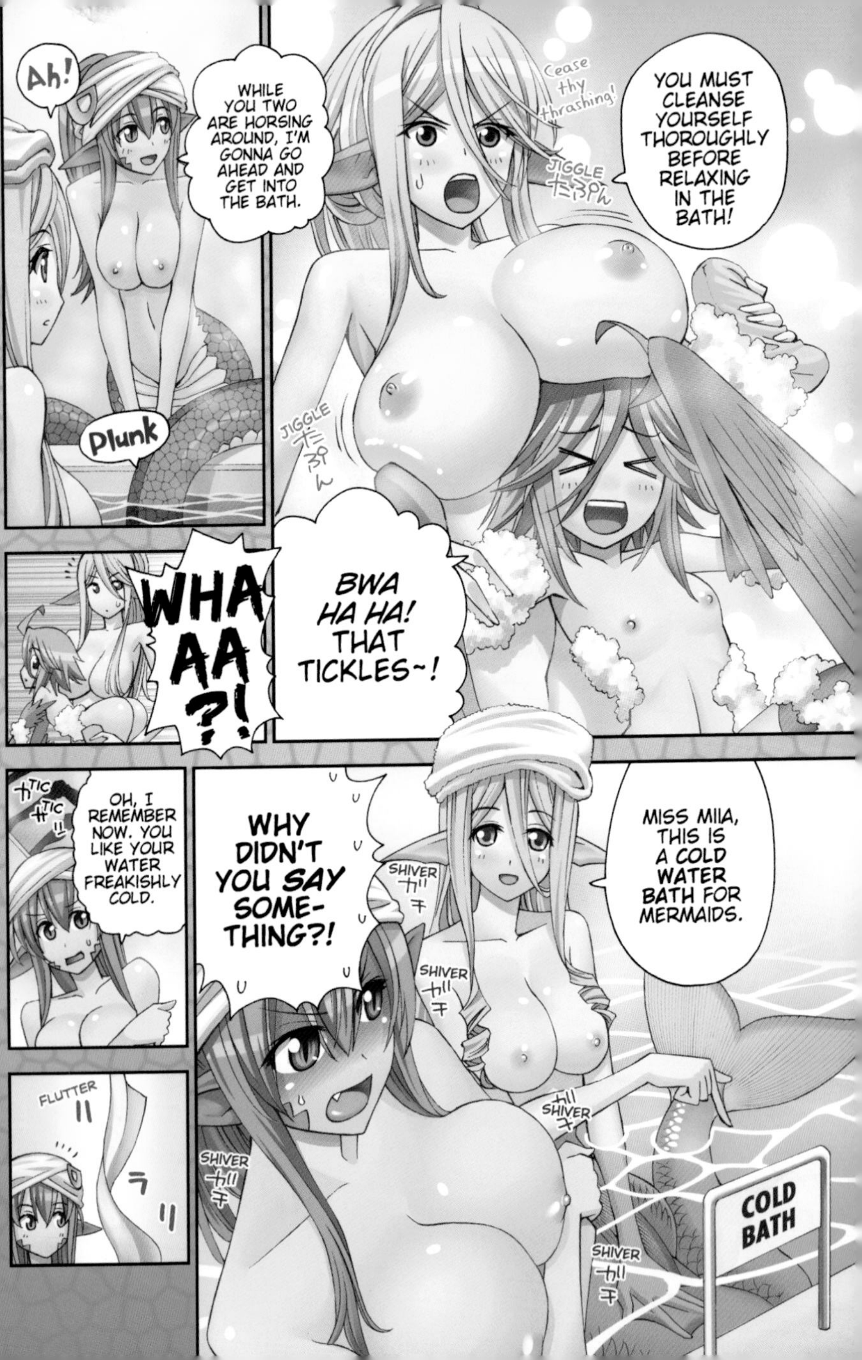

Cease thy thrashing!
YOU MUST CLEANSE YOURSELF THOROUGHLY BEFORE RELAXING IN THE BATH!
JIGGLE たぷん
JIGGLE たぷん
BWA HA HA! THAT TICKLES~!
WHILE YOU TWO ARE HORSING AROUND, I'M GONNA GO AHEAD AND GET INTO THE BATH.
Ah!
Plunk
WHAAA?!
MISS MIIA, THIS IS A COLD WATER BATH FOR MERMAIDS.
WHY DIDN'T YOU SAY SOMETHING?!
SHIVER ガチ
SHIVER ガチ
SHIVER ガチ
SHIVER ガチ
SHIVER ガチ
COLD BATH
ガTIC ガTIC
OH, I REMEMBER NOW. YOU LIKE YOUR WATER FREAKISHLY COLD.
FLUTTER

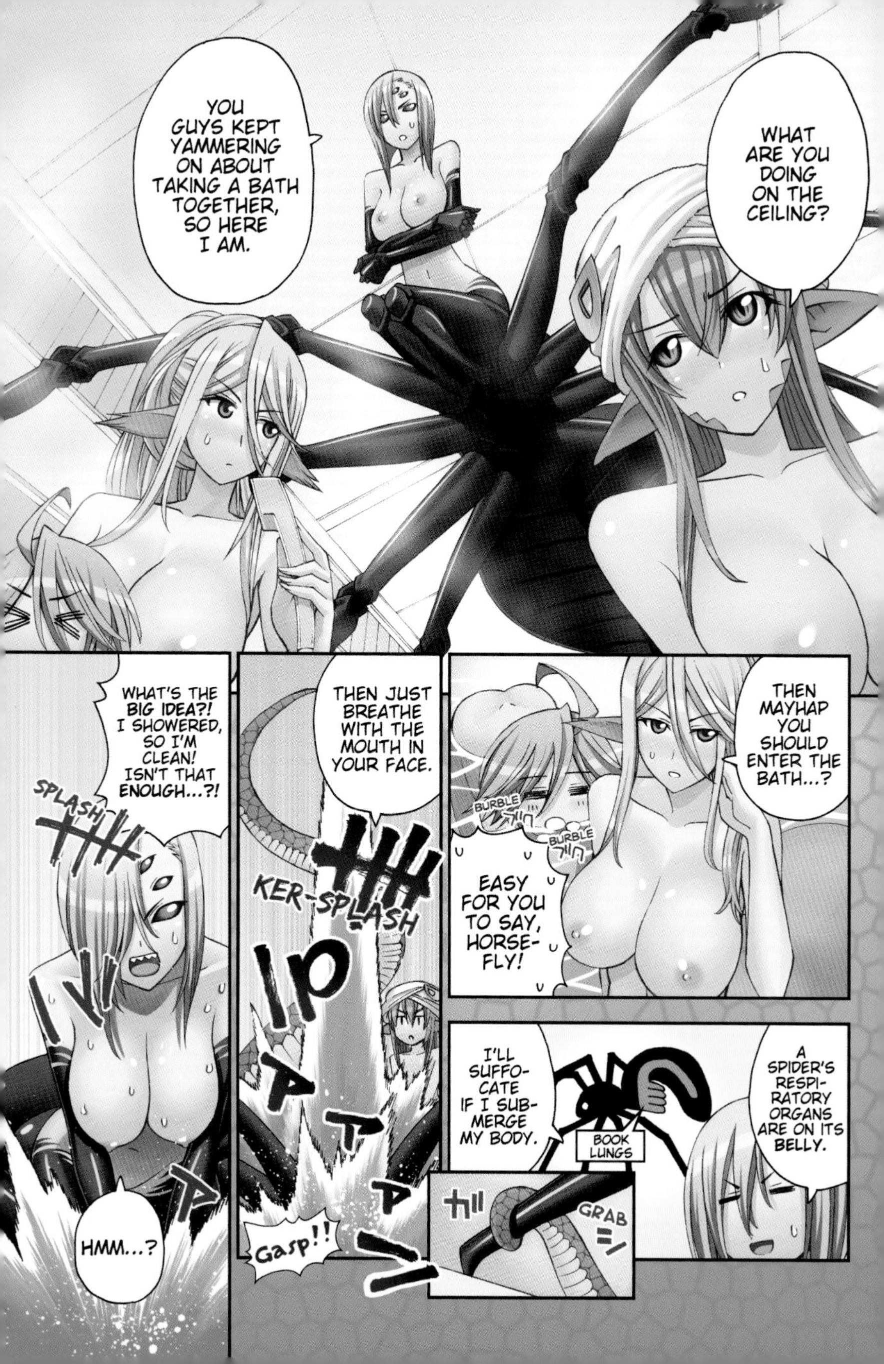
WHAT ARE YOU DOING ON THE CEILING?
YOU GUYS KEPT YAMMERING ON ABOUT TAKING A BATH TOGETHER, SO HERE I AM.
THEN MAYHAP YOU SHOULD ENTER THE BATH...?
BURBLE
BURBLE
EASY FOR YOU TO SAY, HORSE-FLY!
A SPIDER'S RESPI-RATORY ORGANS ARE ON ITS BELLY.
BOOK LUNGS
I'LL SUFFO-CATE IF I SUB-MERGE MY BODY.
GRAB
THEN JUST BREATHE WITH THE MOUTH IN YOUR FACE.
KER-SPLASH
Gasp!!
WHAT'S THE BIG IDEA?! I SHOWERED, SO I'M CLEAN! ISN'T THAT ENOUGH...?!
SPLASH
HMM...?

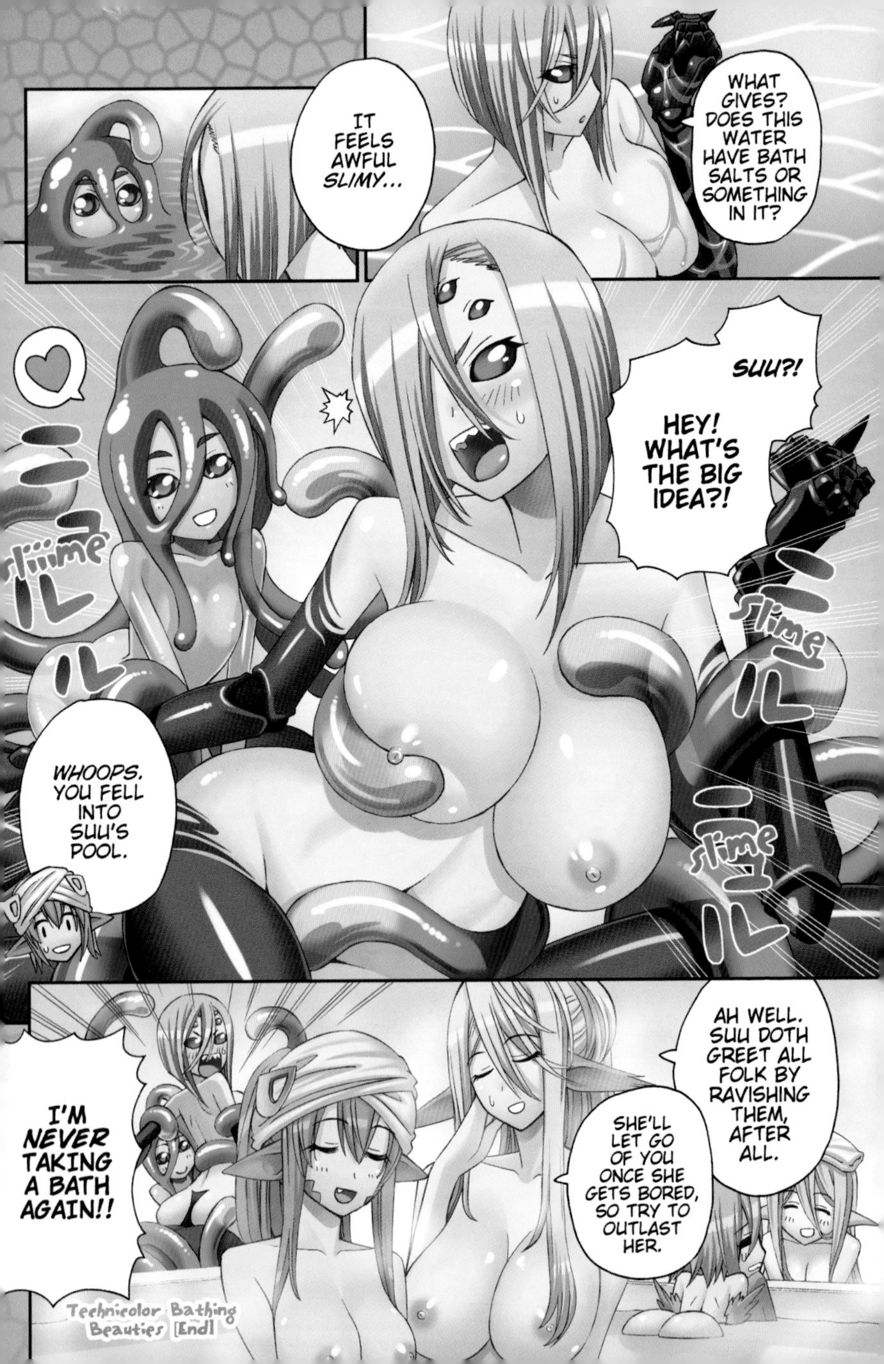
WHAT GIVES? DOES THIS WATER HAVE BATH SALTS OR SOMETHING IN IT?
IT FEELS AWFUL *SLIMY*...
SUU?!
HEY! WHAT'S THE BIG IDEA?!
slime
slime
sliiime
WHOOPS. YOU FELL INTO SUU'S POOL.
AH WELL. SUU DOTH GREET ALL FOLK BY RAVISHING THEM, AFTER ALL.
SHE'LL LET GO OF YOU ONCE SHE GETS BORED, SO TRY TO OUTLAST HER.
I'M *NEVER* TAKING A BATH AGAIN!!
Technicolor Bathing Beauties [End]

Chapter 19

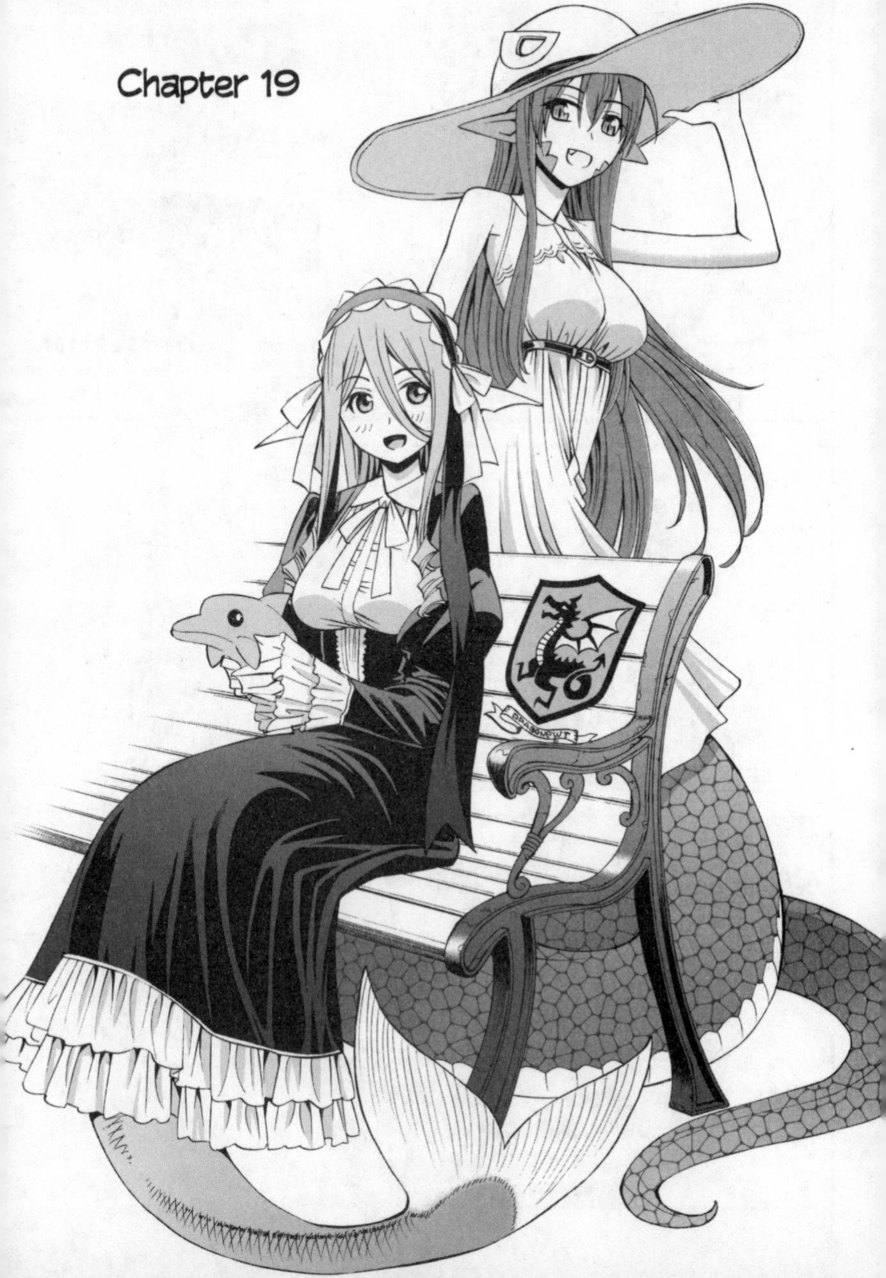
DRAGONEWT

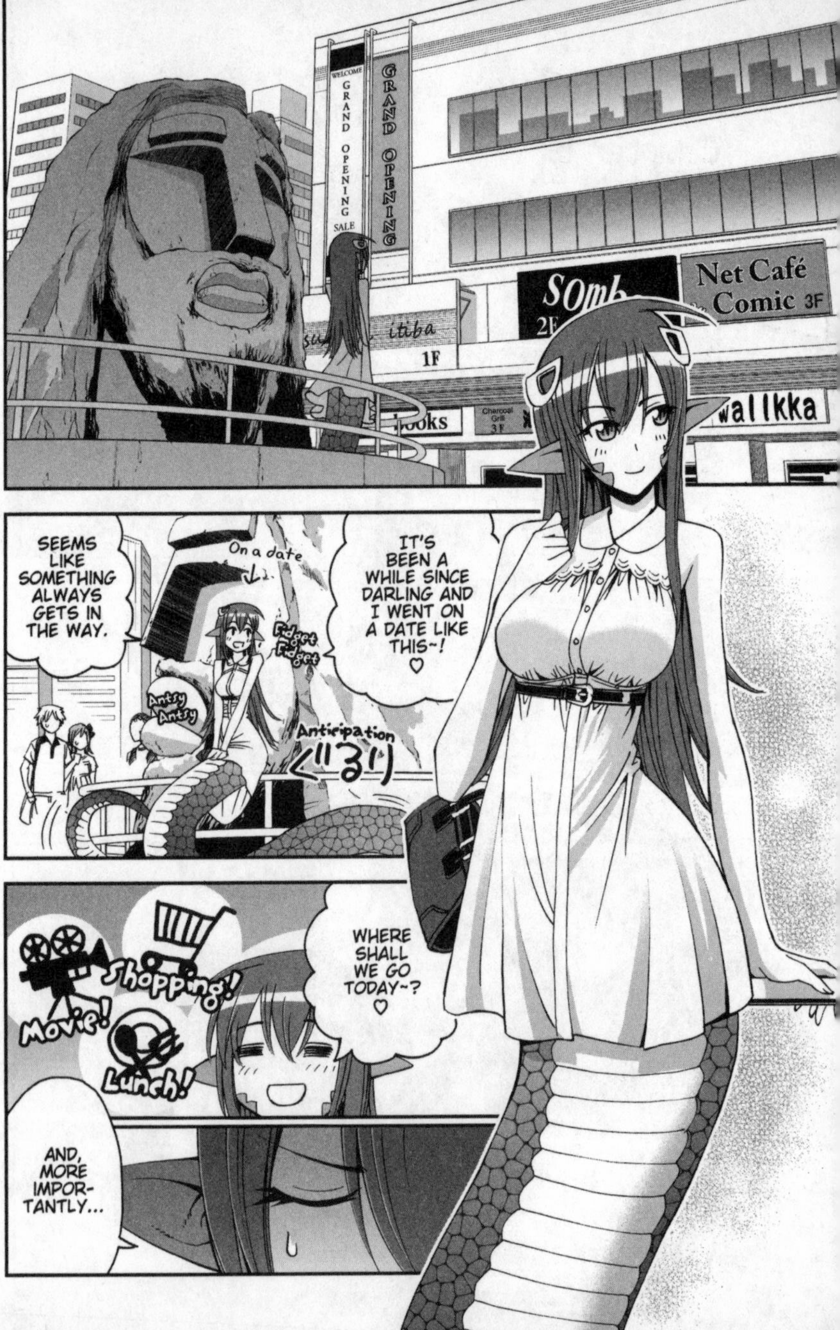
WELCOME
GRAND OPENING SALE
GRAND OPENING
Net Café
Comic 3F
1F
Charcoal Grill 3F
wallkka
IT'S BEEN A WHILE SINCE DARLING AND I WENT ON A DATE LIKE THIS~! ♡
On a date
Fidget Fidget
SEEMS LIKE SOMETHING ALWAYS GETS IN THE WAY.
Antsy Antsy
Anticipation
WHERE SHALL WE GO TODAY~? ♡
Shopping!
Movie!
Lunch!
AND, MORE IMPOR-TANTLY...

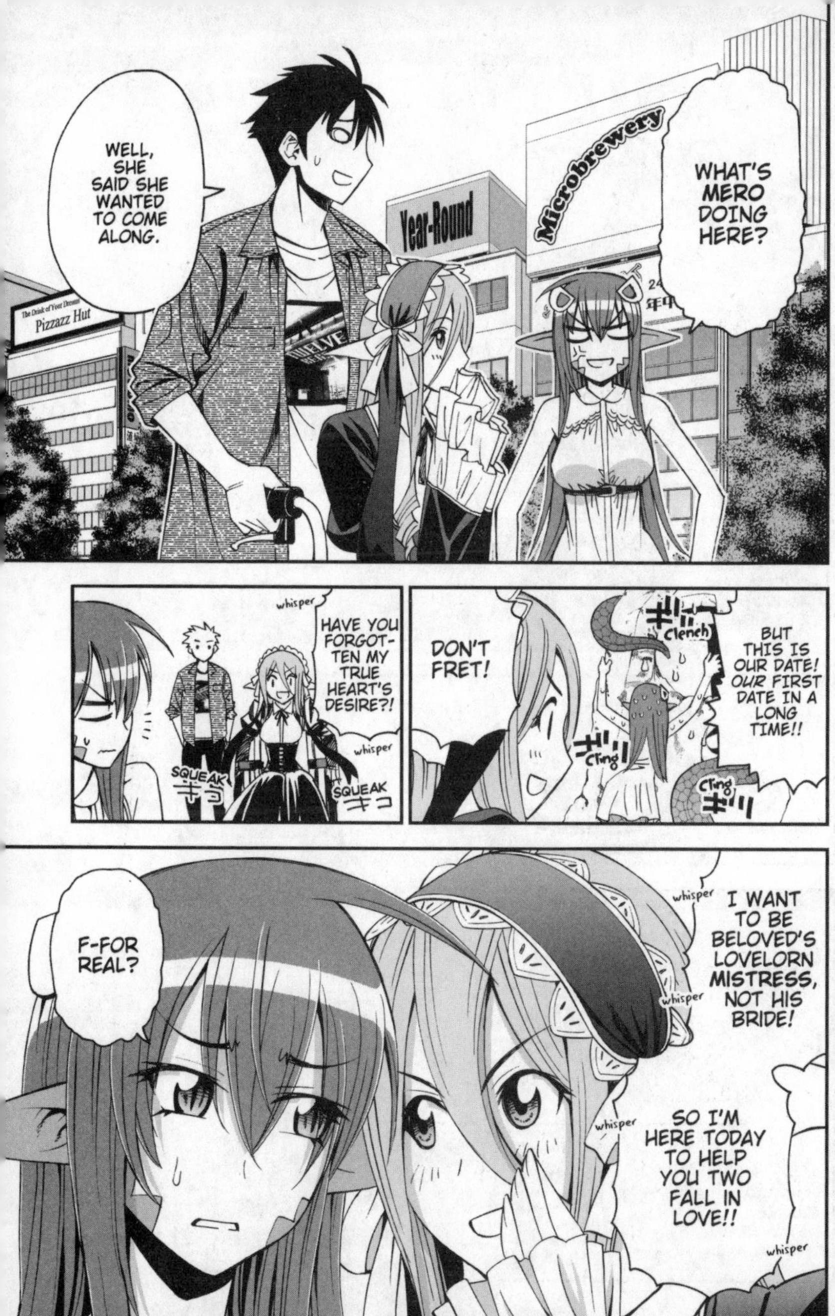
WHAT'S MERO DOING HERE?
Microbrewery
Year-Round
Pizzazz Hut
WELL, SHE SAID SHE WANTED TO COME ALONG.
BUT THIS IS OUR DATE! OUR FIRST DATE IN A LONG TIME!!
Clench
Cling
Cling
DON'T FRET!
whisper
HAVE YOU FORGOT-TEN MY TRUE HEART'S DESIRE?!
whisper
SQUEAK
SQUEAK
whisper
I WANT TO BE BELOVED'S LOVELORN MISTRESS, NOT HIS BRIDE!
whisper
whisper
SO I'M HERE TODAY TO HELP YOU TWO FALL IN LOVE!!
whisper
F-FOR REAL?

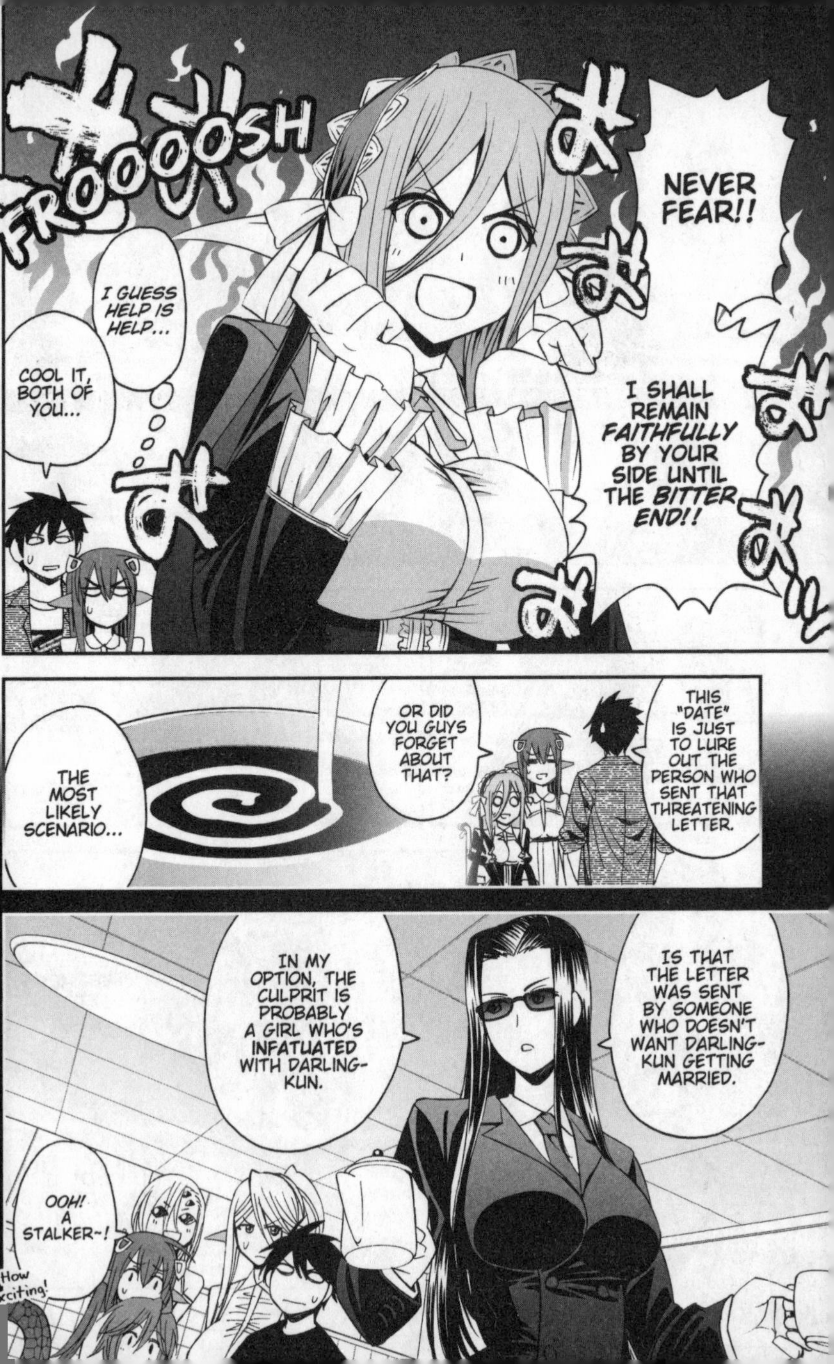
NEVER FEAR!!
I SHALL REMAIN *FAITHFULLY* BY YOUR SIDE UNTIL THE *BITTER END!!*
FROOOOSH
I GUESS HELP IS HELP...
COOL IT, BOTH OF YOU...
THIS "DATE" IS JUST TO LURE OUT THE PERSON WHO SENT THAT THREATENING LETTER.
OR DID YOU GUYS FORGET ABOUT THAT?
THE MOST LIKELY SCENARIO...
IS THAT THE LETTER WAS SENT BY SOMEONE WHO DOESN'T WANT DARLING-KUN GETTING MARRIED.
IN MY OPTION, THE CULPRIT IS PROBABLY A GIRL WHO'S INFATUATED WITH DARLING-KUN.
OOH! A STALKER~!
How exciting!

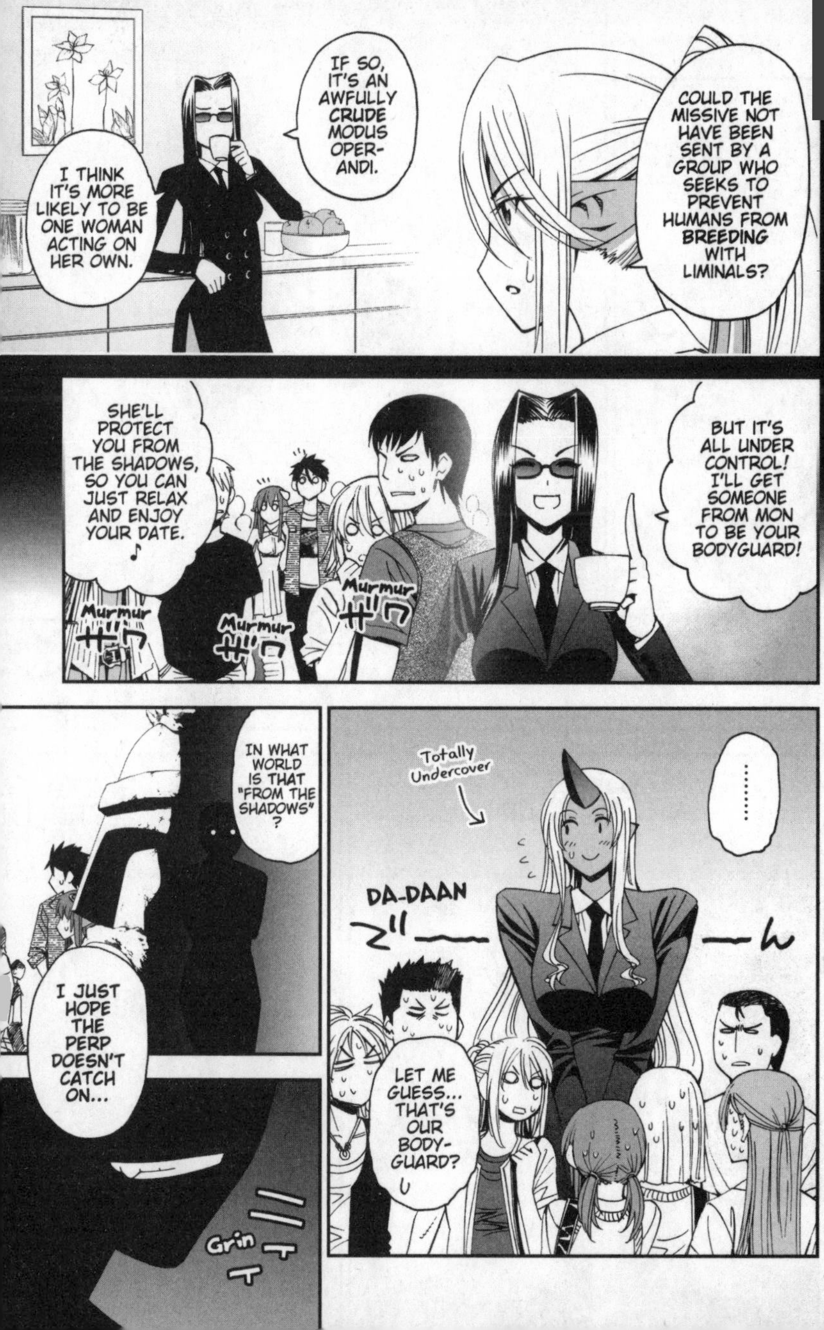
COULD THE MISSIVE NOT HAVE BEEN SENT BY A GROUP WHO SEEKS TO PREVENT HUMANS FROM BREEDING WITH LIMINALS?
IF SO, IT'S AN AWFULLY CRUDE MODUS OPER-ANDI.
I THINK IT'S MORE LIKELY TO BE ONE WOMAN ACTING ON HER OWN.
BUT IT'S ALL UNDER CONTROL! I'LL GET SOMEONE FROM MON TO BE YOUR BODYGUARD!
SHE'LL PROTECT YOU FROM THE SHADOWS, SO YOU CAN JUST RELAX AND ENJOY YOUR DATE. ♪
Murmur
Murmur
Murmur
......
Totally Undercover
DA-DAAN
LET ME GUESS... THAT'S OUR BODY-GUARD?
IN WHAT WORLD IS THAT "FROM THE SHADOWS"?
I JUST HOPE THE PERP DOESN'T CATCH ON...
Grin

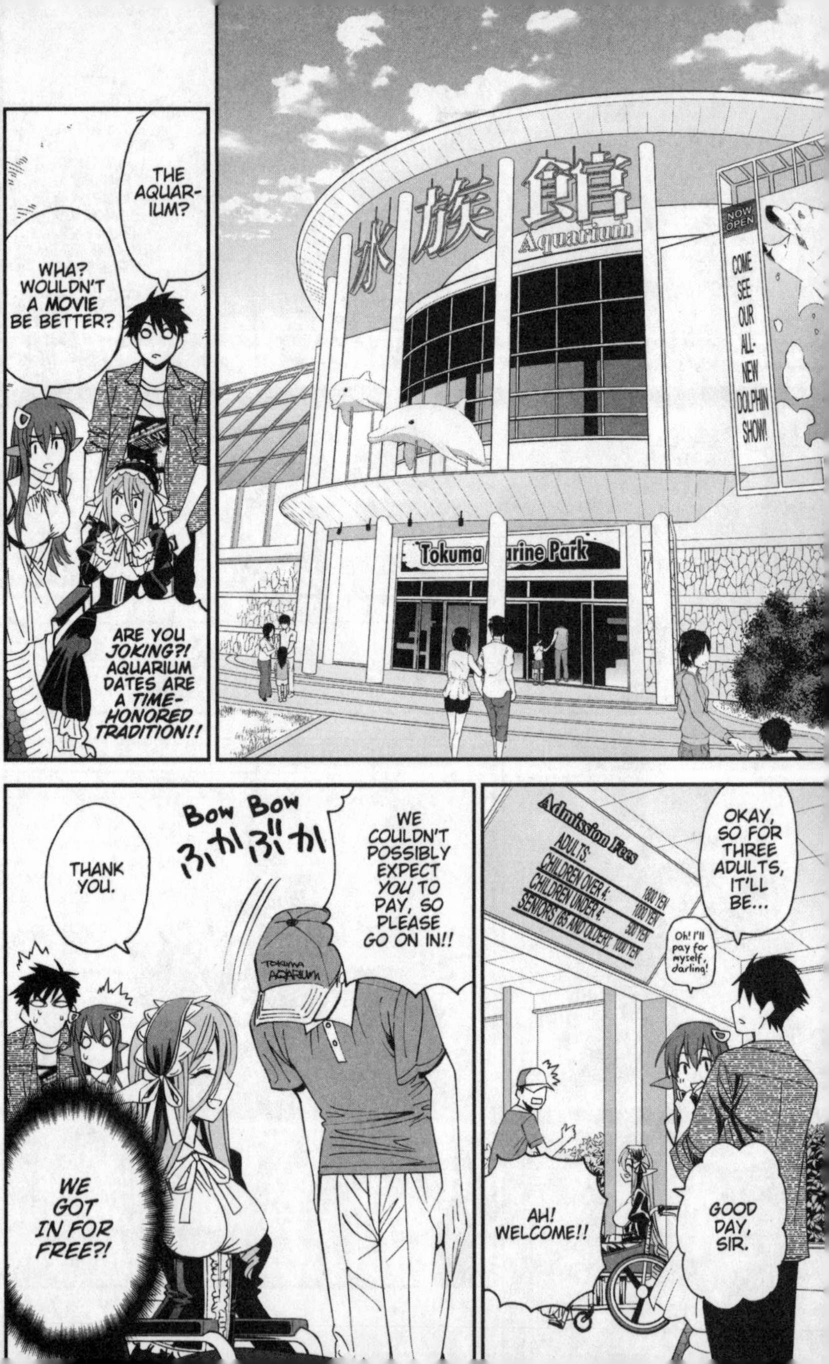

水族館
Aquarium
NOW OPEN
COME SEE OUR ALL-NEW DOLPHIN SHOW!
Tokuma arine Park
THE AQUARIUM?
WHA? WOULDN'T A MOVIE BE BETTER?
ARE YOU *JOKING*?! AQUARIUM DATES ARE A *TIME-HONORED TRADITION*!!
Admission Fees
ADULTS: 1800 YEN
CHILDREN OVER 4: 1000 YEN
CHILDREN UNDER 4: 500 YEN
SENIORS (65 AND OLDER): 1000 YEN
OKAY, SO FOR THREE ADULTS, IT'LL BE...
Oh! I'll pay for myself, darling!
GOOD DAY, SIR.
AH! WELCOME!!
Bow Bow
ふかぶか
WE COULDN'T POSSIBLY EXPECT *YOU* TO PAY, SO PLEASE GO ON IN!!
TOKUMA AQUARIUM
THANK YOU.
WE GOT IN FOR FREE?!

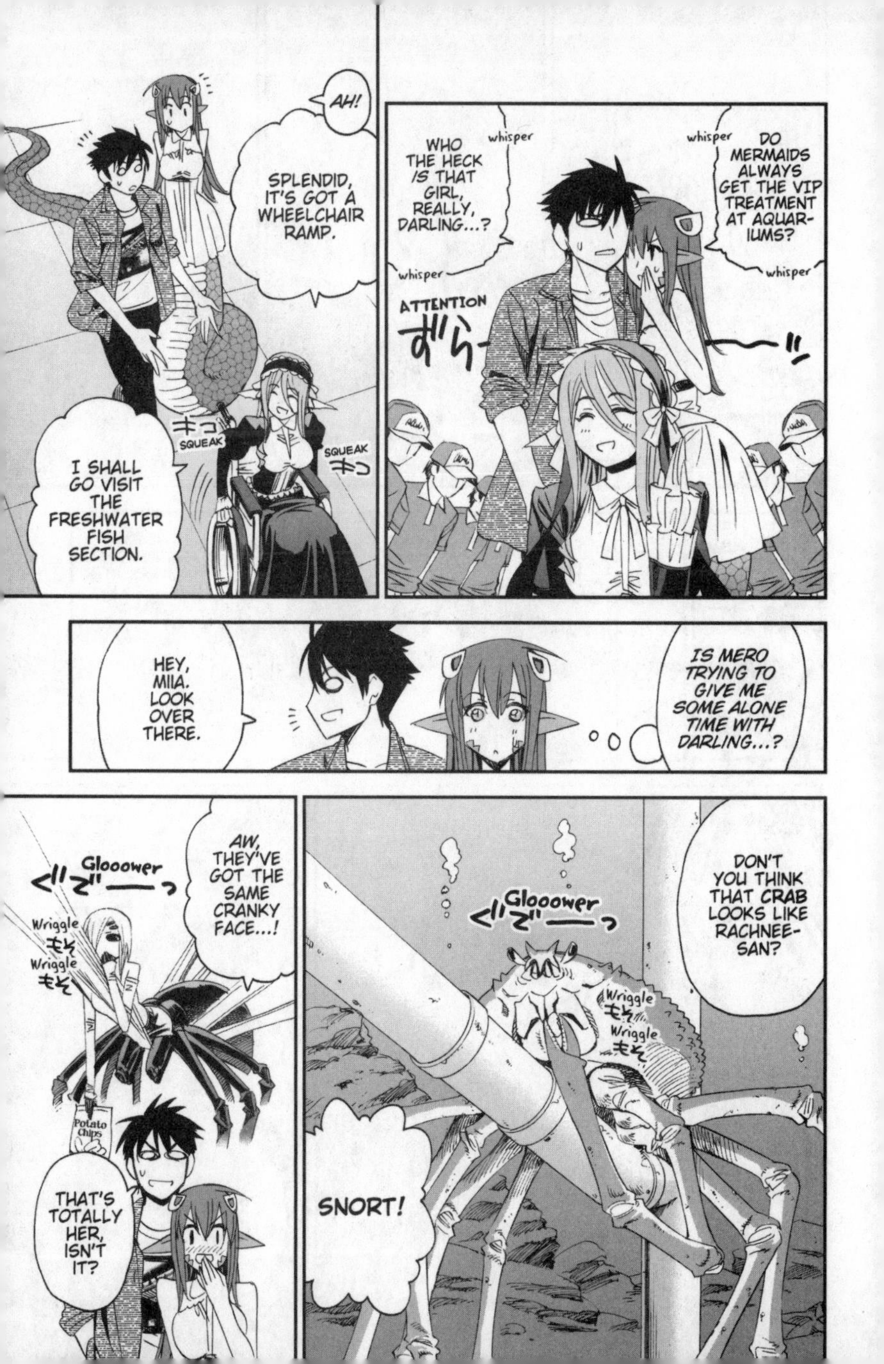
whisper
DO MERMAIDS ALWAYS GET THE VIP TREATMENT AT AQUARIUMS?
whisper
whisper
WHO THE HECK IS THAT GIRL, REALLY, DARLING...?
whisper
ATTENTION
ずら〜〜〜
AH!
SPLENDID, IT'S GOT A WHEELCHAIR RAMP.
SQUEAK
キコ
SQUEAK
キコ
I SHALL GO VISIT THE FRESHWATER FISH SECTION.
IS MERO TRYING TO GIVE ME SOME ALONE TIME WITH DARLING...?
HEY, MIIA. LOOK OVER THERE.
DON'T YOU THINK THAT CRAB LOOKS LIKE RACHNEE-SAN?
Gloooower
ぐぞ〜っ
Wriggle
もそ
Wriggle
もそ
SNORT!
AW, THEY'VE GOT THE SAME CRANKY FACE...!
Gloooower
ぐぞ〜っ
Wriggle
もそ
Wriggle
もそ
Potato Chips
THAT'S TOTALLY HER, ISN'T IT?

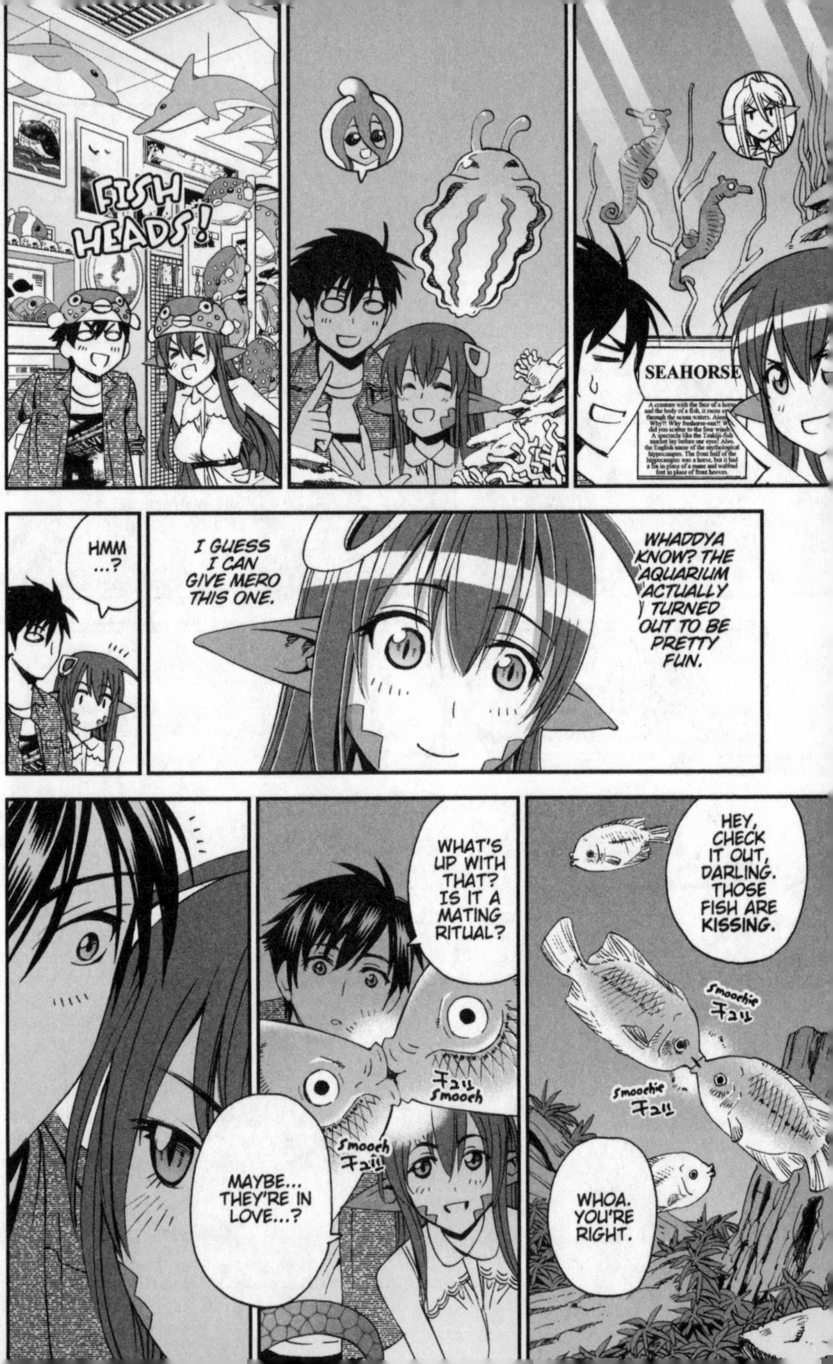
SEAHORSE
A creature with the face of a hors
and the body of a fish, it races s
through the ocean waters. Aiee
Why?! Why Seahorse-san?! W
did you scatter to the four winds
A spectacle like the Tsukiji-fish market lay before our eyes! Also, the English name of the mythological hippocampus. The front half of the hippocampus was a horse, but it had a fin in place of a mane and webbed feet in place of front hooves.
FISH HEADS!
WHADDYA KNOW? THE AQUARIUM ACTUALLY TURNED OUT TO BE PRETTY FUN.
I GUESS I CAN GIVE MERO THIS ONE.
HMM ...?
HEY, CHECK IT OUT, DARLING. THOSE FISH ARE KISSING.
Smoochie
Smoochie
WHOA. YOU'RE RIGHT.
WHAT'S UP WITH THAT? IS IT A MATING RITUAL?
Smooch
Smooch
MAYBE... THEY'RE IN LOVE...?

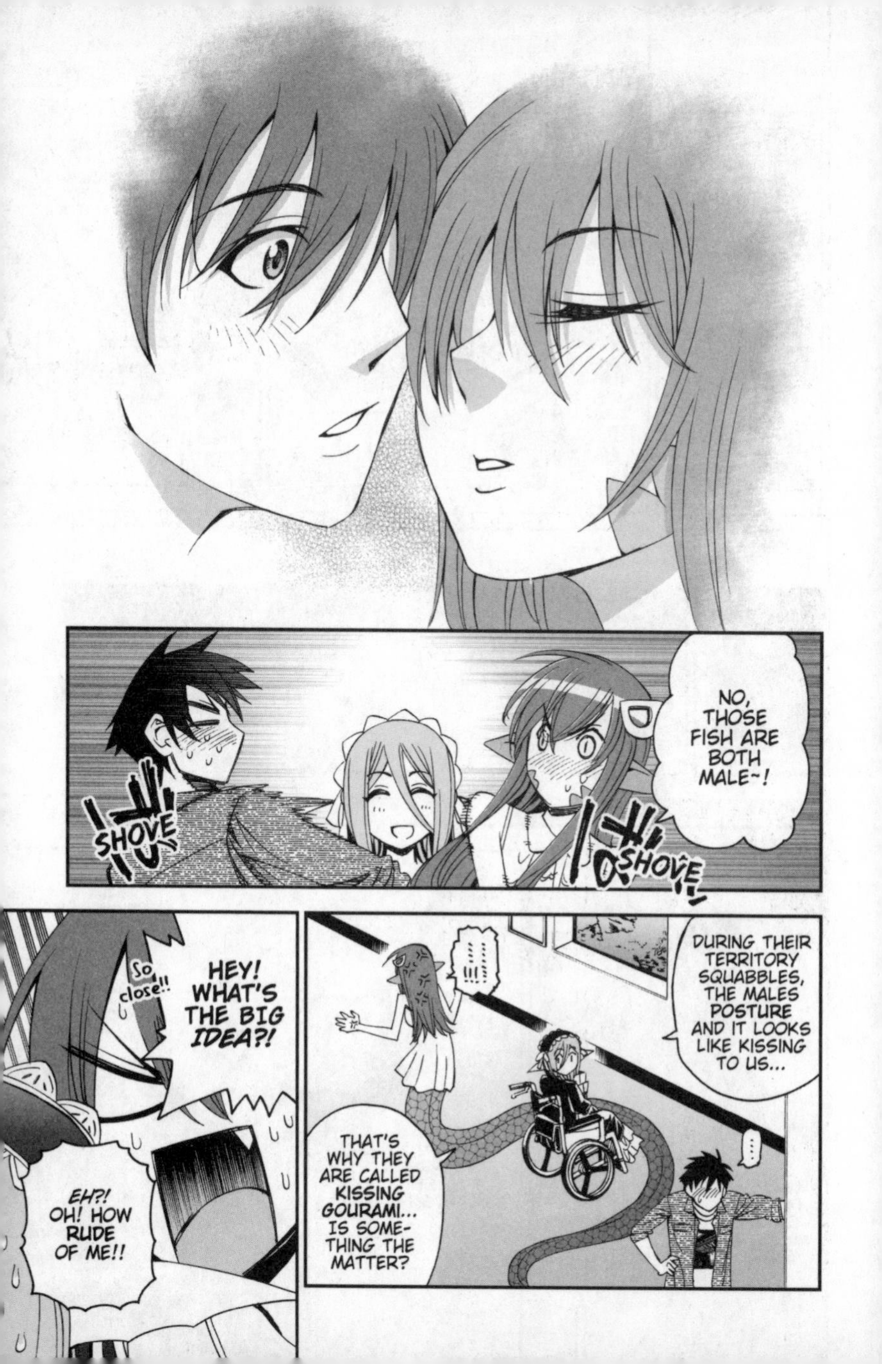
NO, THOSE FISH ARE BOTH MALE~!
SHOVE
SHOVE
DURING THEIR TERRITORY SQUABBLES, THE MALES POSTURE AND IT LOOKS LIKE KISSING TO US...
...!!!
THAT'S WHY THEY ARE CALLED KISSING GOURAMI... IS SOMETHING THE MATTER?
...
HEY! WHAT'S THE BIG IDEA?!
So close!!
EH?! OH! HOW RUDE OF ME!!

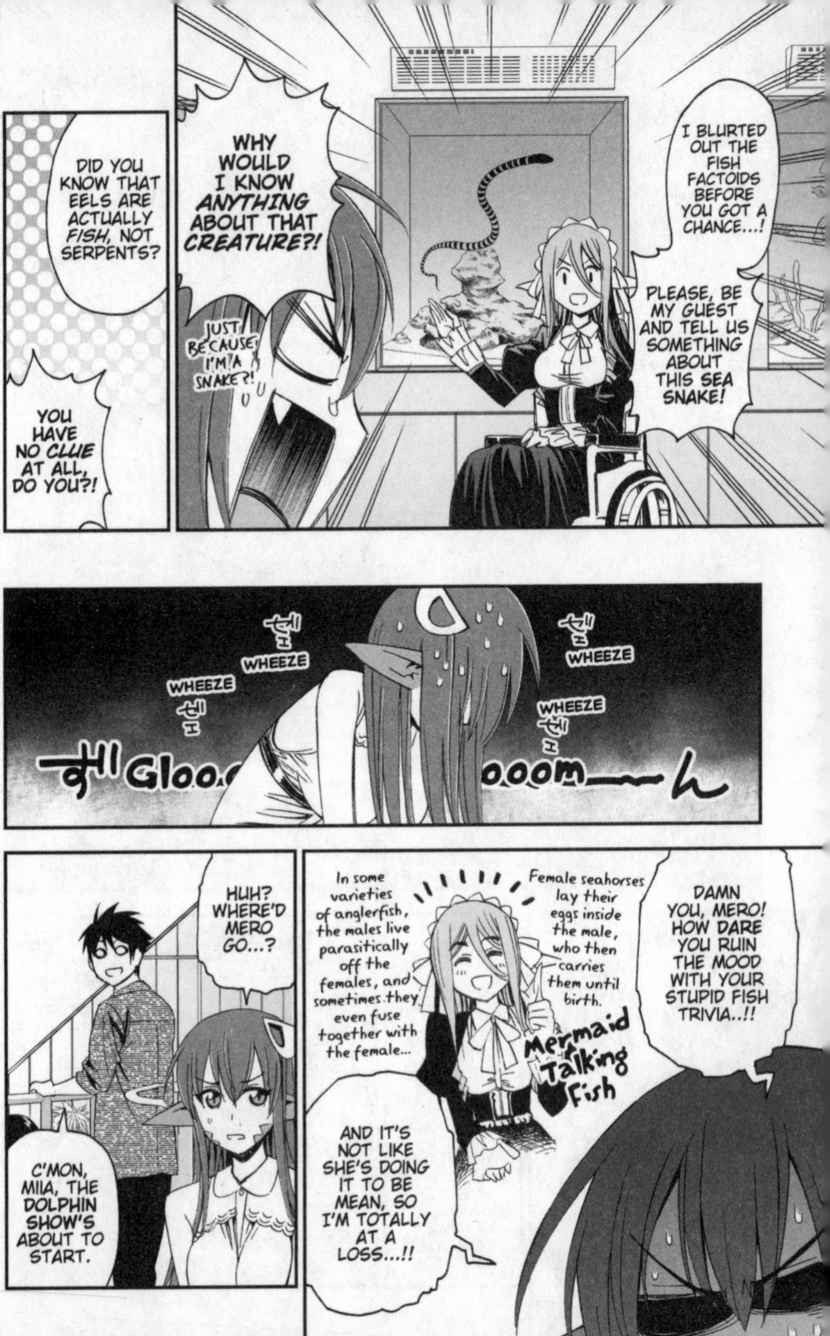
I BLURTED OUT THE FISH FACTOIDS BEFORE YOU GOT A CHANCE...!
PLEASE, BE MY GUEST AND TELL US SOMETHING ABOUT THIS SEA SNAKE!
WHY WOULD I KNOW *ANYTHING* ABOUT THAT *CREATURE?!*
JUST BECAUSE I'M A SNAKE?!
DID YOU KNOW THAT EELS ARE ACTUALLY *FISH*, NOT SERPENTS?
YOU HAVE NO *CLUE* AT ALL, DO YOU?!
WHEEZE
WHEEZE
WHEEZE
WHEEZE
Gloo
ooom
DAMN YOU, MERO! HOW DARE YOU RUIN THE MOOD WITH YOUR STUPID FISH TRIVIA..!!
Female seahorses lay their eggs inside the male, who then carries them until birth.
In some varieties of anglerfish, the males live parasitically off the females, and sometimes they even fuse together with the female...
Mermaid Talking Fish
AND IT'S NOT LIKE SHE'S DOING IT TO BE MEAN, SO I'M TOTALLY AT A LOSS...!!
HUH? WHERE'D MERO GO...?
C'MON, MIIA, THE DOLPHIN SHOW'S ABOUT TO START.

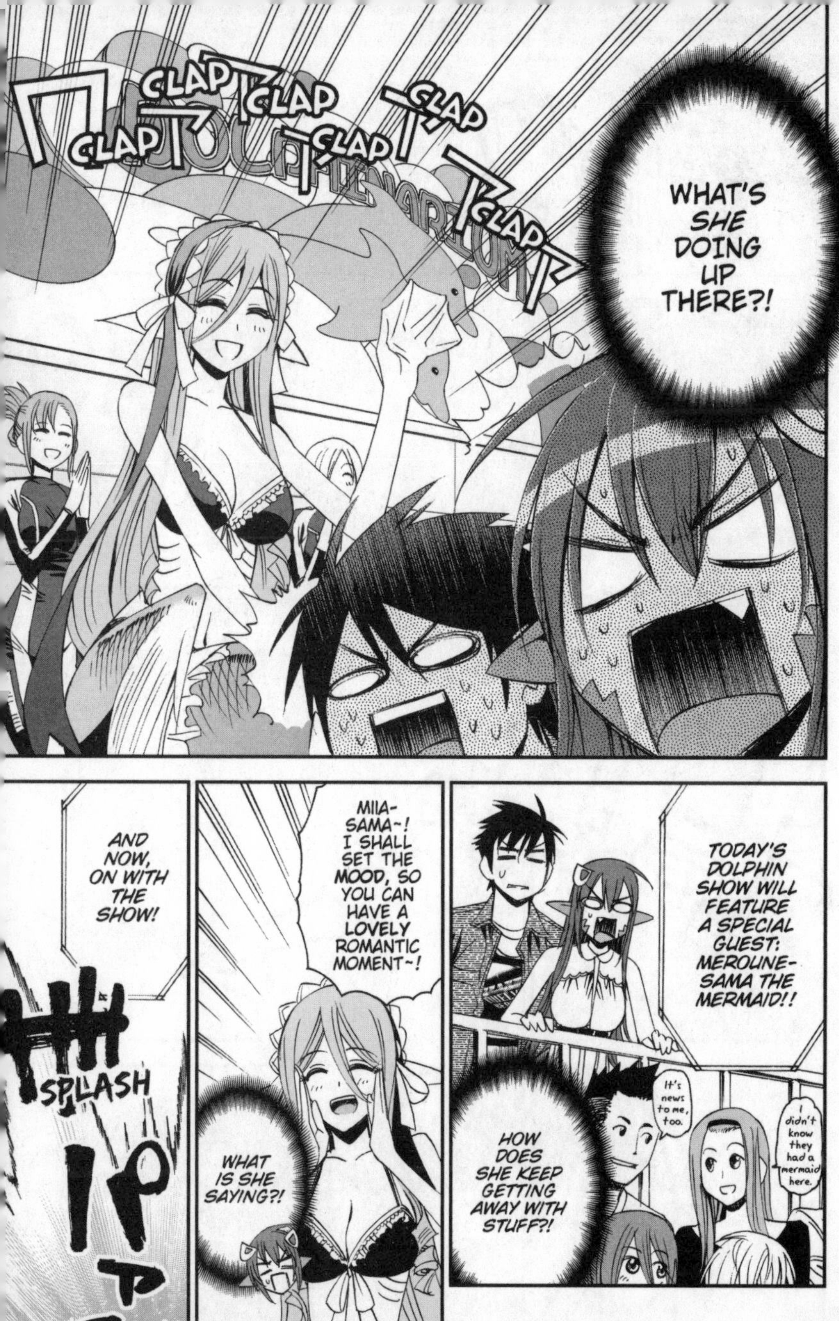
CLAP
CLAP
CLAP
CLAP
CLAP
CLAP
WHAT'S SHE DOING UP THERE?!
TODAY'S DOLPHIN SHOW WILL FEATURE A SPECIAL GUEST: MEROUNE-SAMA THE MERMAID!!
I didn't know they had a mermaid here.
It's news to me, too.
HOW DOES SHE KEEP GETTING AWAY WITH STUFF?!
MIIA-SAMA~! I SHALL SET THE MOOD, SO YOU CAN HAVE A LOVELY ROMANTIC MOMENT~!
WHAT IS SHE SAYING?!
AND NOW, ON WITH THE SHOW!
SPLASH

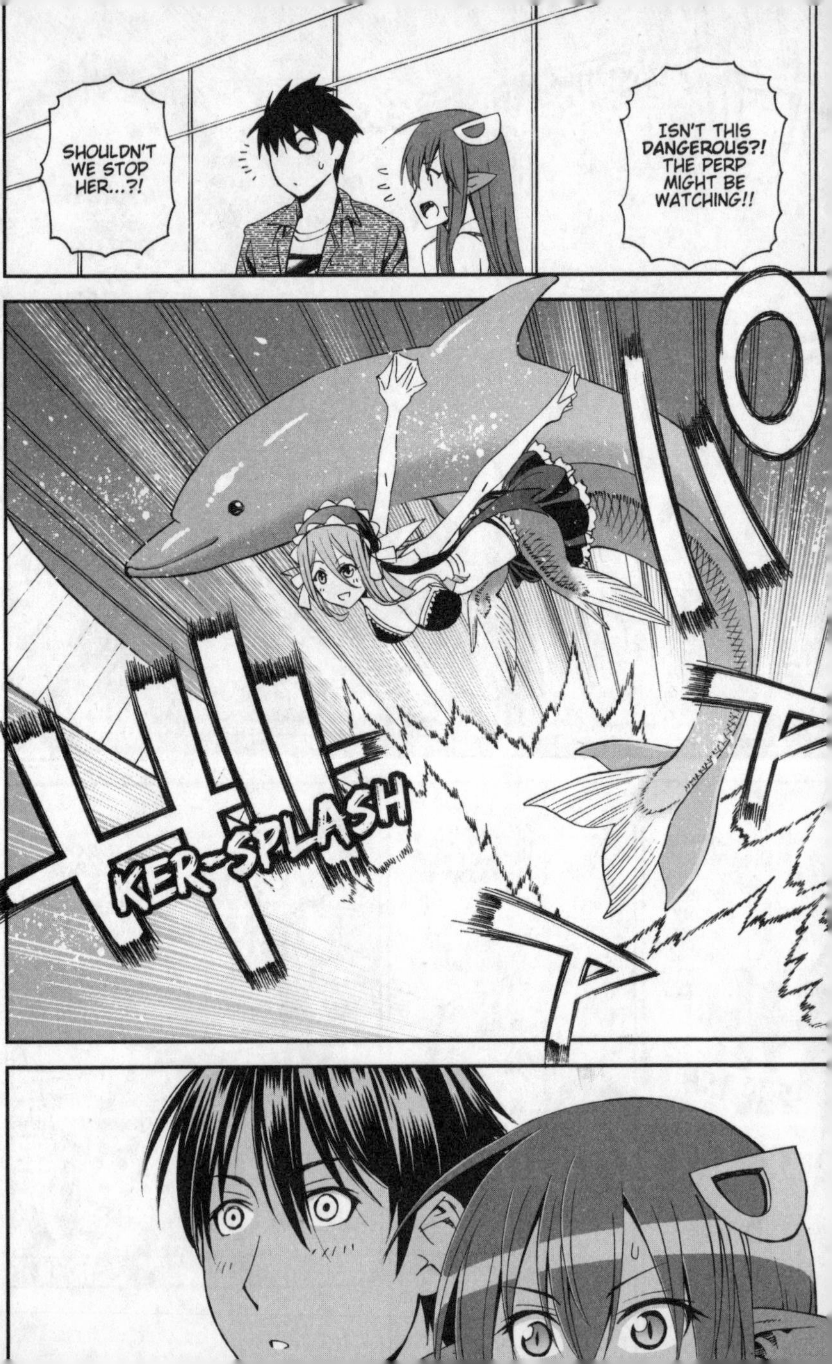
ISN'T THIS DANGEROUS?! THE PERP MIGHT BE WATCHING!!
SHOULDN'T WE STOP HER...?!
KER-SPLASH

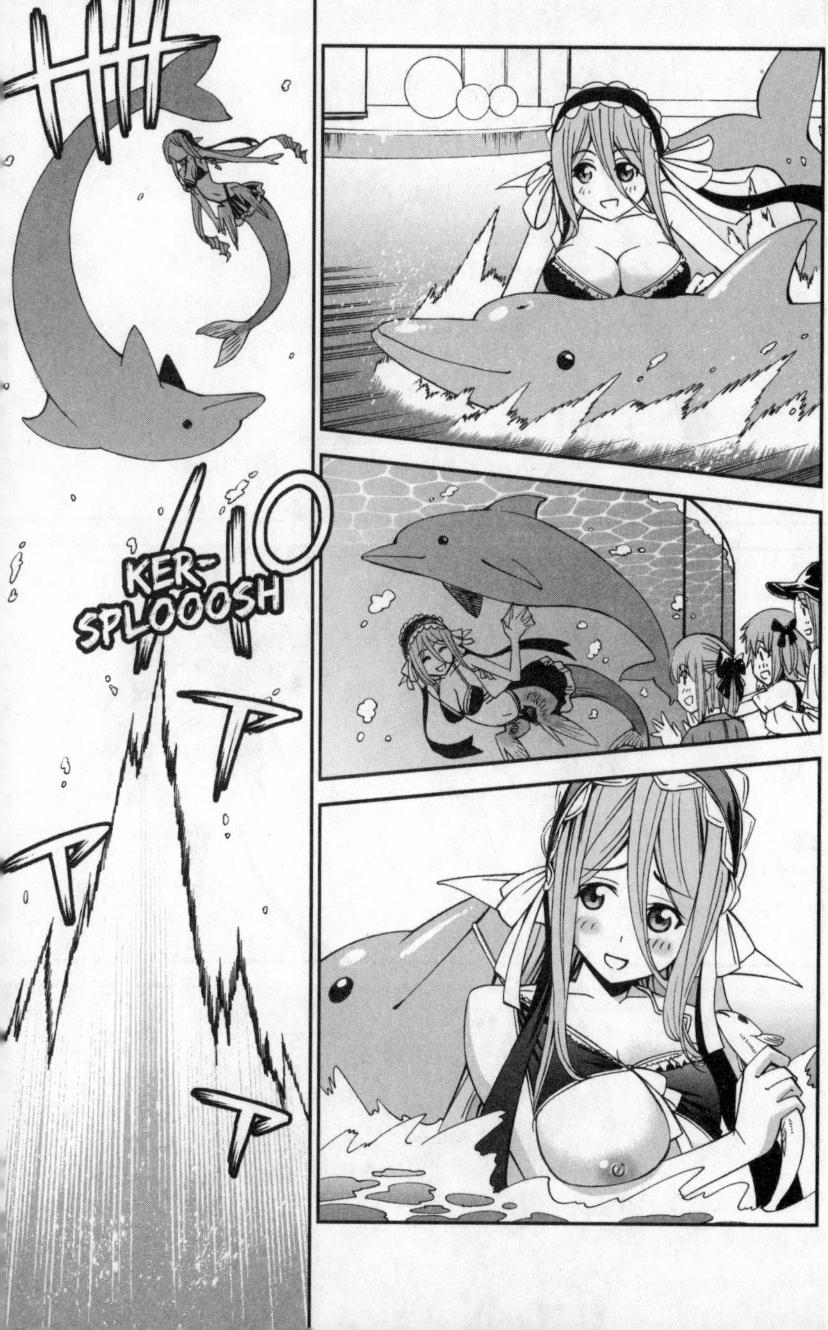
KER-
SPLOOOSH

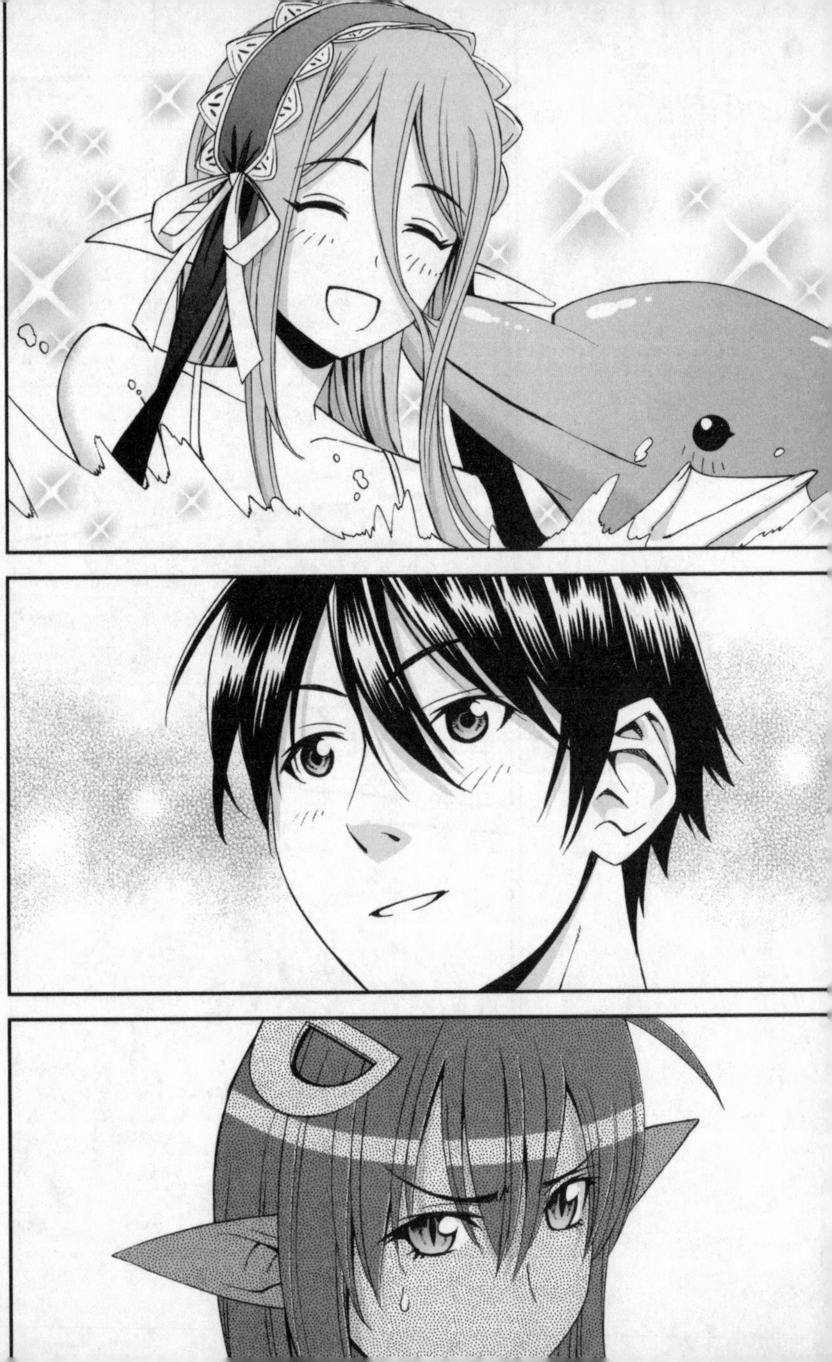

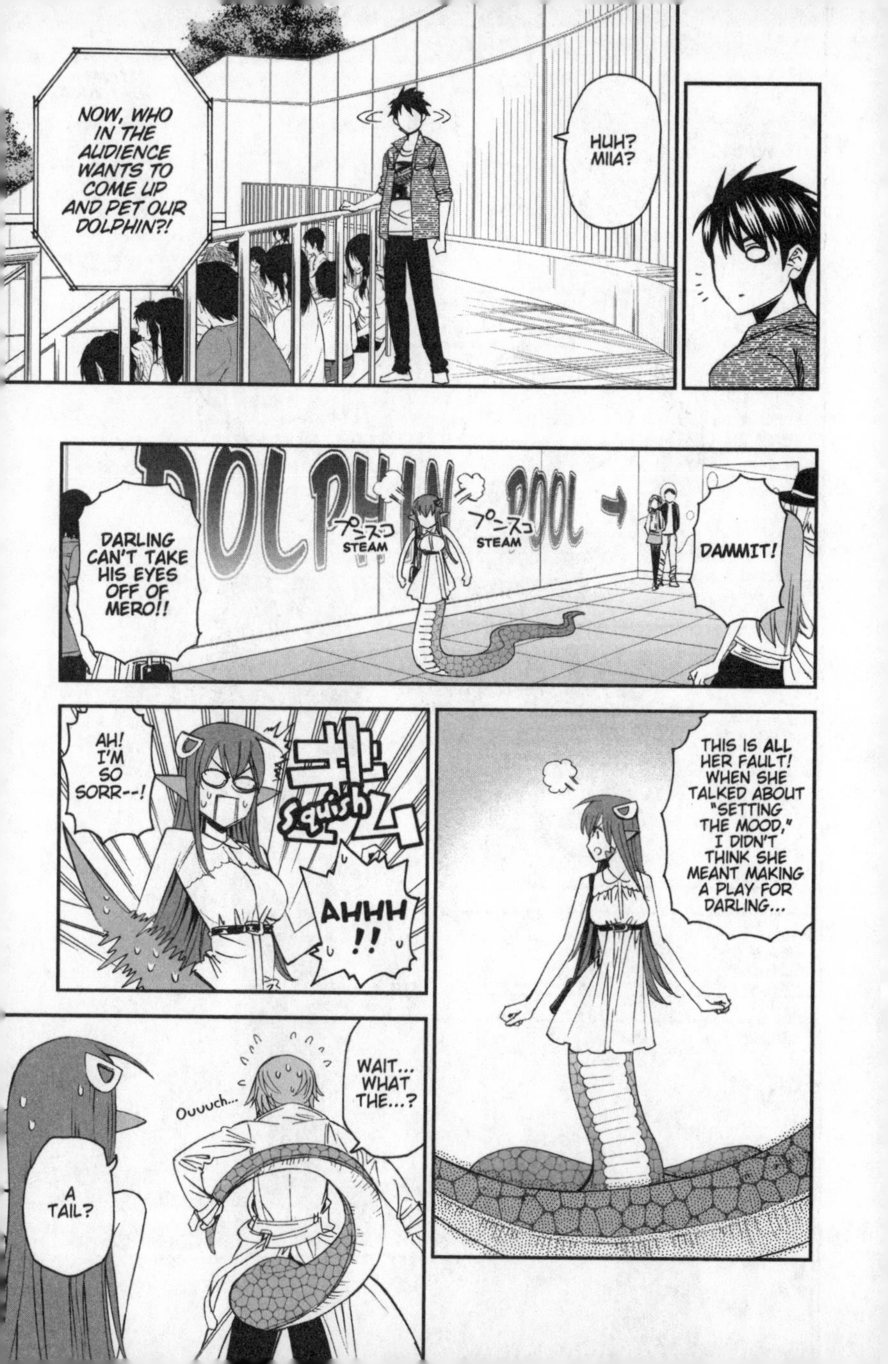
HUH? MIIA?
NOW, WHO IN THE AUDIENCE WANTS TO COME UP AND PET OUR DOLPHIN?!
DAMMIT!
DOLPHIN POOL
プンスコ STEAM
プンスコ STEAM
DARLING CAN'T TAKE HIS EYES OFF OF MERO!!
THIS IS ALL HER FAULT! WHEN SHE TALKED ABOUT "SETTING THE MOOD," I DIDN'T THINK SHE MEANT MAKING A PLAY FOR DARLING...
AH! I'M SO SORR--!
Squish
AHHH!!
WAIT... WHAT THE...?
Ouuuch...
A TAIL?

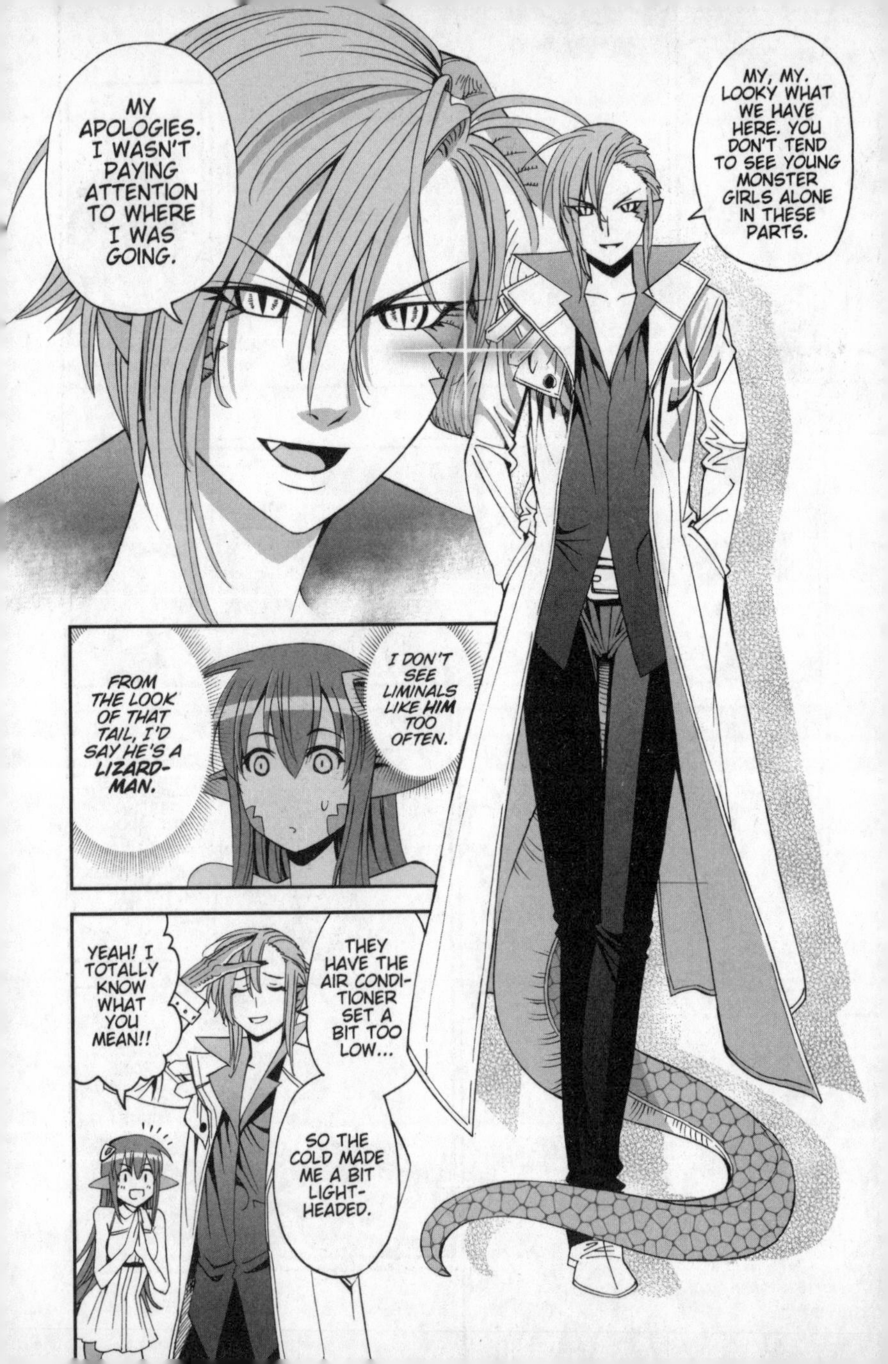
MY, MY. LOOKY WHAT WE HAVE HERE. YOU DON'T TEND TO SEE YOUNG MONSTER GIRLS ALONE IN THESE PARTS.
MY APOLOGIES. I WASN'T PAYING ATTENTION TO WHERE I WAS GOING.
I DON'T SEE LIMINALS LIKE HIM TOO OFTEN.
FROM THE LOOK OF THAT TAIL, I'D SAY HE'S A LIZARD-MAN.
THEY HAVE THE AIR CONDI-TIONER SET A BIT TOO LOW...
SO THE COLD MADE ME A BIT LIGHT-HEADED.
YEAH! I TOTALLY KNOW WHAT YOU MEAN!!

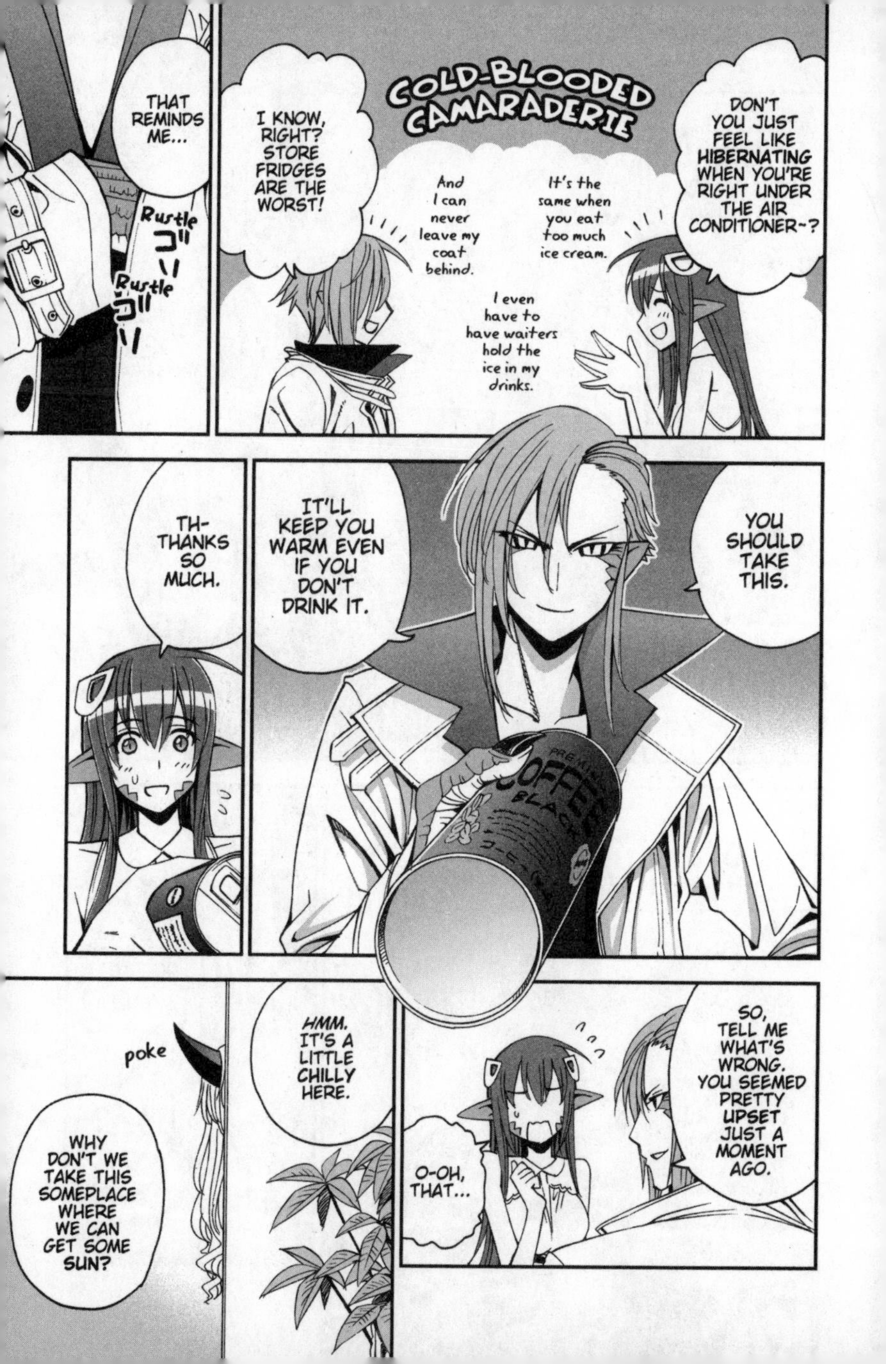
COLD-BLOODED CAMARADERIE
DON'T YOU JUST FEEL LIKE HIBERNATING WHEN YOU'RE RIGHT UNDER THE AIR CONDITIONER~?
I KNOW, RIGHT? STORE FRIDGES ARE THE WORST!
It's the same when you eat too much ice cream.
And I can never leave my coat behind.
I even have to have waiters hold the ice in my drinks.
THAT REMINDS ME...
Rustle ゴソ
Rustle ゴソ
YOU SHOULD TAKE THIS.
IT'LL KEEP YOU WARM EVEN IF YOU DON'T DRINK IT.
PREMIUM COFFEE BLACK
TH-THANKS SO MUCH.
SO, TELL ME WHAT'S WRONG. YOU SEEMED PRETTY UPSET JUST A MOMENT AGO.
O-OH, THAT...
HMM. IT'S A LITTLE CHILLY HERE.
poke
WHY DON'T WE TAKE THIS SOMEPLACE WHERE WE CAN GET SOME SUN?

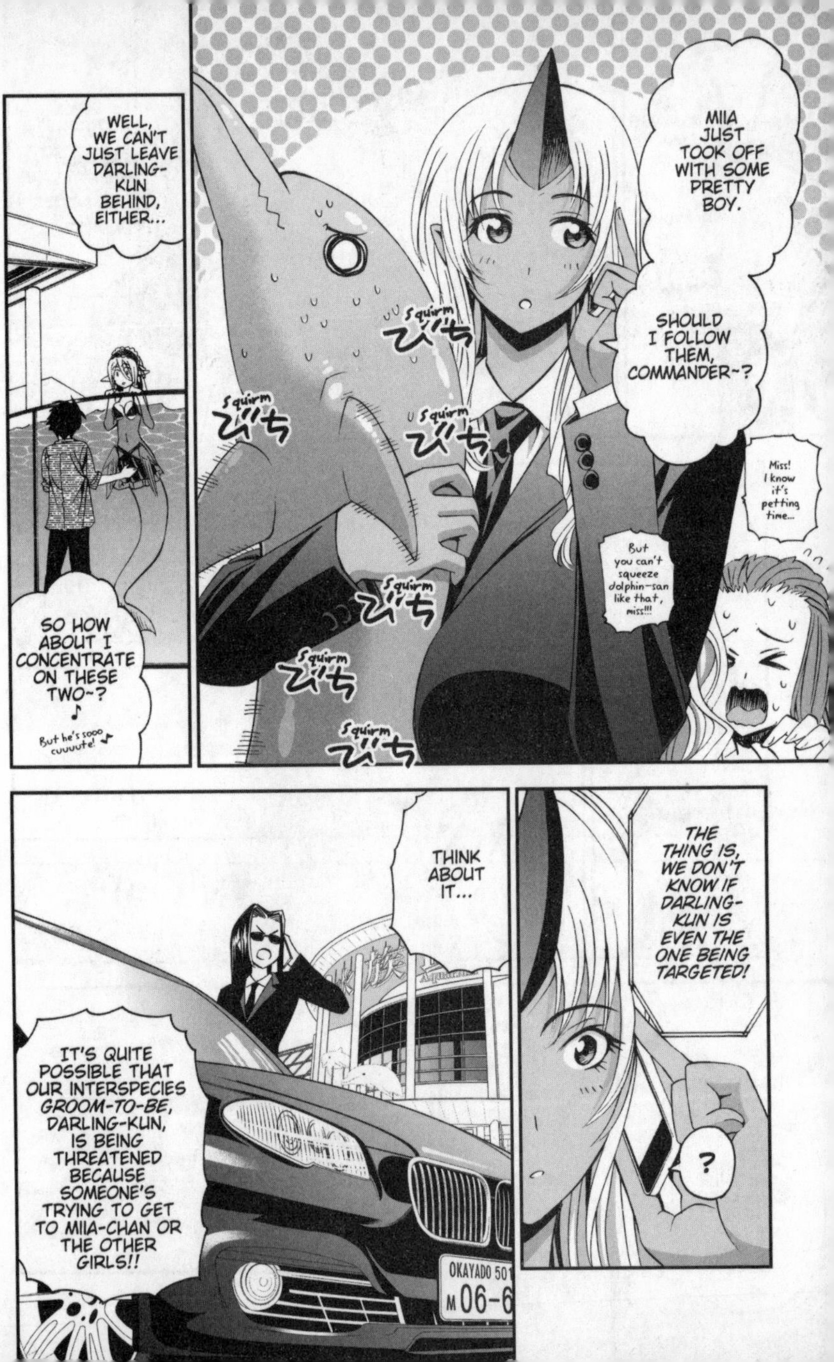
MIIA JUST TOOK OFF WITH SOME PRETTY BOY.
SHOULD I FOLLOW THEM, COMMANDER~?
squirm ぴち
squirm ぴち
squirm ぴち
squirm ぴち
squirm ぴち
squirm ぴち
Miss! I know it's petting time...
But you can't squeeze dolphin-san like that, miss!!!
WELL, WE CAN'T JUST LEAVE DARLING-KUN BEHIND, EITHER...
SO HOW ABOUT I CONCENTRATE ON THESE TWO~? ♪
But he's sooo cuuuute! ♪
THE THING IS, WE DON'T KNOW IF DARLING-KUN IS EVEN THE ONE BEING TARGETED!
?
THINK ABOUT IT...
IT'S QUITE POSSIBLE THAT OUR INTERSPECIES *GROOM-TO-BE*, DARLING-KUN, IS BEING THREATENED BECAUSE SOMEONE'S TRYING TO GET TO MIIA-CHAN OR THE OTHER GIRLS!!

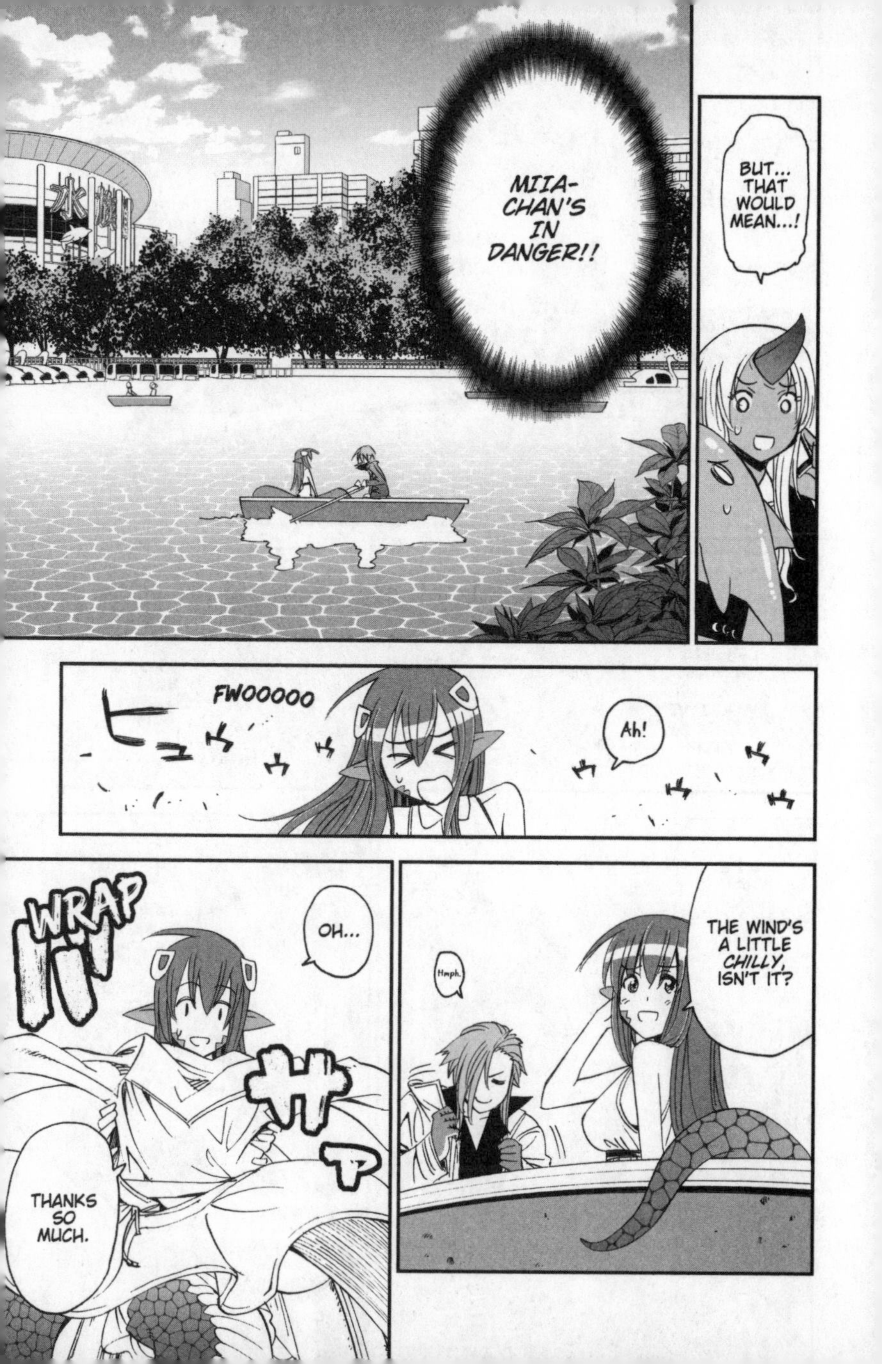
BUT... THAT WOULD MEAN...!
MIIA-CHAN'S IN DANGER!!
FWOOOOO
Ah!
THE WIND'S A LITTLE *CHILLY*, ISN'T IT?
Hmph.
OH...
WRAP
THANKS SO MUCH.

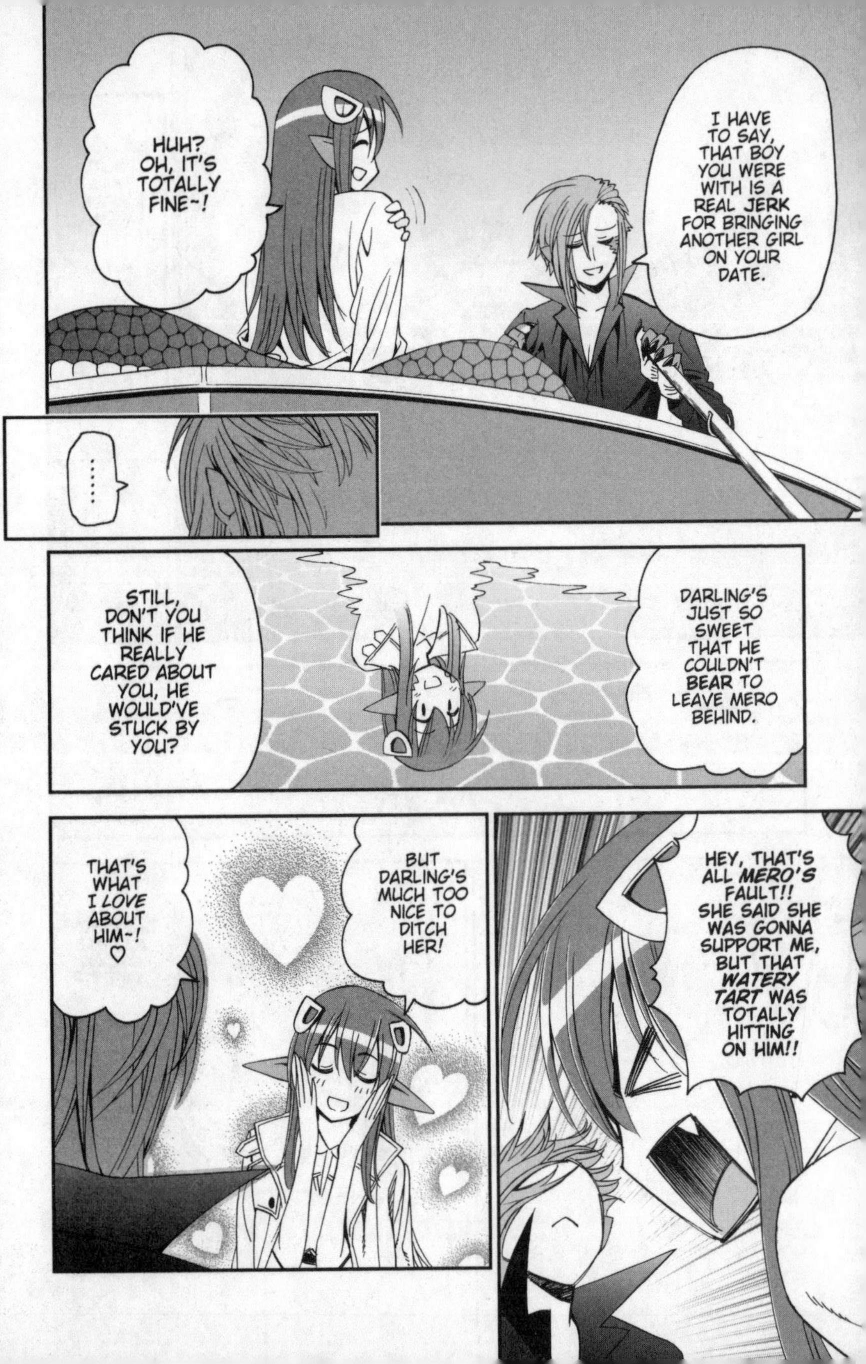
I HAVE TO SAY, THAT BOY YOU WERE WITH IS A REAL JERK FOR BRINGING ANOTHER GIRL ON YOUR DATE.
HUH? OH, IT'S TOTALLY FINE~!
......
DARLING'S JUST SO SWEET THAT HE COULDN'T BEAR TO LEAVE MERO BEHIND.
STILL, DON'T YOU THINK IF HE REALLY CARED ABOUT YOU, HE WOULD'VE STUCK BY YOU?
HEY, THAT'S ALL *MERO'S* FAULT!! SHE SAID SHE WAS GONNA SUPPORT ME, BUT THAT *WATERY TART* WAS TOTALLY HITTING ON HIM!!
BUT DARLING'S MUCH TOO NICE TO DITCH HER!
THAT'S WHAT I *LOVE* ABOUT HIM~! ♡

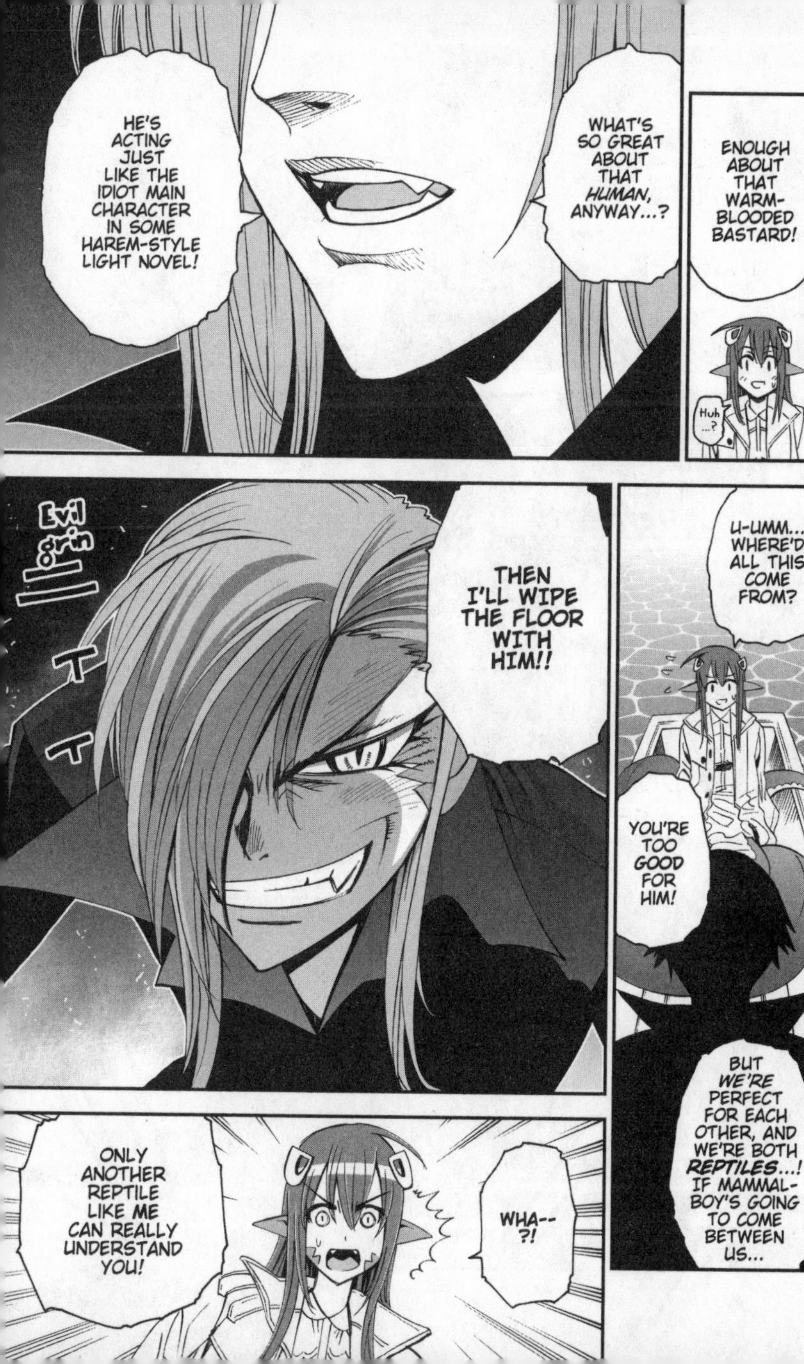
ENOUGH ABOUT THAT WARM-BLOODED BASTARD!
Huh...?
WHAT'S SO GREAT ABOUT THAT HUMAN, ANYWAY...?
HE'S ACTING JUST LIKE THE IDIOT MAIN CHARACTER IN SOME HAREM-STYLE LIGHT NOVEL!
U-UMM... WHERE'D ALL THIS COME FROM?
YOU'RE TOO GOOD FOR HIM!
BUT WE'RE PERFECT FOR EACH OTHER, AND WE'RE BOTH REPTILES...! IF MAMMAL-BOY'S GOING TO COME BETWEEN US...
THEN I'LL WIPE THE FLOOR WITH HIM!!
Evil grin
T
T
WHA--?!
ONLY ANOTHER REPTILE LIKE ME CAN REALLY UNDERSTAND YOU!

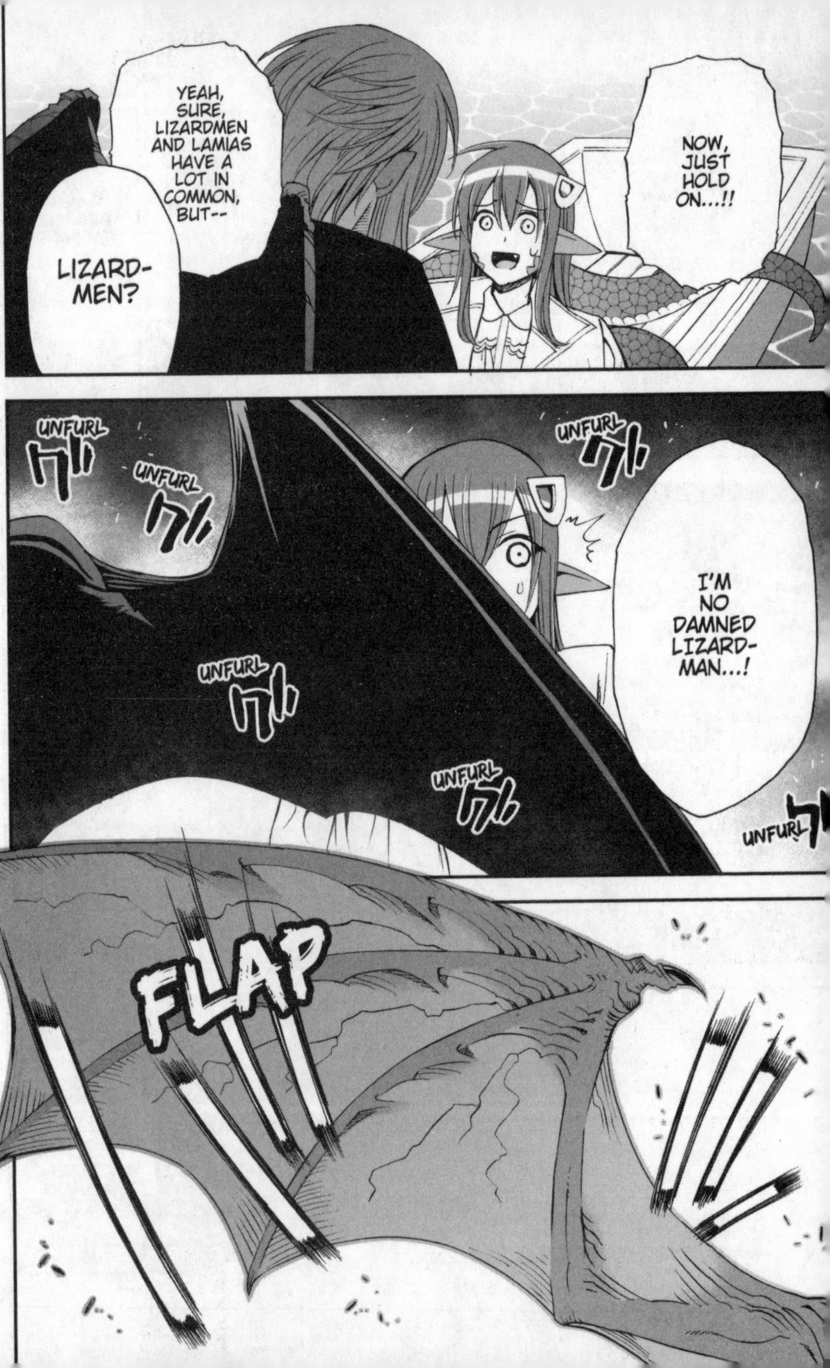
NOW, JUST HOLD ON...!!
YEAH, SURE, LIZARDMEN AND LAMIAS HAVE A LOT IN COMMON, BUT--
LIZARD-MEN?
UNFURL
I'M NO DAMNED LIZARD-MAN...!
UNFURL
UNFURL
UNFURL
UNFURL
UNFURL
FLAP

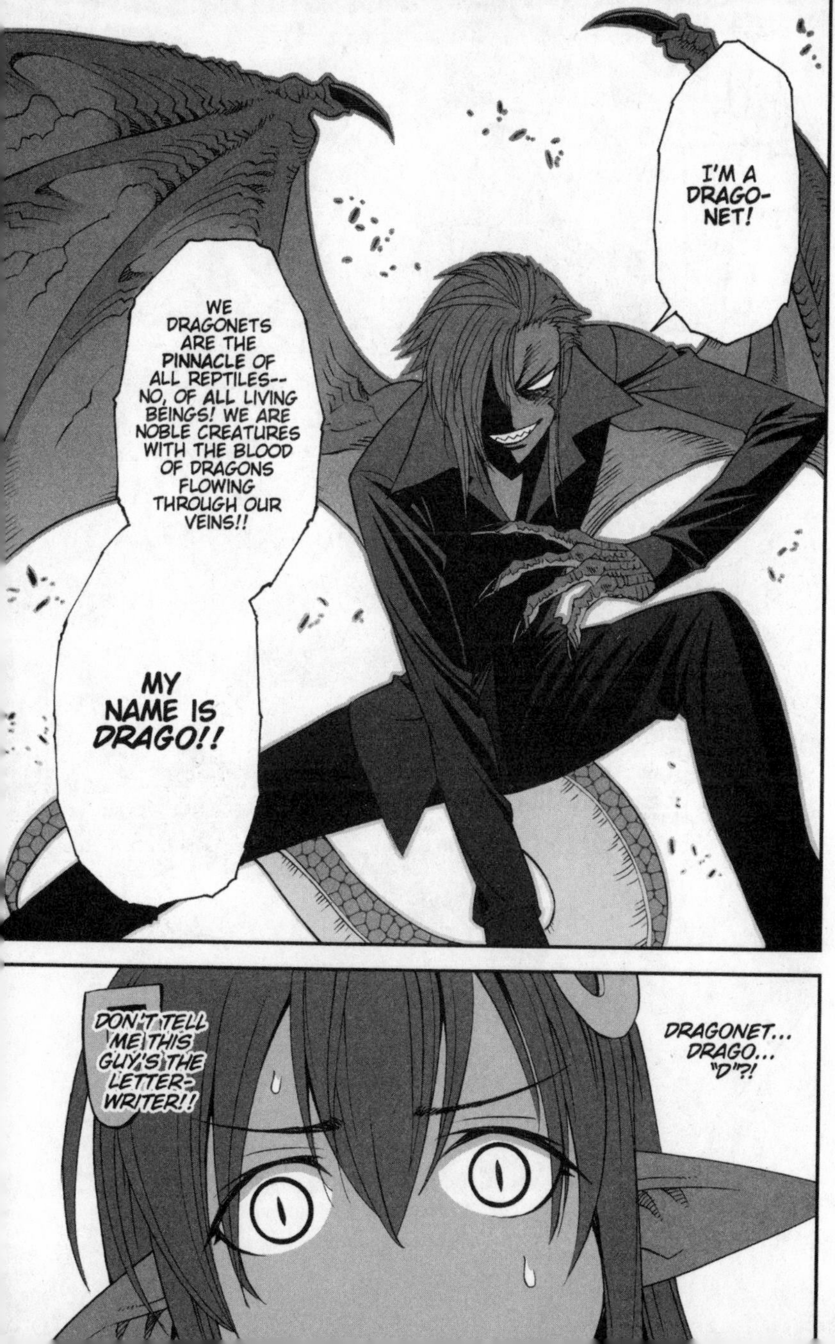
I'M A DRAGONET!
WE DRAGONETS ARE THE PINNACLE OF ALL REPTILES--NO, OF ALL LIVING BEINGS! WE ARE NOBLE CREATURES WITH THE BLOOD OF DRAGONS FLOWING THROUGH OUR VEINS!!
MY NAME IS DRAGO!!
DRAGONET... DRAGO... "D"?!
DON'T TELL ME THIS GUY'S THE LETTER-WRITER!!

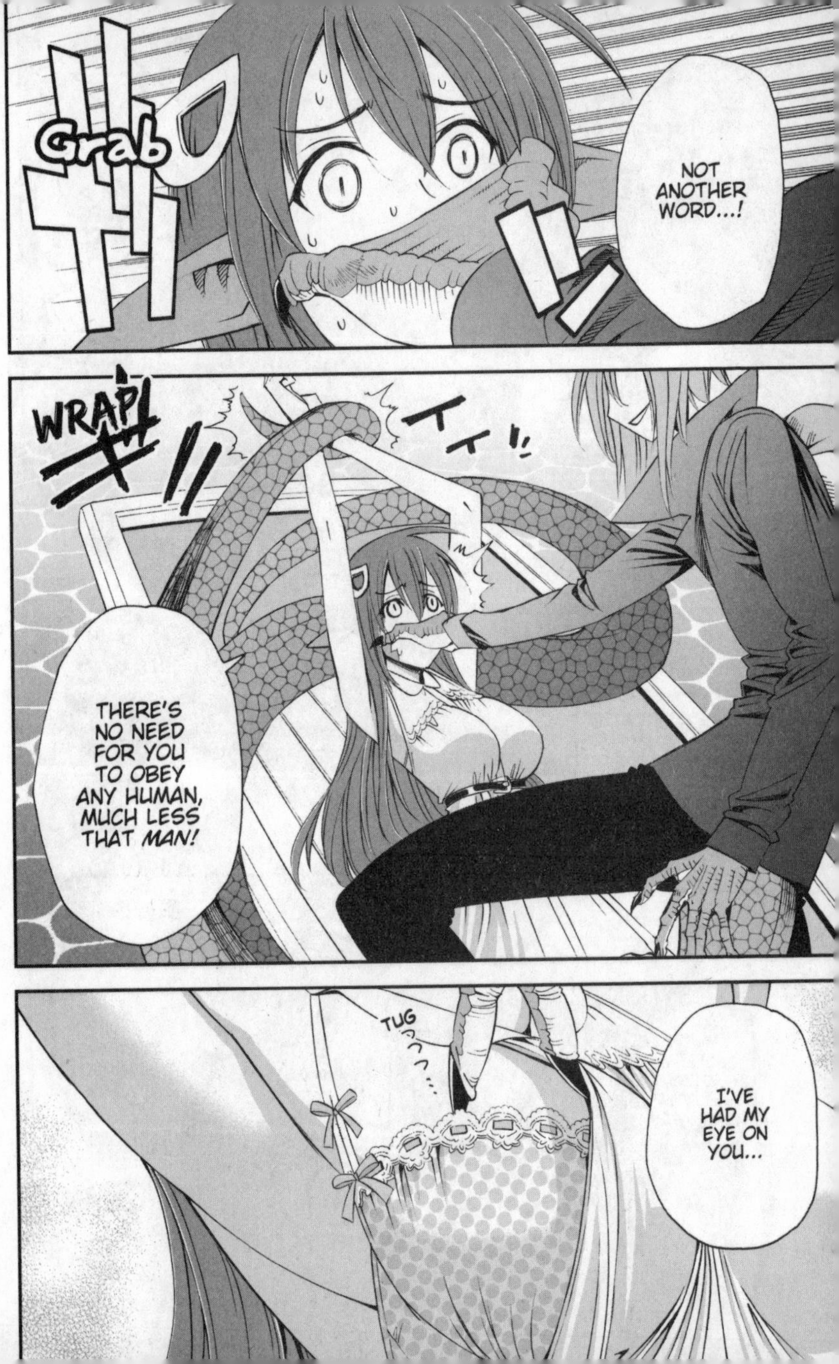
NOT ANOTHER WORD...!
Grab
WRAP!
THERE'S NO NEED FOR YOU TO OBEY ANY HUMAN, MUCH LESS THAT MAN!
I'VE HAD MY EYE ON YOU...
TUG

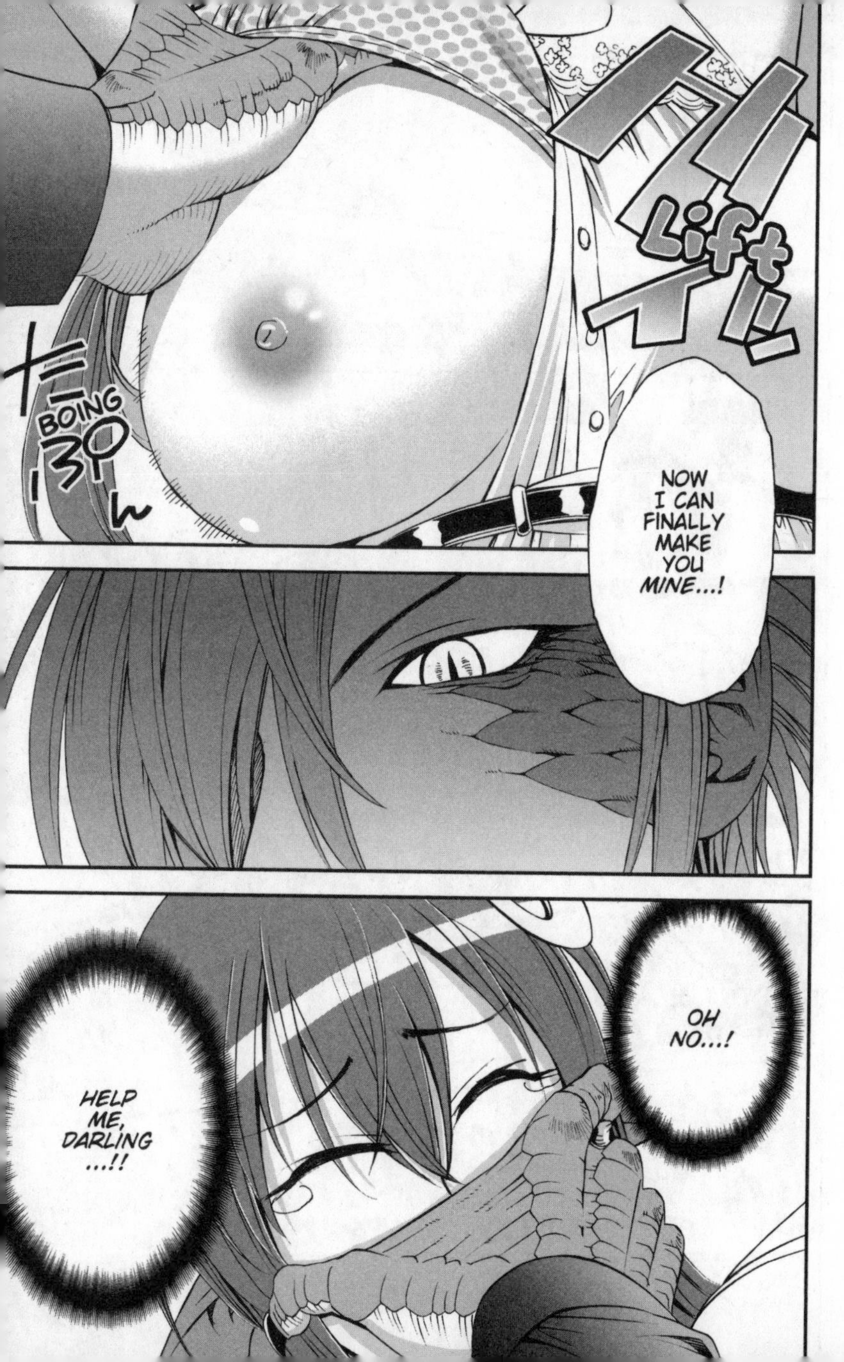
Lift
BOING
NOW I CAN FINALLY MAKE YOU MINE...!
OH NO...!
HELP ME, DARLING ...!!

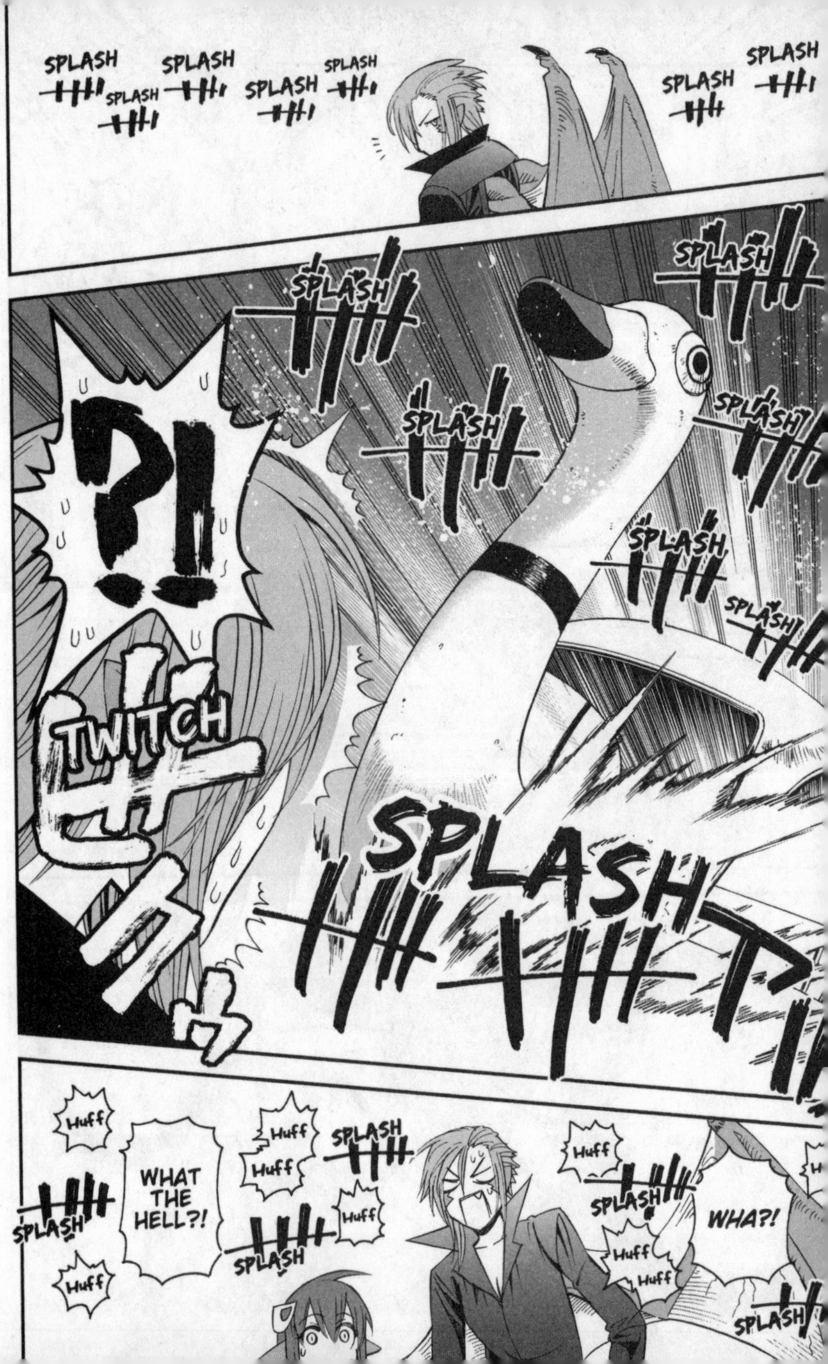
SPLASH
SPLASH
SPLASH
SPLASH
SPLASH
SPLASH
SPLASH
SPLASH
SPLASH
SPLASH
SPLASH
SPLASH
SPLASH
?!!
TWITCH
SPLASH
SPLASH
WHA?!
Huff
Huff
Huff
SPLASH
SPLASH
Huff
Huff
Huff
SPLASH
SPLASH
WHAT THE HELL?!
Huff
SPLASH
Huff

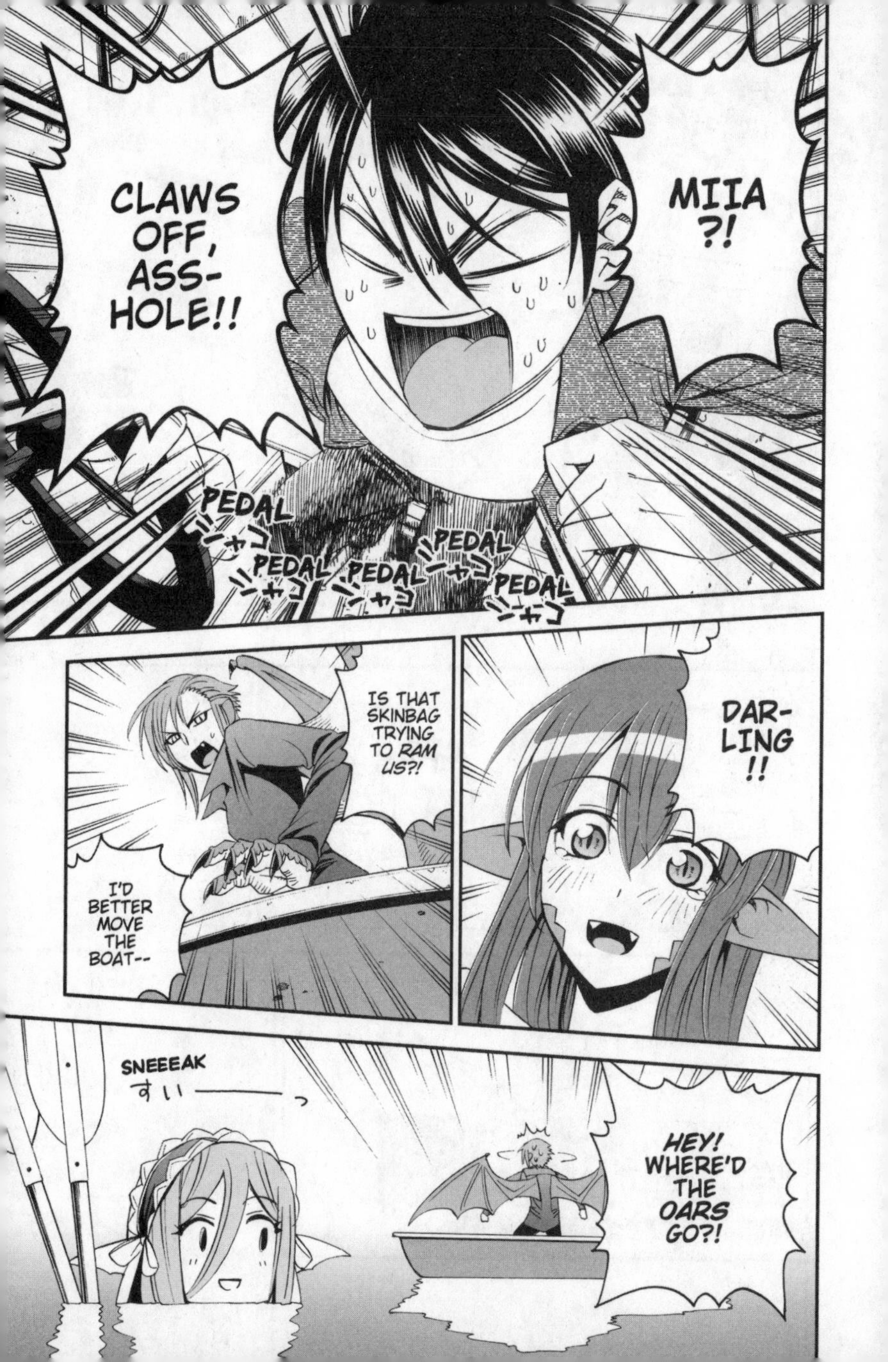
MIIA?!
CLAWS OFF, ASS-HOLE!!
PEDAL
シャコ
PEDAL
シャコ
PEDAL
シャコ
PEDAL
シャコ
PEDAL
シャコ
DAR-LING!!
IS THAT SKINBAG TRYING TO *RAM* US?!
I'D BETTER MOVE THE BOAT--
SNEEEAK
すいーーっ
HEY! WHERE'D THE OARS GO?!

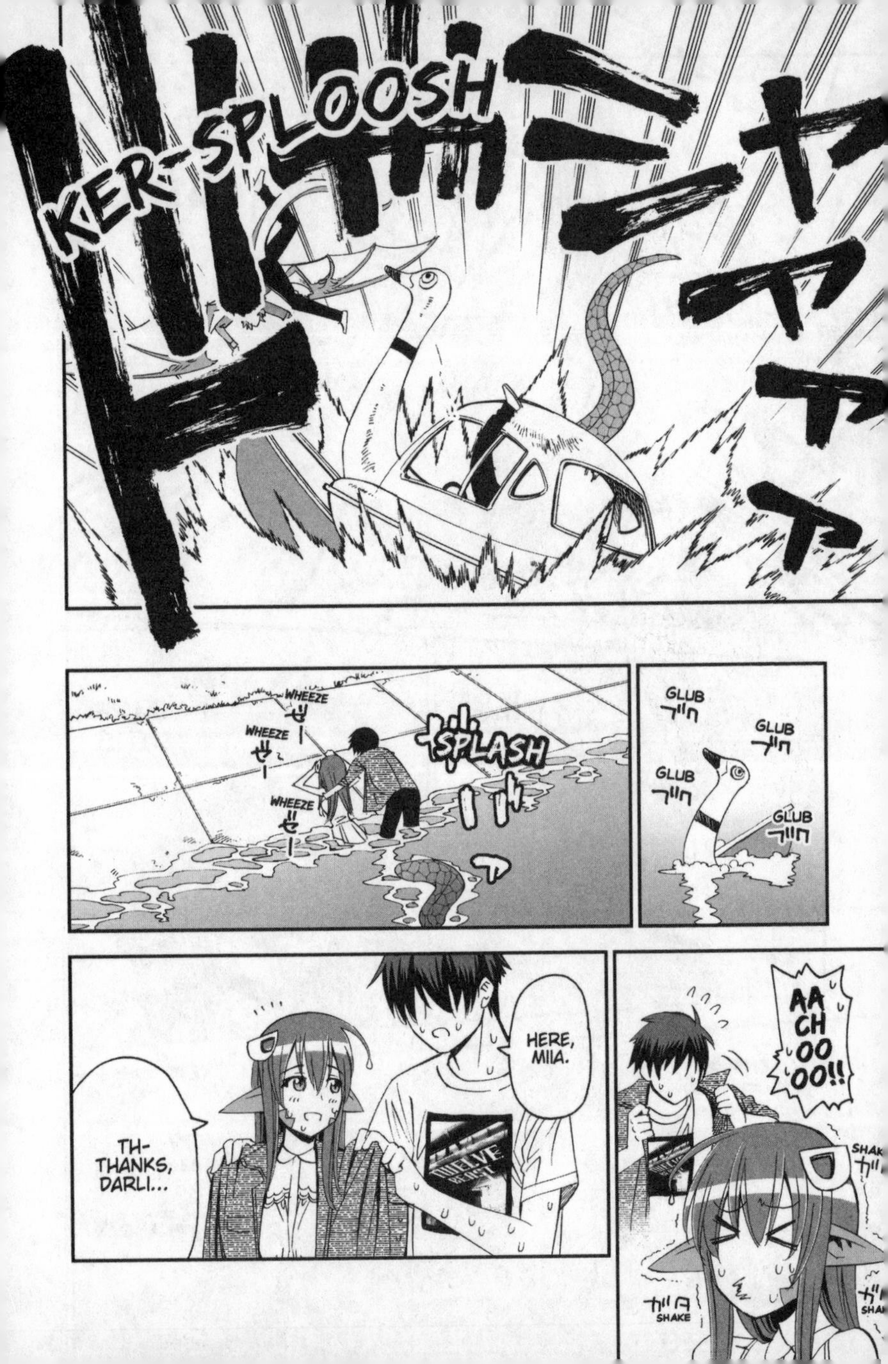
KER-SPLOOSH
GLUB
GLUB
GLUB
GLUB
WHEEZE
WHEEZE
WHEEZE
SPLASH
AA CH OO OO!!
SHAKE
SHAKE
SHAKE
HERE, MIIA.
TH-THANKS, DARLI...

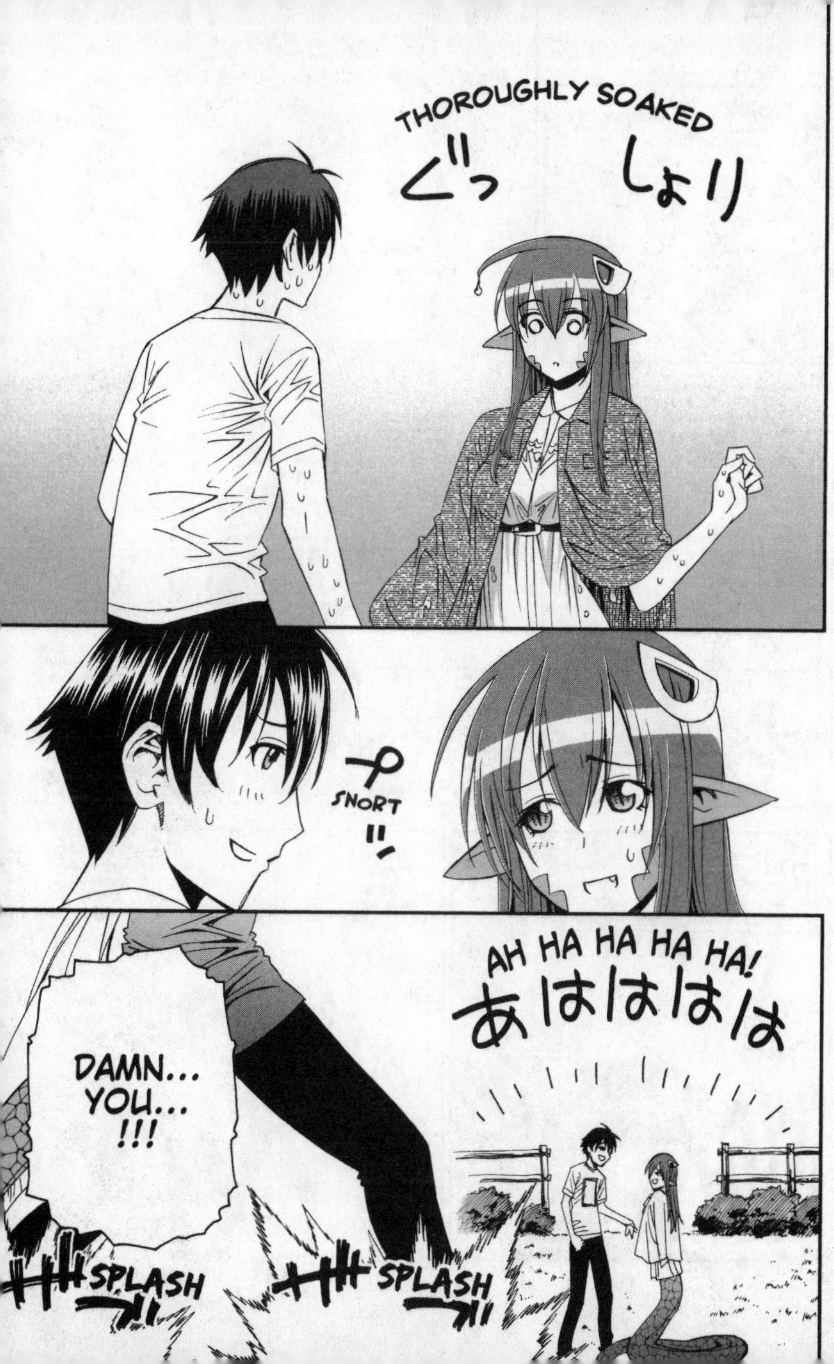
THOROUGHLY SOAKED
ぐっしょり
SNORT
AH HA HA HA HA!
あははははは
DAMN... YOU... !!!
SPLASH
SPLASH

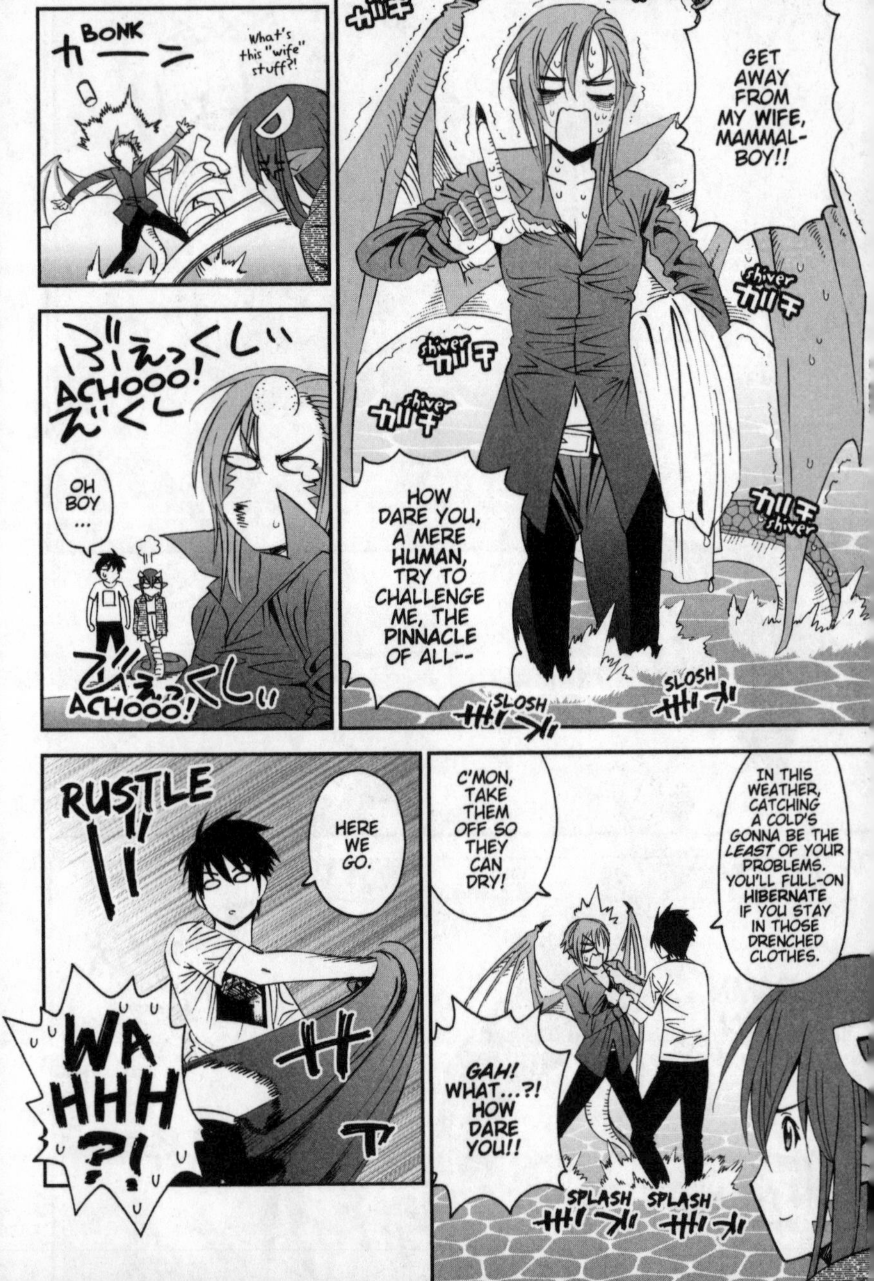
shiver
shiver
GET AWAY FROM MY WIFE, MAMMAL-BOY!!
shiver
shiver
shiver
shiver
HOW DARE YOU, A MERE HUMAN, TRY TO CHALLENGE ME, THE PINNACLE OF ALL--
SLOSH
SLOSH
BONK
What's this "wife" stuff?!
ACHOOO!
OH BOY ...
ACHOOO!
IN THIS WEATHER, CATCHING A COLD'S GONNA BE THE *LEAST* OF YOUR PROBLEMS. YOU'LL FULL-ON HIBERNATE IF YOU STAY IN THOSE DRENCHED CLOTHES.
C'MON, TAKE THEM OFF SO THEY CAN DRY!
GAH! WHAT...?! HOW DARE YOU!!
SPLASH
SPLASH
RUSTLE
HERE WE GO.
WAHHH?!

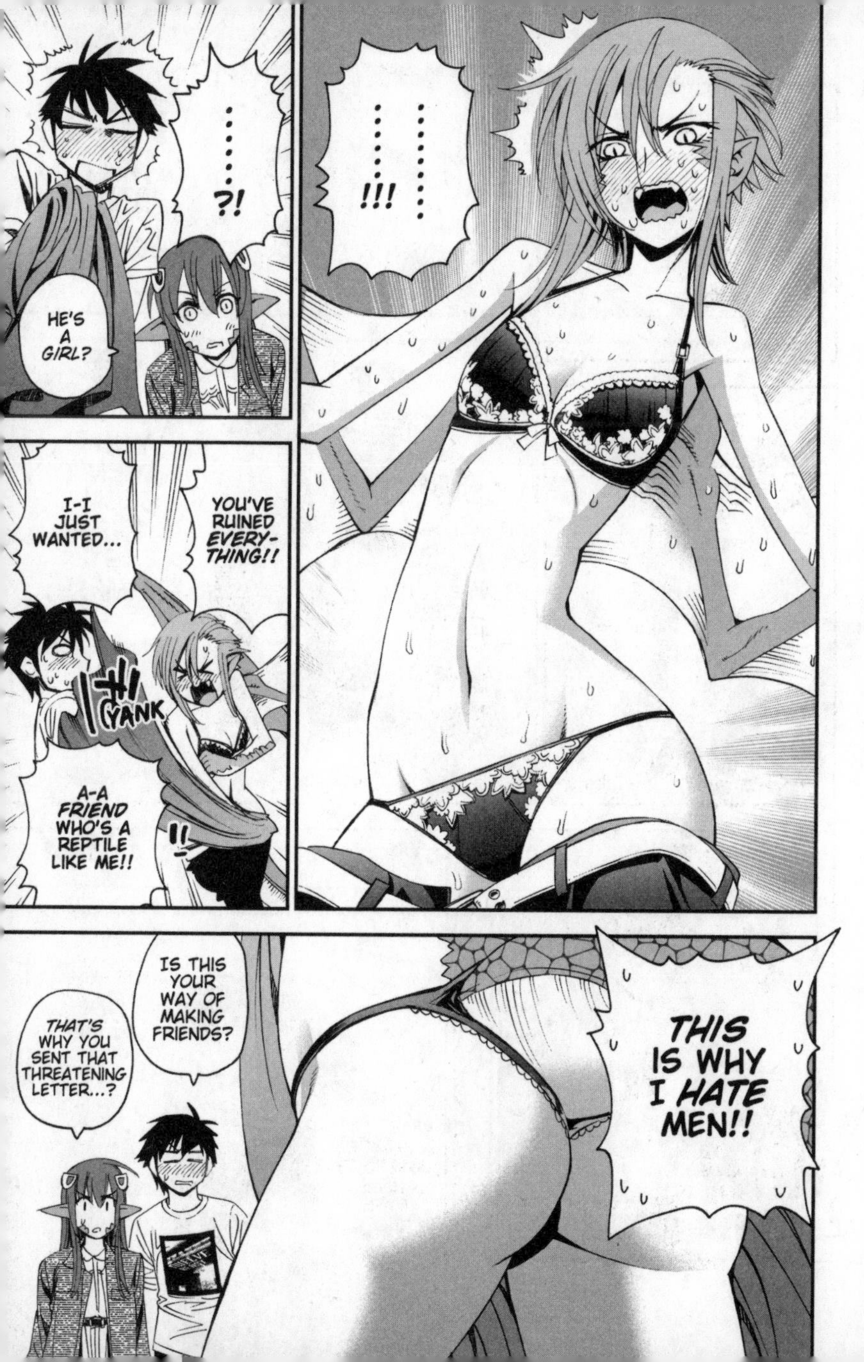
......!!!
......?!
HE'S A GIRL?
YOU'VE RUINED *EVERYTHING*!!
I-I JUST WANTED...
YANK
A-A *FRIEND* WHO'S A REPTILE LIKE ME!!
!!
THIS IS WHY I *HATE* MEN!!
IS THIS YOUR WAY OF MAKING FRIENDS?
THAT'S WHY YOU SENT THAT THREATENING LETTER...?

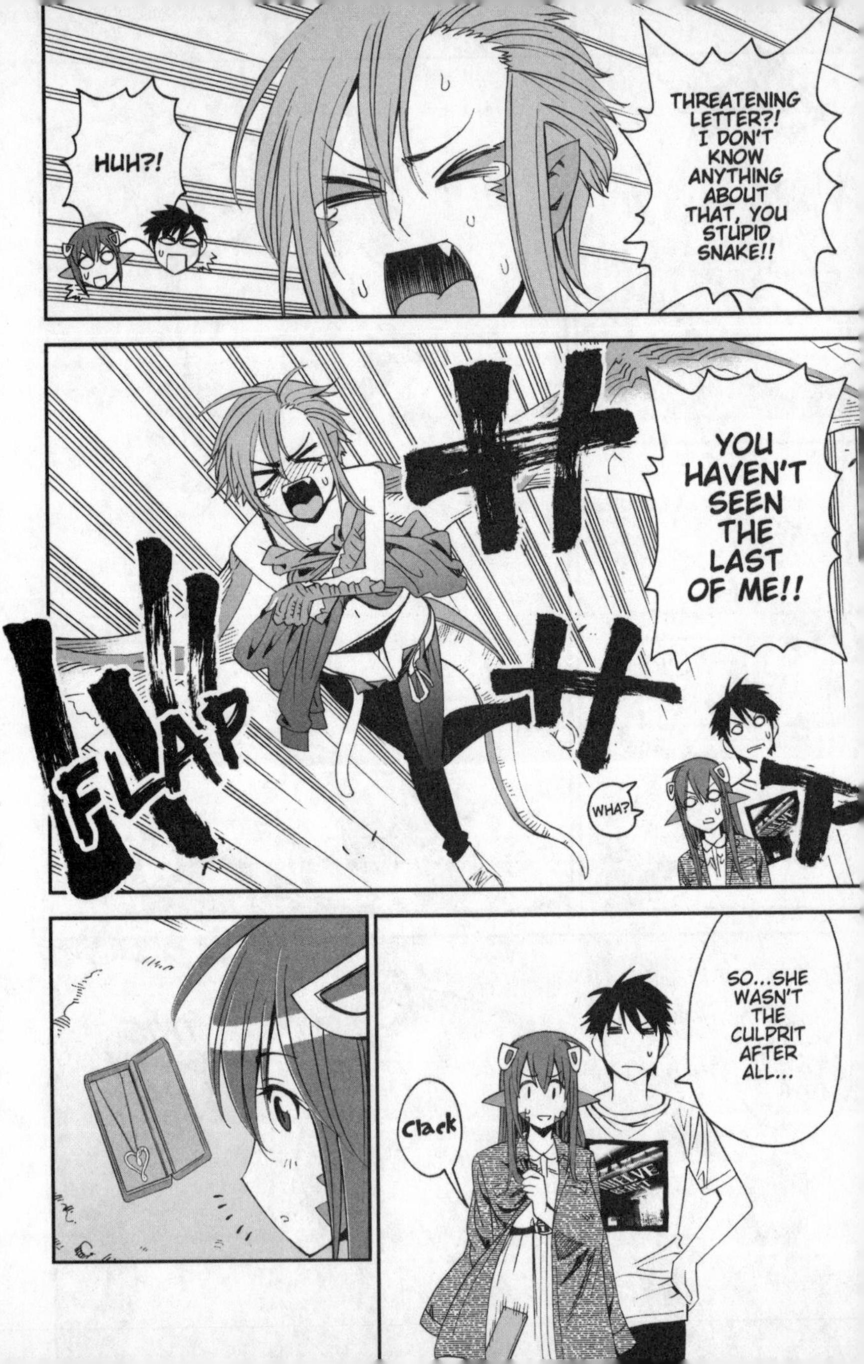
THREATENING LETTER?! I DON'T KNOW ANYTHING ABOUT THAT, YOU STUPID SNAKE!!
HUH?!
YOU HAVEN'T SEEN THE LAST OF ME!!
FLAP
WHA?
SO...SHE WASN'T THE CULPRIT AFTER ALL...
Clack

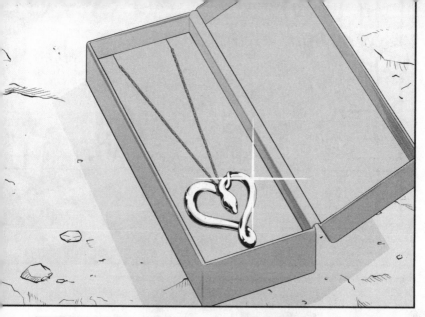

OH! THAT'S... UH--!!

WHAT'S THIS...?

WELL, I SAW IT AT THE AQUARIUM GIFT SHOP, AND IT... MADE ME THINK OF YOU.

BUT I NEVER QUITE GOT UP THE NERVE TO GIVE IT TO YOU.

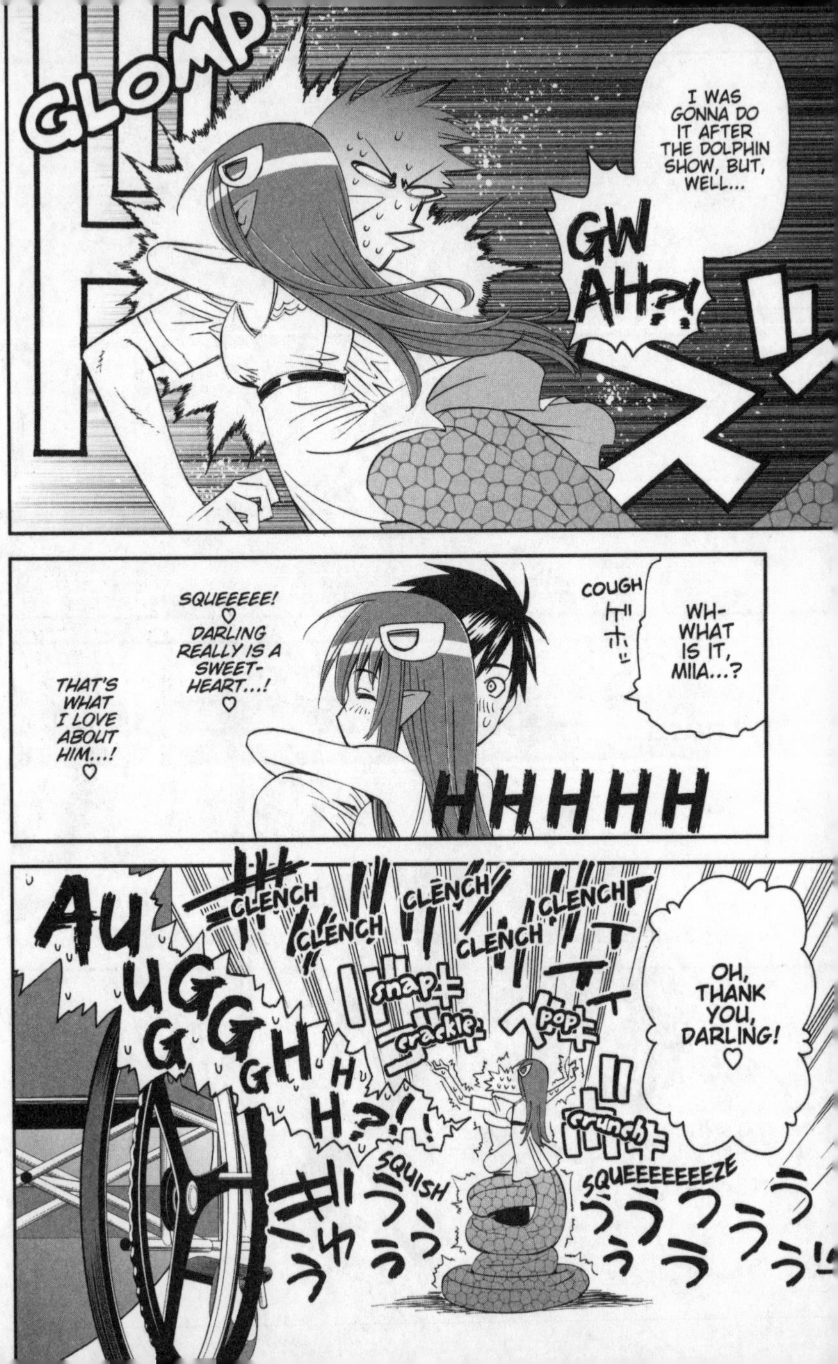
I WAS GONNA DO IT AFTER THE DOLPHIN SHOW, BUT, WELL...
GWAH?!
GLOMP
COUGH
WH-WHAT IS IT, MIIA...?
SQUEEEEE! ♡ DARLING REALLY IS A SWEET-HEART...! ♡
THAT'S WHAT I LOVE ABOUT HIM...! ♡
HHHHH
OH, THANK YOU, DARLING! ♡
CLENCH
CLENCH
CLENCH
CLENCH
CLENCH
CLENCH
snap
crackle
pop
crunch
SQUEEEEEEEEZE
SQUISH
AUUGGGGGHHHH?!!

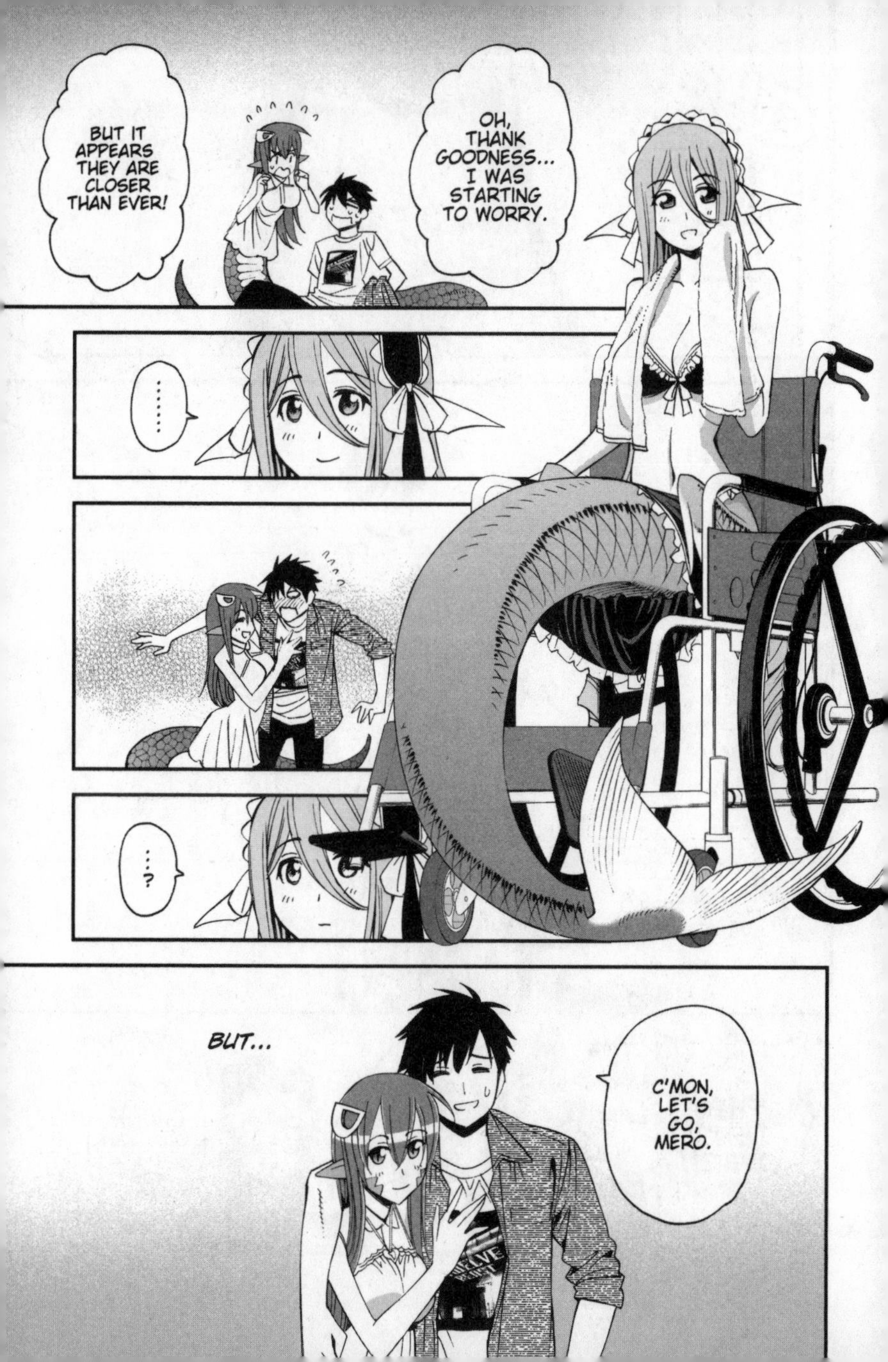
OH, THANK GOODNESS... I WAS STARTING TO WORRY.
BUT IT APPEARS THEY ARE CLOSER THAN EVER!
......
...?
C'MON, LET'S GO, MERO.
BUT...

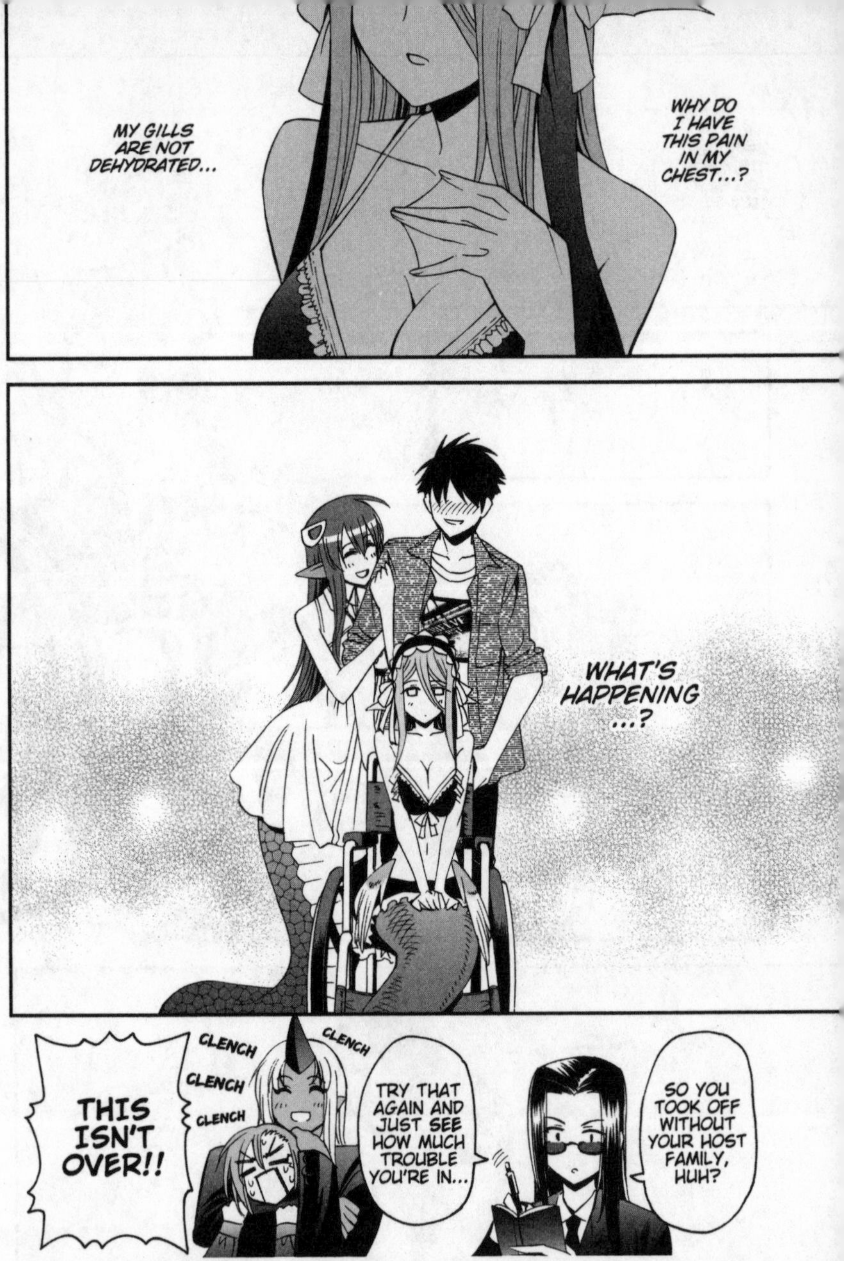
WHY DO I HAVE THIS PAIN IN MY CHEST...?
MY GILLS ARE NOT DEHYDRATED...
WHAT'S HAPPENING ...?
SO YOU TOOK OFF WITHOUT YOUR HOST FAMILY, HUH?
TRY THAT AGAIN AND JUST SEE HOW MUCH TROUBLE YOU'RE IN...
CLENCH
CLENCH
CLENCH
CLENCH
THIS ISN'T OVER!!

Monster Musume

Everyday Life with Monster Girls

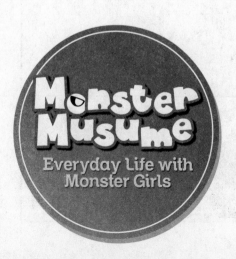

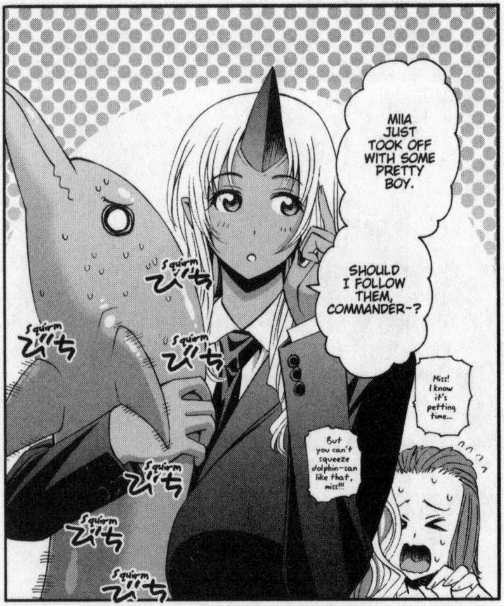
MIIA JUST TOOK OFF WITH SOME PRETTY BOY.
SHOULD I FOLLOW THEM, COMMANDER-?
Miss! I know it's petting time...
But you can't squeeze dolphin-san like that, miss!!!
squirm
squirm
squirm
squirm
squirm
squirm

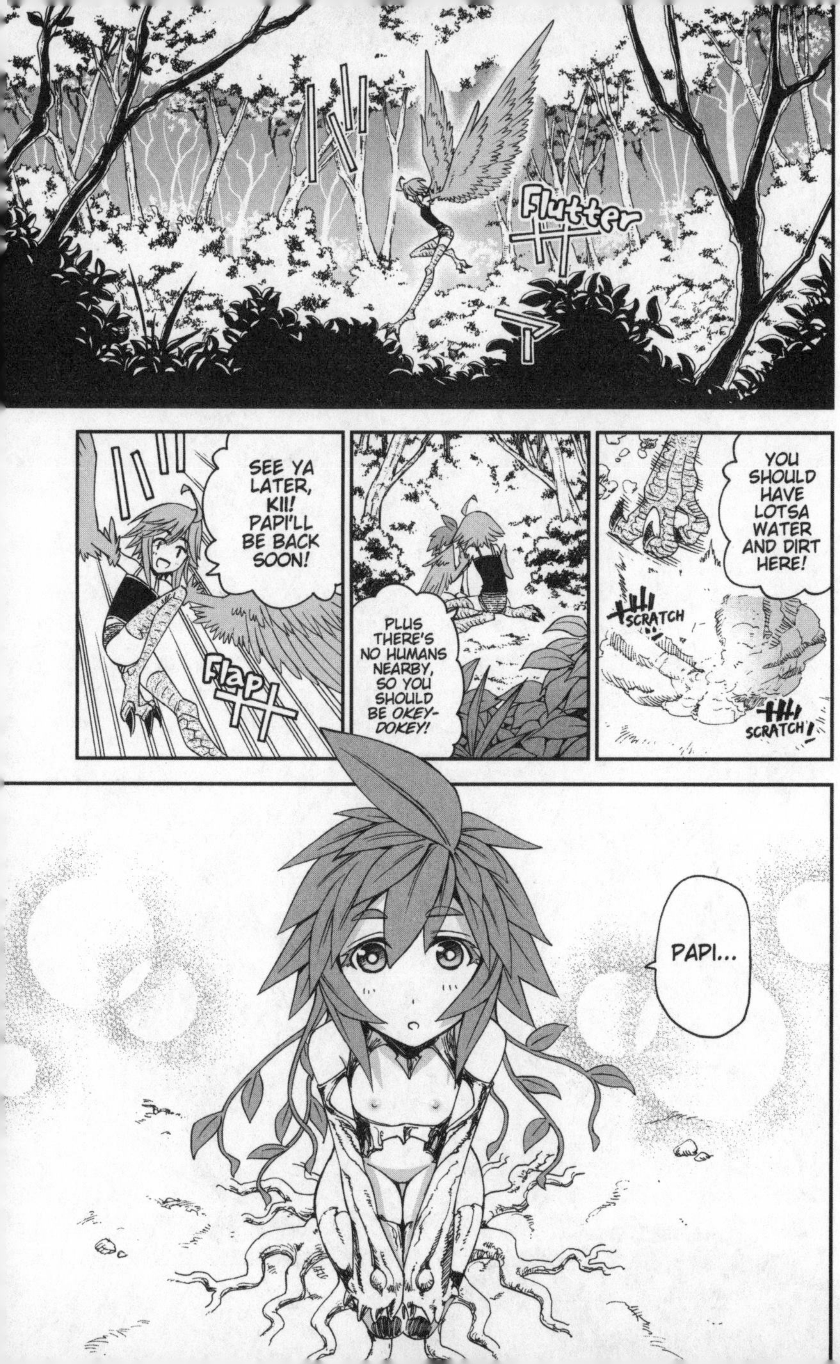
Flutter
YOU SHOULD HAVE LOTSA WATER AND DIRT HERE!
SCRATCH
SCRATCH!
PLUS THERE'S NO HUMANS NEARBY, SO YOU SHOULD BE OKEY-DOKEY!
SEE YA LATER, KII! PAPI'LL BE BACK SOON!
Flap
PAPI...

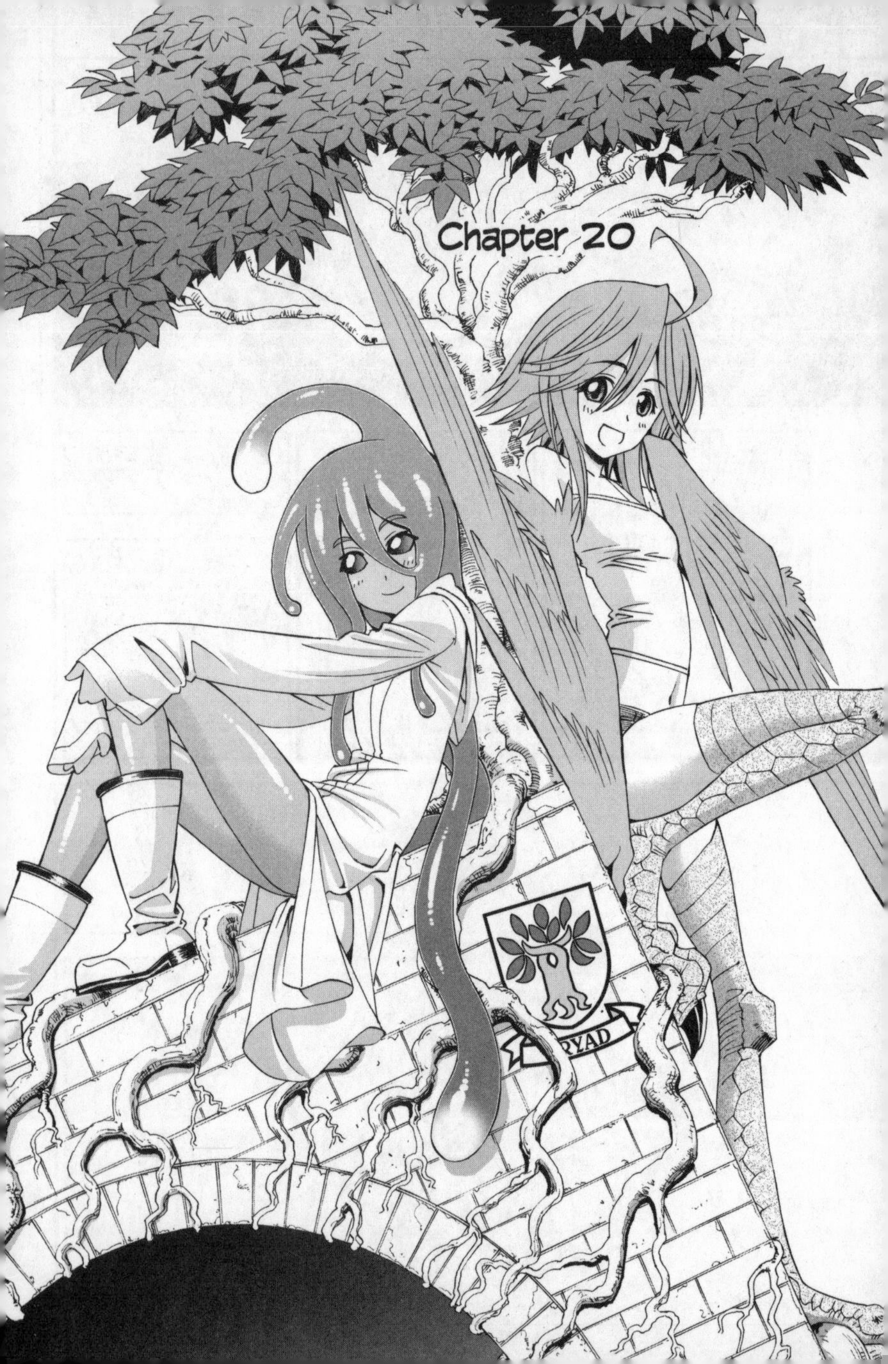
Chapter 20

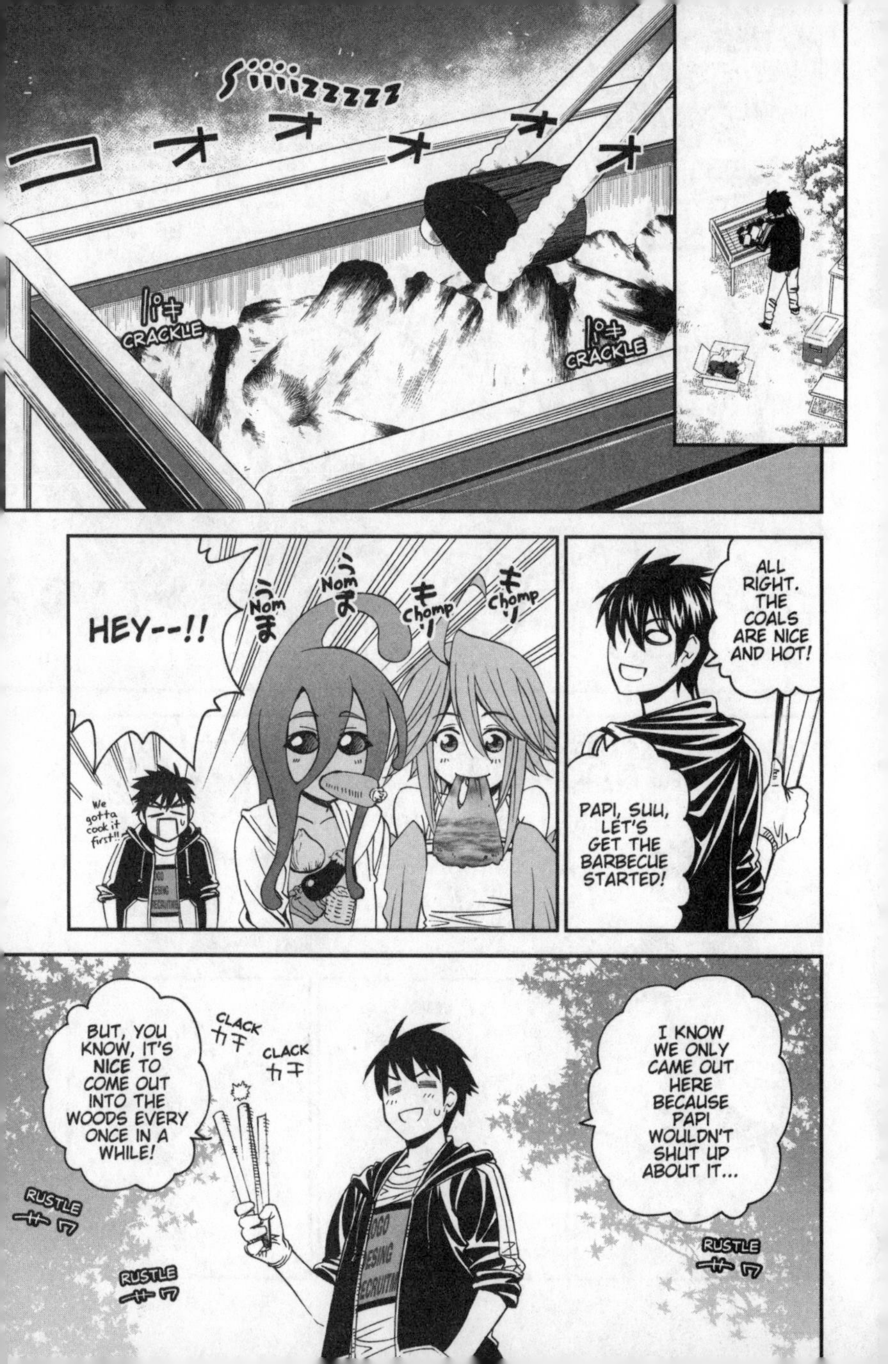
Siiiizzzzz
コオオオオ
パキ CRACKLE
パキ CRACKLE
ALL RIGHT. THE COALS ARE NICE AND HOT!
PAPI, SUU, LET'S GET THE BARBECUE STARTED!
Chomp もり
Chomp もり
Nom うま
Nom うま
HEY--!!
We gotta cook it first!!
I KNOW WE ONLY CAME OUT HERE BECAUSE PAPI WOULDN'T SHUT UP ABOUT IT...
RUSTLE サワ
CLACK カチ
CLACK カチ
BUT, YOU KNOW, IT'S NICE TO COME OUT INTO THE WOODS EVERY ONCE IN A WHILE!
RUSTLE サワ
RUSTLE サワ

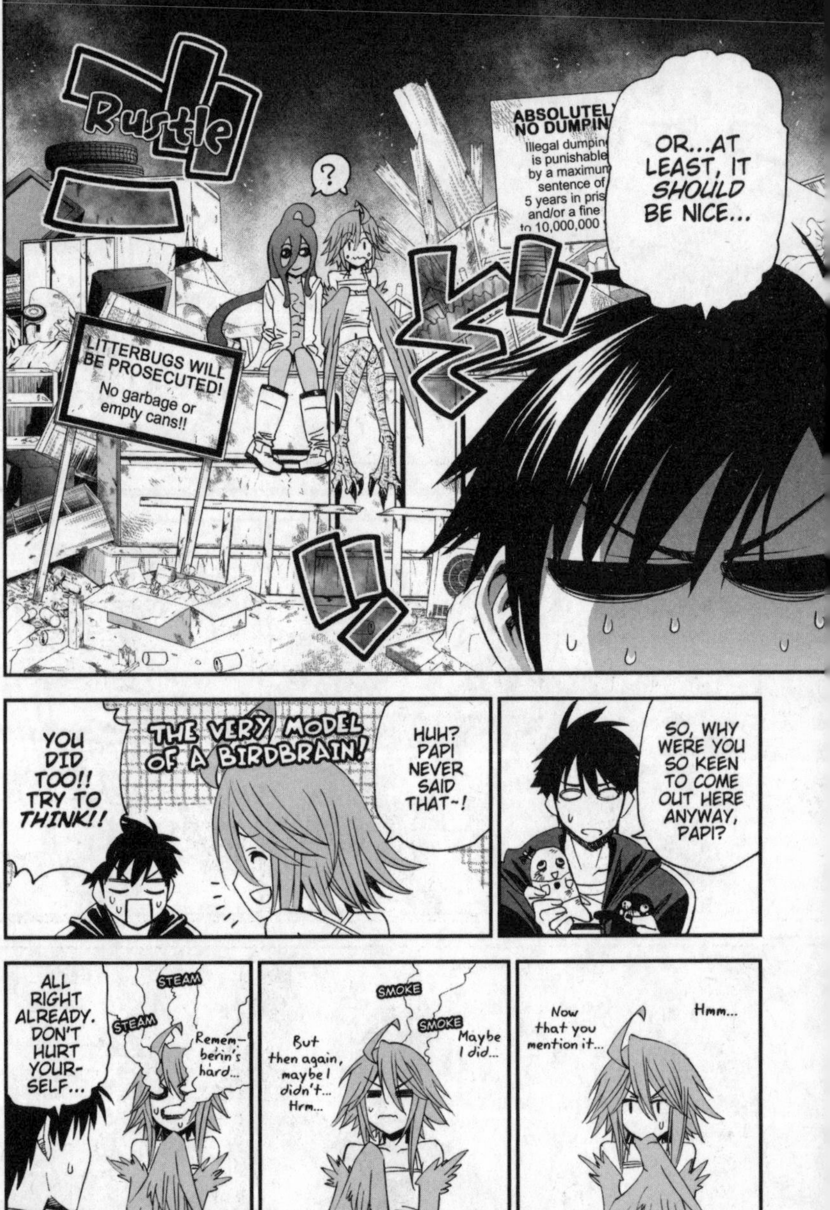
OR...AT LEAST, IT SHOULD BE NICE...
ABSOLUTELY NO DUMPIN
Illegal dumping is punishable by a maximum sentence of 5 years in pris and/or a fine to 10,000,000
?
Rustle
LITTERBUGS WILL BE PROSECUTED! No garbage or empty cans!!
SO, WHY WERE YOU SO KEEN TO COME OUT HERE ANYWAY, PAPI?
HUH? PAPI NEVER SAID THAT~!
THE VERY MODEL OF A BIRDBRAIN!
YOU DID TOO!! TRY TO THINK!!
Hmm...
Now that you mention it...
SMOKE
Maybe I did...
SMOKE
But then again, maybe I didn't... Hrm...
Remem-berin's hard...
STEAM
STEAM
ALL RIGHT ALREADY. DON'T HURT YOUR-SELF...

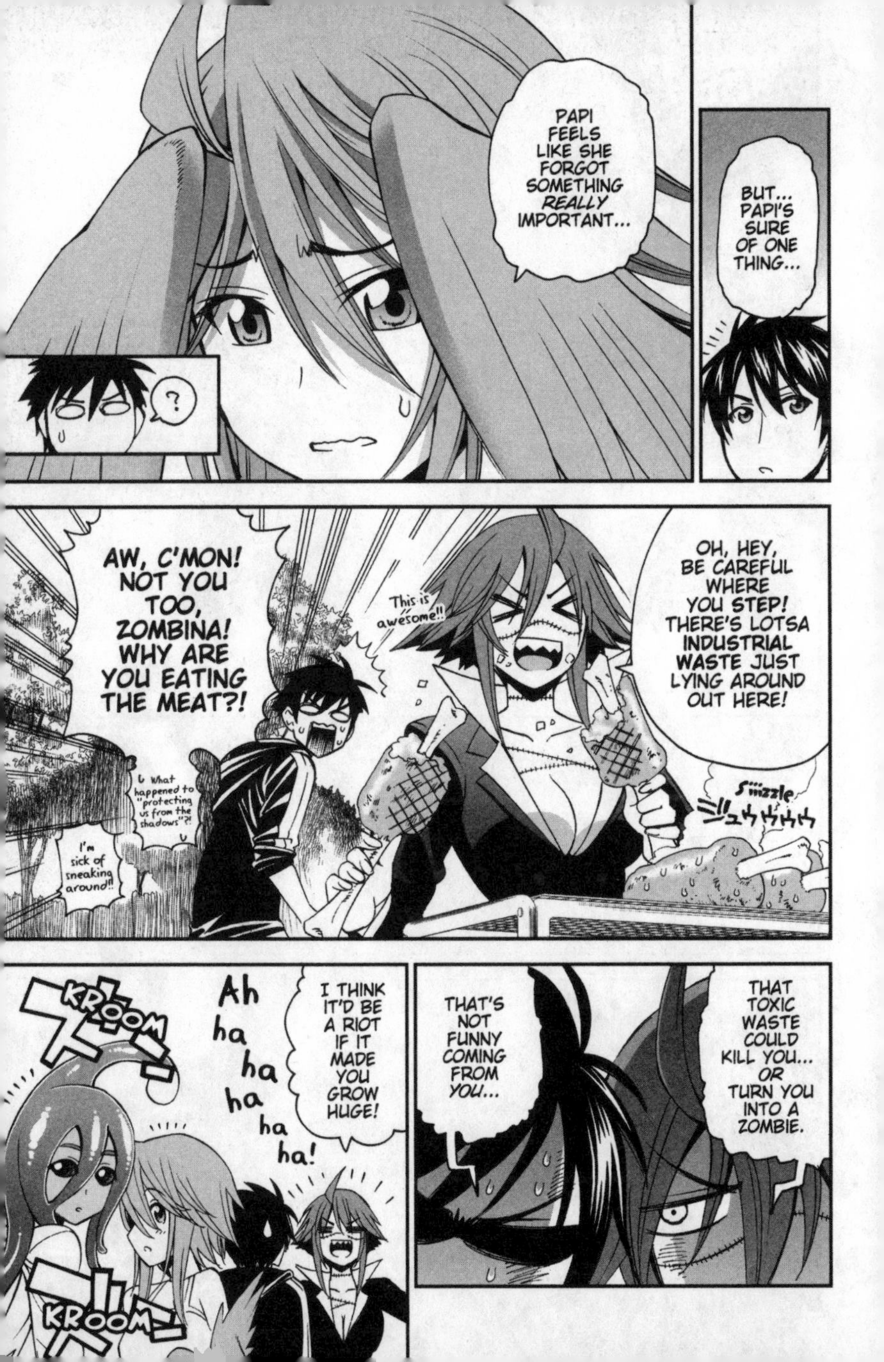
PAPI FEELS LIKE SHE FORGOT SOMETHING *REALLY* IMPORTANT...
?
BUT... PAPI'S SURE OF ONE THING...
OH, HEY, BE CAREFUL WHERE YOU STEP! THERE'S LOTSA INDUSTRIAL WASTE JUST LYING AROUND OUT HERE!
Sizzle
This is awesome!!
AW, C'MON! NOT YOU TOO, ZOMBINA! WHY ARE YOU EATING THE MEAT?!
What happened to "protecting us from the shadows"?!
I'm sick of sneaking around!!
THAT TOXIC WASTE COULD KILL YOU... *OR* TURN YOU INTO A ZOMBIE.
THAT'S NOT FUNNY COMING FROM *YOU*...
I THINK IT'D BE A RIOT IF IT MADE YOU GROW HUGE!
Ah ha ha ha ha ha!
KROOM
KROOM

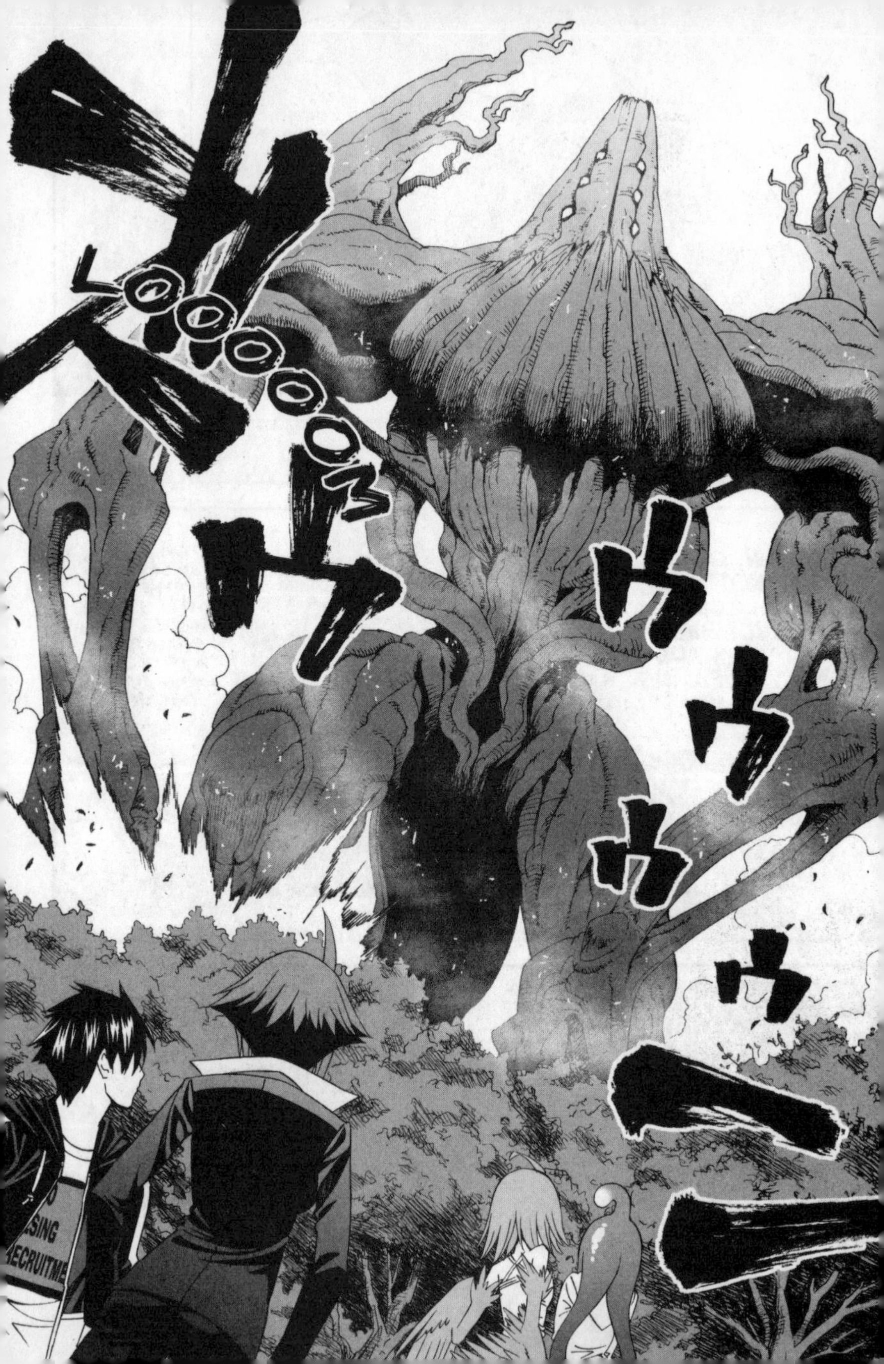
ウウウウーー
LOOOOOM

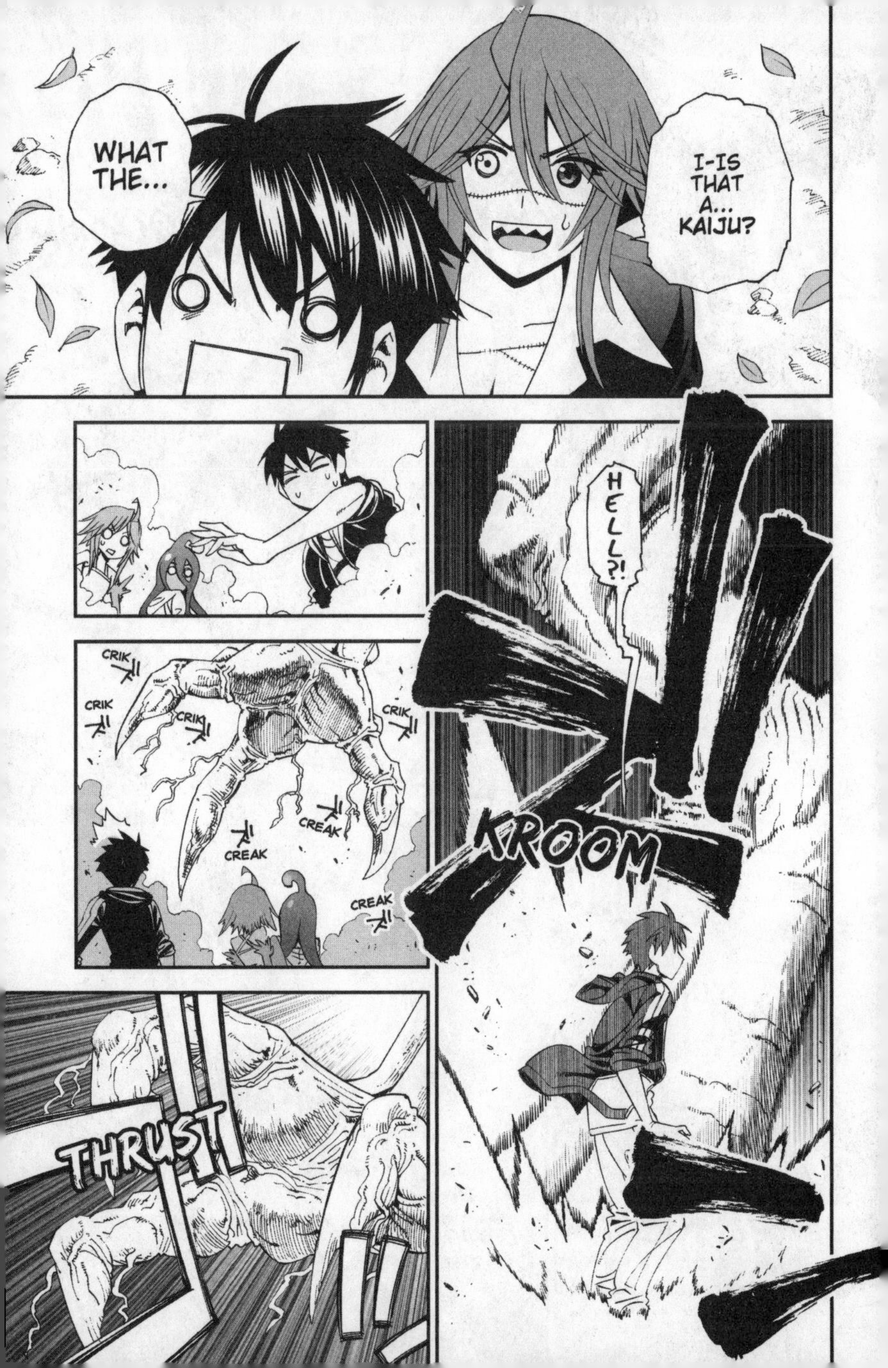
I-IS THAT A... KAIJU?
WHAT THE...
HELL?!
KROOM
CRIK
CRIK
CRIK
CRIK
CREAK
CREAK
CREAK
THRUST

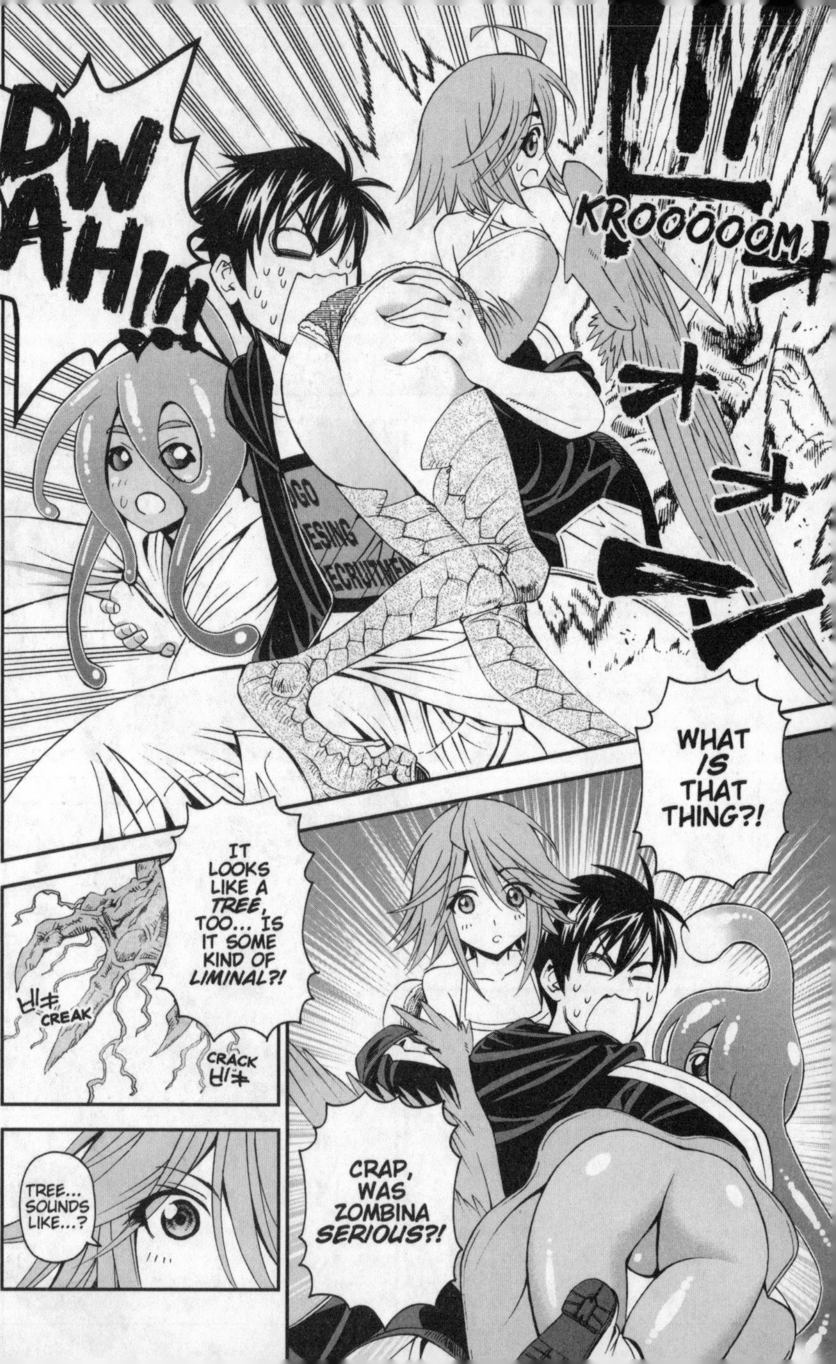
KROOOOOM
DWAH!!!
WHAT *IS* THAT THING?!
CRAP, WAS ZOMBINA *SERIOUS*?!
IT LOOKS LIKE A *TREE*, TOO... IS IT SOME KIND OF *LIMINAL*?!
ビキ CREAK
CRACK ビキ
TREE... SOUNDS LIKE...?

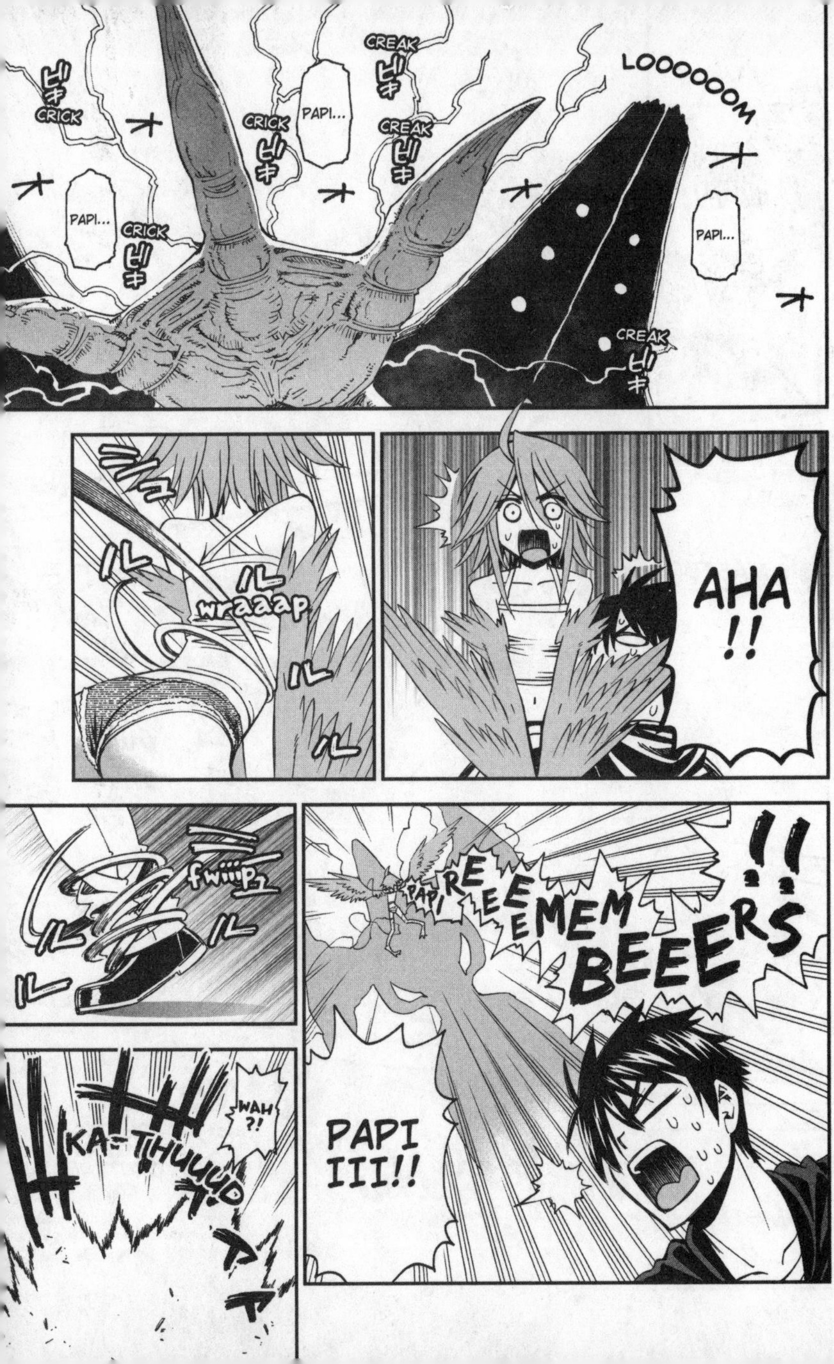
LOOOOOOM
PAPI...
CREAK
ビキ
CREAK
ビキ
CREAK
ビキ
PAPI...
CRICK
ビキ
CRICK
ビキ
PAPI...
CRICK
ビキ
AHA !!
wraaap
PAPI REEEEMEMBEEERS!!
PAPI III!!
fwiiip
WAH ?!
KA-THUUUD

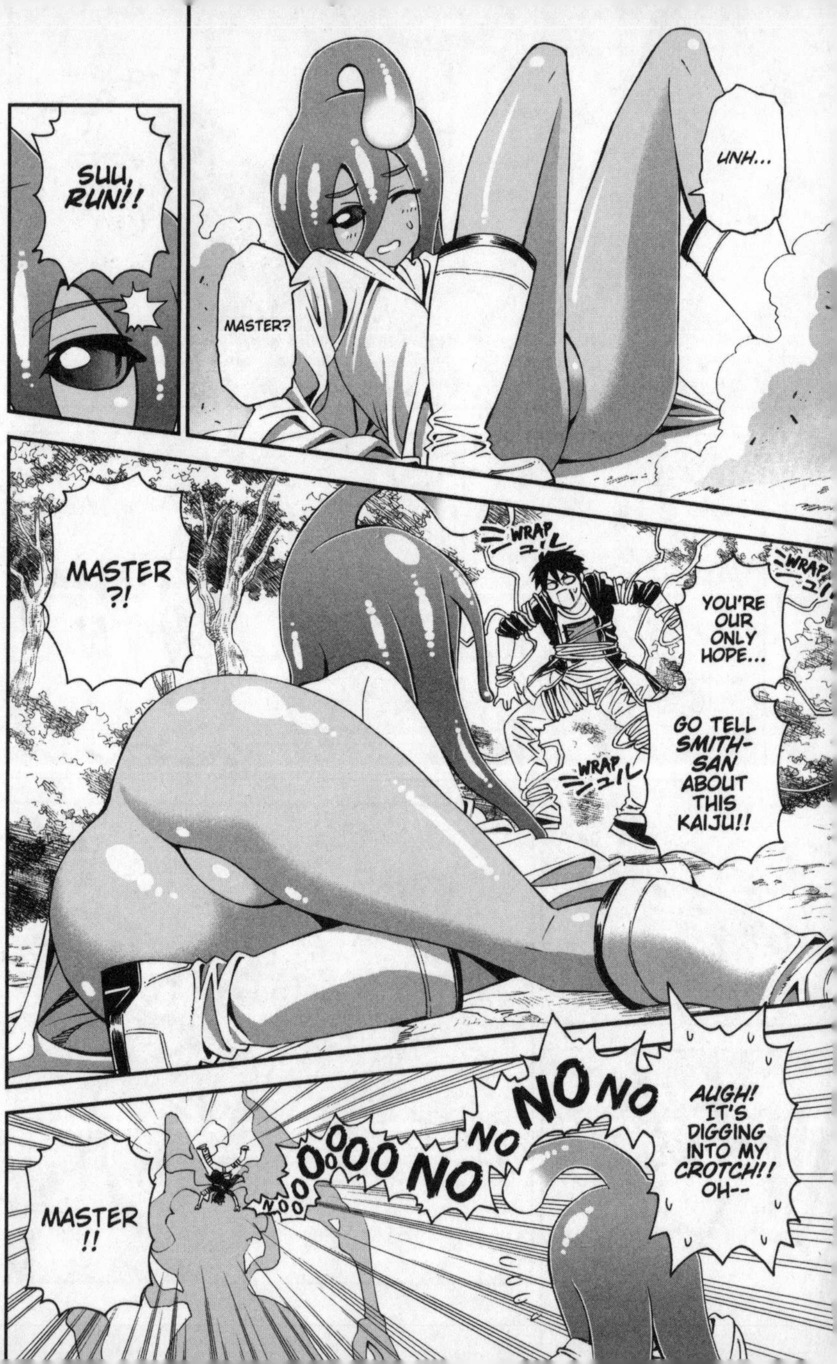
UNH...
MASTER?
SUU, RUN!!
WRAP
WRAP
YOU'RE OUR ONLY HOPE...
GO TELL SMITH-SAN ABOUT THIS KAIJU!!
WRAP
MASTER ?!
AUGH! IT'S DIGGING INTO MY CROTCH!! OH--
NO NO NO NO OOOOO NO
NOOO
MASTER !!

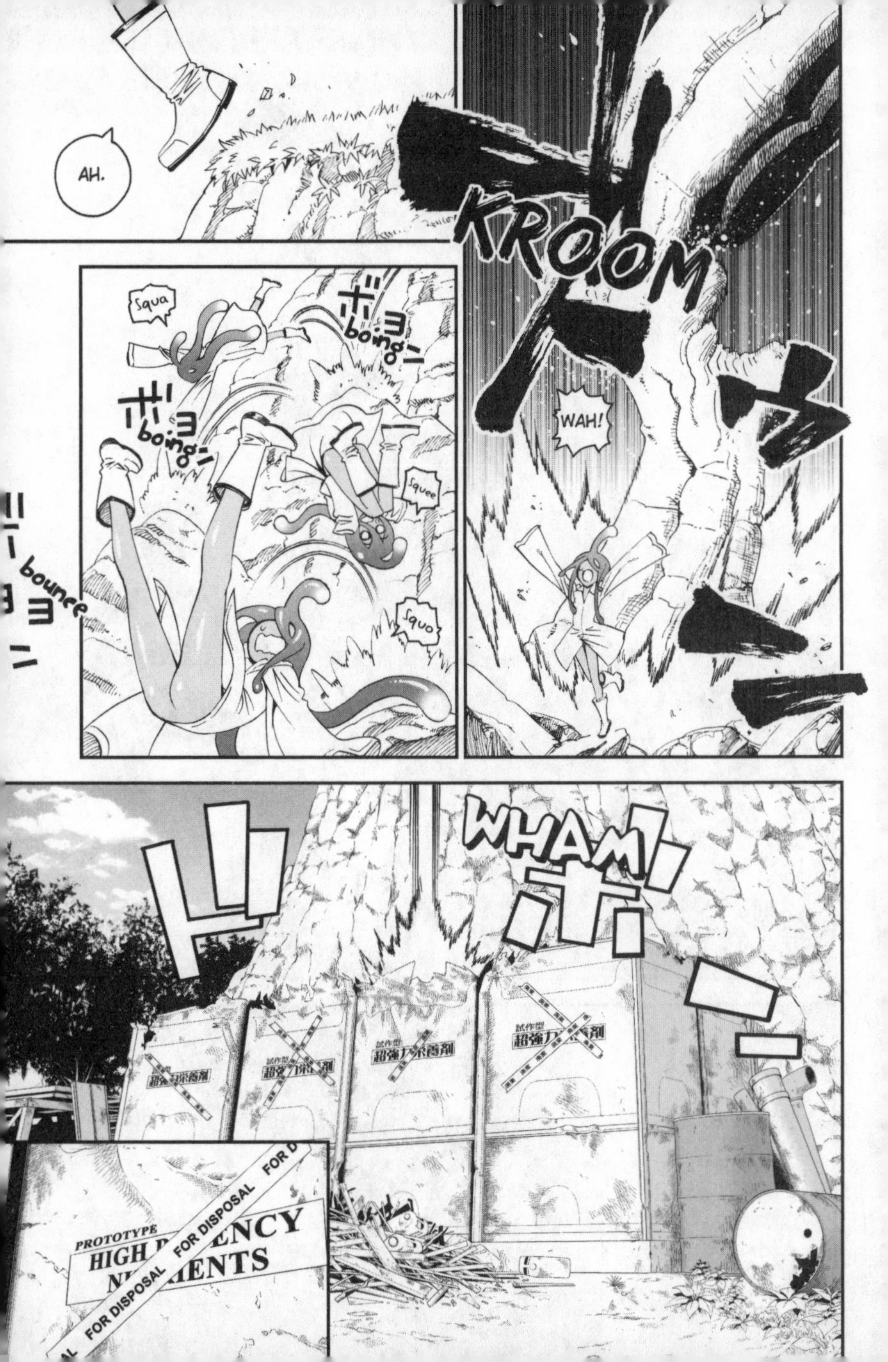

KROOM
WAH!
AH.
Squa
boing
boing
Squee
Squo
bounce
WHAM!
PROTOTYPE
FOR DISPOSAL
FOR DISPOSAL

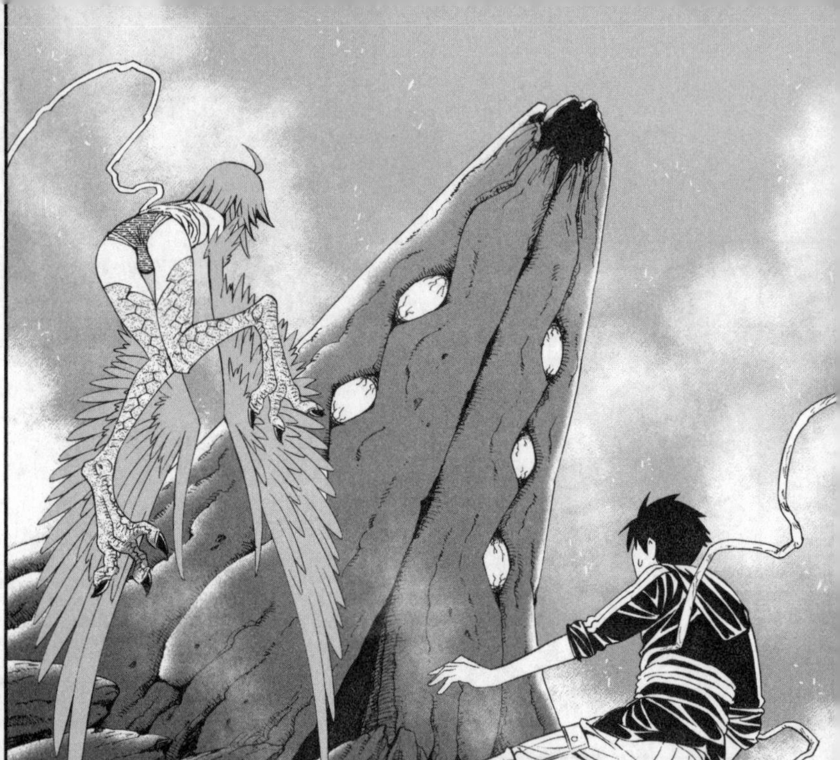

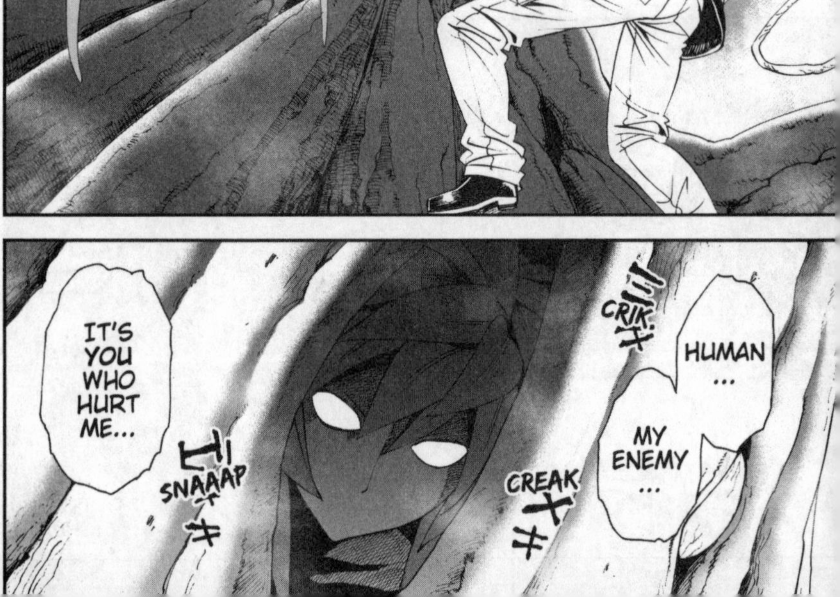
CRIK
HUMAN ...
MY ENEMY ...
CREAK
IT'S YOU WHO HURT ME...
SNAAAP

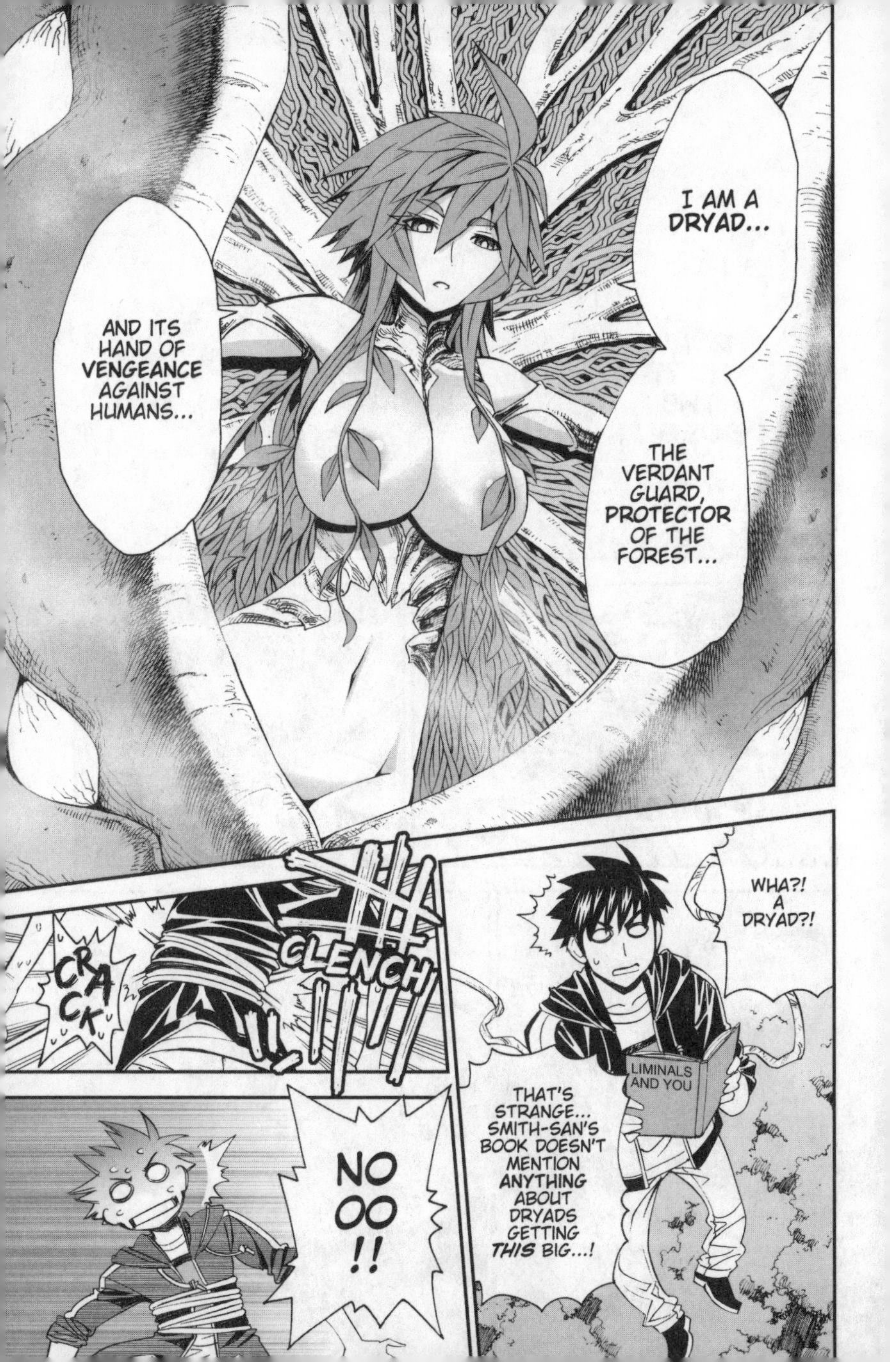
I AM A DRYAD...
THE VERDANT GUARD, PROTECTOR OF THE FOREST...
AND ITS HAND OF VENGEANCE AGAINST HUMANS...
WHA?! A DRYAD?!
LIMINALS AND YOU
THAT'S STRANGE... SMITH-SAN'S BOOK DOESN'T MENTION ANYTHING ABOUT DRYADS GETTING *THIS* BIG...!
CLENCH
CRACK
NOOO!!

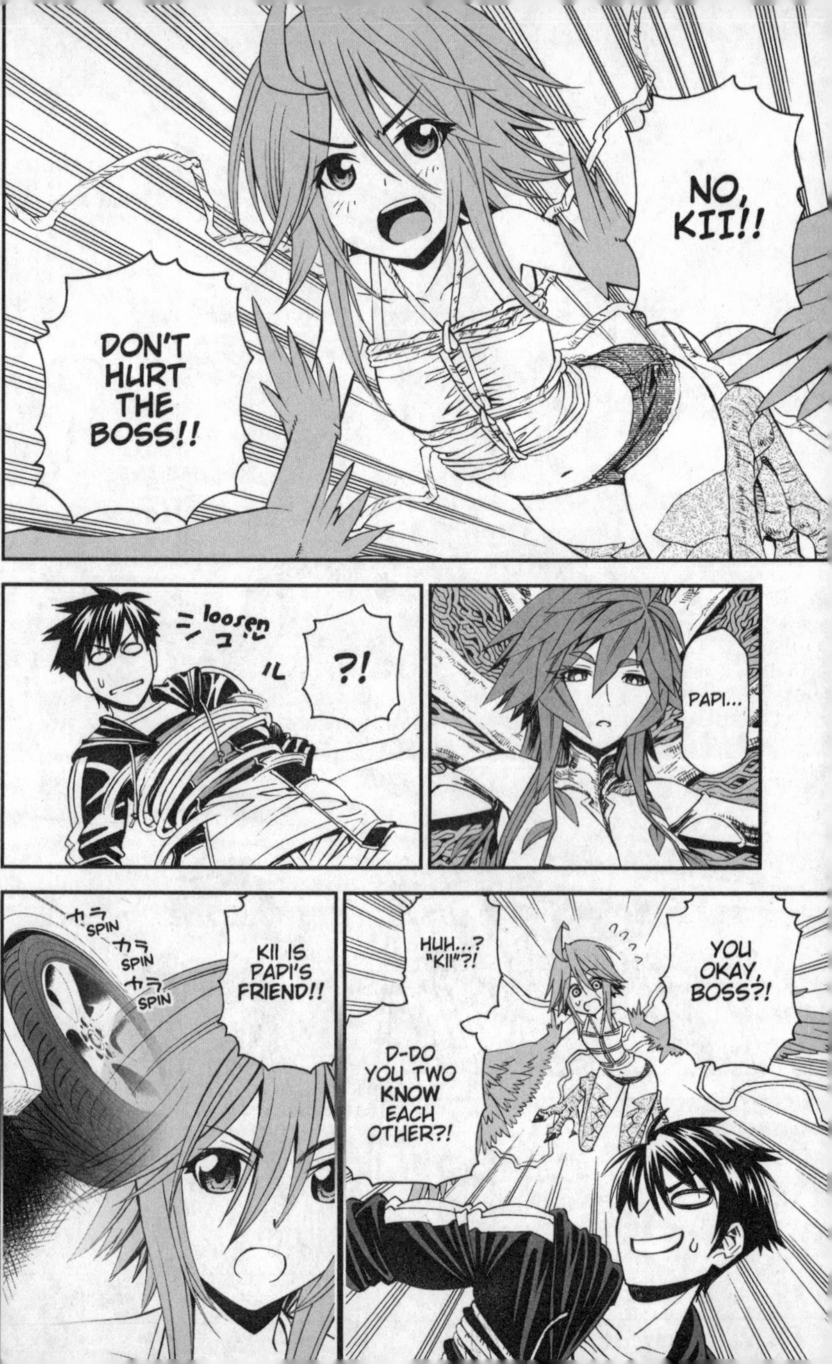
NO, KII!!
DON'T HURT THE BOSS!!
PAPI...
シュル loosen
?!
YOU OKAY, BOSS?!
HUH...? "KII"?!
D-DO YOU TWO KNOW EACH OTHER?!
KII IS PAPI'S FRIEND!!
カラ SPIN
カラ SPIN
カラ SPIN

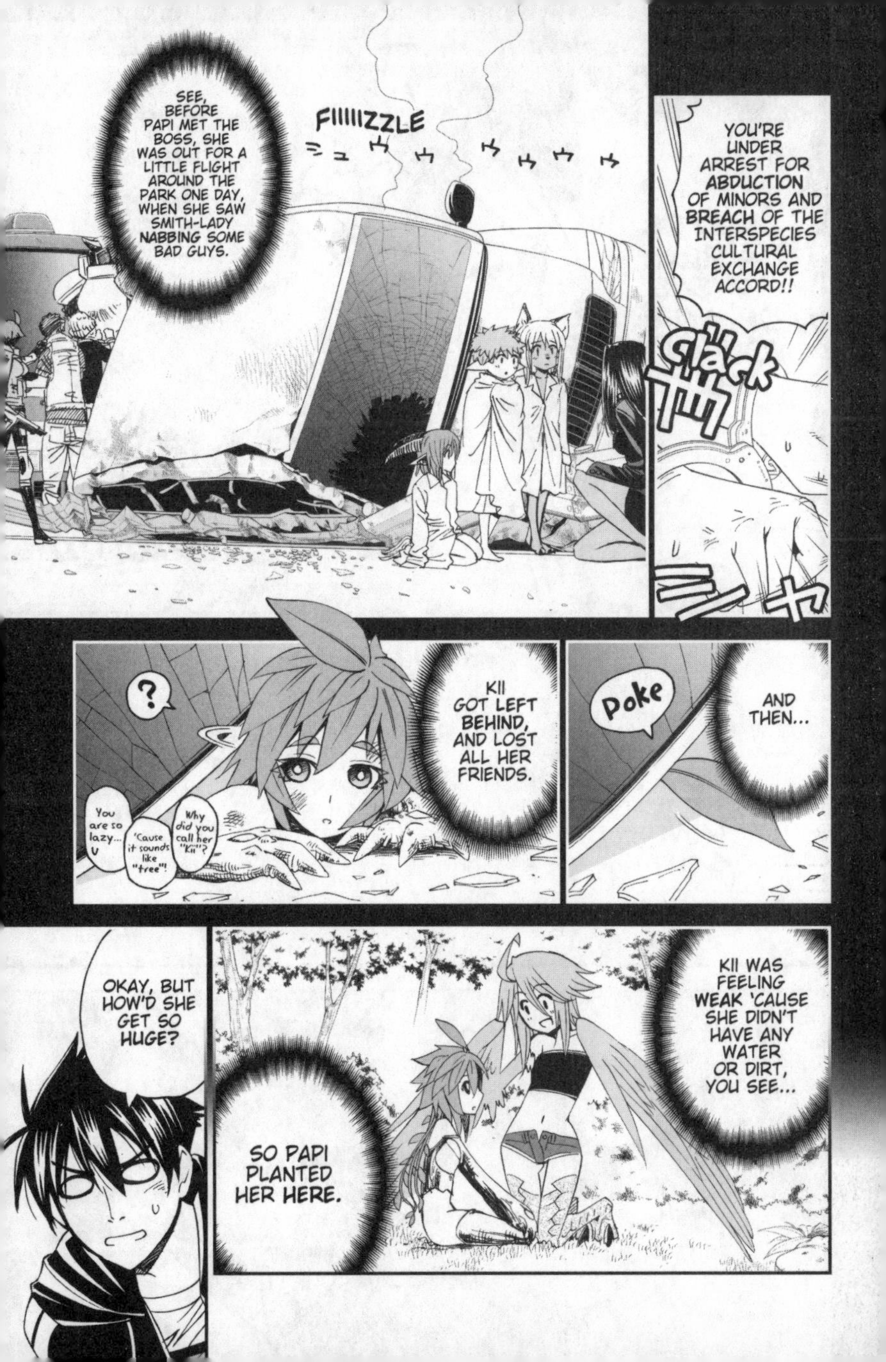
YOU'RE UNDER ARREST FOR ABDUCTION OF MINORS AND BREACH OF THE INTERSPECIES CULTURAL EXCHANGE ACCORD!!
clack
SEE, BEFORE PAPI MET THE BOSS, SHE WAS OUT FOR A LITTLE FLIGHT AROUND THE PARK ONE DAY, WHEN SHE SAW SMITH-LADY NABBING SOME BAD GUYS.
FIIIIZZLE
AND THEN...
Poke
KII GOT LEFT BEHIND, AND LOST ALL HER FRIENDS.
?
Why did you call her "Kii"?
'Cause it sounds like "tree"!
You are so lazy...
KII WAS FEELING WEAK 'CAUSE SHE DIDN'T HAVE ANY WATER OR DIRT, YOU SEE...
SO PAPI PLANTED HER HERE.
OKAY, BUT HOW'D SHE GET SO HUGE?

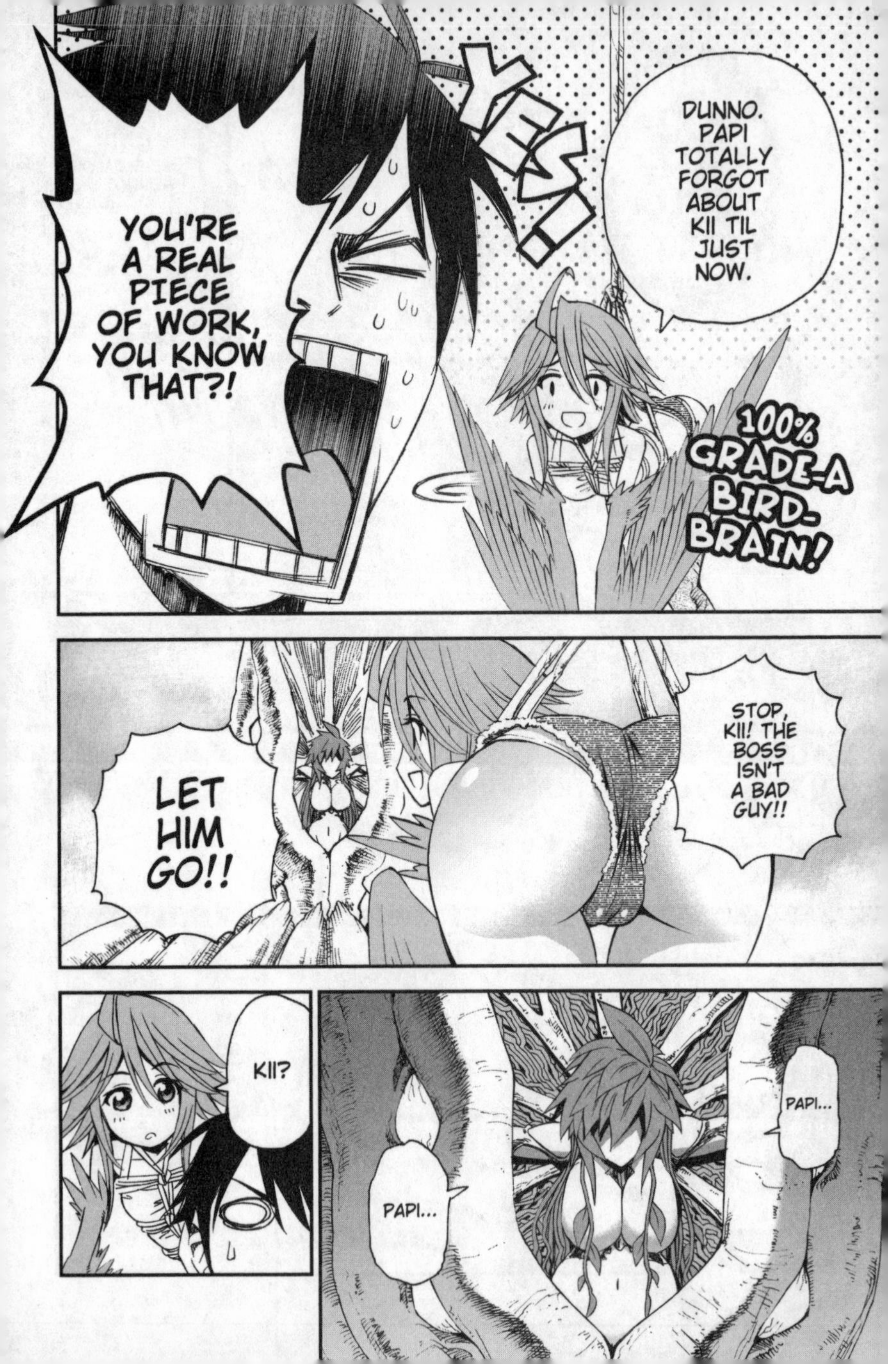

DUNNO. PAPI TOTALLY FORGOT ABOUT KII TIL JUST NOW.
YES!
100% GRADE-A BIRD-BRAIN!
YOU'RE A REAL PIECE OF WORK, YOU KNOW THAT?!
STOP, KII! THE BOSS ISN'T A BAD GUY!!
LET HIM GO!!
PAPI...
PAPI...
KII?

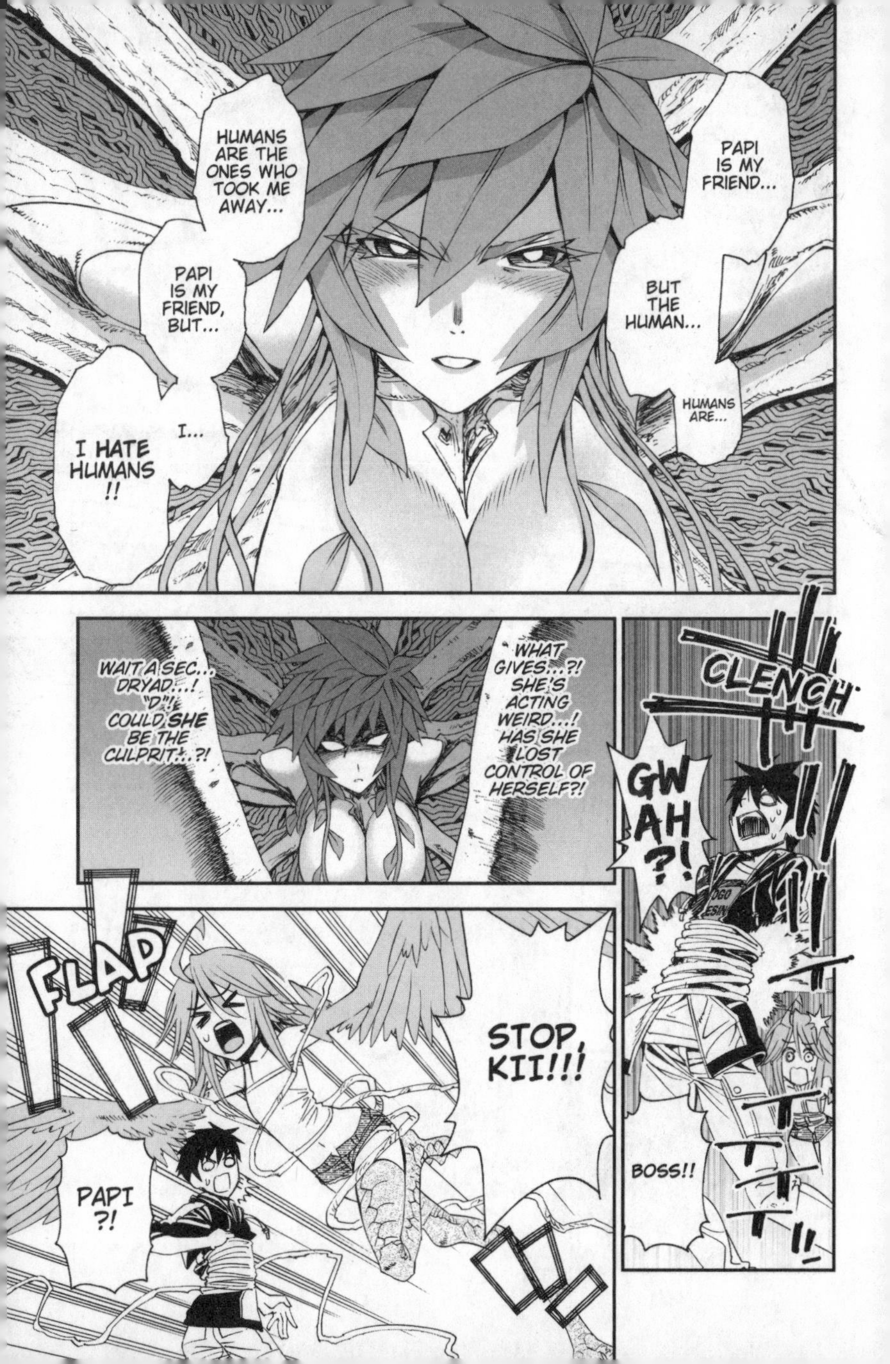
PAPI IS MY FRIEND...
BUT THE HUMAN...
HUMANS ARE...
HUMANS ARE THE ONES WHO TOOK ME AWAY...
PAPI IS MY FRIEND, BUT...
I...
I HATE HUMANS!!
CLENCH
GWAH?!
BOSS!!
WHAT GIVES...?! SHE'S ACTING WEIRD...! HAS SHE LOST CONTROL OF HERSELF?!
WAIT A SEC... DRYAD...! "D"! COULD SHE BE THE CULPRIT...?!
STOP, KII!!!
FLAP
PAPI ?!

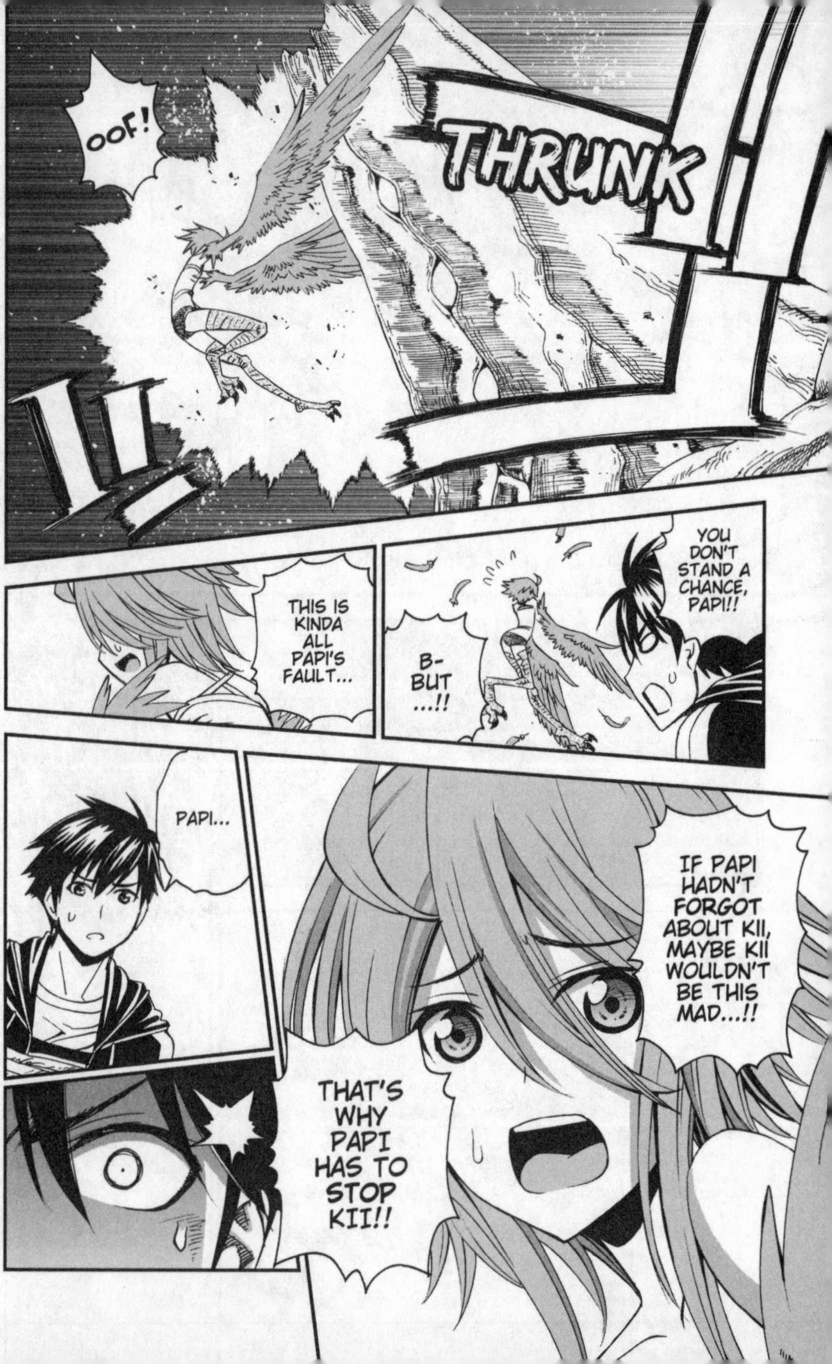
THRUNK
OOF!
YOU DON'T STAND A CHANCE, PAPI!!
B-BUT...!!
THIS IS KINDA ALL PAPI'S FAULT...
IF PAPI HADN'T FORGOT ABOUT KII, MAYBE KII WOULDN'T BE THIS MAD...!!
THAT'S WHY PAPI HAS TO STOP KII!!
PAPI...

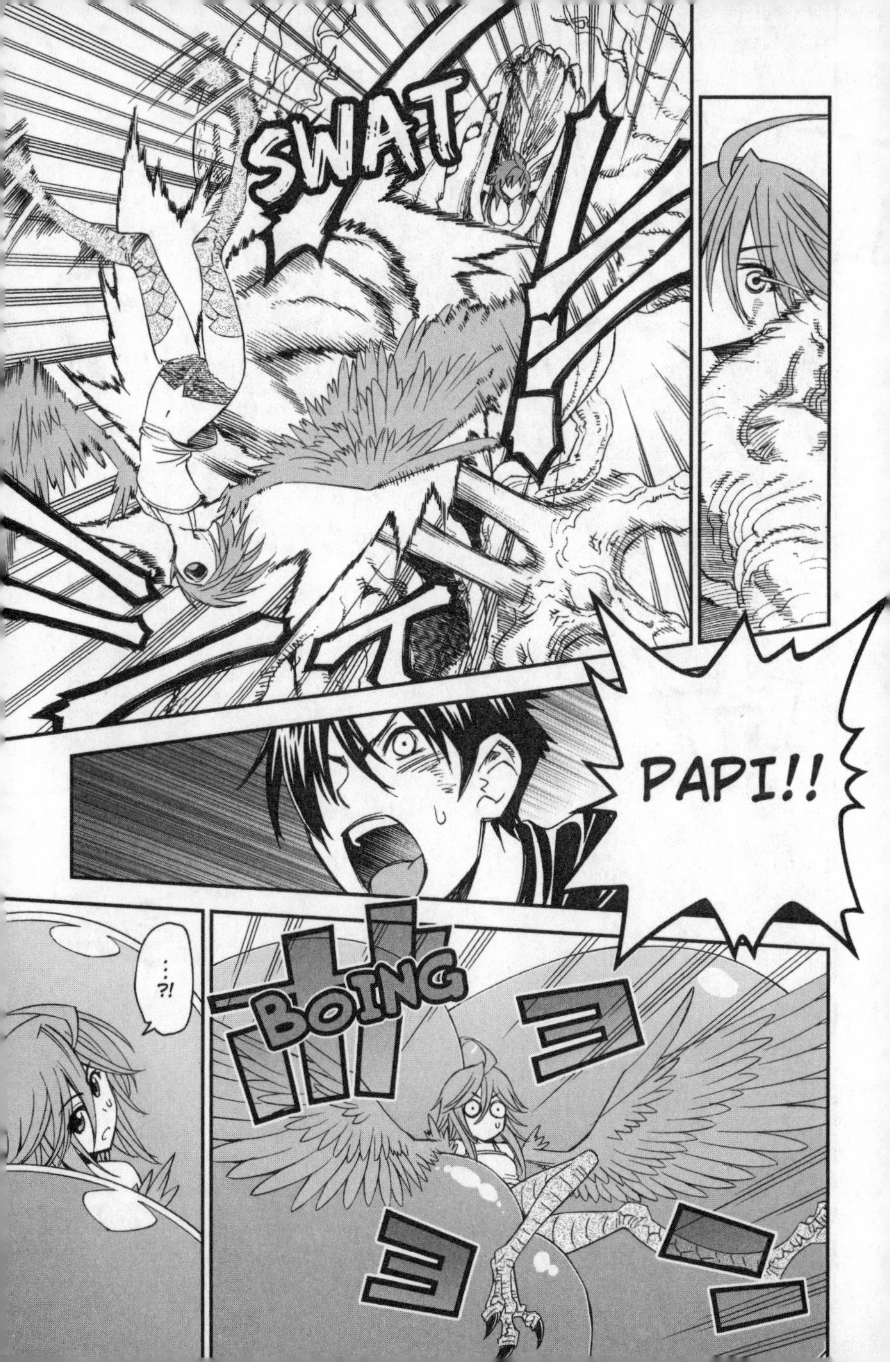
SWAT
PAPI!!
BOING
…?!

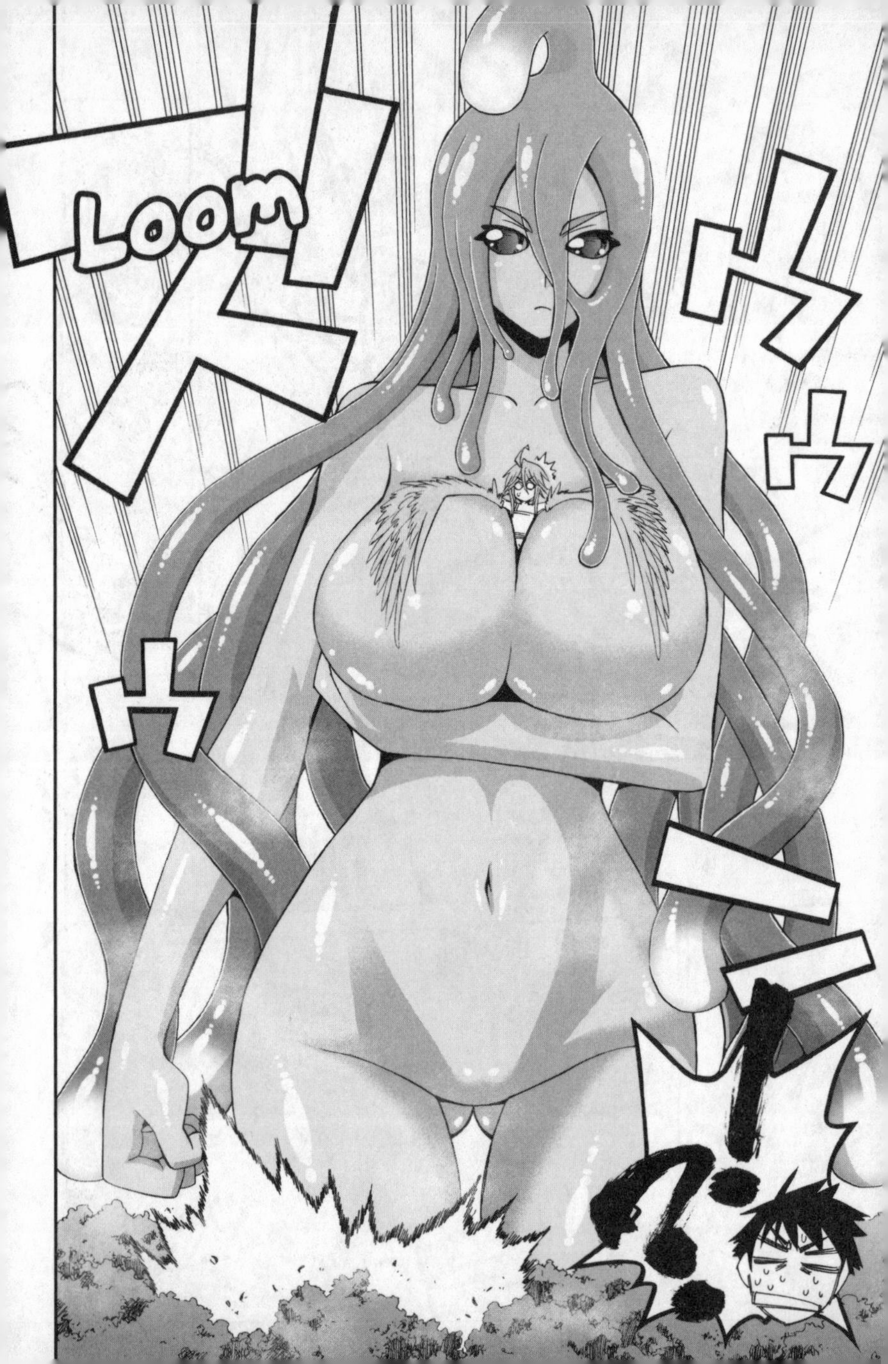
LOOM
!?

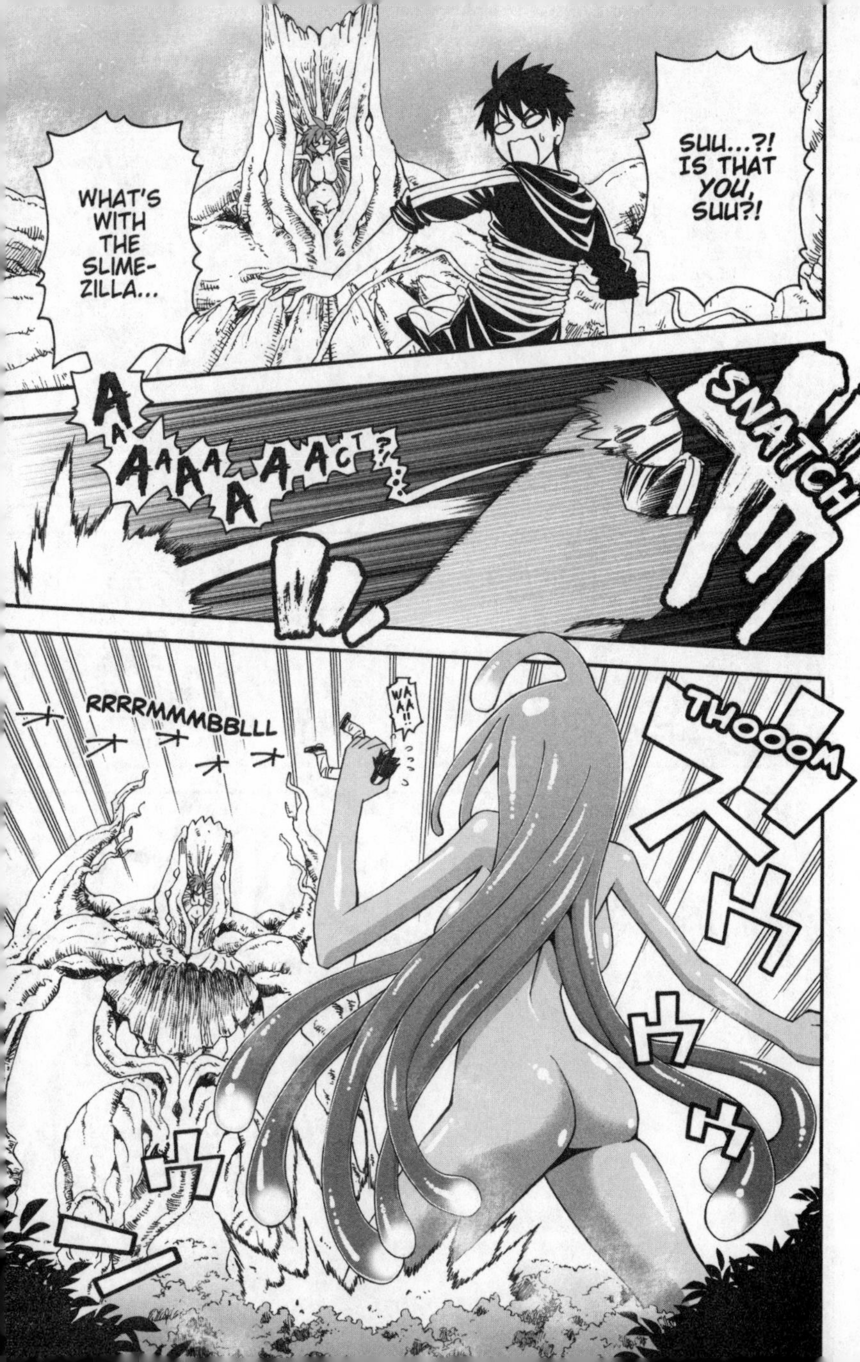
SUU...?! IS THAT YOU, SUU?!
WHAT'S WITH THE SLIME-ZILLA...
SNATCH
AAAAAAAAAACT?!...
THOOOM
WAAA!!
RRRRMMMBBLLL

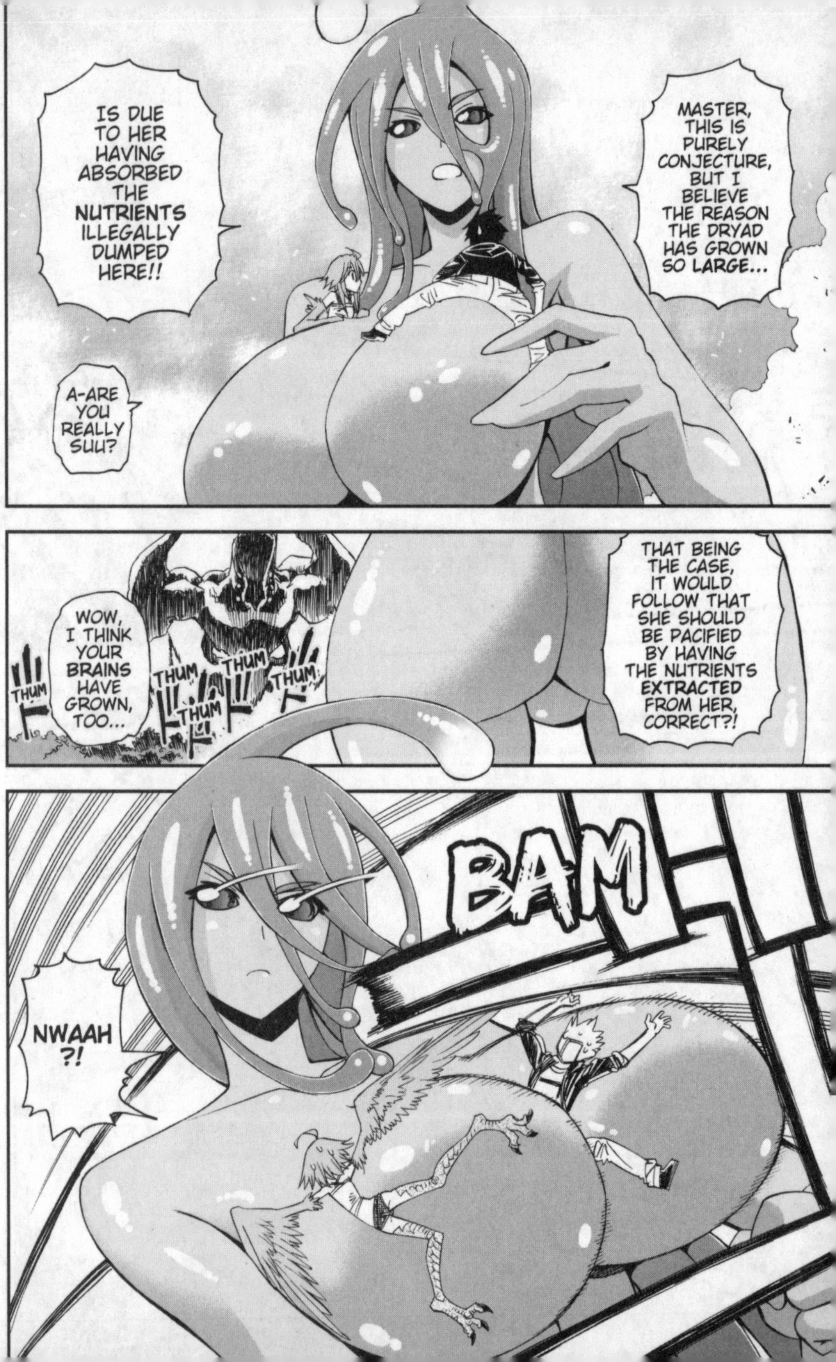

MASTER, THIS IS PURELY CONJECTURE, BUT I BELIEVE THE REASON THE DRYAD HAS GROWN SO LARGE...
IS DUE TO HER HAVING ABSORBED THE NUTRIENTS ILLEGALLY DUMPED HERE!!
A-ARE YOU REALLY SUU?
THAT BEING THE CASE, IT WOULD FOLLOW THAT SHE SHOULD BE PACIFIED BY HAVING THE NUTRIENTS EXTRACTED FROM HER, CORRECT?!
THUM THUM THUM THUM THUM
WOW, I THINK YOUR BRAINS HAVE GROWN, TOO...
BAM
NWAAH ?!

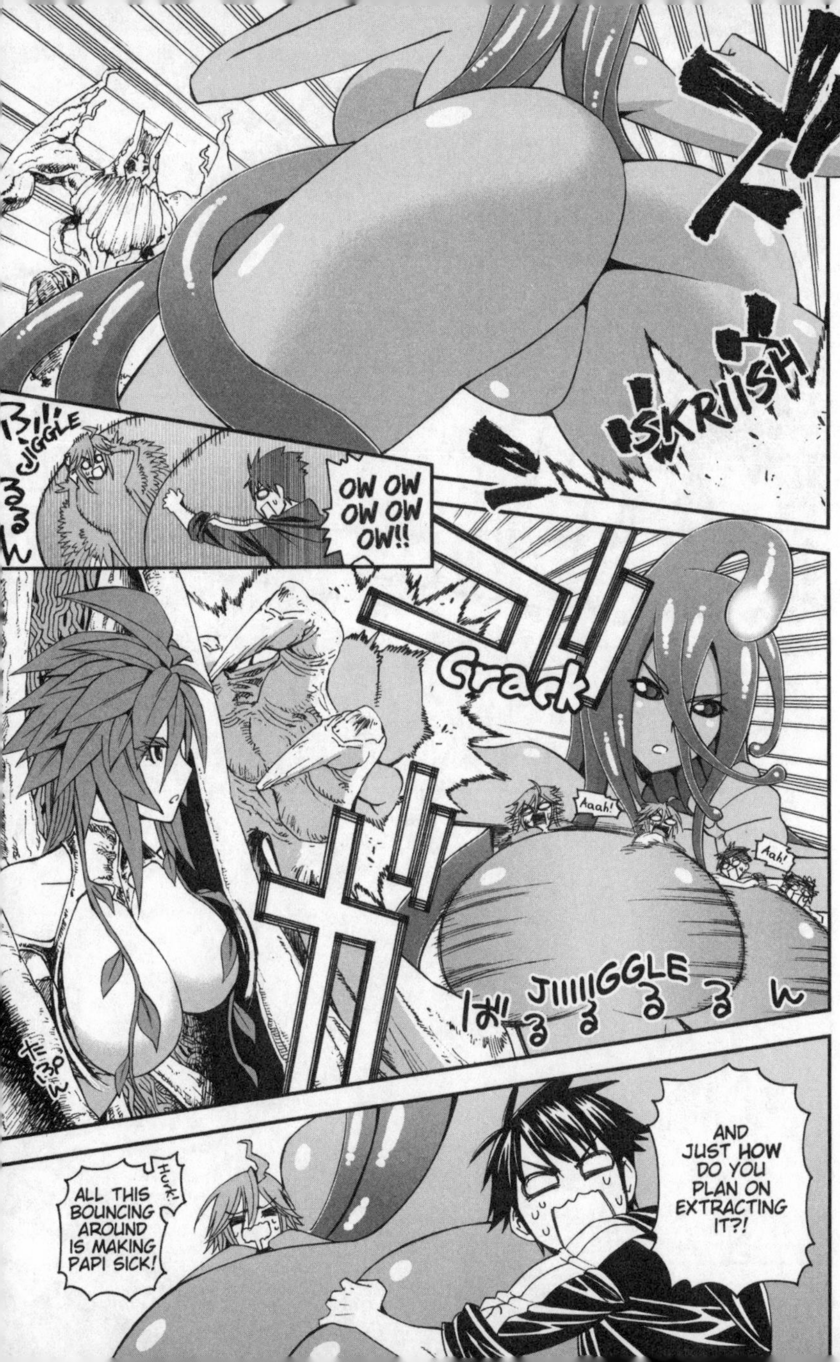
SKRIISH
OW OW OW OW OW!!
JIGGLE
Crack
Aaah!
Aah!
JIIIIGGLE
AND JUST HOW DO YOU PLAN ON EXTRACTING IT?!
Hurk!
ALL THIS BOUNCING AROUND IS MAKING PAPI SICK!

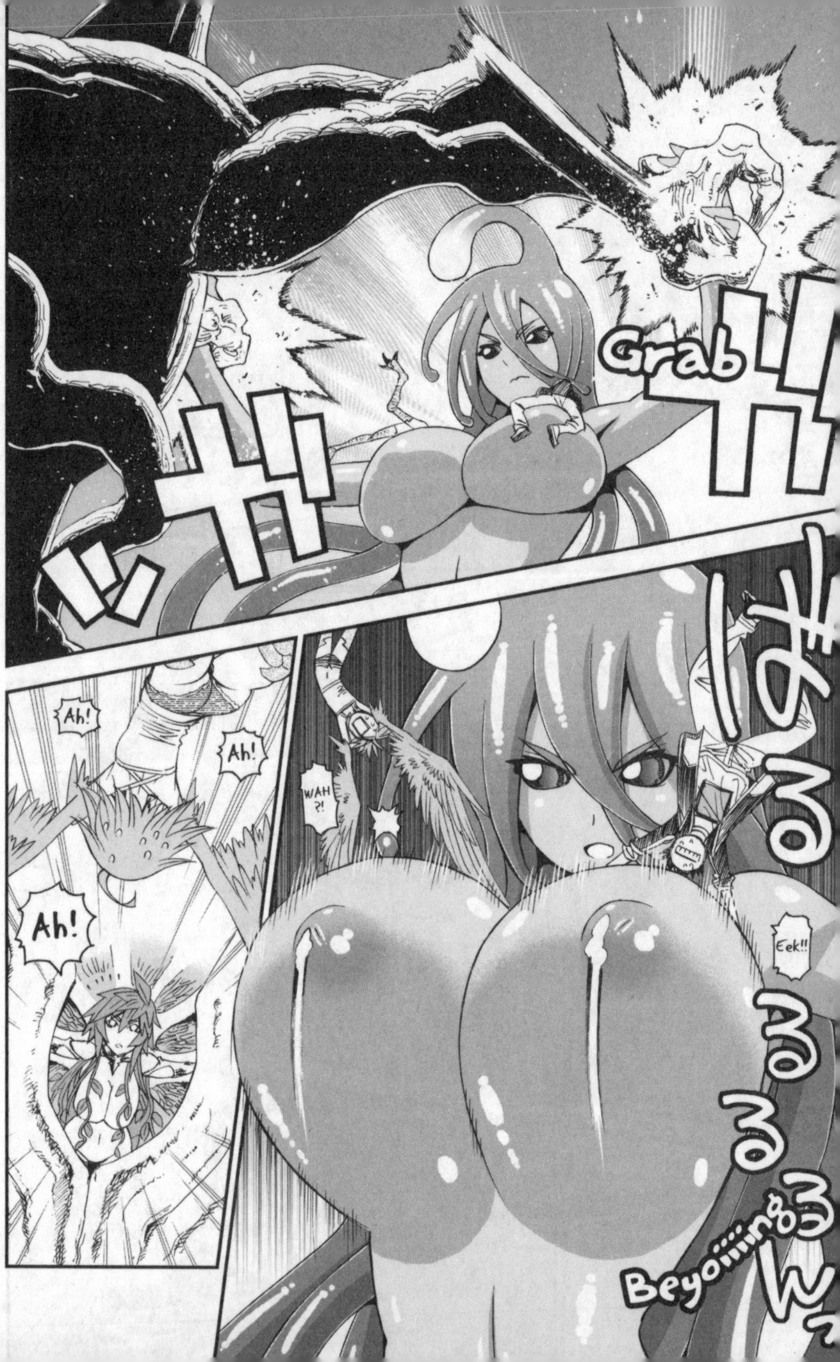
Grab
WAH ?!
Eek!!
Beyoiiiing
Ah!
Ah!
Ah!

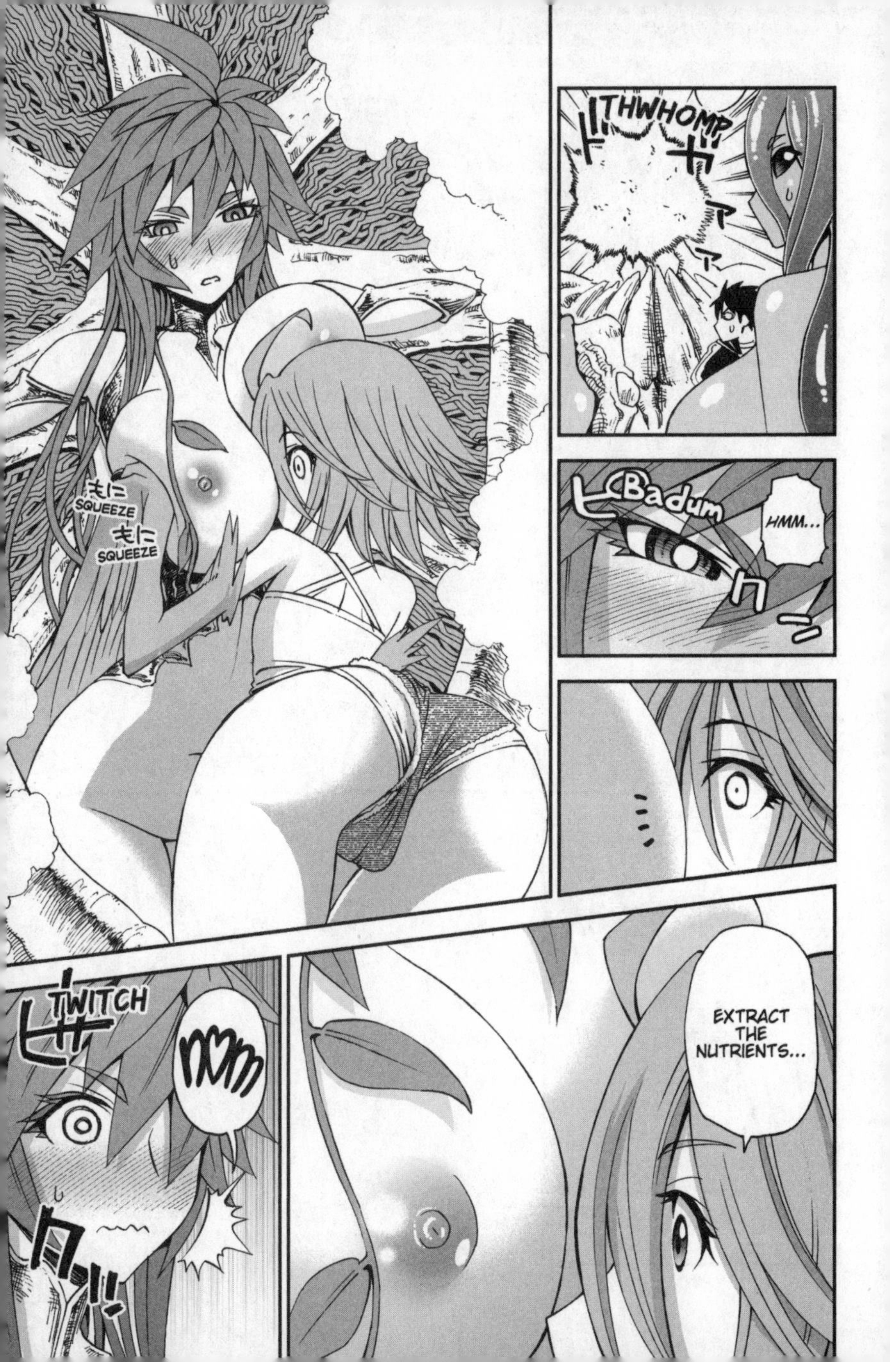
THWHOMP
Badum
HMM...
もに
SQUEEZE
もに
SQUEEZE
EXTRACT THE NUTRIENTS...
TWITCH
nom

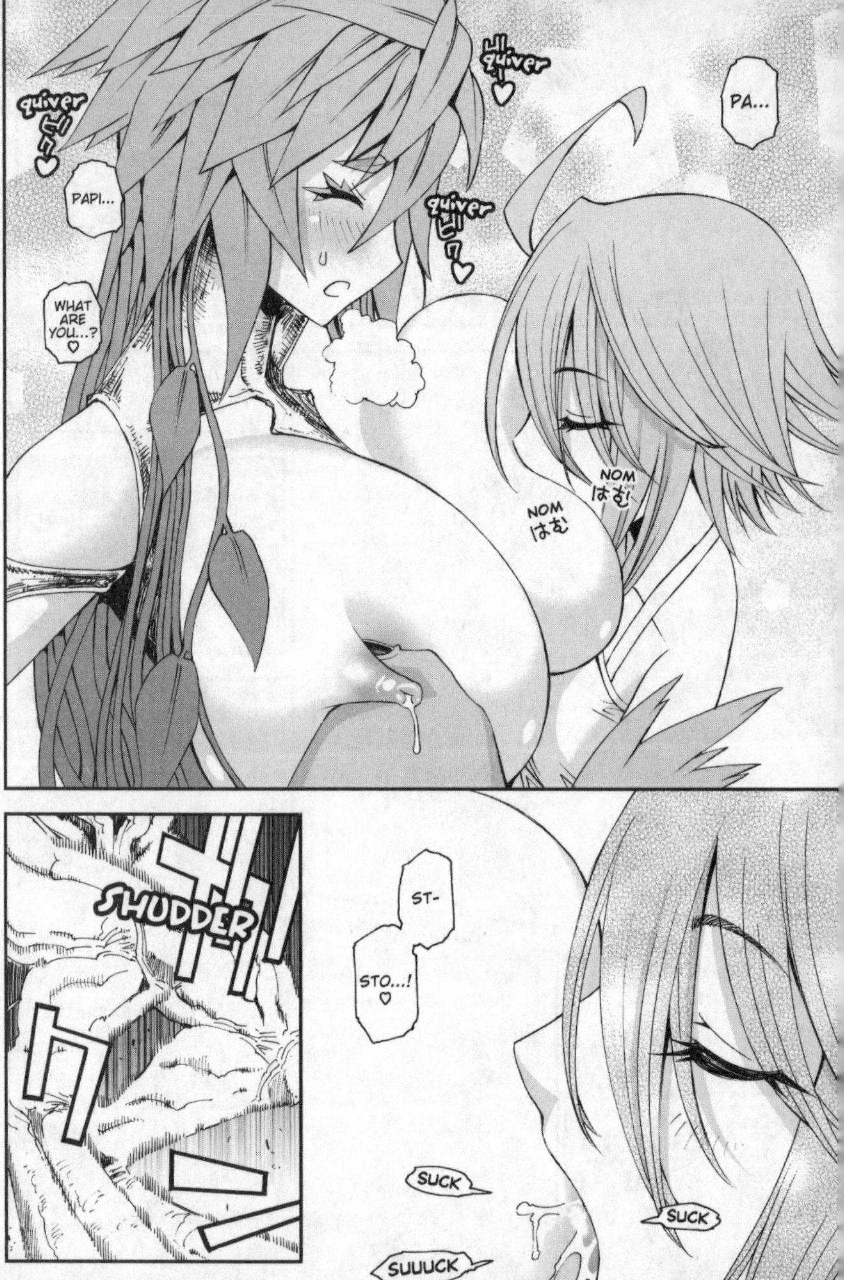
PA...
quiver ビク♡
quiver ビク♡
quiver ビク♡
PAPI...
WHAT ARE YOU...?♡
NOM はむ!
NOM はむ
ST-
STO...!♡
SUCK
SUCK
SUUUCK
SHUDDER

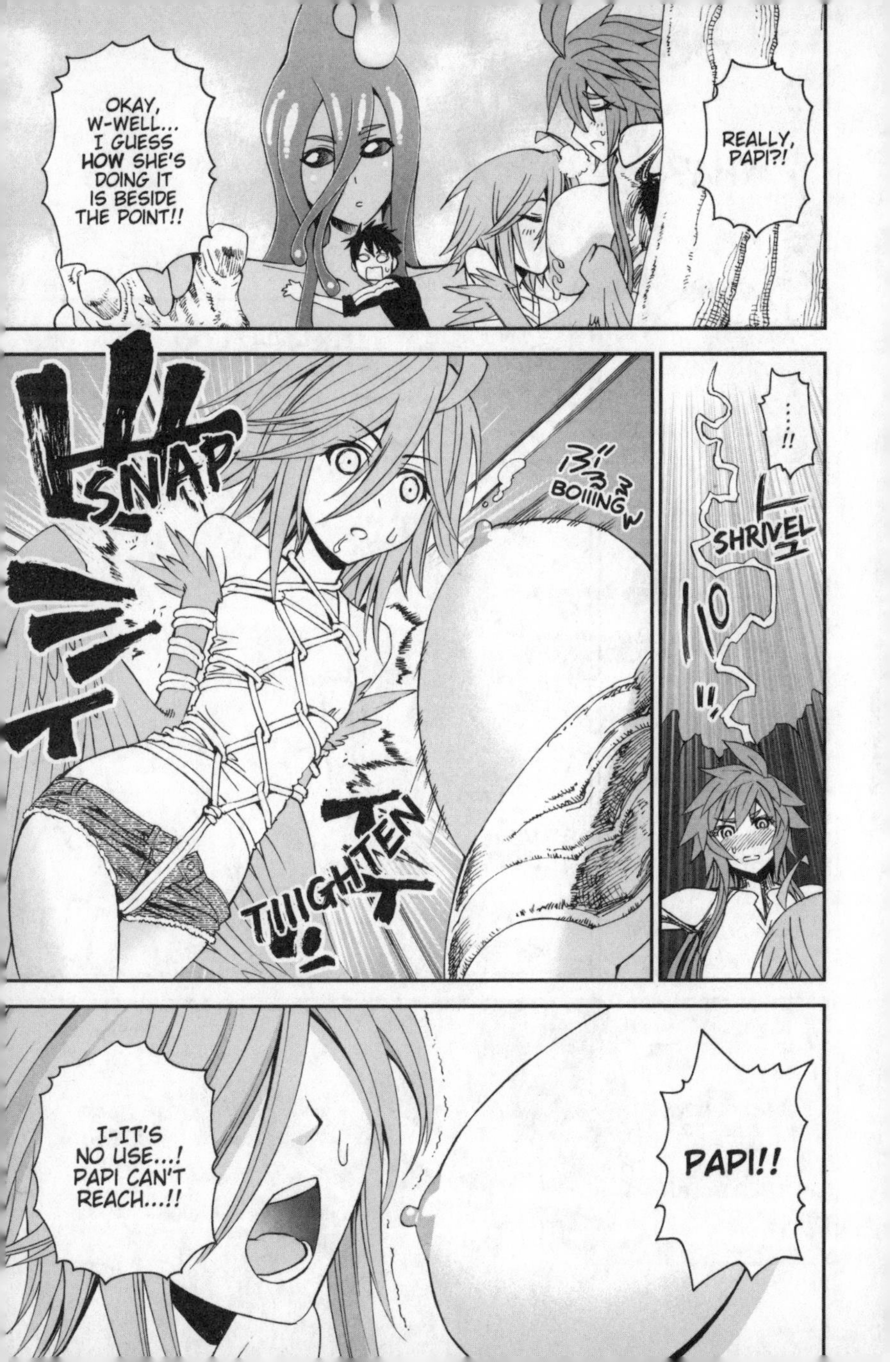
REALLY, PAPI?!
OKAY, W-WELL... I GUESS HOW SHE'S DOING IT IS BESIDE THE POINT!!
...!!
SHRIVEL
BOIIING
SNAP
TIIIGHTEN
PAPI!!
I-IT'S NO USE...! PAPI CAN'T REACH...!!

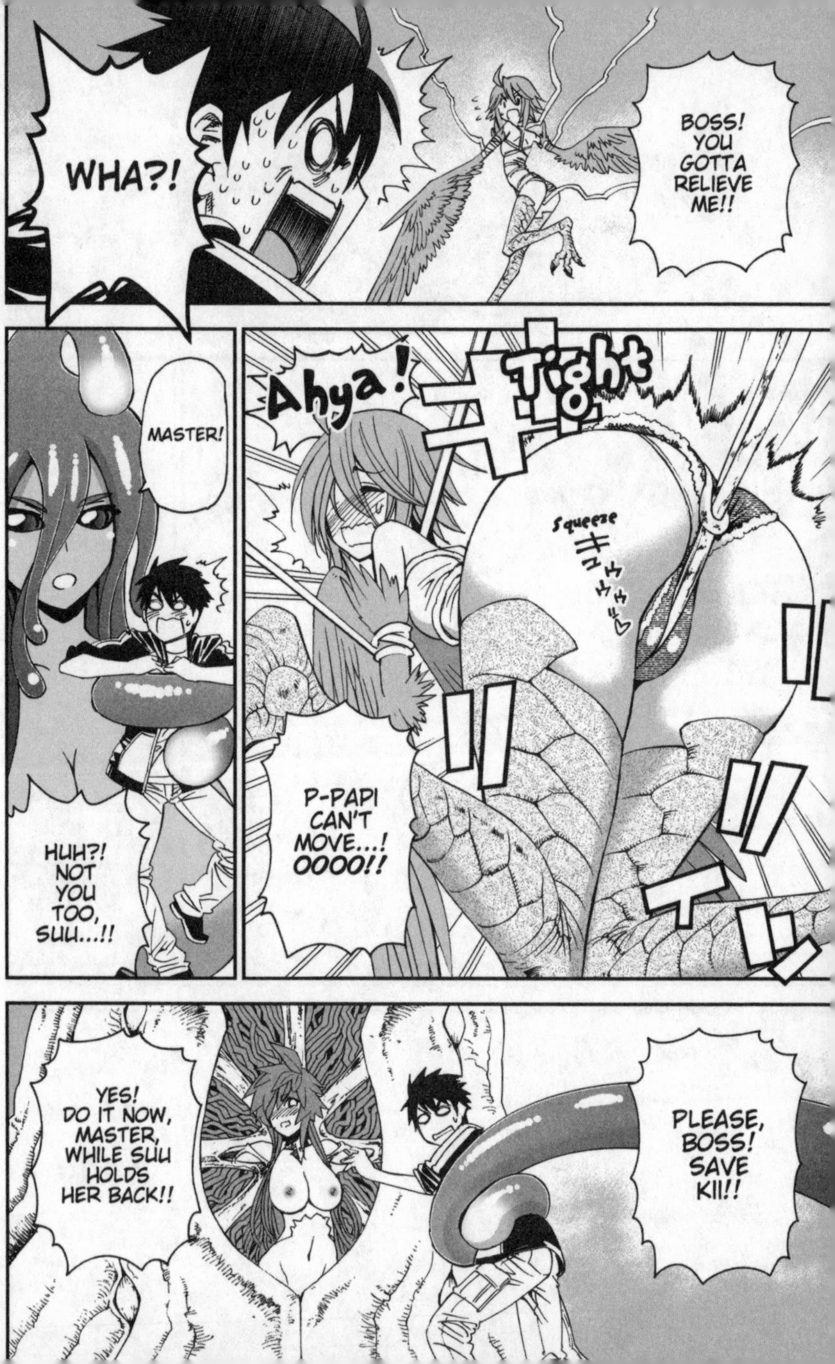
BOSS! YOU GOTTA RELIEVE ME!!
WHA?!
Ahya!
Tight
Squeeze
P-PAPI CAN'T MOVE...! OOOO!!
MASTER!
HUH?! NOT YOU TOO, SUU...!!
PLEASE, BOSS! SAVE KII!!
YES! DO IT NOW, MASTER, WHILE SUU HOLDS HER BACK!!

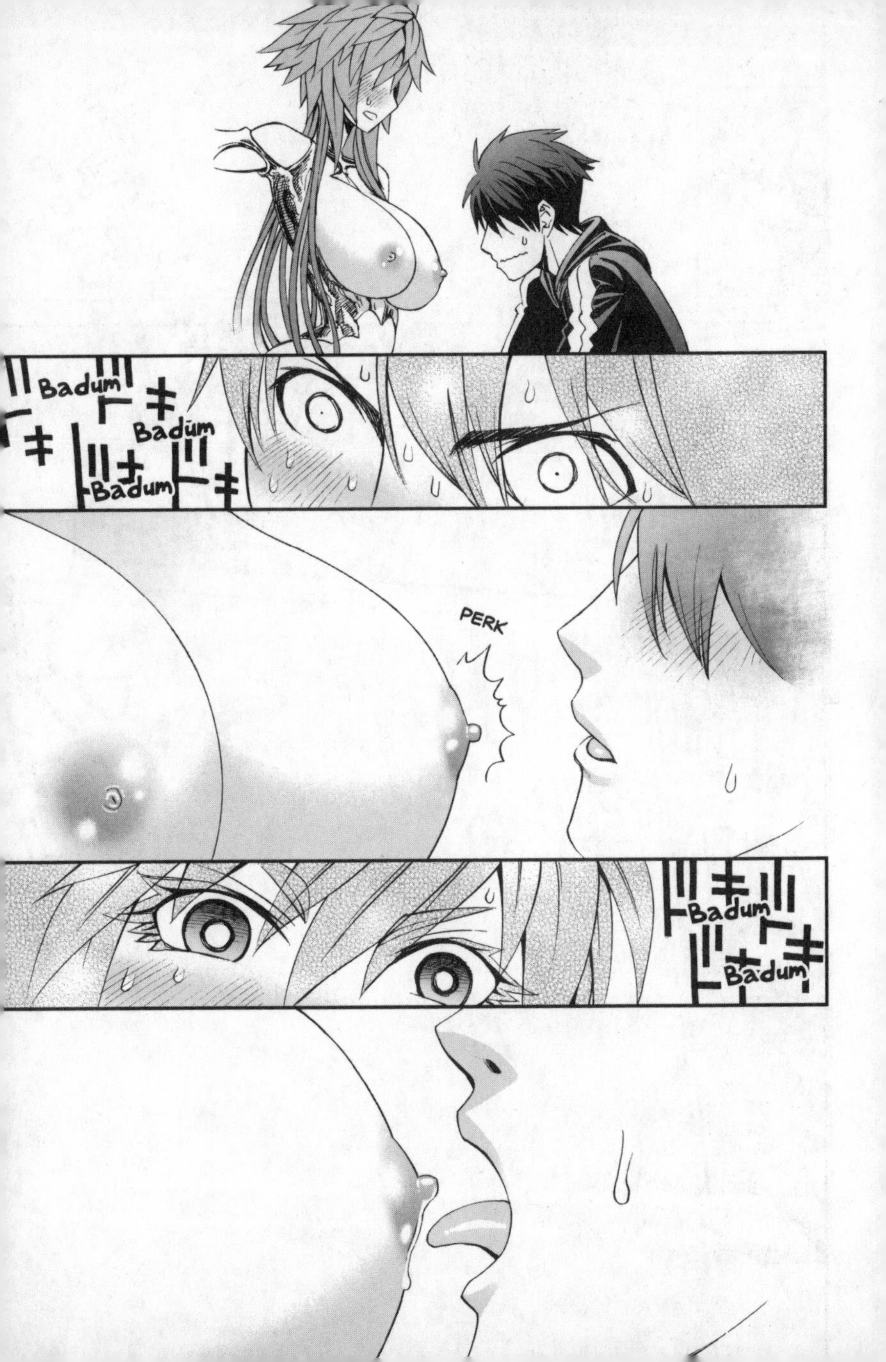
ドキ
Badum
ドキ
Badum
ドキ
Badum
ドキ
PERK
ドキ
Badum
ドキ
Badum

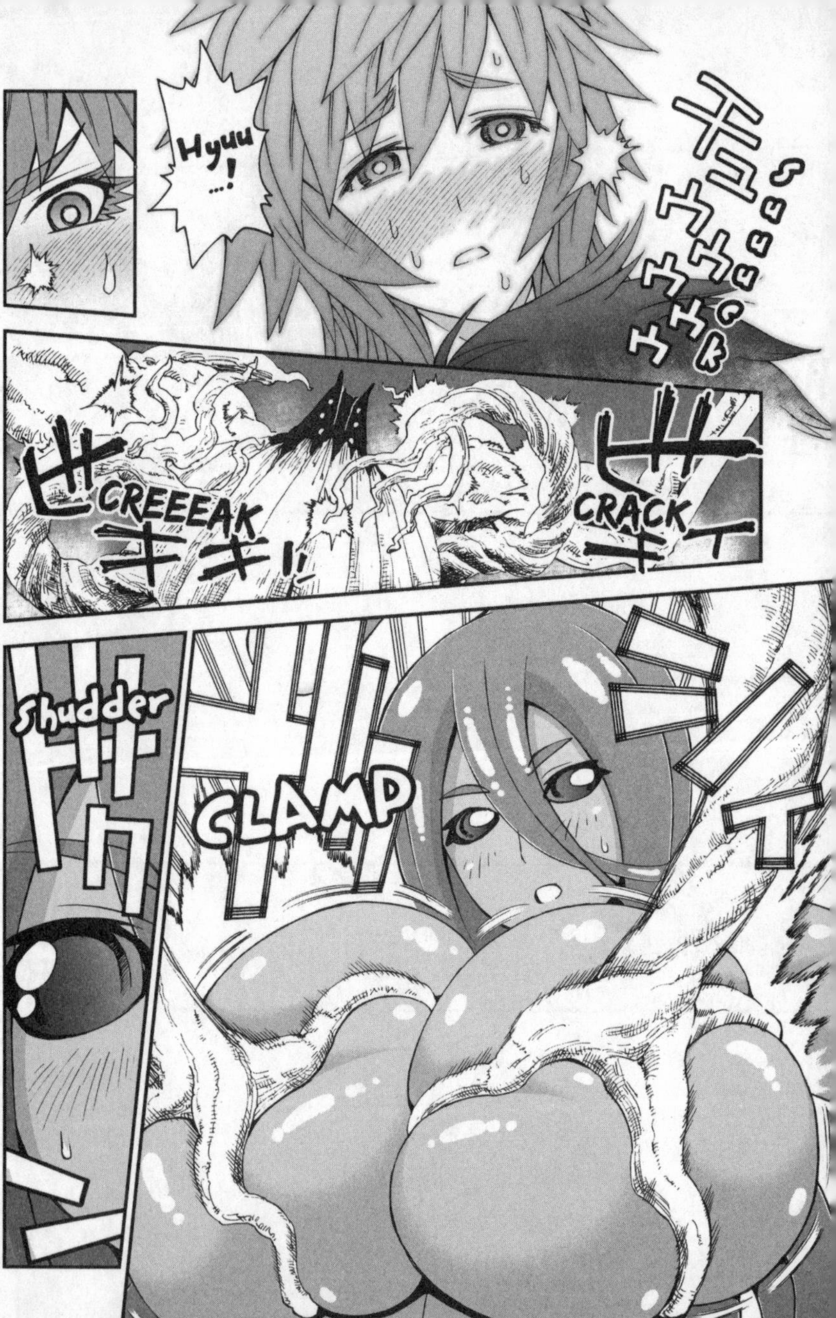
suuuuuck
Hyuu...!
CRACK
CREEEAK
CLAMP
Shudder

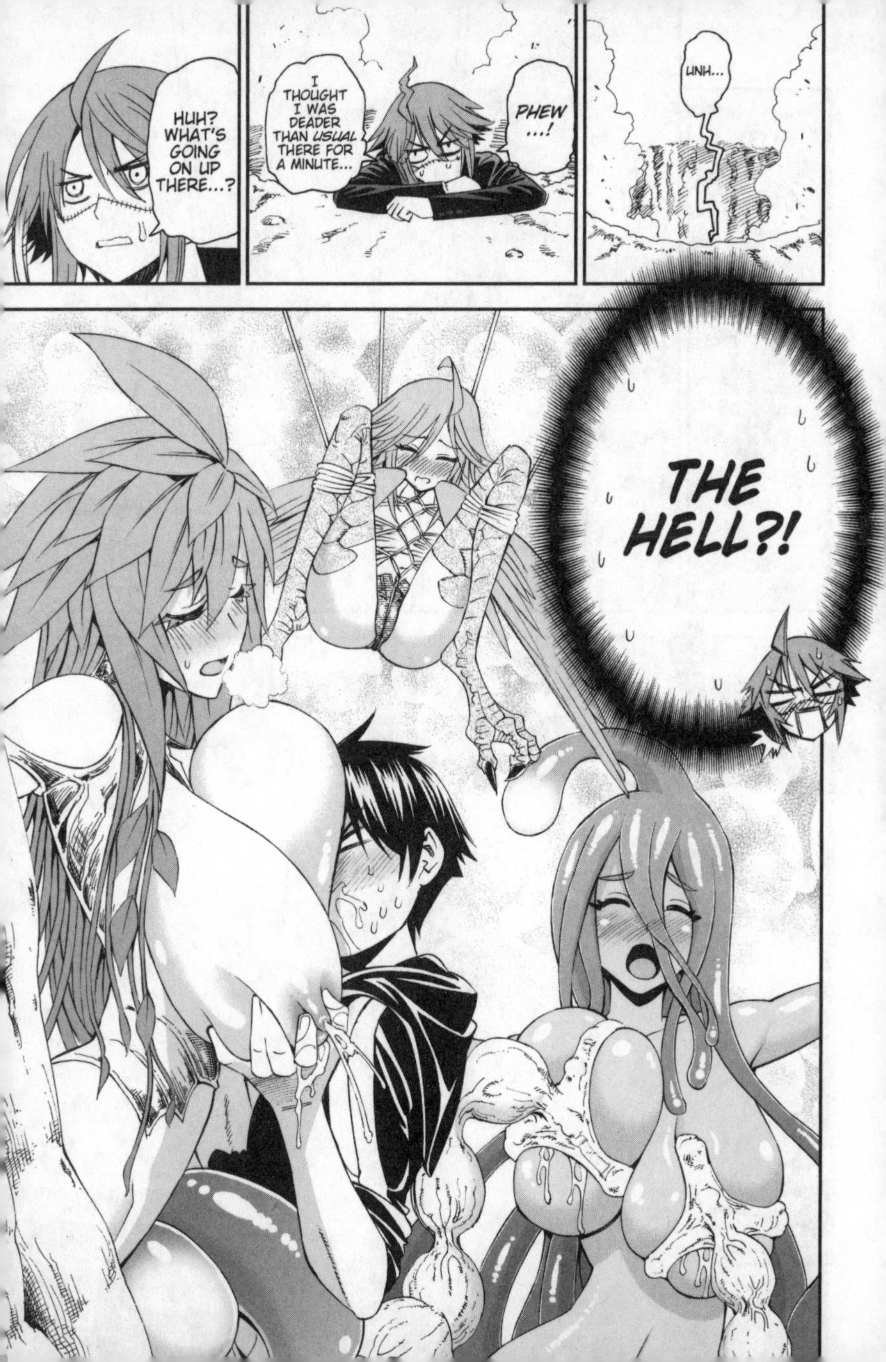
UNH...
PHEW ...!
I THOUGHT I WAS DEADER THAN *USUAL* THERE FOR A MINUTE...
HUH? WHAT'S GOING ON UP THERE...?
THE HELL?!

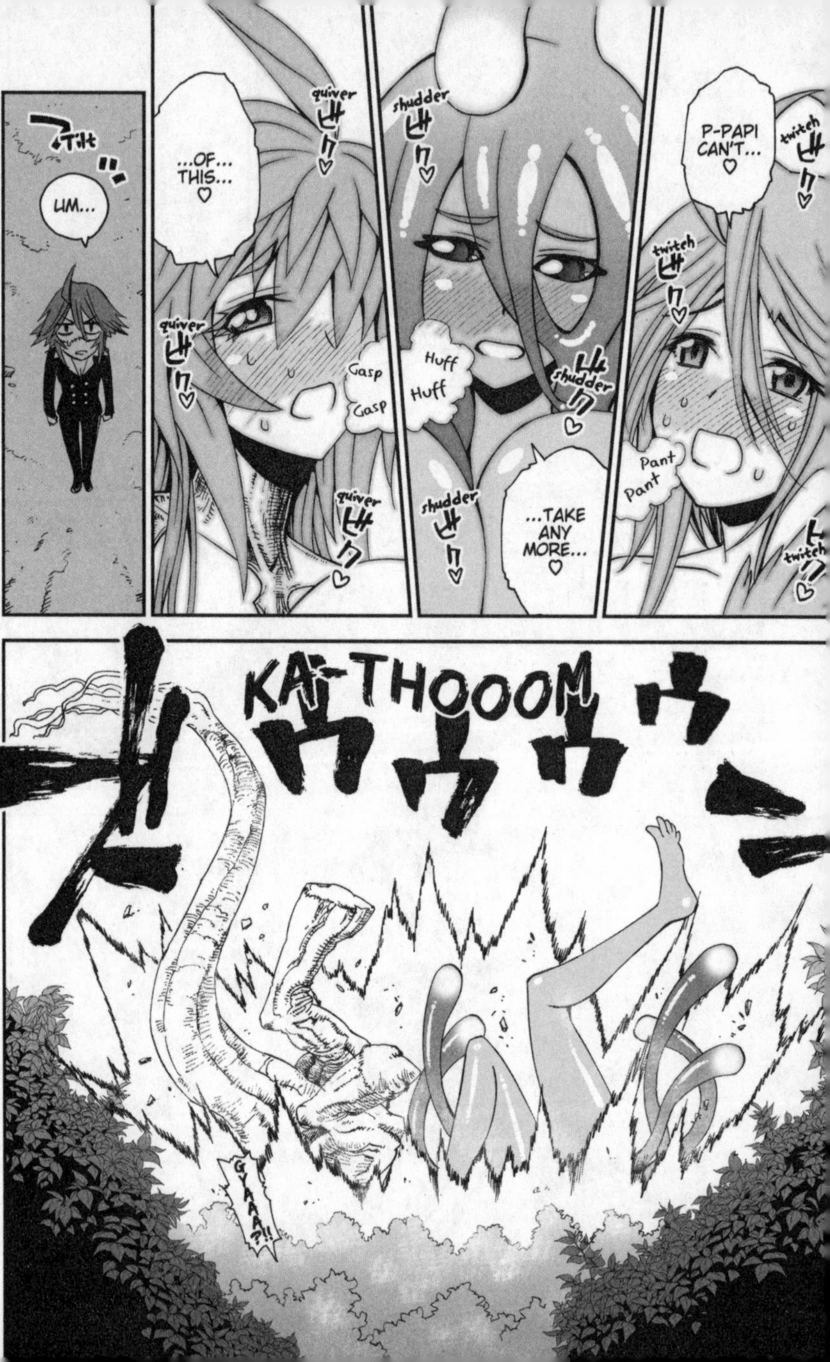

P-PAPI CAN'T... ♡
twitch
twitch
Pant Pant
twitch
shudder
shudder
Huff Huff
...TAKE ANY MORE... ♡
shudder
quiver
...OF... THIS... ♡
quiver
Gasp Gasp
quiver
Tilt
UM...
KA-THOOOM
GYAAAA?!!

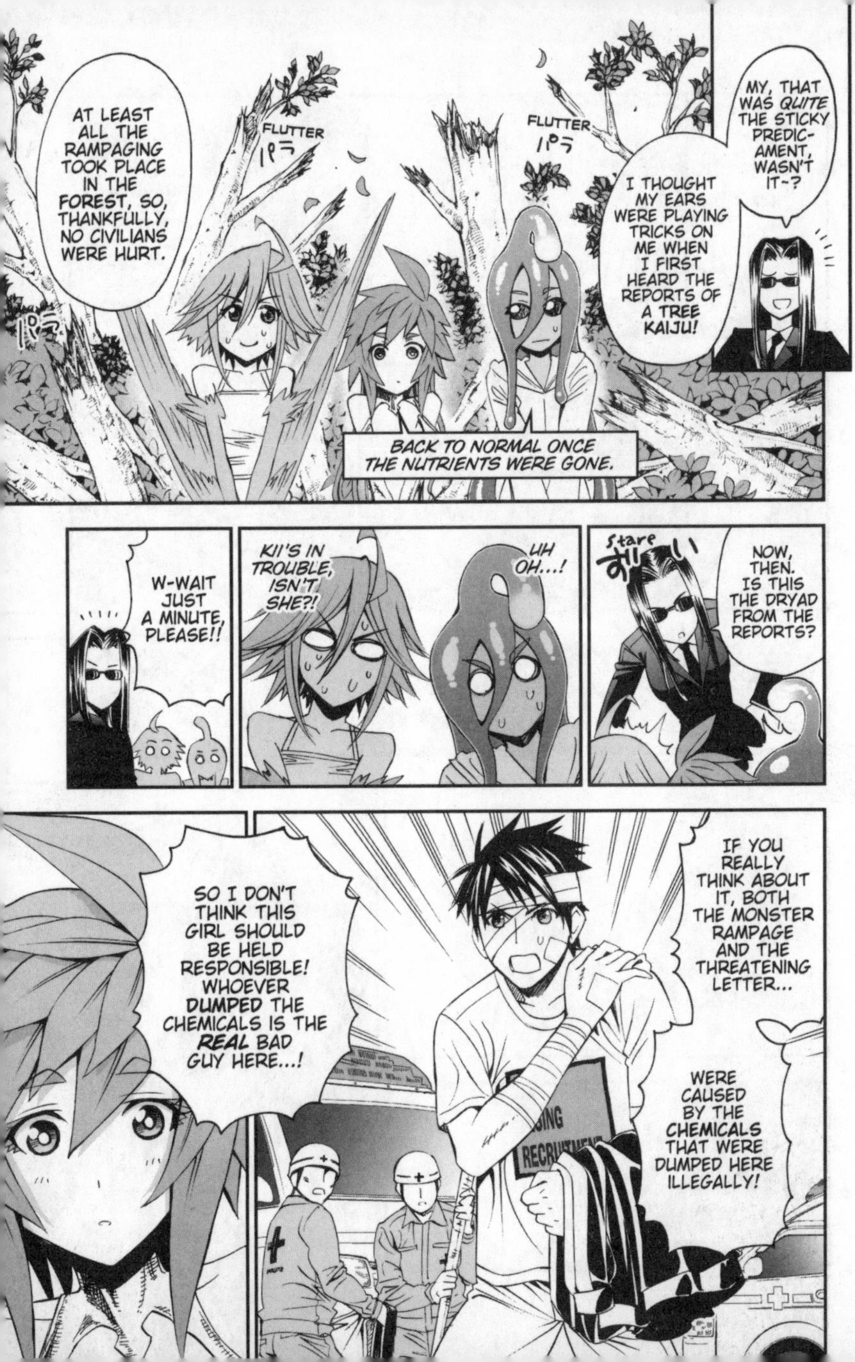
MY, THAT WAS *QUITE* THE STICKY PREDICAMENT, WASN'T IT~?
I THOUGHT MY EARS WERE PLAYING TRICKS ON ME WHEN I FIRST HEARD THE REPORTS OF A TREE KAIJU!
FLUTTER
パラ
FLUTTER
パラ
AT LEAST ALL THE RAMPAGING TOOK PLACE IN THE FOREST, SO, THANKFULLY, NO CIVILIANS WERE HURT.
パラ
BACK TO NORMAL ONCE THE NUTRIENTS WERE GONE.
NOW, THEN. IS THIS THE DRYAD FROM THE REPORTS?
Stare
UH OH...!
KII'S IN TROUBLE, ISN'T SHE?!
W-WAIT JUST A MINUTE, PLEASE!!
IF YOU REALLY THINK ABOUT IT, BOTH THE MONSTER RAMPAGE AND THE THREATENING LETTER...
WERE CAUSED BY THE CHEMICALS THAT WERE DUMPED HERE ILLEGALLY!
SO I DON'T THINK THIS GIRL SHOULD BE HELD RESPONSIBLE! WHOEVER **DUMPED** THE CHEMICALS IS THE ***REAL*** BAD GUY HERE...!

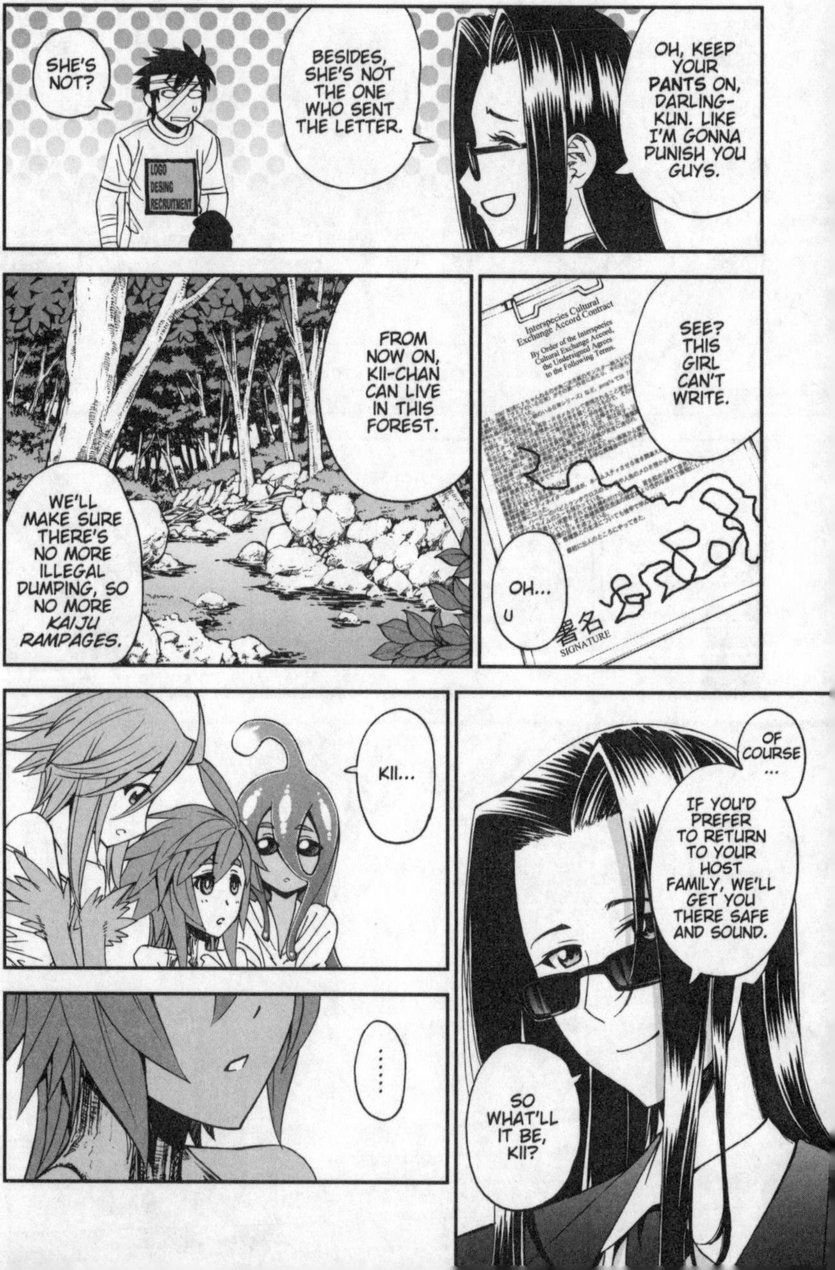
OH, KEEP YOUR PANTS ON, DARLING-KUN. LIKE I'M GONNA PUNISH YOU GUYS.
BESIDES, SHE'S NOT THE ONE WHO SENT THE LETTER.
SHE'S NOT?
LOGO DESING RECRUITMENT
SEE? THIS GIRL CAN'T WRITE.
Interspecies Cultural Exchange Accord Contract
By Order of the Interspecies Cultural Exchange Accord, the Undersigned Agrees to the Following Terms.
署名 SIGNATURE
OH...
FROM NOW ON, KII-CHAN CAN LIVE IN THIS FOREST.
WE'LL MAKE SURE THERE'S NO MORE ILLEGAL DUMPING, SO NO MORE *KAIJU* RAMPAGES.
OF COURSE...
IF YOU'D PREFER TO RETURN TO YOUR HOST FAMILY, WE'LL GET YOU THERE SAFE AND SOUND.
SO WHAT'LL IT BE, KII?
KII...
......

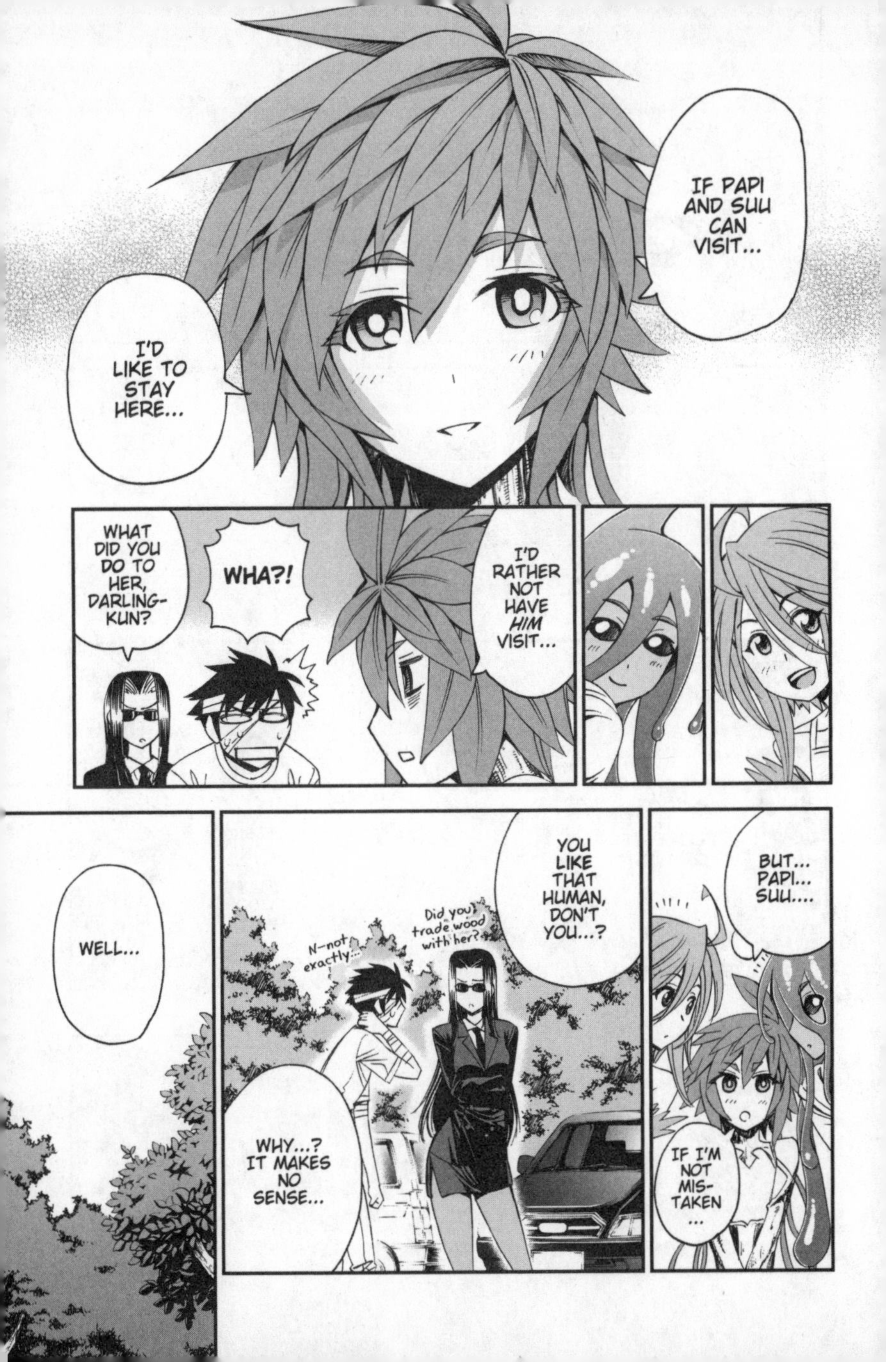
IF PAPI AND SUU CAN VISIT...
I'D LIKE TO STAY HERE...
I'D RATHER NOT HAVE *HIM* VISIT...
WHA?!
WHAT DID YOU DO TO HER, DARLING-KUN?
BUT... PAPI... SUU....
IF I'M NOT MIS-TAKEN ...
YOU LIKE THAT HUMAN, DON'T YOU...?
Did you trade wood with her?
N-not exactly...
WHY...? IT MAKES NO SENSE...
WELL...

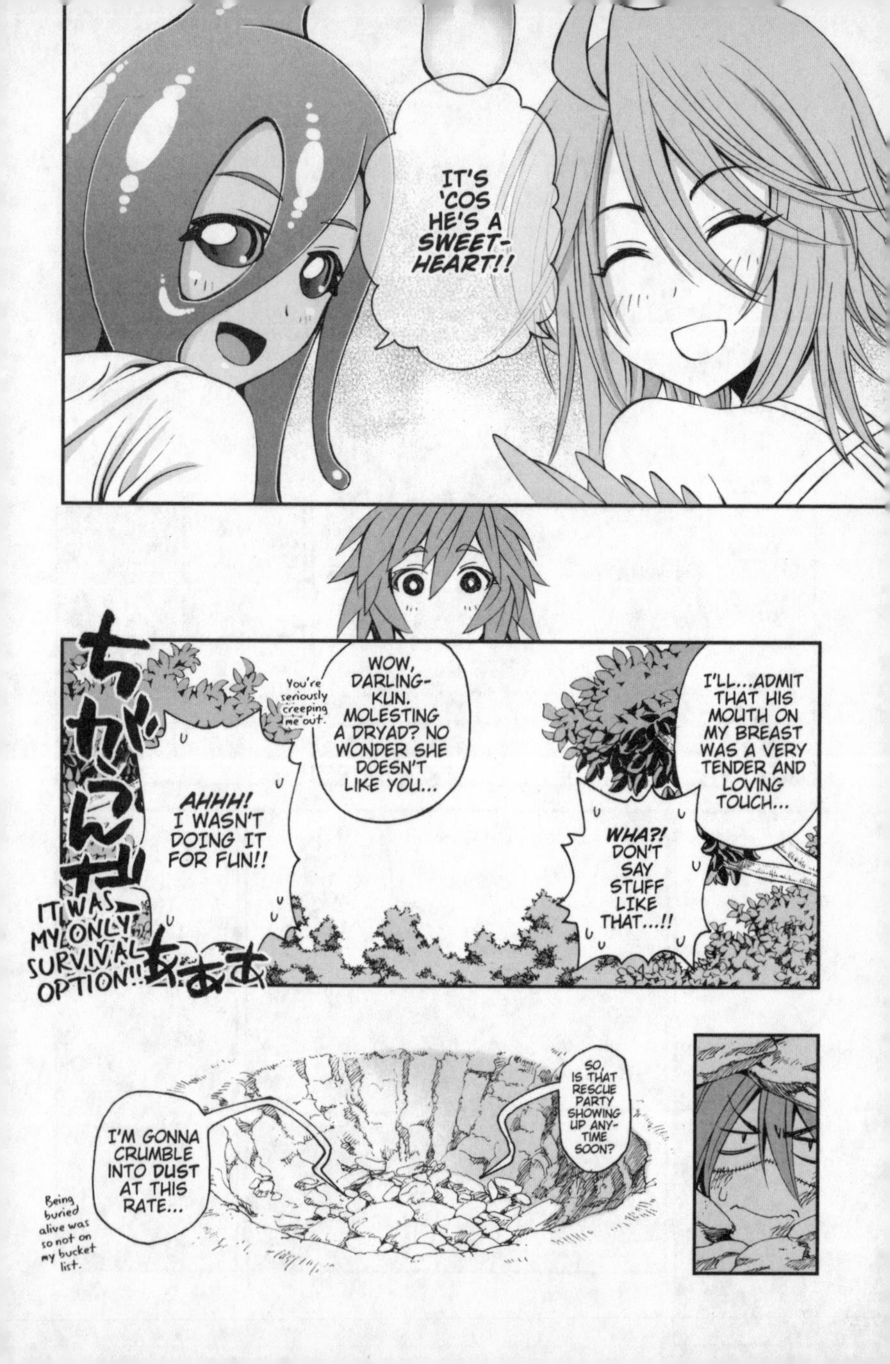
IT'S 'COS HE'S A SWEET-HEART!!
I'LL...ADMIT THAT HIS MOUTH ON MY BREAST WAS A VERY TENDER AND LOVING TOUCH...
WHA?! DON'T SAY STUFF LIKE THAT...!!
WOW, DARLING-KUN. MOLESTING A DRYAD? NO WONDER SHE DOESN'T LIKE YOU...
You're seriously creeping me out.
AHHH! I WASN'T DOING IT FOR FUN!!
IT WAS MY ONLY SURVIVAL OPTION!!
SO, IS THAT RESCUE PARTY SHOWING UP ANY-TIME SOON?
I'M GONNA CRUMBLE INTO DUST AT THIS RATE...
Being buried alive was so not on my bucket list.

Monster Musume

Everyday Life with Monster Girls

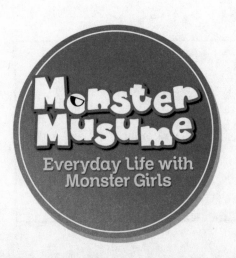

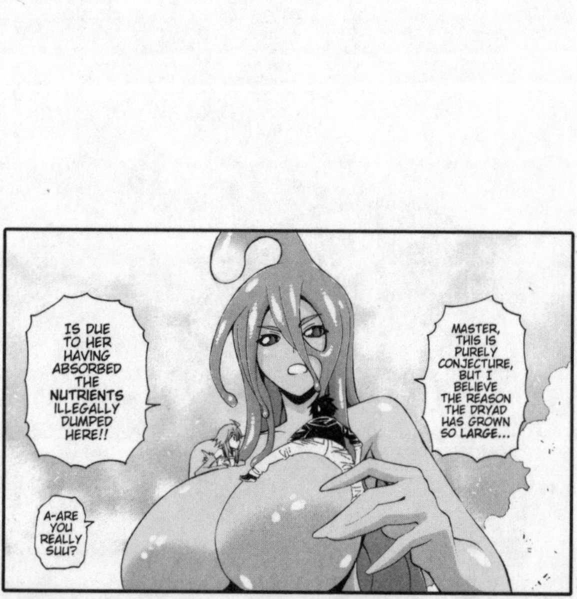
MASTER, THIS IS PURELY CONJECTURE, BUT I BELIEVE THE REASON THE DRYAD HAS GROWN SO LARGE...
IS DUE TO HER HAVING ABSORBED THE NUTRIENTS ILLEGALLY DUMPED HERE!!
A-ARE YOU REALLY SUU?

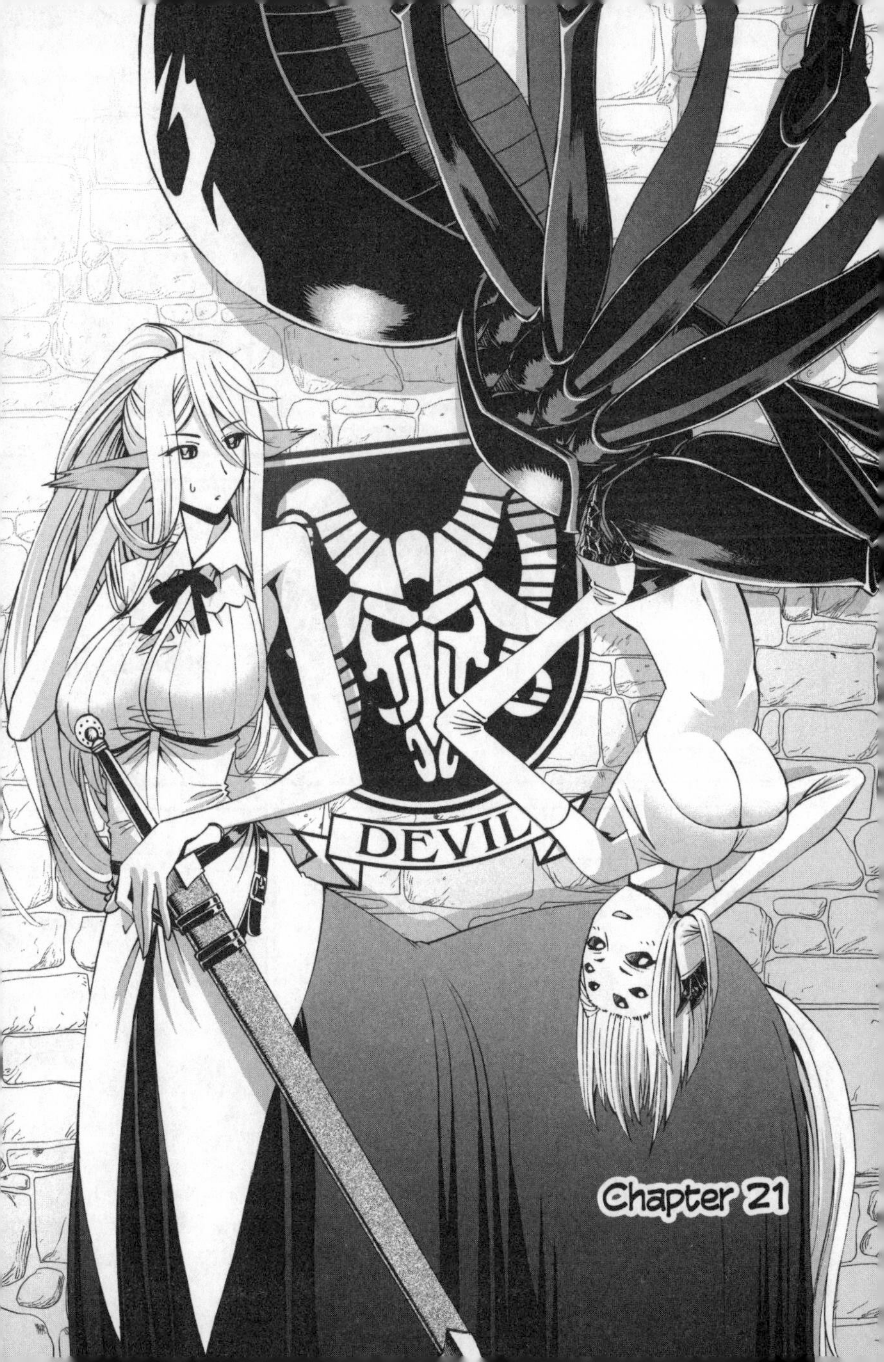
DEVIL
Chapter 21

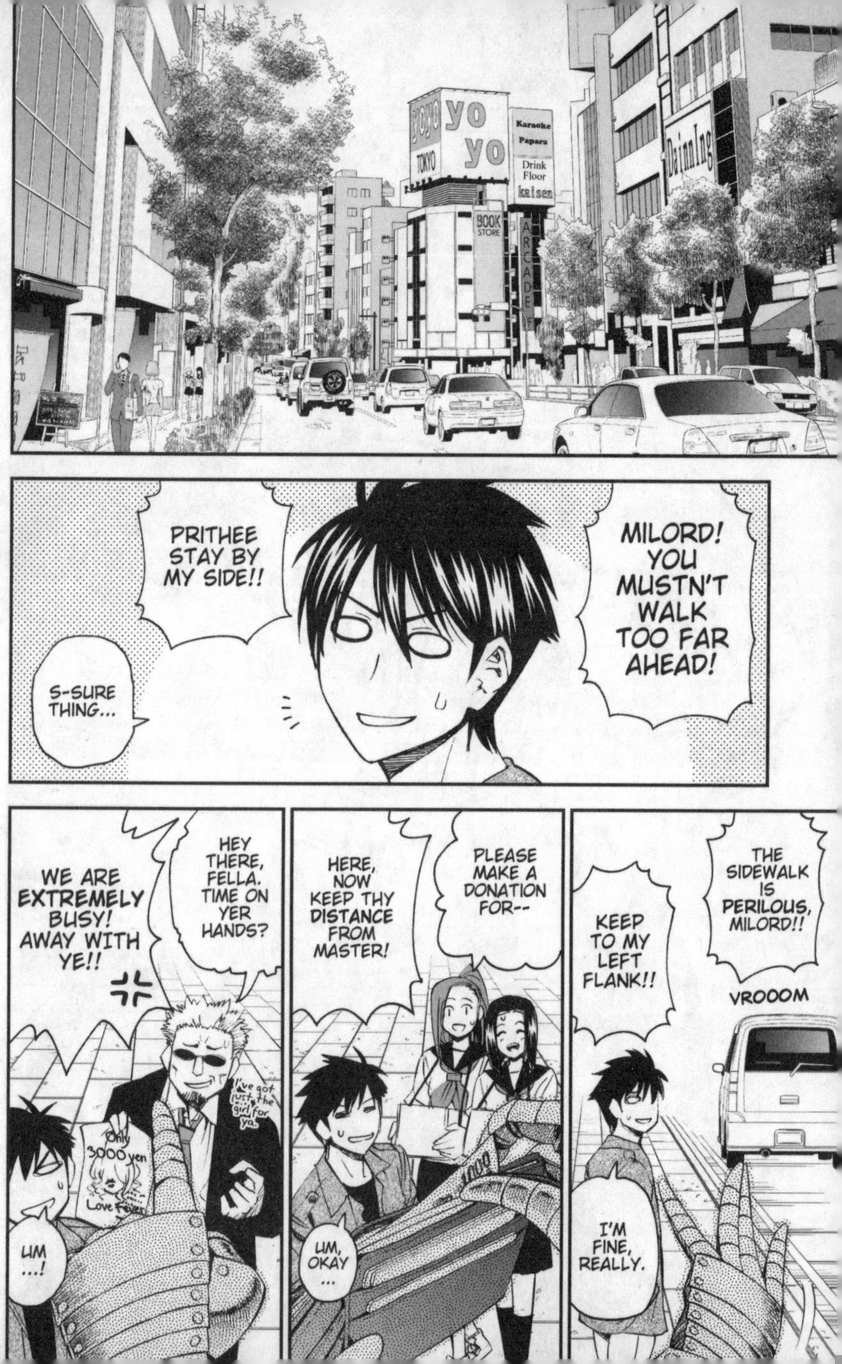
yoyo
TOKYO
yo yo
Karaoke Papara
Drink Floor
kaisen
BOOK STORE
ARCADE
DainnIng
MILORD! YOU MUSTN'T WALK TOO FAR AHEAD!
PRITHEE STAY BY MY SIDE!!
S-SURE THING...
THE SIDEWALK IS PERILOUS, MILORD!!
KEEP TO MY LEFT FLANK!!
VROOOM
I'M FINE, REALLY.
PLEASE MAKE A DONATION FOR--
HERE, NOW KEEP THY DISTANCE FROM MASTER!
UM, OKAY ...
HEY THERE, FELLA. TIME ON YER HANDS?
I've got just the girl for ya.
Only 3000 yen
Love Fever
WE ARE EXTREMELY BUSY! AWAY WITH YE!!
UM ...!

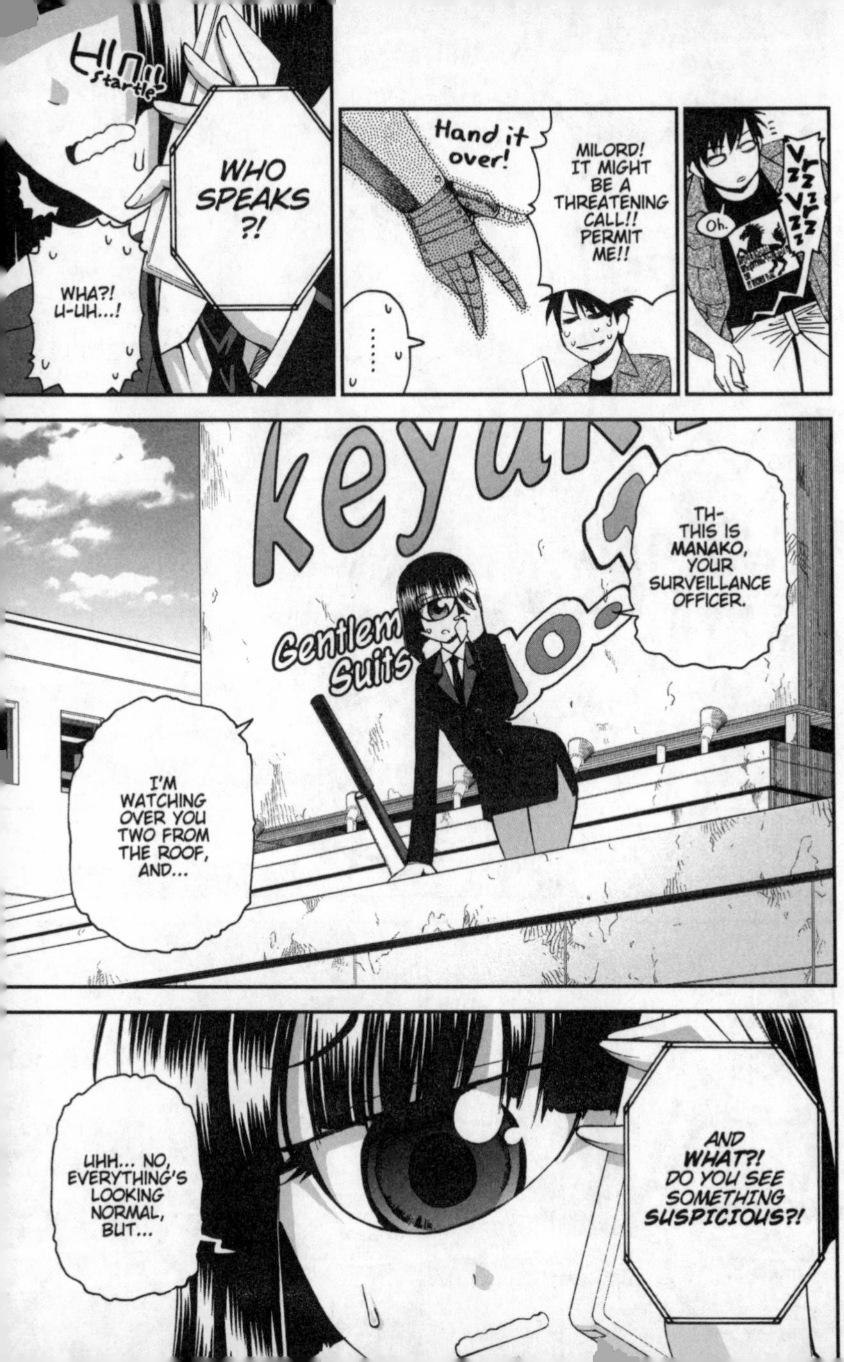

Vrzz Vrzz
Oh.
MILORD! IT MIGHT BE A THREATENING CALL!! PERMIT ME!!
Hand it over!
......
startle
WHO SPEAKS ?!
WHA?! U-UH...!
TH- THIS IS MANAKO, YOUR SURVEILLANCE OFFICER.
I'M WATCHING OVER YOU TWO FROM THE ROOF, AND...
AND WHAT?! DO YOU SEE SOMETHING SUSPICIOUS?!
UHH... NO, EVERYTHING'S LOOKING NORMAL, BUT...

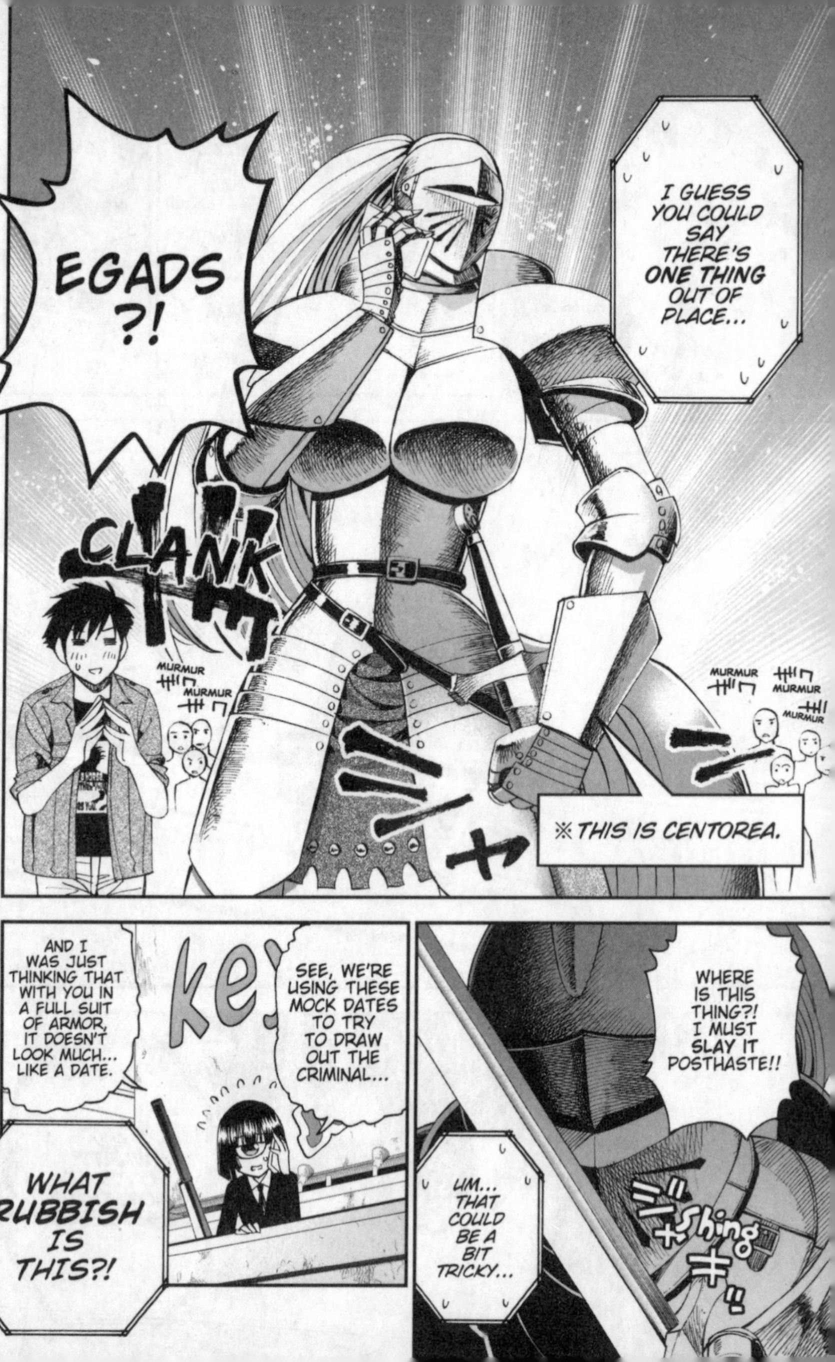
I GUESS YOU COULD SAY THERE'S ONE THING OUT OF PLACE...
EGADS ?!
CLANK
MURMUR
MURMUR
MURMUR
MURMUR
MURMUR
※THIS IS CENTOREA.
WHERE IS THIS THING?! I MUST SLAY IT POSTHASTE!!
UM... THAT COULD BE A BIT TRICKY...
shing
SEE, WE'RE USING THESE MOCK DATES TO TRY TO DRAW OUT THE CRIMINAL...
AND I WAS JUST THINKING THAT WITH YOU IN A FULL SUIT OF ARMOR, IT DOESN'T LOOK MUCH... LIKE A DATE.
WHAT RUBBISH IS THIS?!

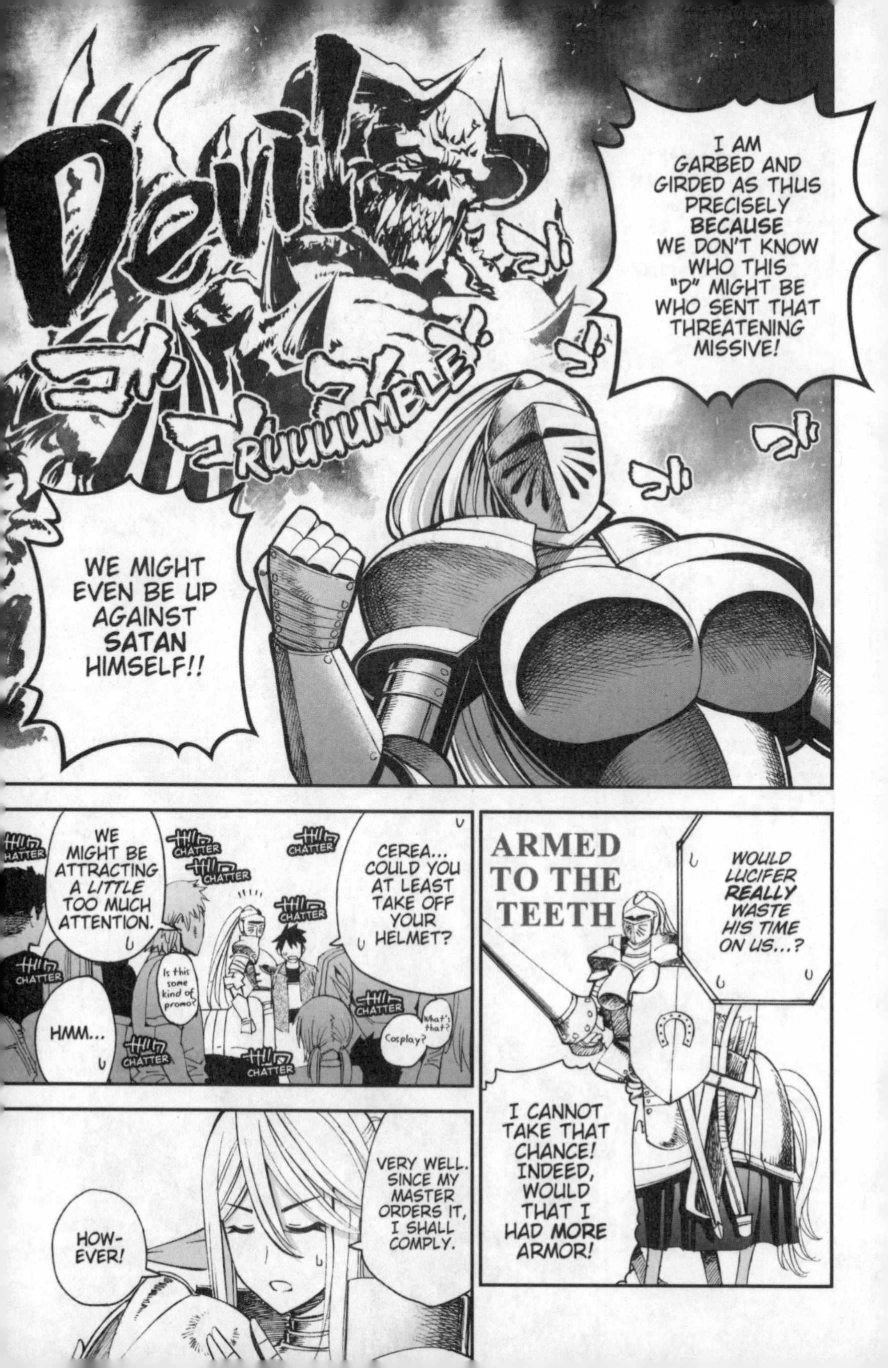
I AM GARBED AND GIRDED AS THUS PRECISELY BECAUSE WE DON'T KNOW WHO THIS "D" MIGHT BE WHO SENT THAT THREATENING MISSIVE!
Devil!
RUUUUMBLE
WE MIGHT EVEN BE UP AGAINST SATAN HIMSELF!!
ARMED TO THE TEETH
WOULD LUCIFER REALLY WASTE HIS TIME ON US...?
I CANNOT TAKE THAT CHANCE! INDEED, WOULD THAT I HAD MORE ARMOR!
CEREA... COULD YOU AT LEAST TAKE OFF YOUR HELMET?
WE MIGHT BE ATTRACTING A LITTLE TOO MUCH ATTENTION.
CHATTER
CHATTER
CHATTER
CHATTER
What's that?
Cosplay?
Is this some kind of promo?
HMM...
CHATTER
CHATTER
CHATTER
CHATTER
VERY WELL. SINCE MY MASTER ORDERS IT, I SHALL COMPLY.
HOW-EVER!

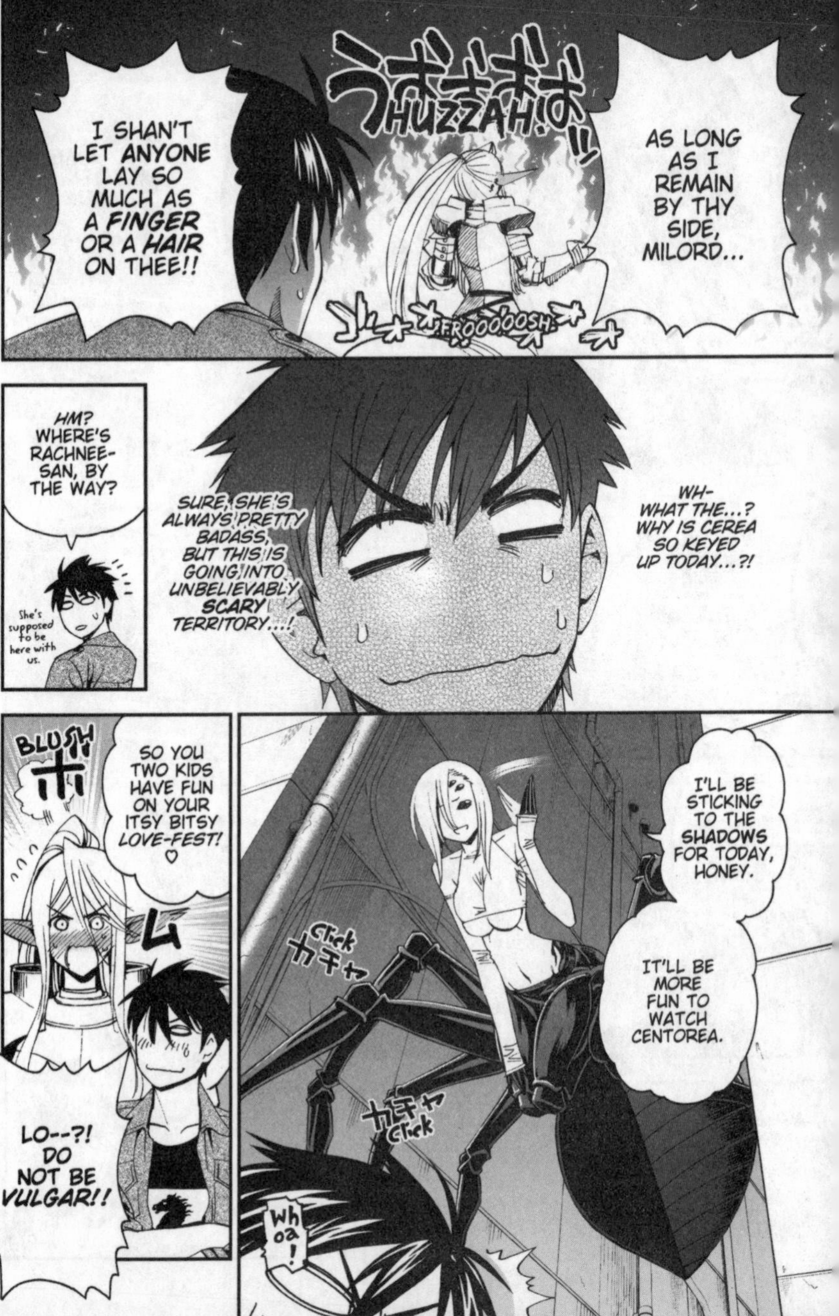

HUZZAH!!
AS LONG AS I REMAIN BY THY SIDE, MILORD...
I SHAN'T LET ANYONE LAY SO MUCH AS A FINGER OR A HAIR ON THEE!!
FROOOOOSH
WH- WHAT THE...? WHY IS CEREA SO KEYED UP TODAY...?!
SURE, SHE'S ALWAYS PRETTY BADASS, BUT THIS IS GOING INTO UNBELIEVABLY SCARY TERRITORY...!
HM? WHERE'S RACHNEE-SAN, BY THE WAY?
She's supposed to be here with us.
I'LL BE STICKING TO THE SHADOWS FOR TODAY, HONEY.
IT'LL BE MORE FUN TO WATCH CENTOREA.
Click
Click
Whoa!
SO YOU TWO KIDS HAVE FUN ON YOUR ITSY BITSY LOVE-FEST! ♡
BLUSH
LO--?! DO NOT BE VULGAR!!

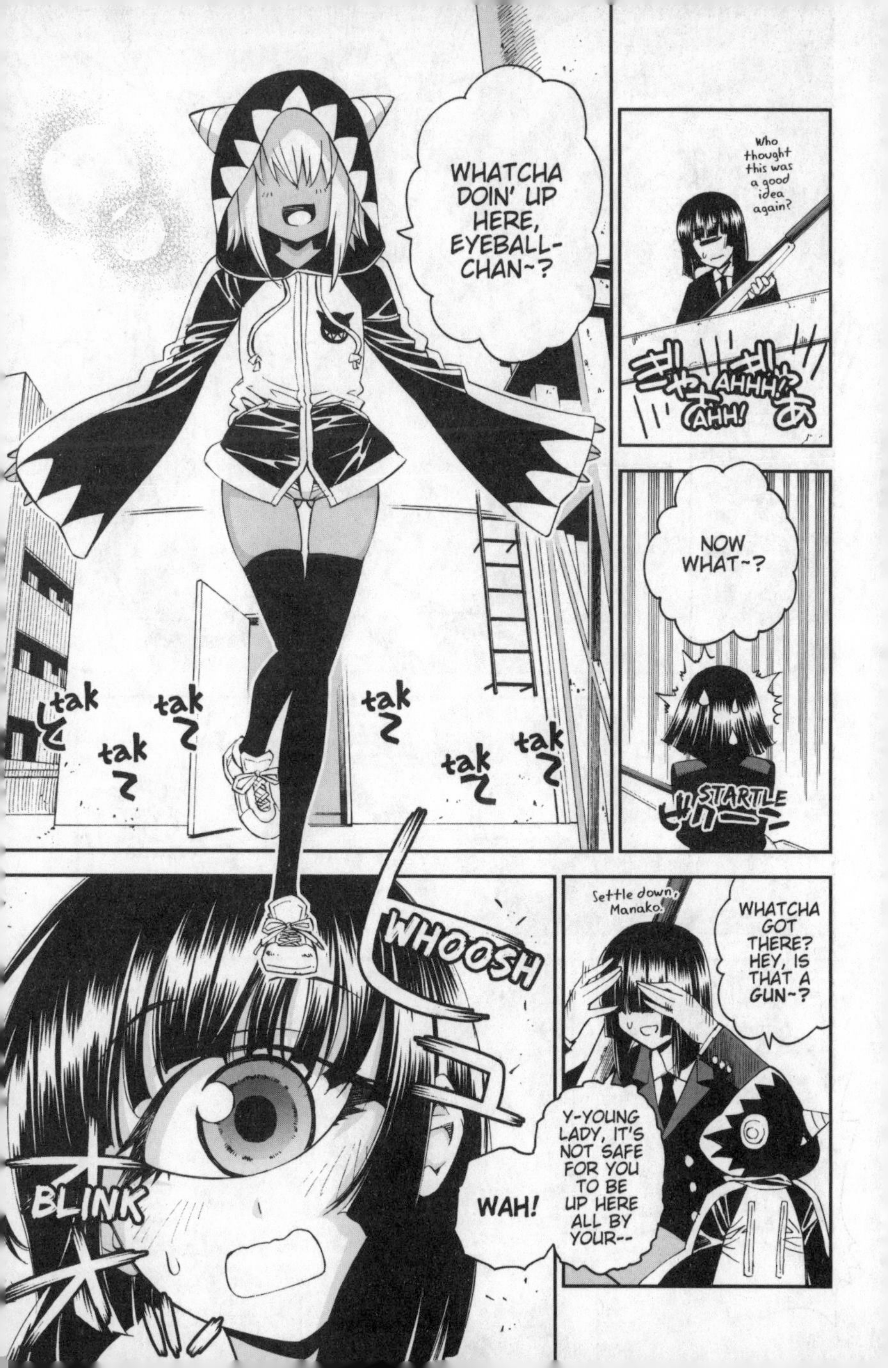

Who thought this was a good idea again?
AHHH!?
AHH!
NOW WHAT~?
STARTLE
WHATCHA DOIN' UP HERE, EYEBALL-CHAN~?
tak
tak
tak
tak
tak
tak
Settle down, Manako.
WHATCHA GOT THERE? HEY, IS THAT A GUN~?
Y-YOUNG LADY, IT'S NOT SAFE FOR YOU TO BE UP HERE ALL BY YOUR--
WHOOSH
WAH!
BLINK

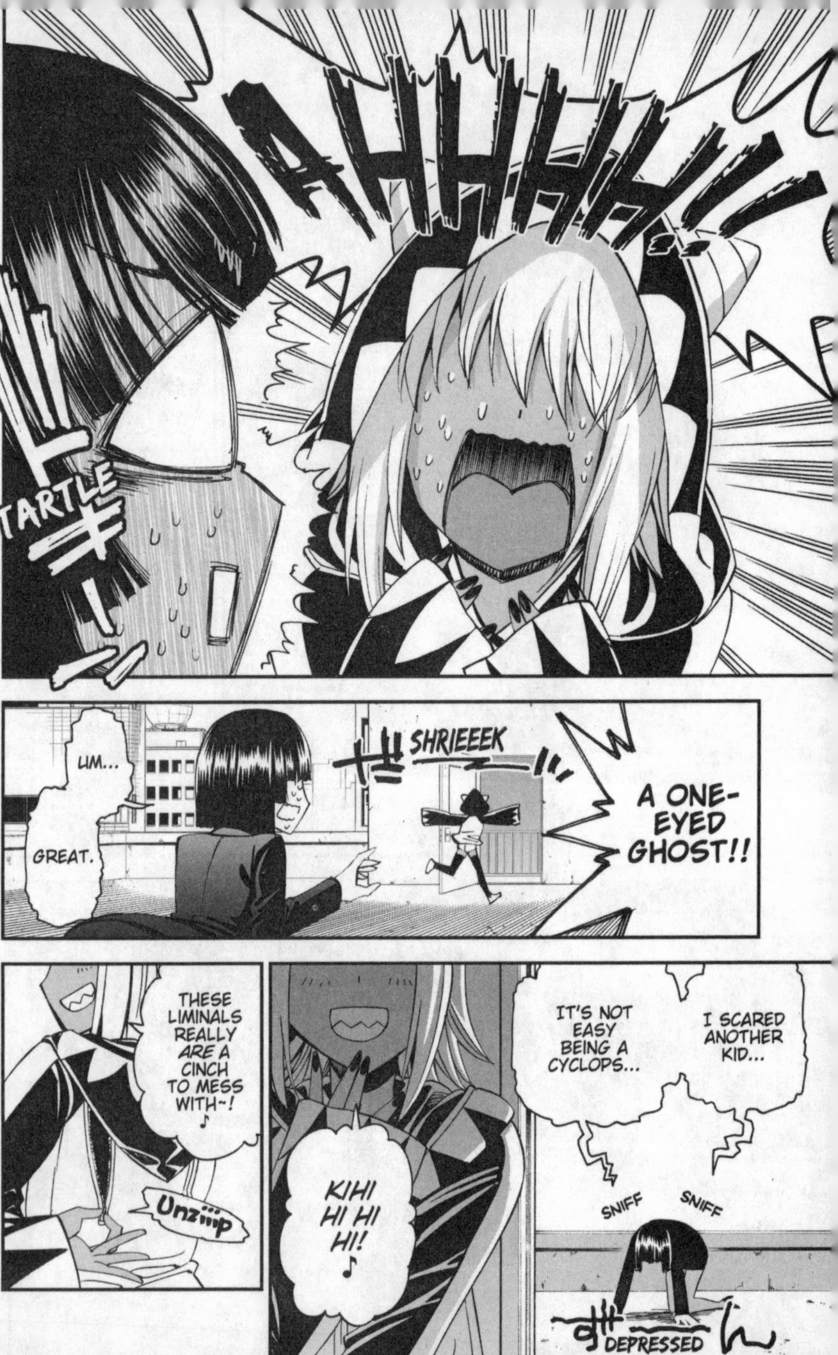
AHHHHH!!
STARTLE
A ONE-EYED GHOST!!
SHRIEEEK
UM... GREAT.
I SCARED ANOTHER KID...
IT'S NOT EASY BEING A CYCLOPS...
SNIFF
SNIFF
DEPRESSED
KIHI HI HI HI! ♪
THESE LIMINALS REALLY ARE A CINCH TO MESS WITH~! ♪
Unziiip

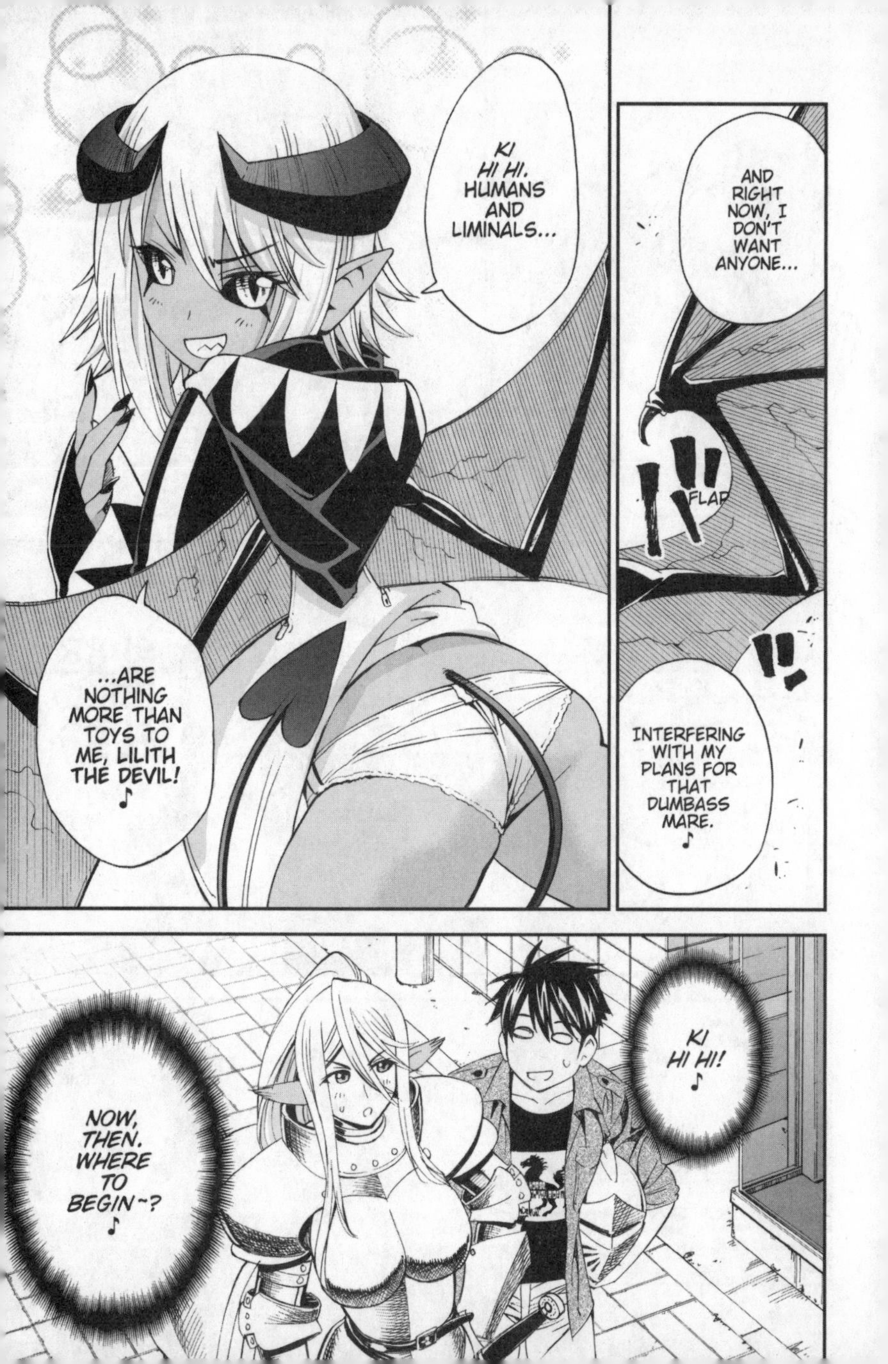
KI HI HI. HUMANS AND LIMINALS...
...ARE NOTHING MORE THAN TOYS TO ME, LILITH THE DEVIL! ♪
AND RIGHT NOW, I DON'T WANT ANYONE...
FLAP
INTERFERING WITH MY PLANS FOR THAT DUMBASS MARE. ♪
KI HI HI! ♪
NOW, THEN. WHERE TO BEGIN~? ♪

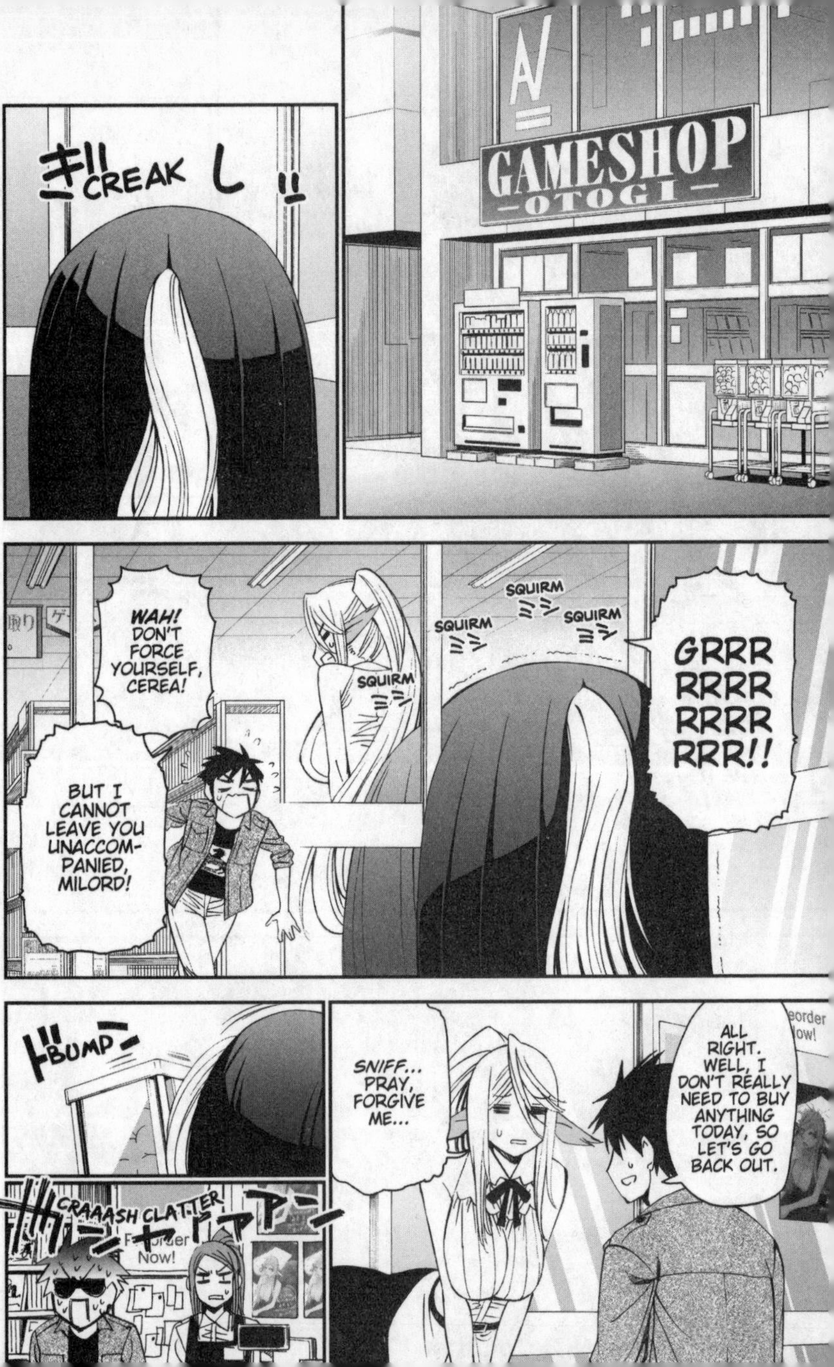
GAMESHOP
-OTOGI-
CREAK
GRRR RRRR RRRR RRR!!
SQUIRM
SQUIRM
SQUIRM
SQUIRM
WAH! DON'T FORCE YOURSELF, CEREA!
BUT I CANNOT LEAVE YOU UNACCOMPANIED, MILORD!
ALL RIGHT. WELL, I DON'T REALLY NEED TO BUY ANYTHING TODAY, SO LET'S GO BACK OUT.
SNIFF... PRAY, FORGIVE ME...
BUMP
CRAAASH CLATTER
Now!

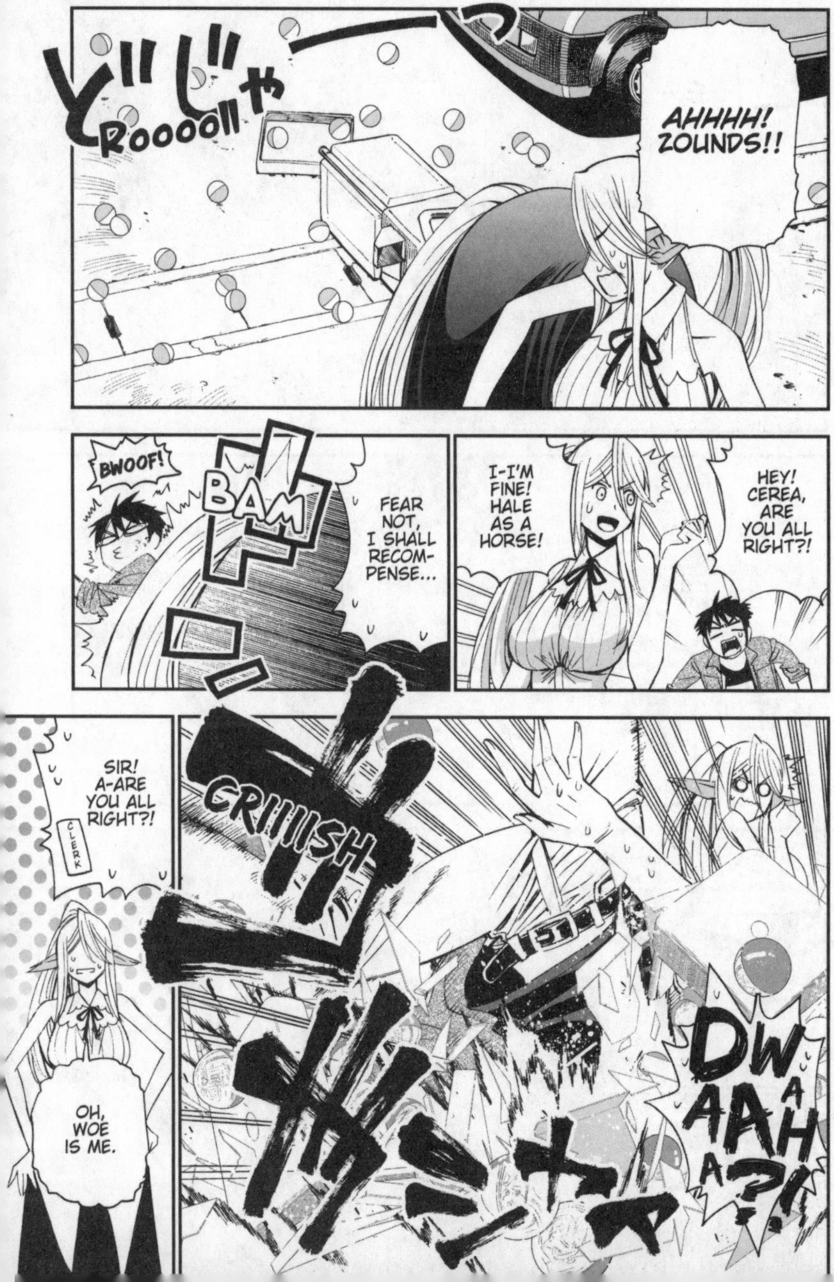

どじゃーっ
ROOOOLL
AHHHH! ZOUNDS!!
HEY! CEREA, ARE YOU ALL RIGHT?!
I-I'M FINE! HALE AS A HORSE!
FEAR NOT, I SHALL RECOMPENSE...
BAM
BWOOF!
CRIIIISH
DWAAAHA?!
SIR! A-ARE YOU ALL RIGHT?!
CLERK
OH, WOE IS ME.

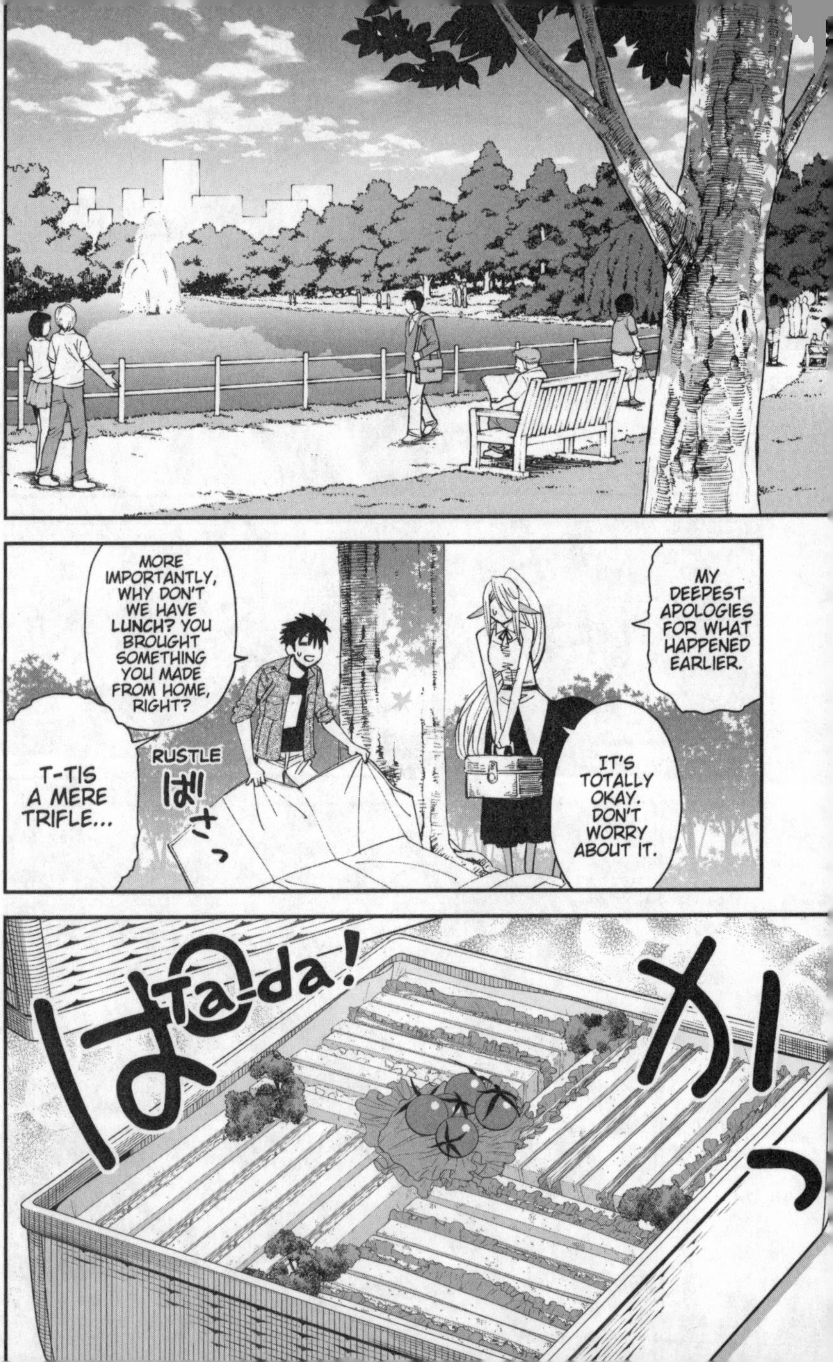
MY DEEPEST APOLOGIES FOR WHAT HAPPENED EARLIER.
IT'S TOTALLY OKAY. DON'T WORRY ABOUT IT.
T-TIS A MERE TRIFLE...
MORE IMPORTANTLY, WHY DON'T WE HAVE LUNCH? YOU BROUGHT SOMETHING YOU MADE FROM HOME, RIGHT?
RUSTLE
ばさっ
ぱかっ
TA-DA!

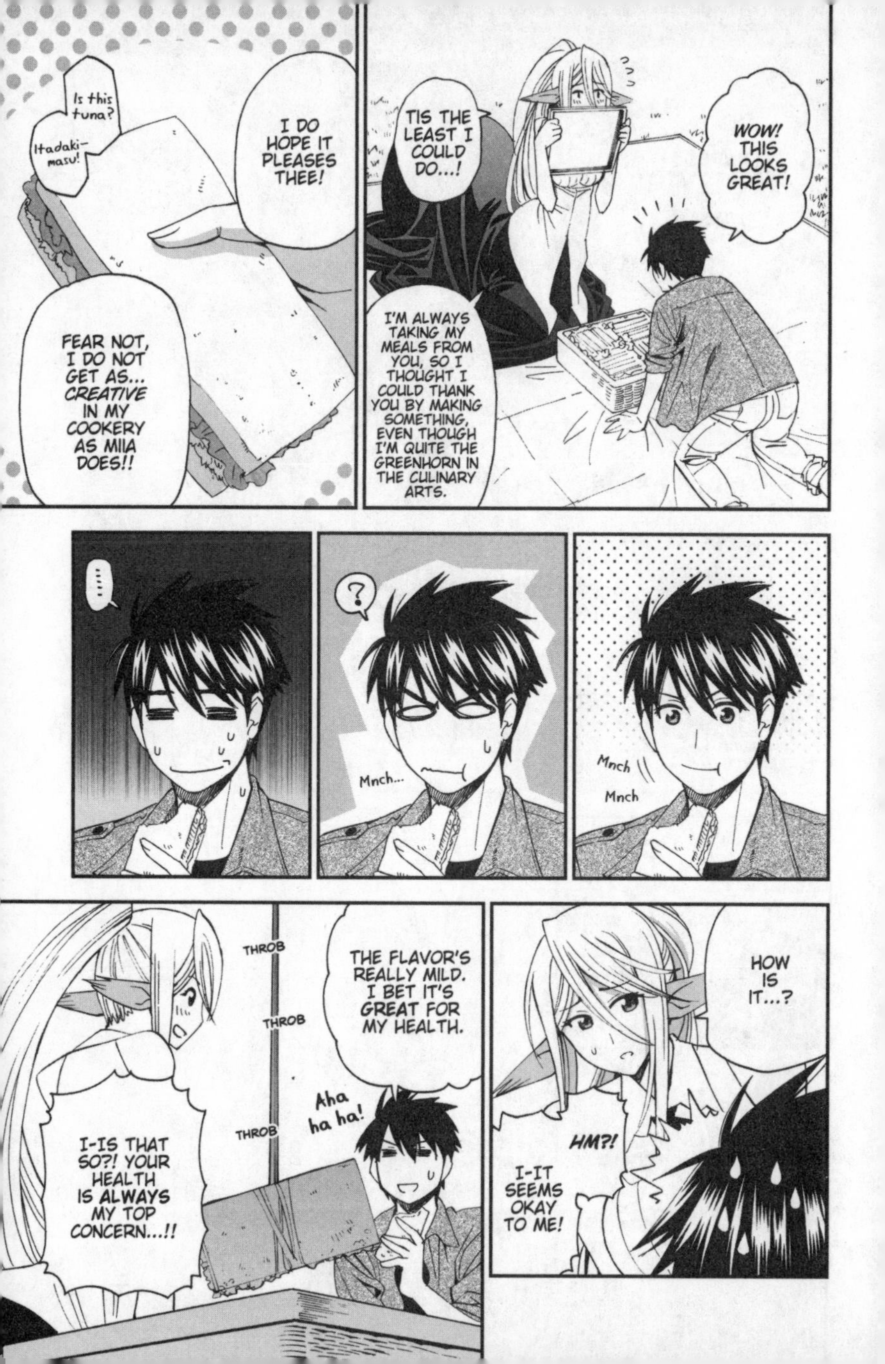
WOW! THIS LOOKS GREAT!
TIS THE LEAST I COULD DO...!
I'M ALWAYS TAKING MY MEALS FROM YOU, SO I THOUGHT I COULD THANK YOU BY MAKING SOMETHING, EVEN THOUGH I'M QUITE THE GREENHORN IN THE CULINARY ARTS.
I DO HOPE IT PLEASES THEE!
Itadaki-masu!
Is this tuna?
FEAR NOT, I DO NOT GET AS... CREATIVE IN MY COOKERY AS MIIA DOES!!
Mnch
Mnch
?
Mnch...
......
HOW IS IT...?
HM?!
I-IT SEEMS OKAY TO ME!
THE FLAVOR'S REALLY MILD. I BET IT'S GREAT FOR MY HEALTH.
Aha ha ha!
THROB
THROB
THROB
I-IS THAT SO?! YOUR HEALTH IS ALWAYS MY TOP CONCERN...!!

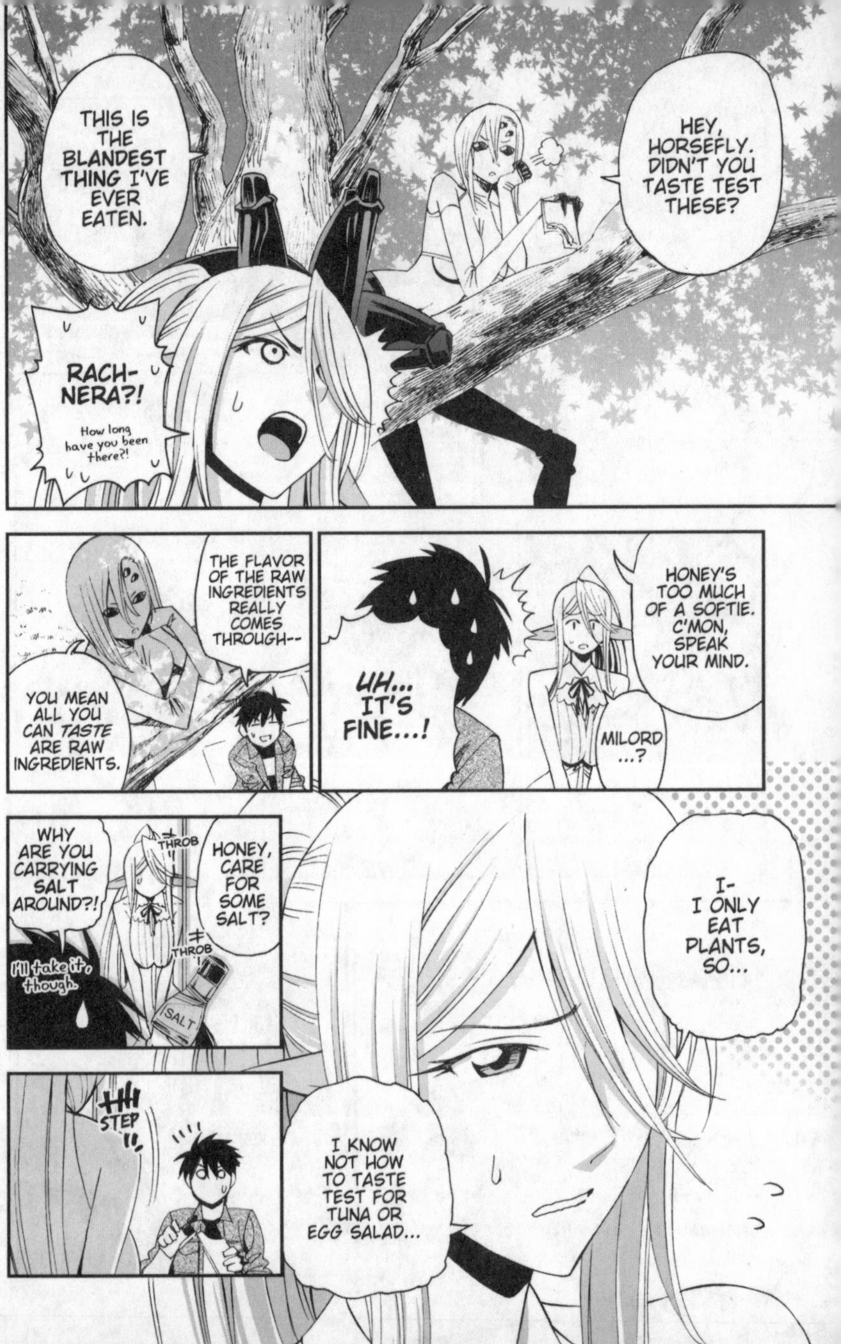
HEY, HORSEFLY. DIDN'T YOU TASTE TEST THESE?
THIS IS THE BLANDEST THING I'VE EVER EATEN.
RACH-NERA?!
How long have you been there?!
HONEY'S TOO MUCH OF A SOFTIE. C'MON, SPEAK YOUR MIND.
UH... IT'S FINE...!
MILORD ...?
THE FLAVOR OF THE RAW INGREDIENTS REALLY COMES THROUGH--
YOU MEAN ALL YOU CAN TASTE ARE RAW INGREDIENTS.
I- I ONLY EAT PLANTS, SO...
I KNOW NOT HOW TO TASTE TEST FOR TUNA OR EGG SALAD...
HONEY, CARE FOR SOME SALT?
THROB
THROB
WHY ARE YOU CARRYING SALT AROUND?!
I'll take it, though.
SALT
STEP

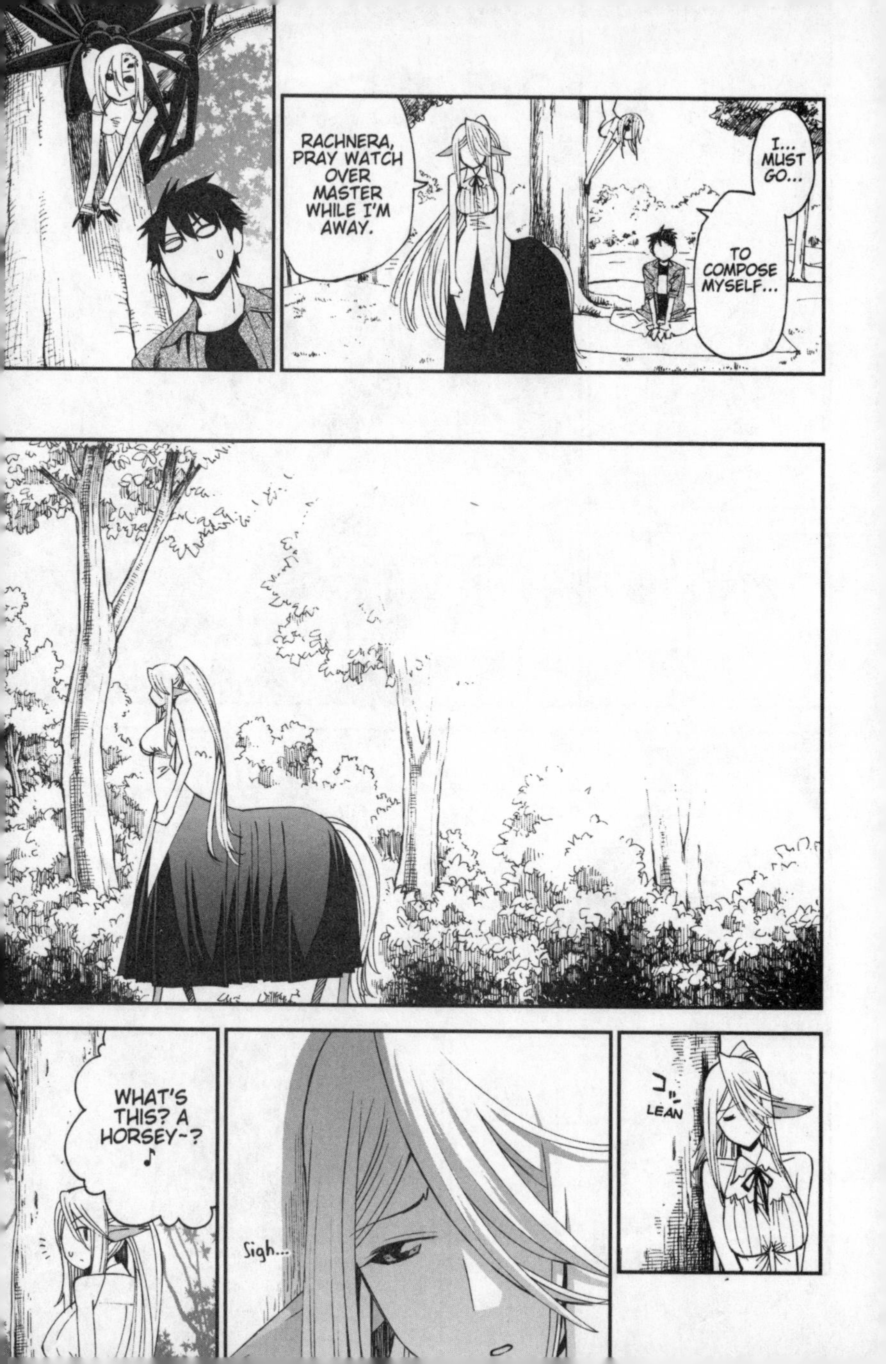
I... MUST GO...
TO COMPOSE MYSELF...
RACHNERA, PRAY WATCH OVER MASTER WHILE I'M AWAY.
コッ
LEAN
Sigh...
WHAT'S THIS? A HORSEY~? ♪

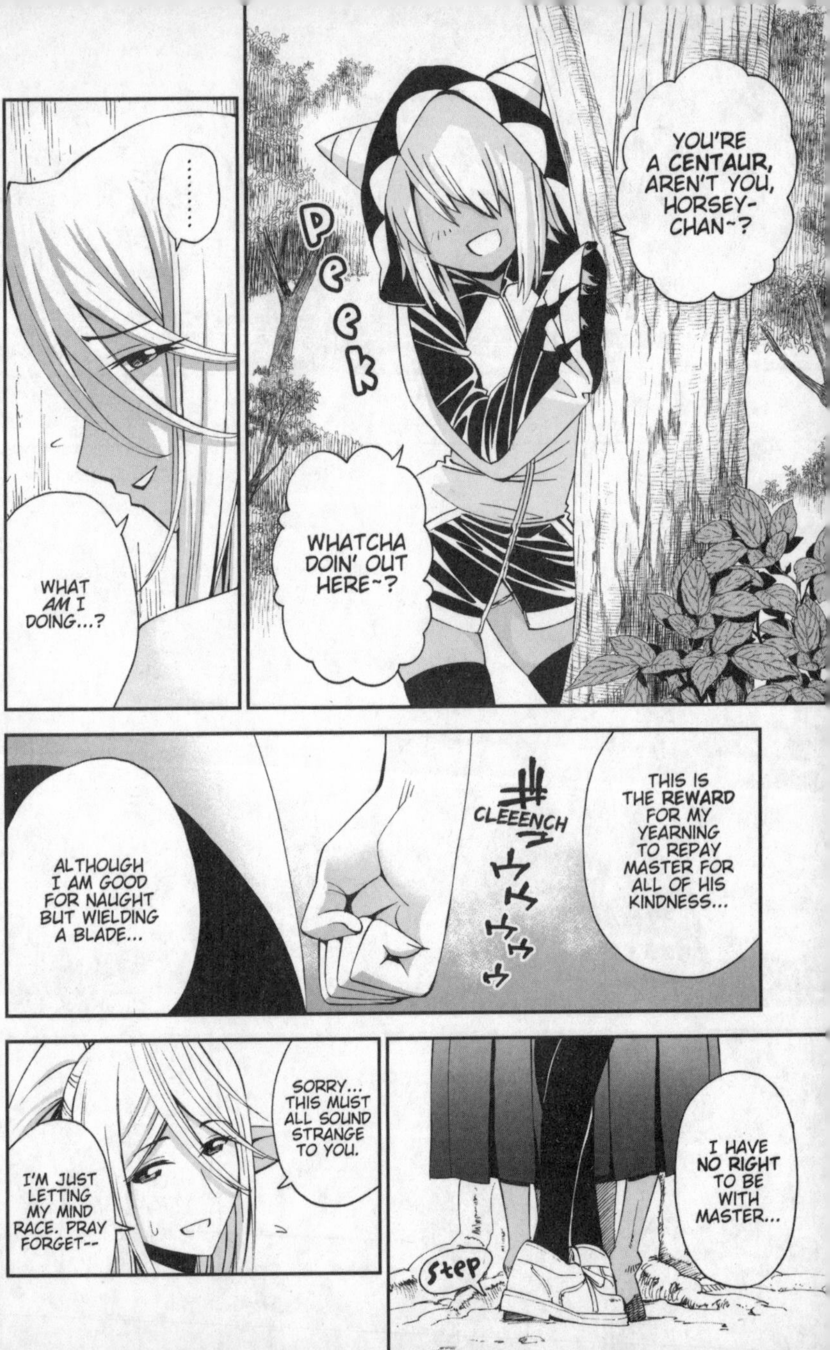
YOU'RE A CENTAUR, AREN'T YOU, HORSEY-CHAN~?
Peek
WHATCHA DOIN' OUT HERE~?
......
WHAT AM I DOING...?
THIS IS THE REWARD FOR MY YEARNING TO REPAY MASTER FOR ALL OF HIS KINDNESS...
CLEEENCH
ALTHOUGH I AM GOOD FOR NAUGHT BUT WIELDING A BLADE...
I HAVE NO RIGHT TO BE WITH MASTER...
Step
SORRY... THIS MUST ALL SOUND STRANGE TO YOU.
I'M JUST LETTING MY MIND RACE. PRAY FORGET--

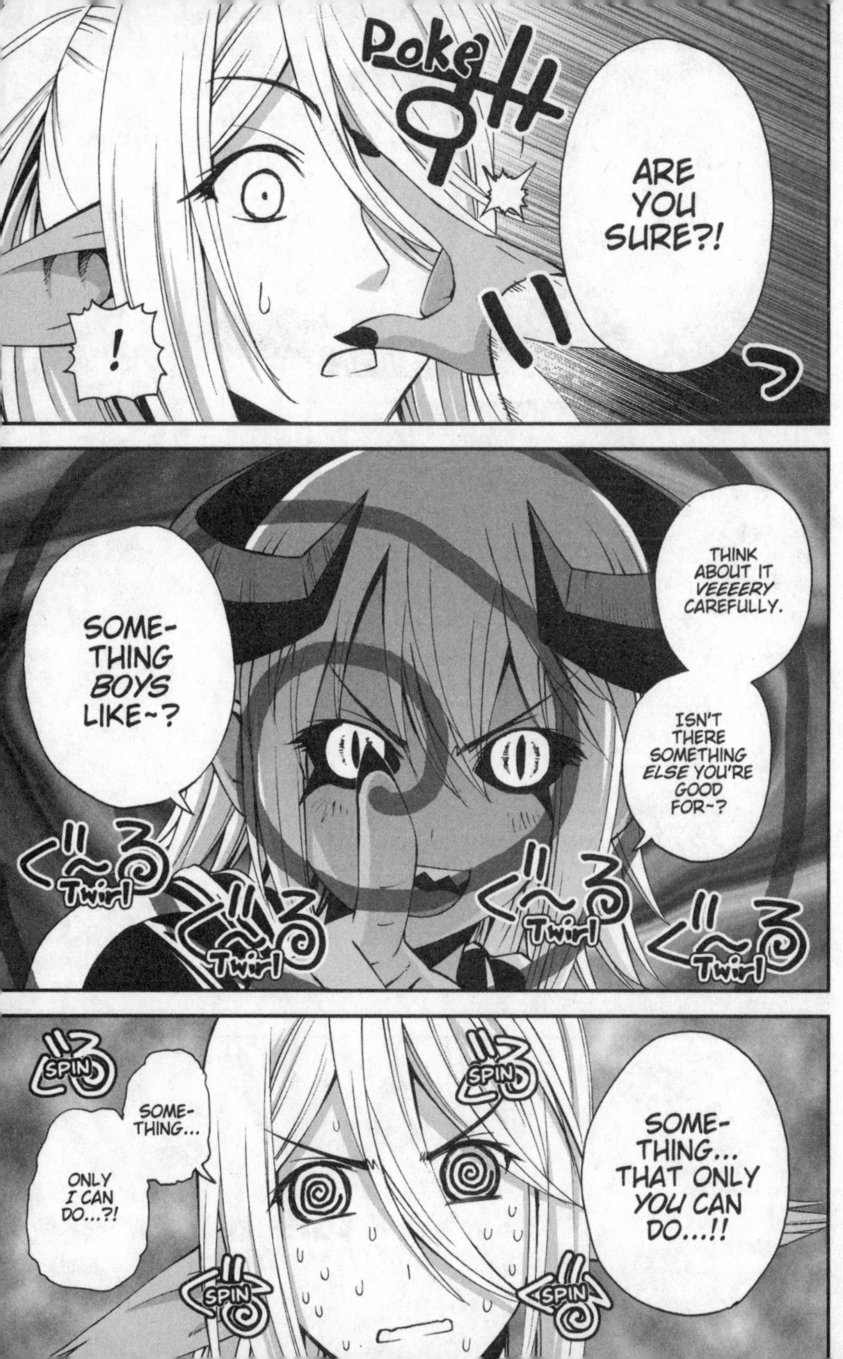

Poke
ARE YOU SURE?!
!
THINK ABOUT IT VEEEERY CAREFULLY.
ISN'T THERE SOMETHING ELSE YOU'RE GOOD FOR~?
SOME-THING BOYS LIKE~?
Twirl
Twirl
Twirl
Twirl
SOME-THING... THAT ONLY YOU CAN DO...!!
SOME-THING...
ONLY I CAN DO...?!
SPIN
SPIN
SPIN
SPIN

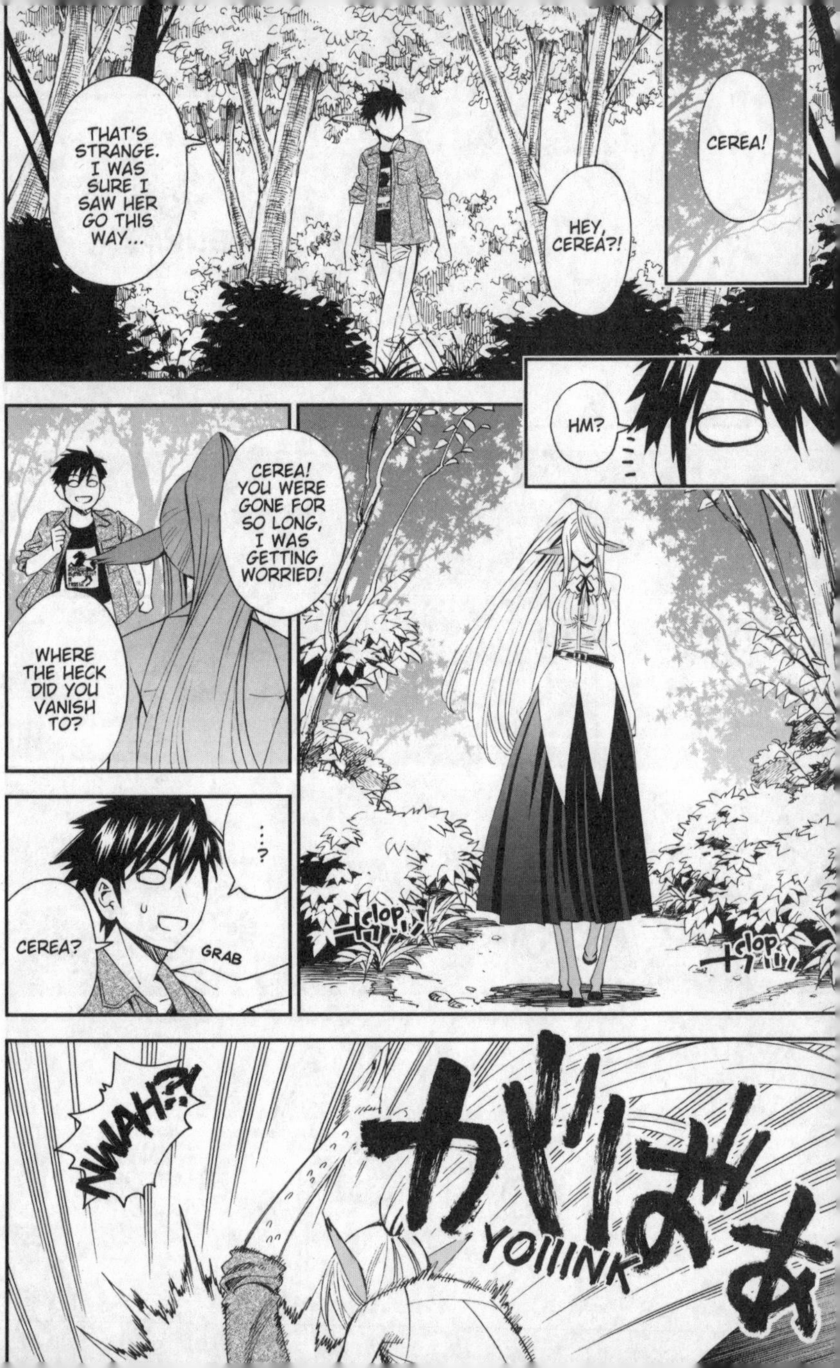
CEREA!
HEY, CEREA?!
THAT'S STRANGE. I WAS SURE I SAW HER GO THIS WAY...
HM?
clop
clop
CEREA! YOU WERE GONE FOR SO LONG, I WAS GETTING WORRIED!
WHERE THE HECK DID YOU VANISH TO?
...?
CEREA?
GRAB
YOIIINK
NWAH?!

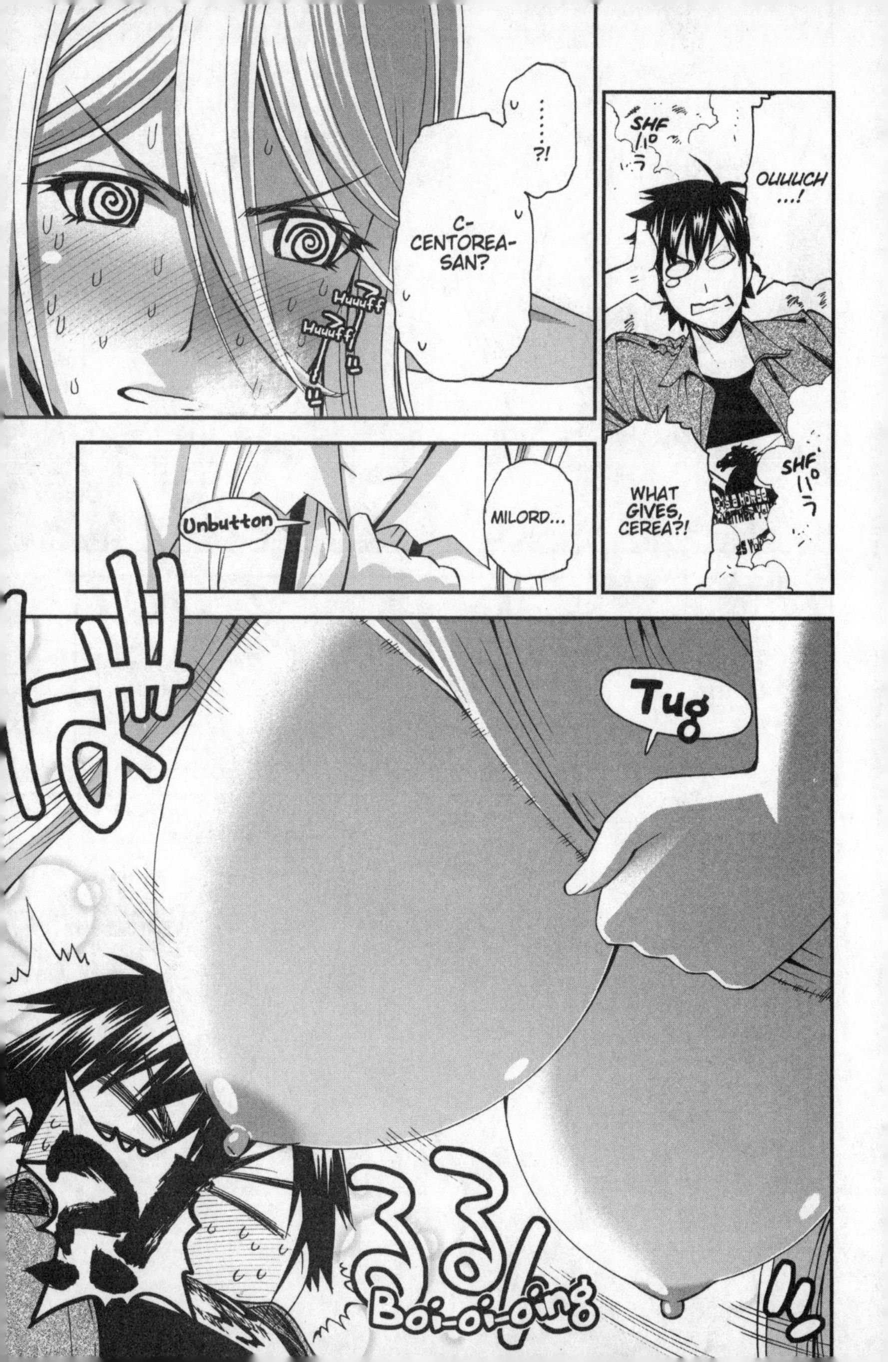

SHF
OUUUCH ...!
WHAT GIVES, CEREA?!
SHF
......?!
C-CENTOREA-SAN?
Huuuff
Huuuff
MILORD...
Unbutton
Tug
Boi-oi-oing

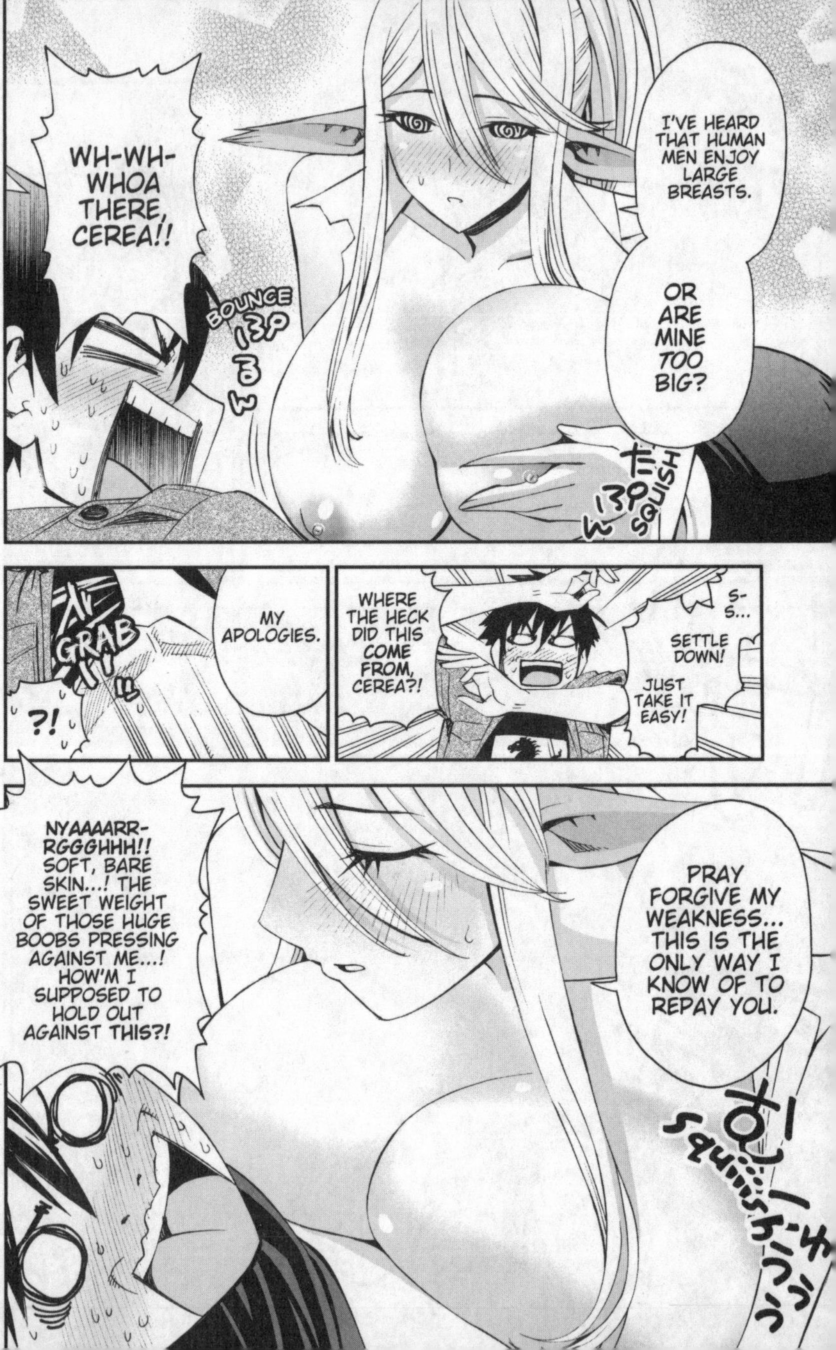
I'VE HEARD THAT HUMAN MEN ENJOY LARGE BREASTS.
OR ARE MINE TOO BIG?
SQUISH
WH-WH-WHOA THERE, CEREA!!
BOUNCE
S-S... SETTLE DOWN!
JUST TAKE IT EASY!
WHERE THE HECK DID THIS COME FROM, CEREA?!
MY APOLOGIES.
GRAB
?!
PRAY FORGIVE MY WEAKNESS... THIS IS THE ONLY WAY I KNOW OF TO REPAY YOU.
squish
NYAAAARR-RGGGHHH!! SOFT, BARE SKIN...! THE SWEET WEIGHT OF THOSE HUGE BOOBS PRESSING AGAINST ME...! HOW'M I SUPPOSED TO HOLD OUT AGAINST THIS?!

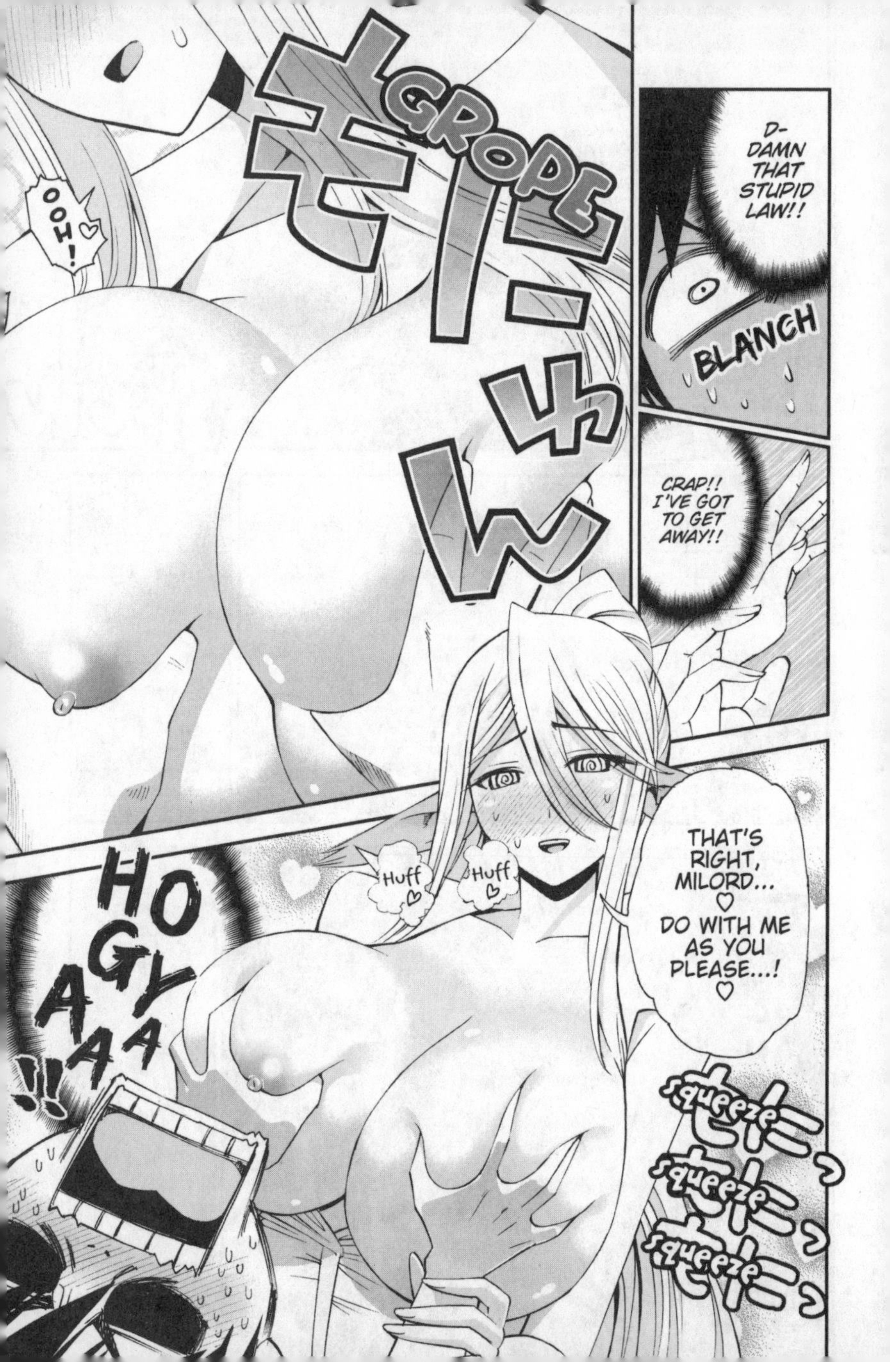
D-DAMN THAT STUPID LAW!!
BLANCH
CRAP!! I'VE GOT TO GET AWAY!!
GROPE
OOH! ♡
THAT'S RIGHT, MILORD... ♡ DO WITH ME AS YOU PLEASE...! ♡
Huff ♡
Huff ♡
squeeze
squeeze
squeeze
HOGYAAAA!!!

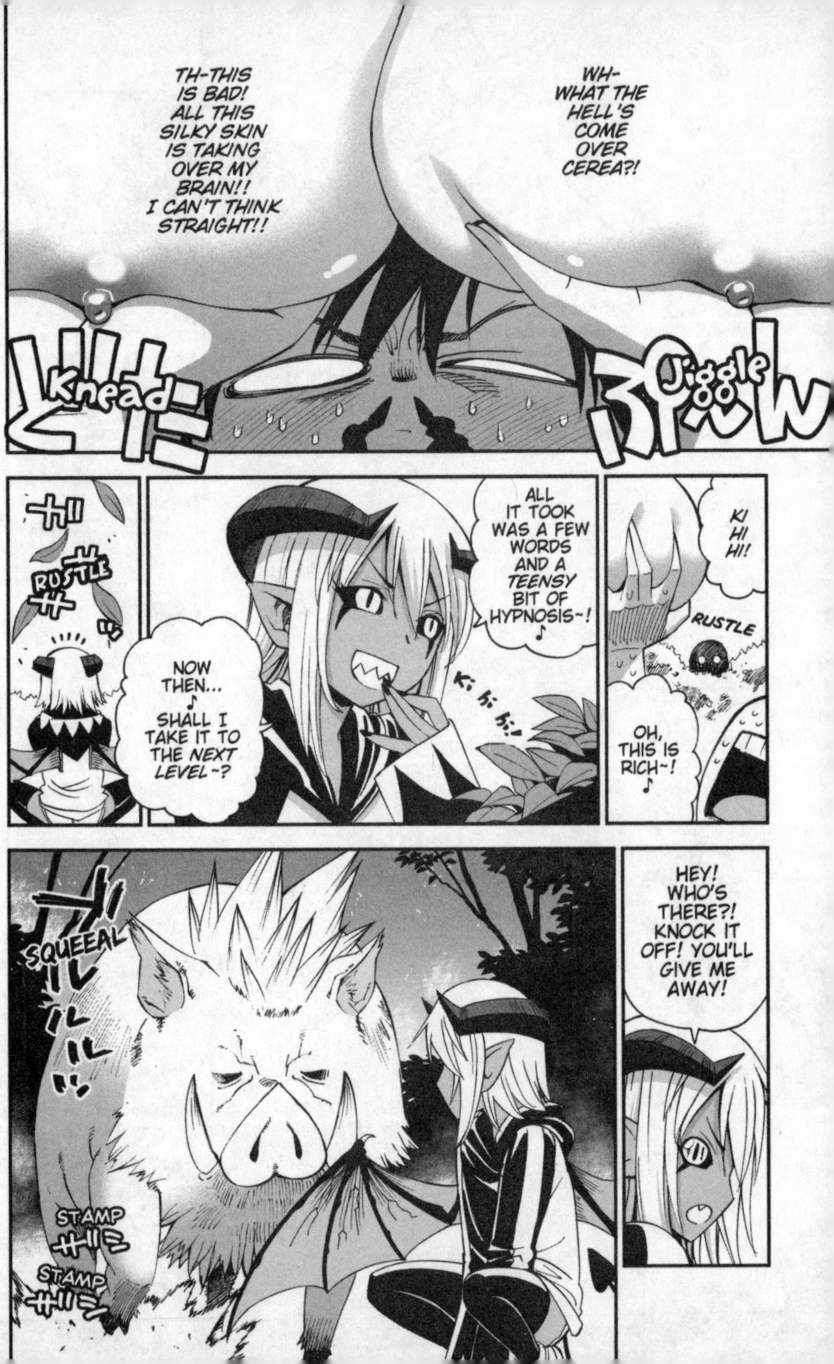
WH- WHAT THE HELL'S COME OVER CEREA?!
TH-THIS IS BAD! ALL THIS SILKY SKIN IS TAKING OVER MY BRAIN!! I CAN'T THINK STRAIGHT!!
Jiggle
Knead
KI HI HI!
RUSTLE
OH, THIS IS RICH~! ♪
ALL IT TOOK WAS A FEW WORDS AND A TEENSY BIT OF HYPNOSIS~! ♪
Ki hi hi!
NOW THEN... ♪ SHALL I TAKE IT TO THE NEXT LEVEL~?
RUSTLE
HEY! WHO'S THERE?! KNOCK IT OFF! YOU'LL GIVE ME AWAY!
SQUEEAL
STAMP
STAMP

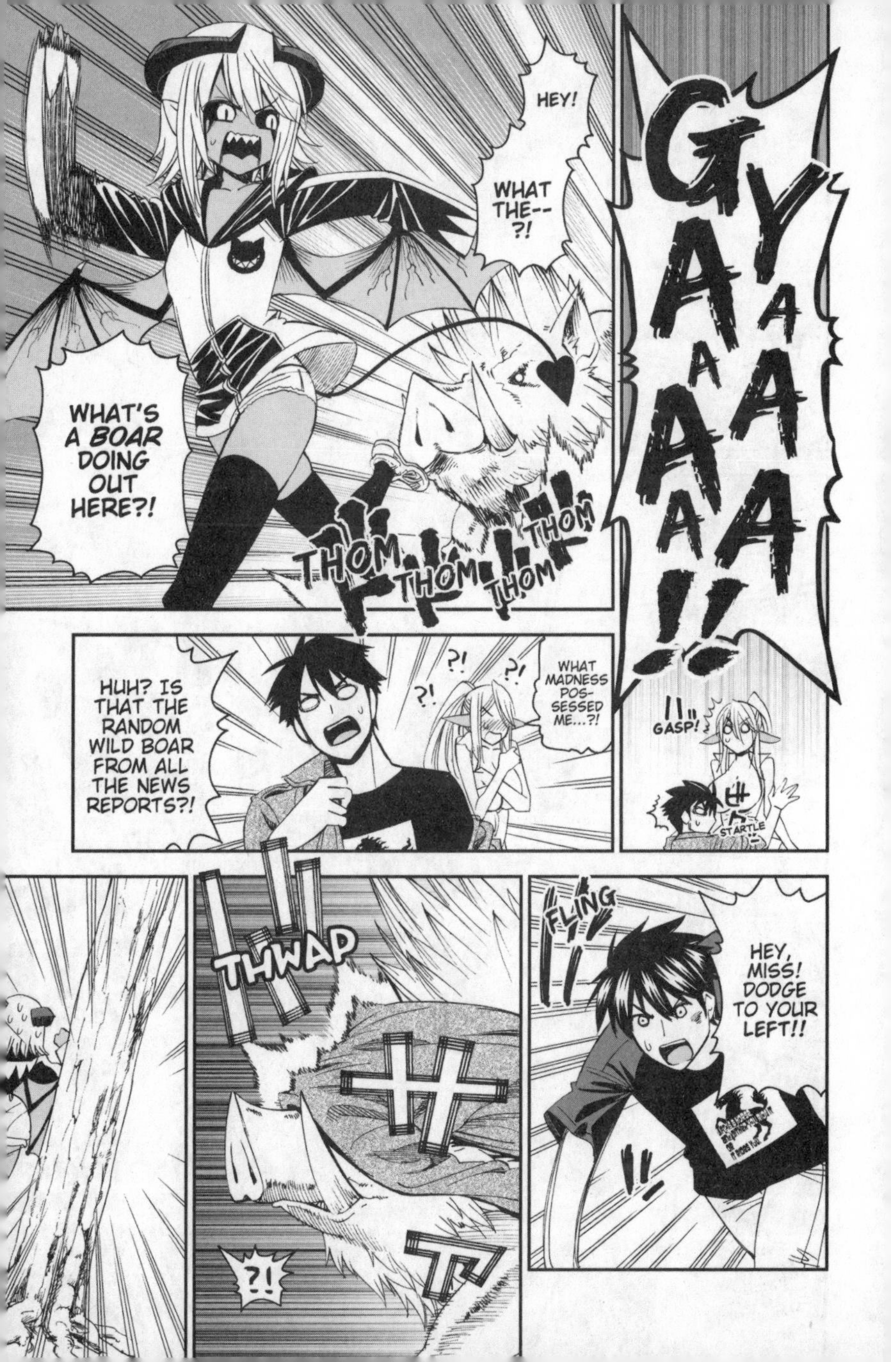
GYAAAAAAAA!!
GASP!
STARTLE
HEY!
WHAT THE-- ?!
WHAT'S A *BOAR* DOING OUT HERE?!
THOM THOM THOM THOM
WHAT MADNESS POS-SESSED ME...?!
?!
?!
?!
HUH? IS THAT THE RANDOM WILD BOAR FROM ALL THE NEWS REPORTS?!
FLING
HEY, MISS! DODGE TO YOUR LEFT!!
THWAP
?!

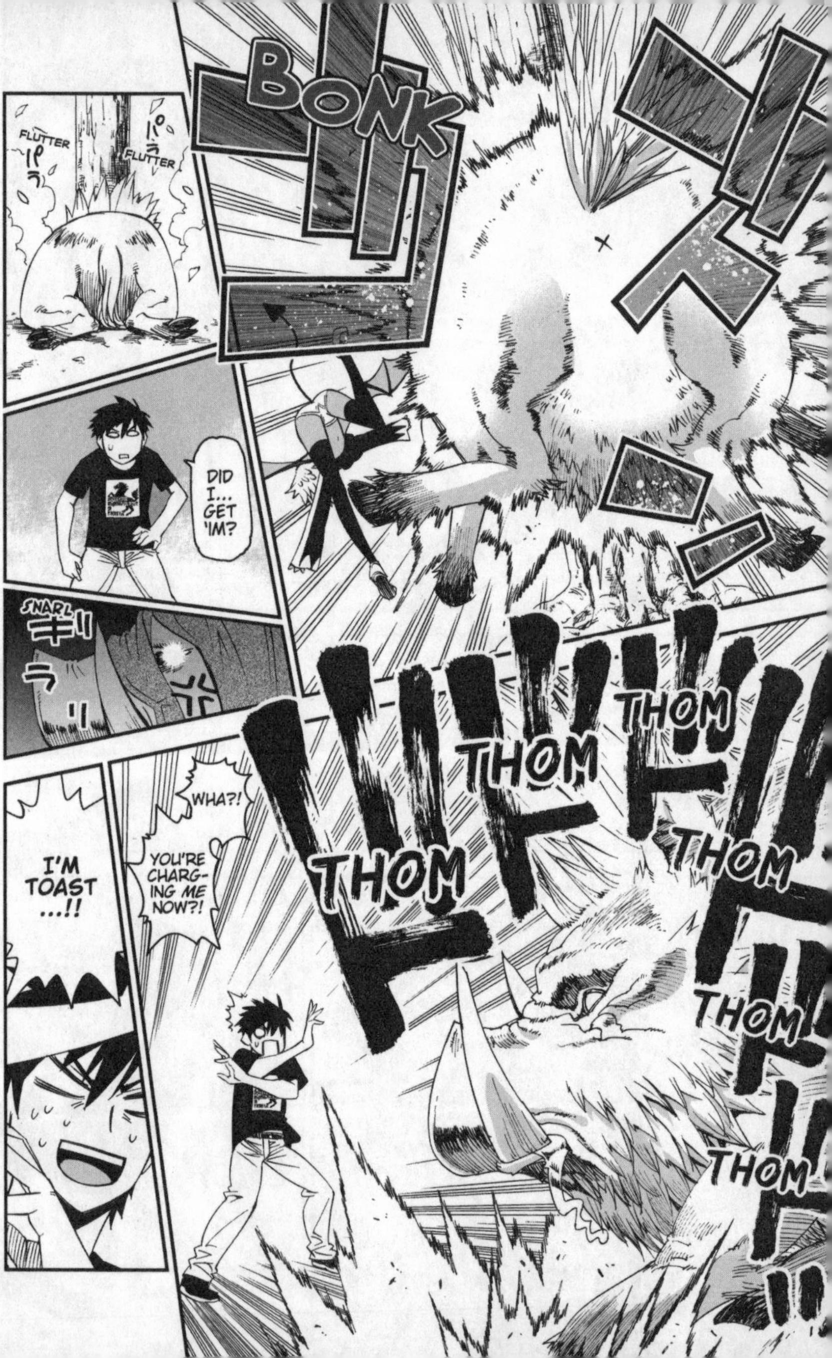
BONK
FLUTTER
FLUTTER
DID I... GET 'IM?
SNARL
THOM THOM THOM THOM THOM THOM
WHA?!
YOU'RE CHARGING ME NOW?!
I'M TOAST ...!!

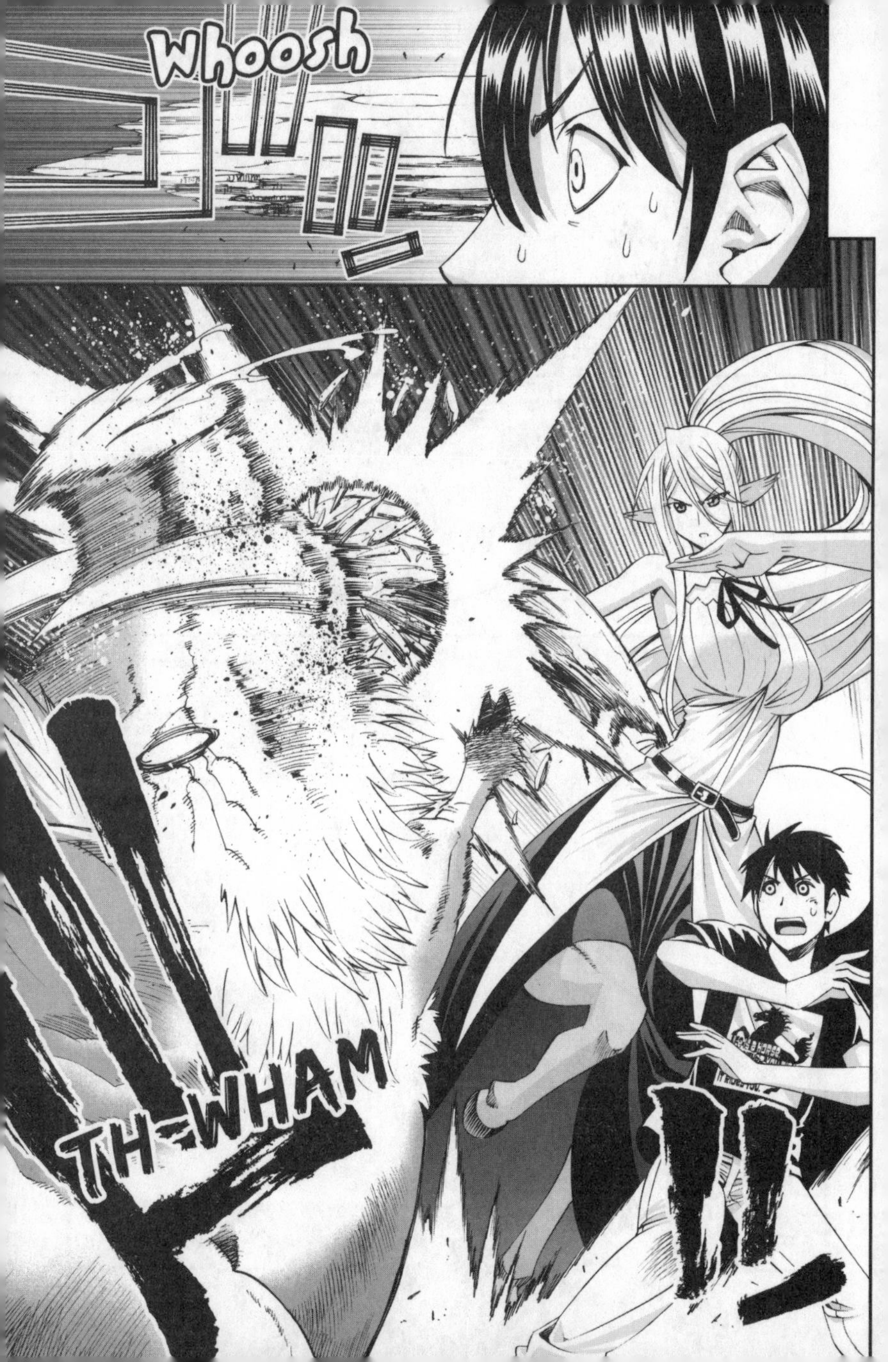
Whoosh
TH-WHAM

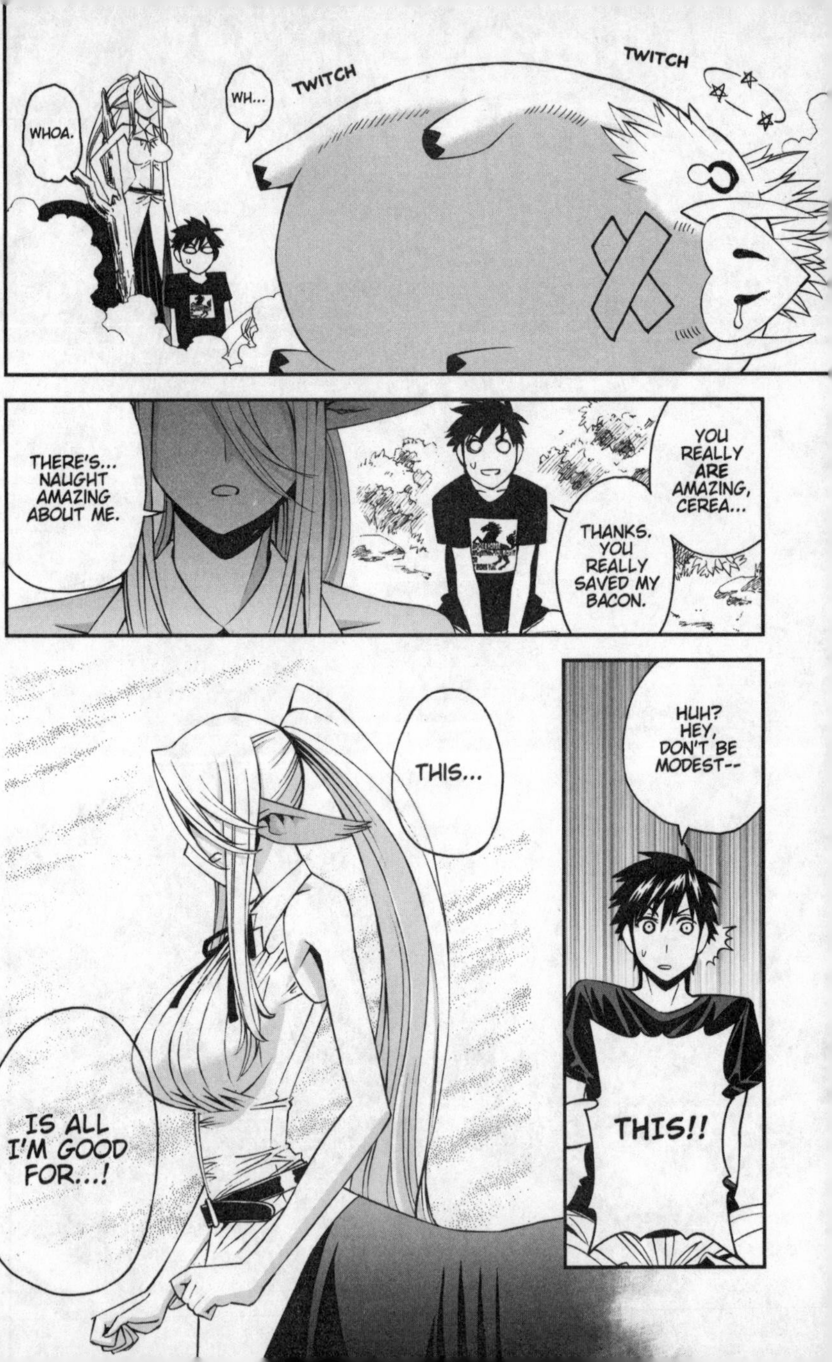
TWITCH
TWITCH
WH...
WHOA.
YOU REALLY ARE AMAZING, CEREA...
THANKS. YOU REALLY SAVED MY BACON.
THERE'S... NAUGHT AMAZING ABOUT ME.
HUH? HEY, DON'T BE MODEST--
THIS!!
THIS...
IS ALL I'M GOOD FOR...!

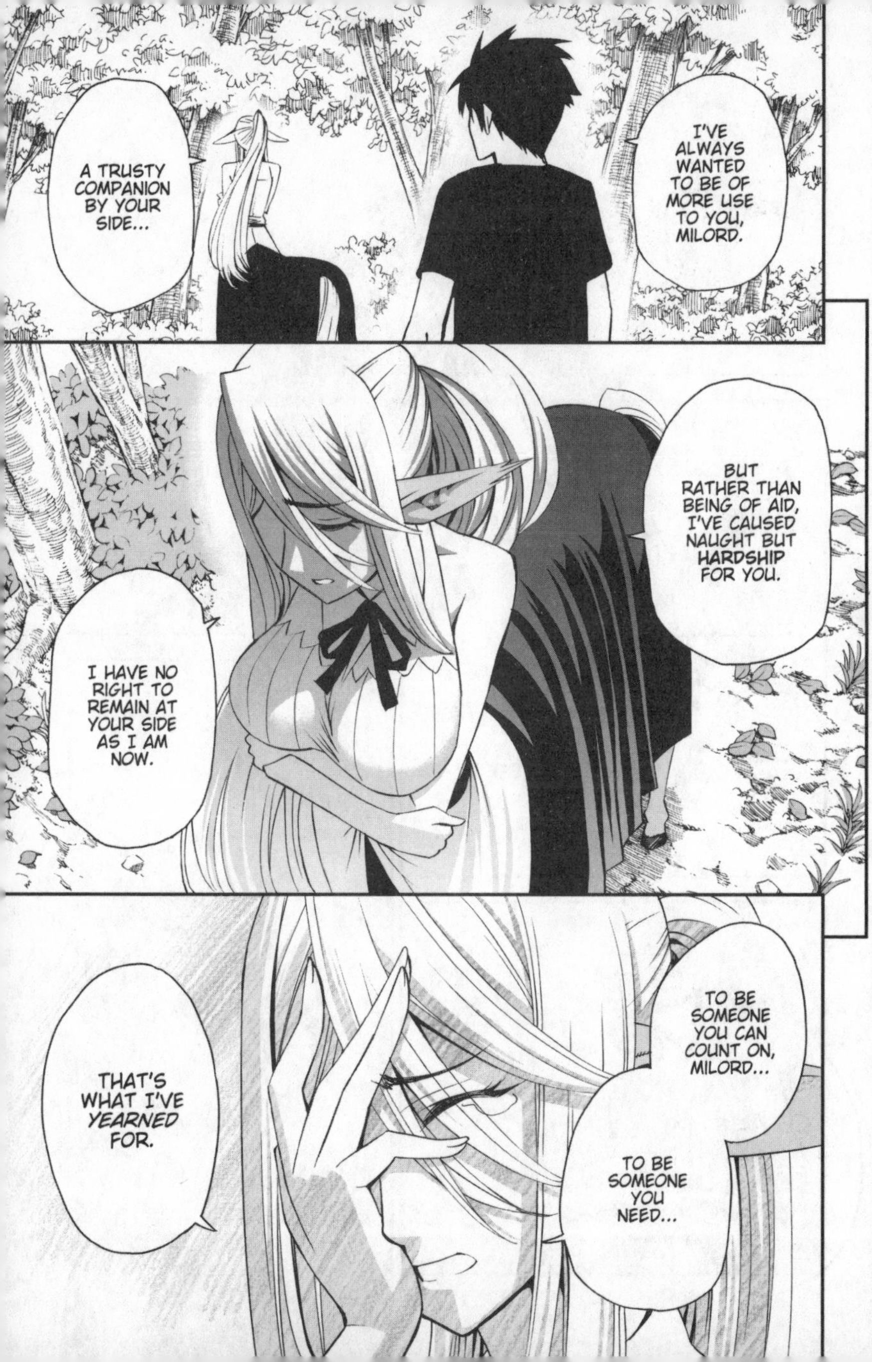
I'VE ALWAYS WANTED TO BE OF MORE USE TO YOU, MILORD.
A TRUSTY COMPANION BY YOUR SIDE...
BUT RATHER THAN BEING OF AID, I'VE CAUSED NAUGHT BUT HARDSHIP FOR YOU.
I HAVE NO RIGHT TO REMAIN AT YOUR SIDE AS I AM NOW.
TO BE SOMEONE YOU CAN COUNT ON, MILORD...
TO BE SOMEONE YOU NEED...
THAT'S WHAT I'VE *YEARNED* FOR.

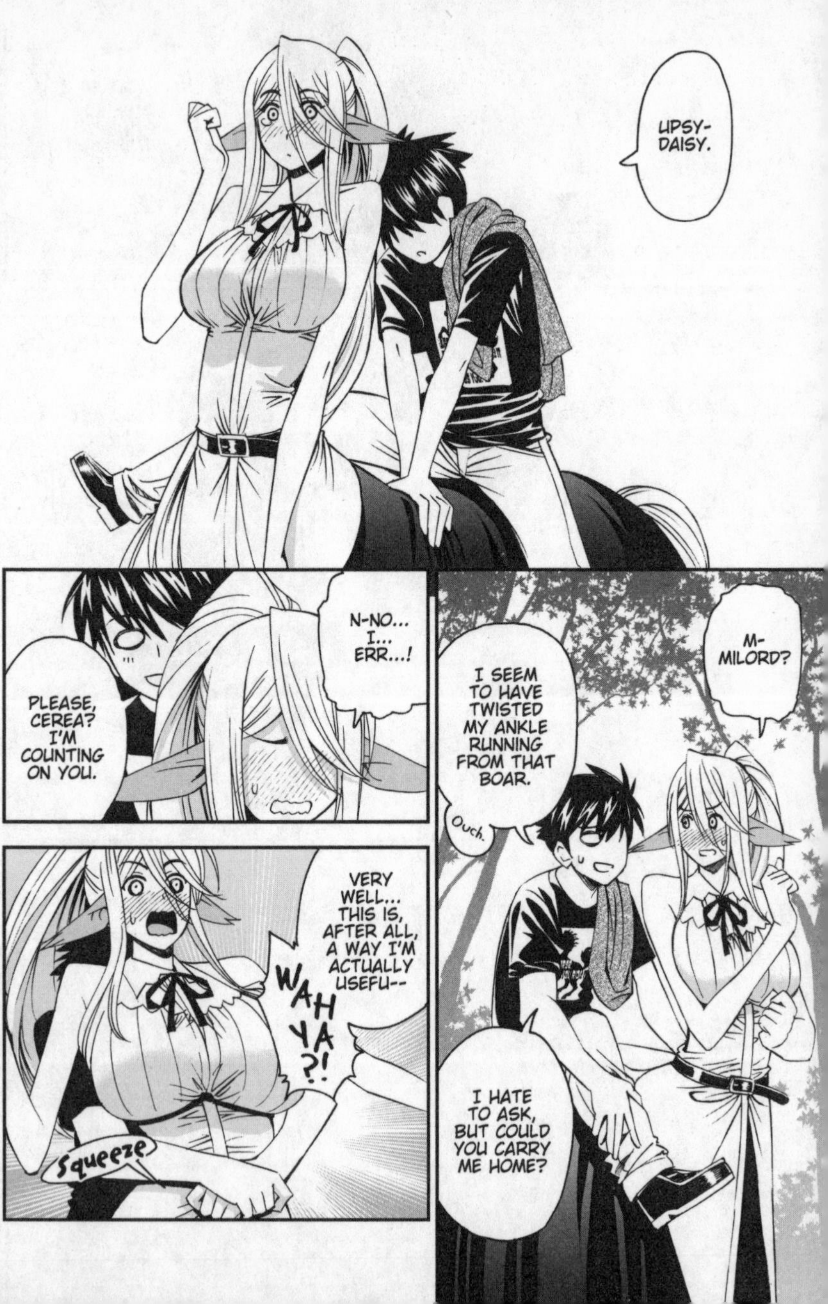
UPSY-DAISY.
M-MILORD?
I SEEM TO HAVE TWISTED MY ANKLE RUNNING FROM THAT BOAR.
Ouch.
I HATE TO ASK, BUT COULD YOU CARRY ME HOME?
N-NO... I... ERR...!
PLEASE, CEREA? I'M COUNTING ON YOU.
VERY WELL... THIS IS, AFTER ALL, A WAY I'M ACTUALLY USEFU--
WAHYA?!
Squeeze

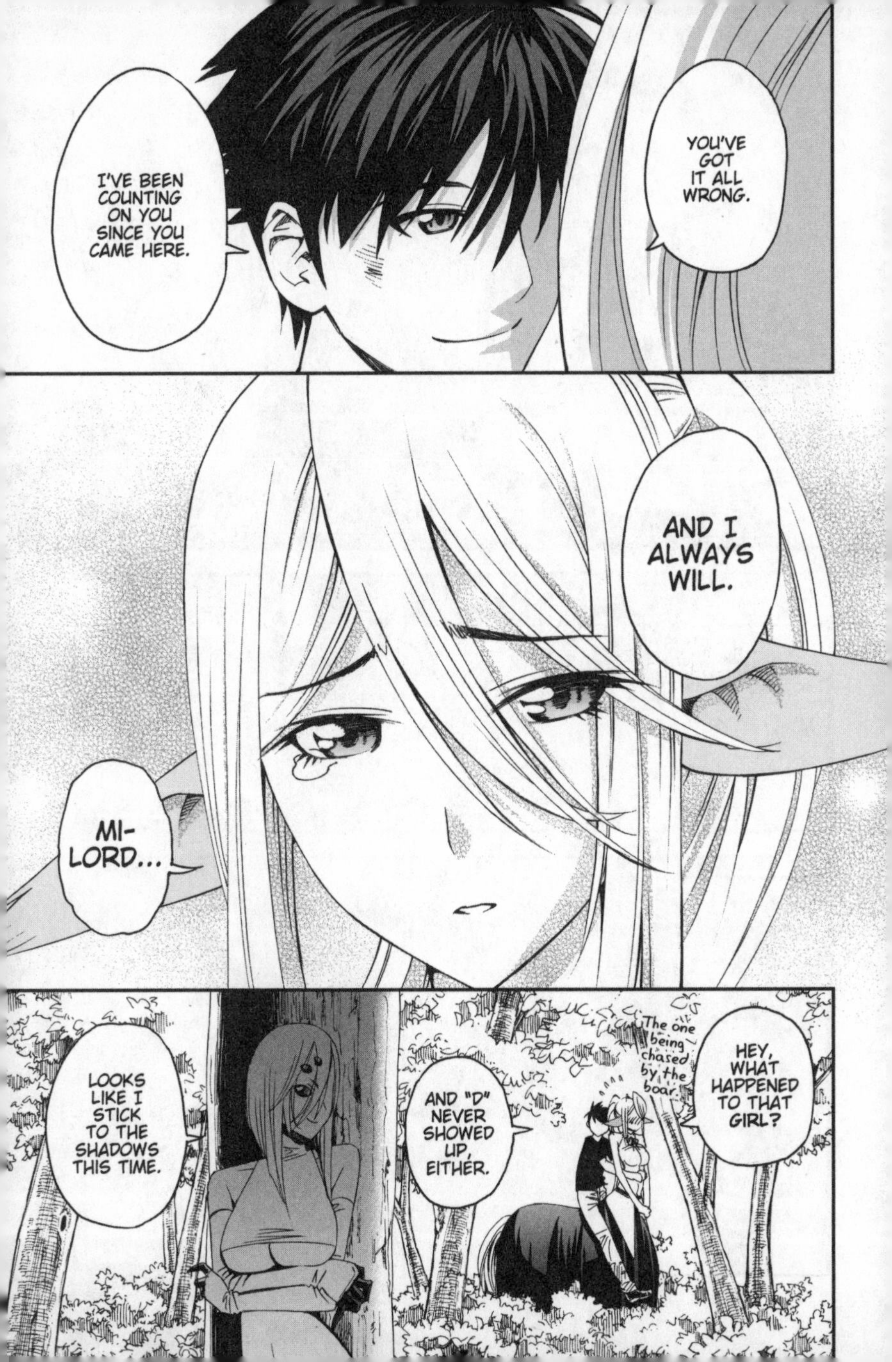
YOU'VE GOT IT ALL WRONG.
I'VE BEEN COUNTING ON YOU SINCE YOU CAME HERE.
AND I ALWAYS WILL.
MI-LORD...
HEY, WHAT HAPPENED TO THAT GIRL?
The one being chased by the boar.
AND "D" NEVER SHOWED UP, EITHER.
LOOKS LIKE I STICK TO THE SHADOWS THIS TIME.

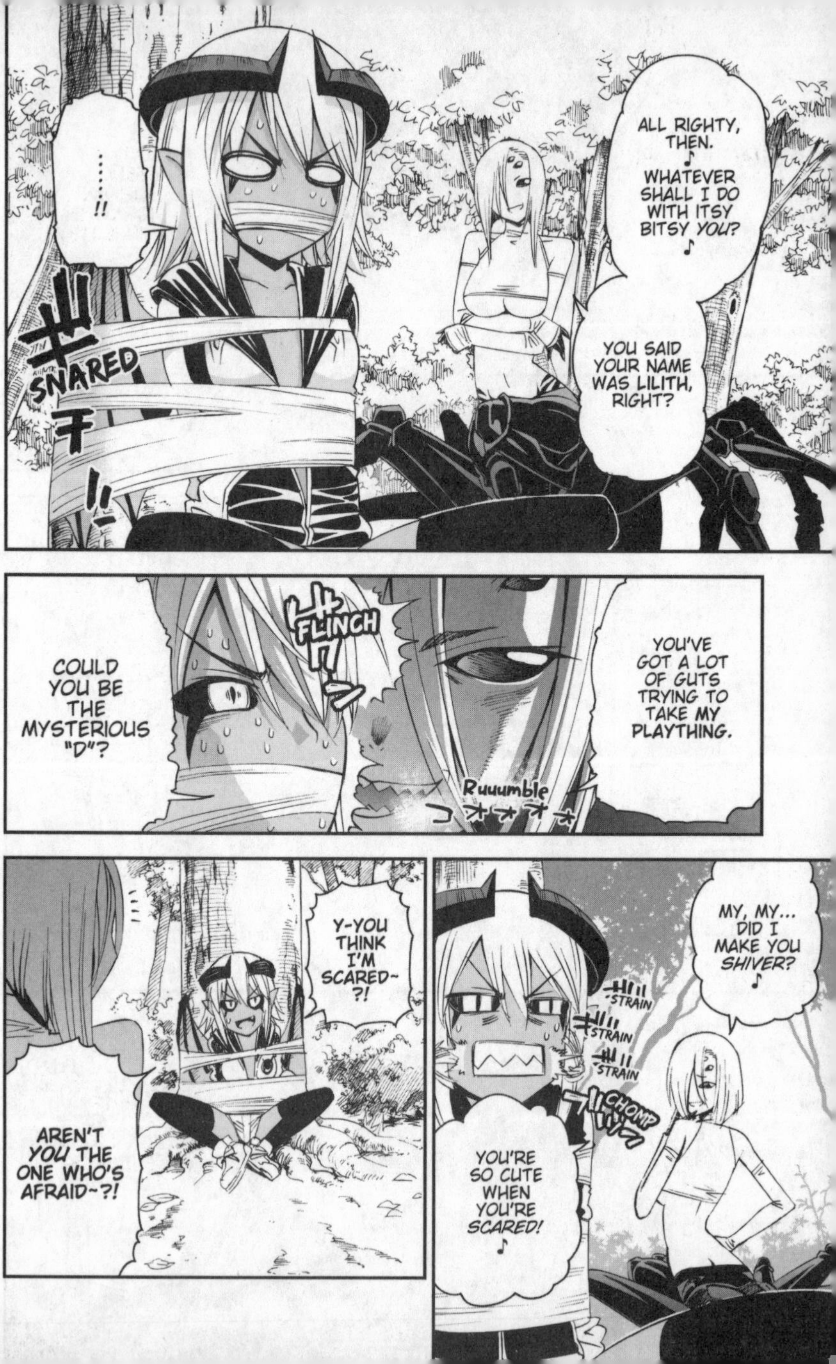

ALL RIGHTY, THEN. ♪ WHATEVER SHALL I DO WITH ITSY BITSY *YOU?* ♪
YOU SAID YOUR NAME WAS LILITH, RIGHT?
......!!
SNARED
YOU'VE GOT A LOT OF GUTS TRYING TO TAKE MY PLAYTHING.
FLINCH
COULD YOU BE THE MYSTERIOUS "D"?
Ruuumble
MY, MY... DID I MAKE YOU *SHIVER?* ♪
STRAIN
STRAIN
STRAIN
CHOMP
YOU'RE SO CUTE WHEN YOU'RE *SCARED!* ♪
Y-YOU THINK I'M SCARED~?!
AREN'T *YOU* THE ONE WHO'S AFRAID~?!

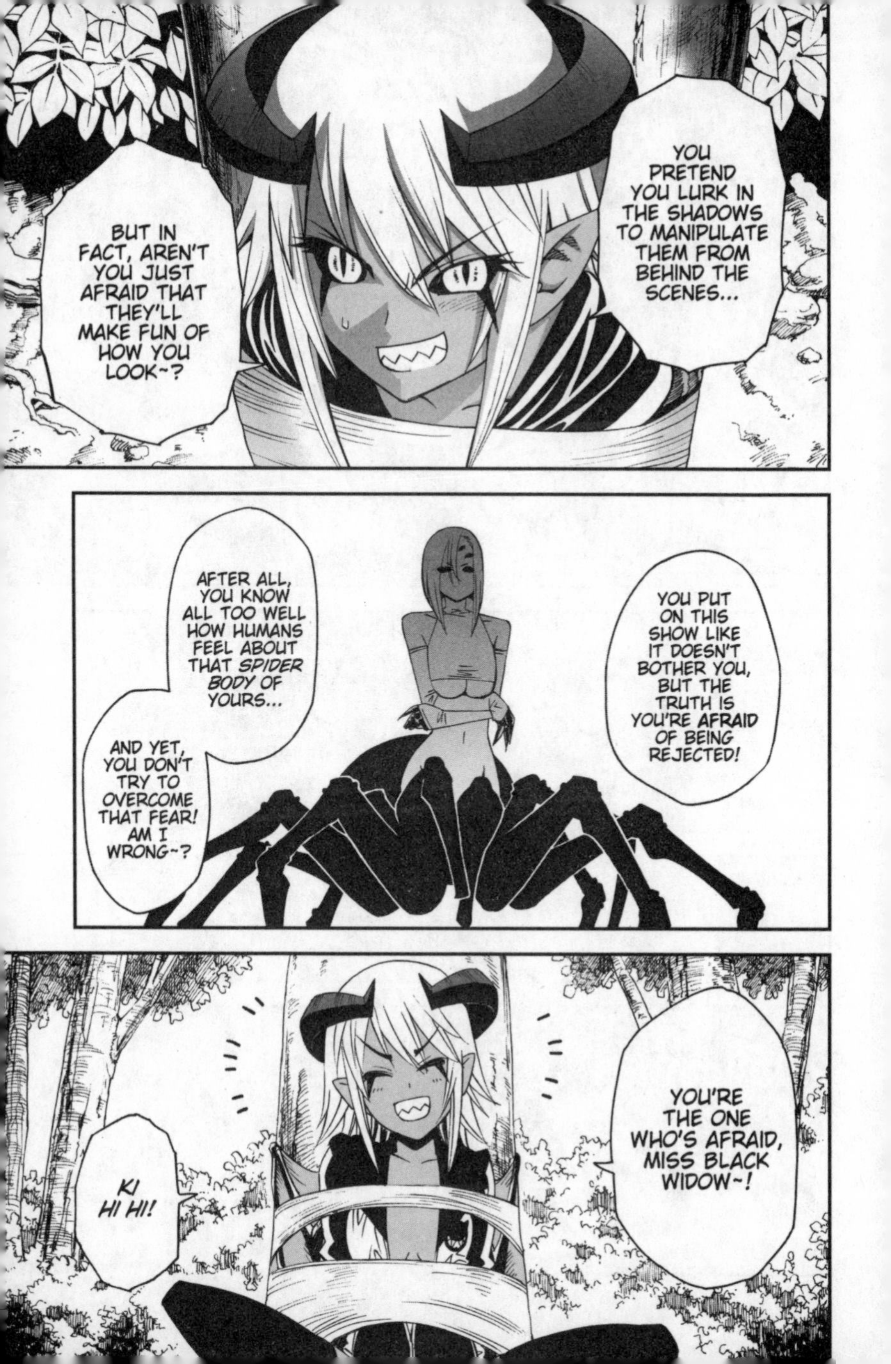
YOU PRETEND YOU LURK IN THE SHADOWS TO MANIPULATE THEM FROM BEHIND THE SCENES...
BUT IN FACT, AREN'T YOU JUST AFRAID THAT THEY'LL MAKE FUN OF HOW YOU LOOK~?
YOU PUT ON THIS SHOW LIKE IT DOESN'T BOTHER YOU, BUT THE TRUTH IS YOU'RE AFRAID OF BEING REJECTED!
AFTER ALL, YOU KNOW ALL TOO WELL HOW HUMANS FEEL ABOUT THAT *SPIDER BODY* OF YOURS...
AND YET, YOU DON'T TRY TO OVERCOME THAT FEAR! AM I WRONG~?
YOU'RE THE ONE WHO'S AFRAID, MISS BLACK WIDOW~!
KI HI HI!

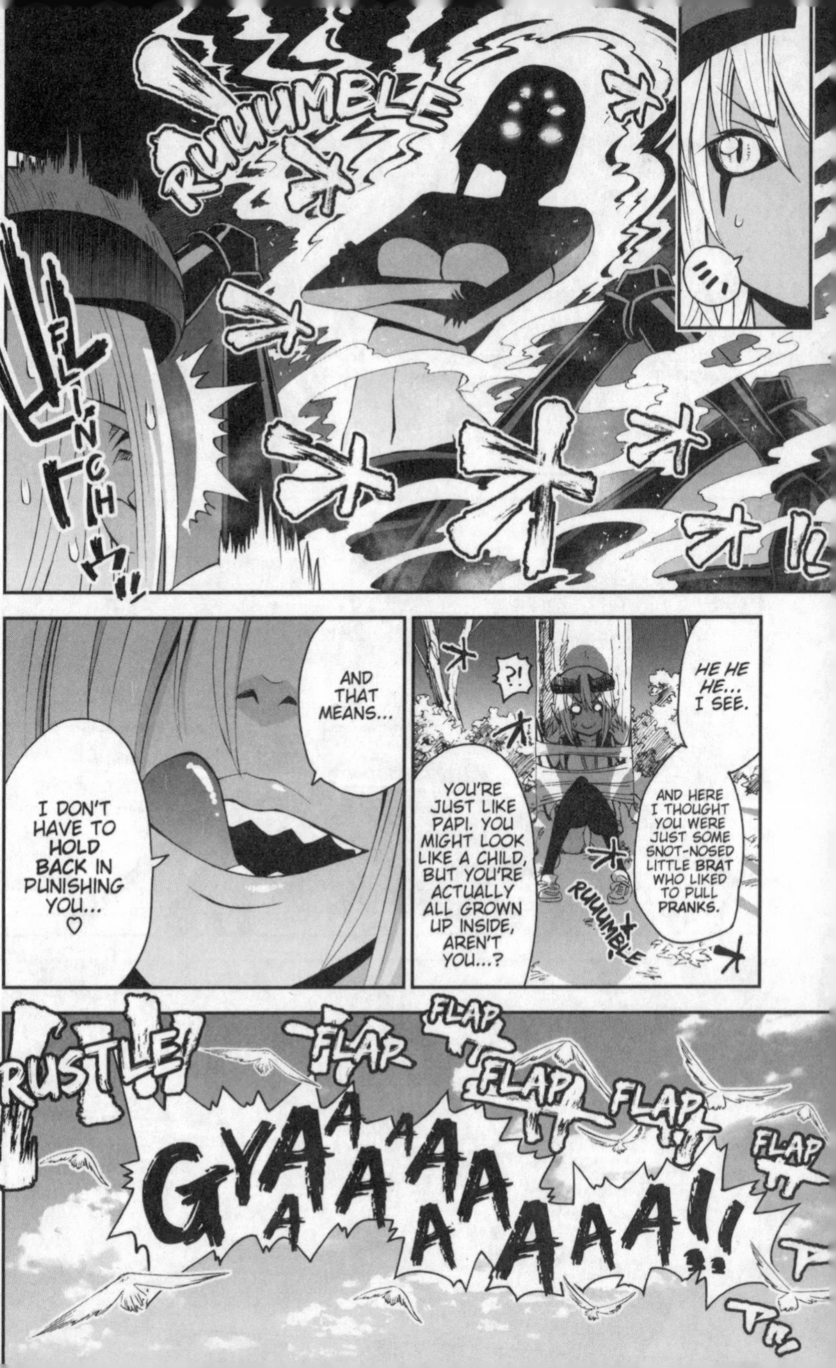

...!!
RUUUMBLE
FLINCH
?!
HE HE HE... I SEE.
AND HERE I THOUGHT YOU WERE JUST SOME SNOT-NOSED LITTLE BRAT WHO LIKED TO PULL PRANKS.
YOU'RE JUST LIKE PAPI. YOU MIGHT LOOK LIKE A CHILD, BUT YOU'RE ACTUALLY ALL GROWN UP INSIDE, AREN'T YOU...?
RUUUMBLE
AND THAT MEANS...
I DON'T HAVE TO HOLD BACK IN PUNISHING YOU... ♡
RUSTLE!
FLAP FLAP FLAP FLAP FLAP
GYAAAAAAAAAAAA!!

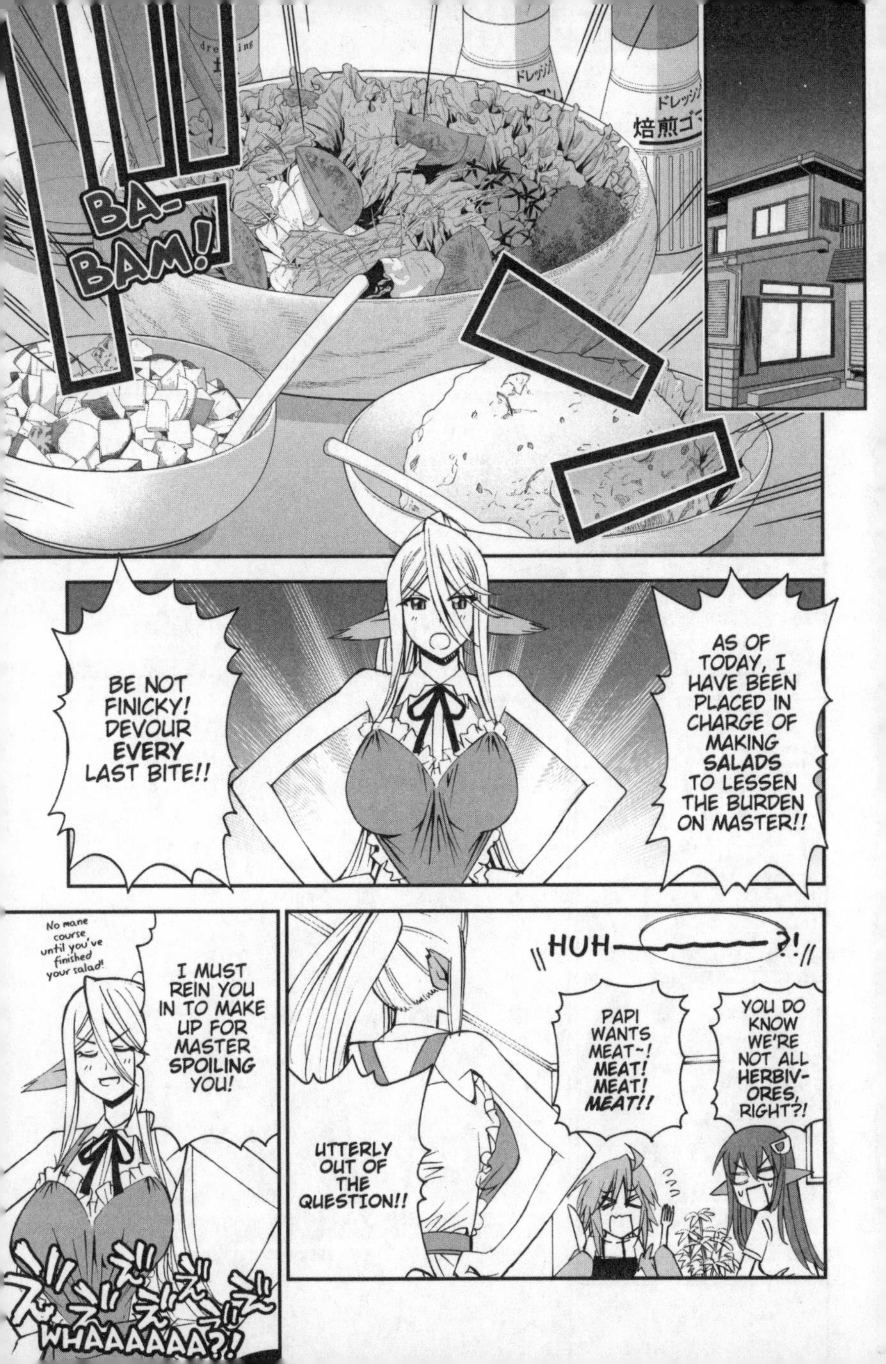
ドレッシング
焙煎ゴマ
BA-BAM!
AS OF TODAY, I HAVE BEEN PLACED IN CHARGE OF MAKING SALADS TO LESSEN THE BURDEN ON MASTER!!
BE NOT FINICKY! DEVOUR EVERY LAST BITE!!
HUH——?!
YOU DO KNOW WE'RE NOT ALL HERBIVORES, RIGHT?!
PAPI WANTS MEAT~! MEAT! MEAT! MEAT!!
UTTERLY OUT OF THE QUESTION!!
I MUST REIN YOU IN TO MAKE UP FOR MASTER SPOILING YOU!
No mane course until you've finished your salad!
WHAAAAAA?!

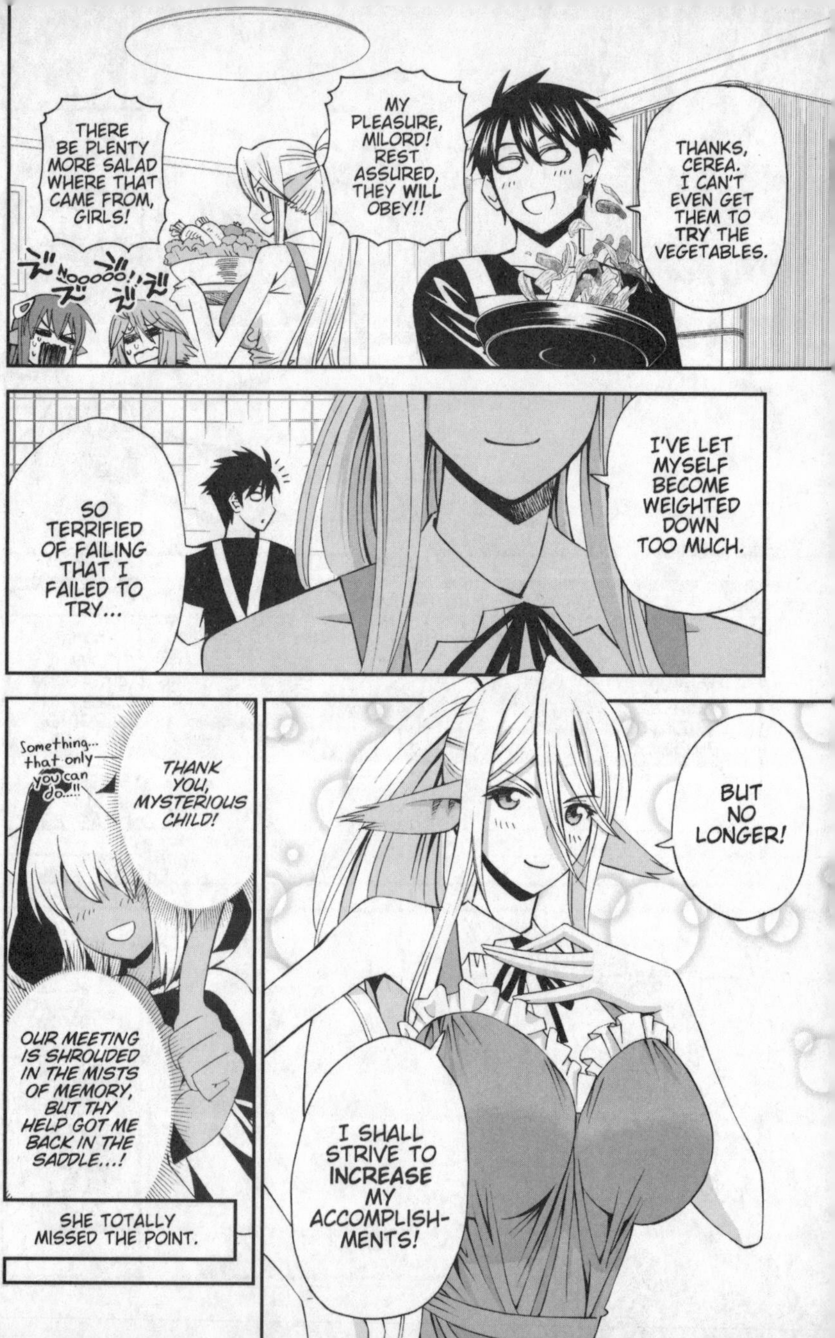
THANKS, CEREA. I CAN'T EVEN GET THEM TO TRY THE VEGETABLES.
MY PLEASURE, MILORD! REST ASSURED, THEY WILL OBEY!!
THERE BE PLENTY MORE SALAD WHERE THAT CAME FROM, GIRLS!
NOOOOOO!!
I'VE LET MYSELF BECOME WEIGHTED DOWN TOO MUCH.
SO TERRIFIED OF FAILING THAT I FAILED TO TRY...
BUT NO LONGER!
I SHALL STRIVE TO INCREASE MY ACCOMPLISHMENTS!
THANK YOU, MYSTERIOUS CHILD!
Something... that only you can do...!!
OUR MEETING IS SHROUDED IN THE MISTS OF MEMORY, BUT THY HELP GOT ME BACK IN THE SADDLE...!
SHE TOTALLY MISSED THE POINT.

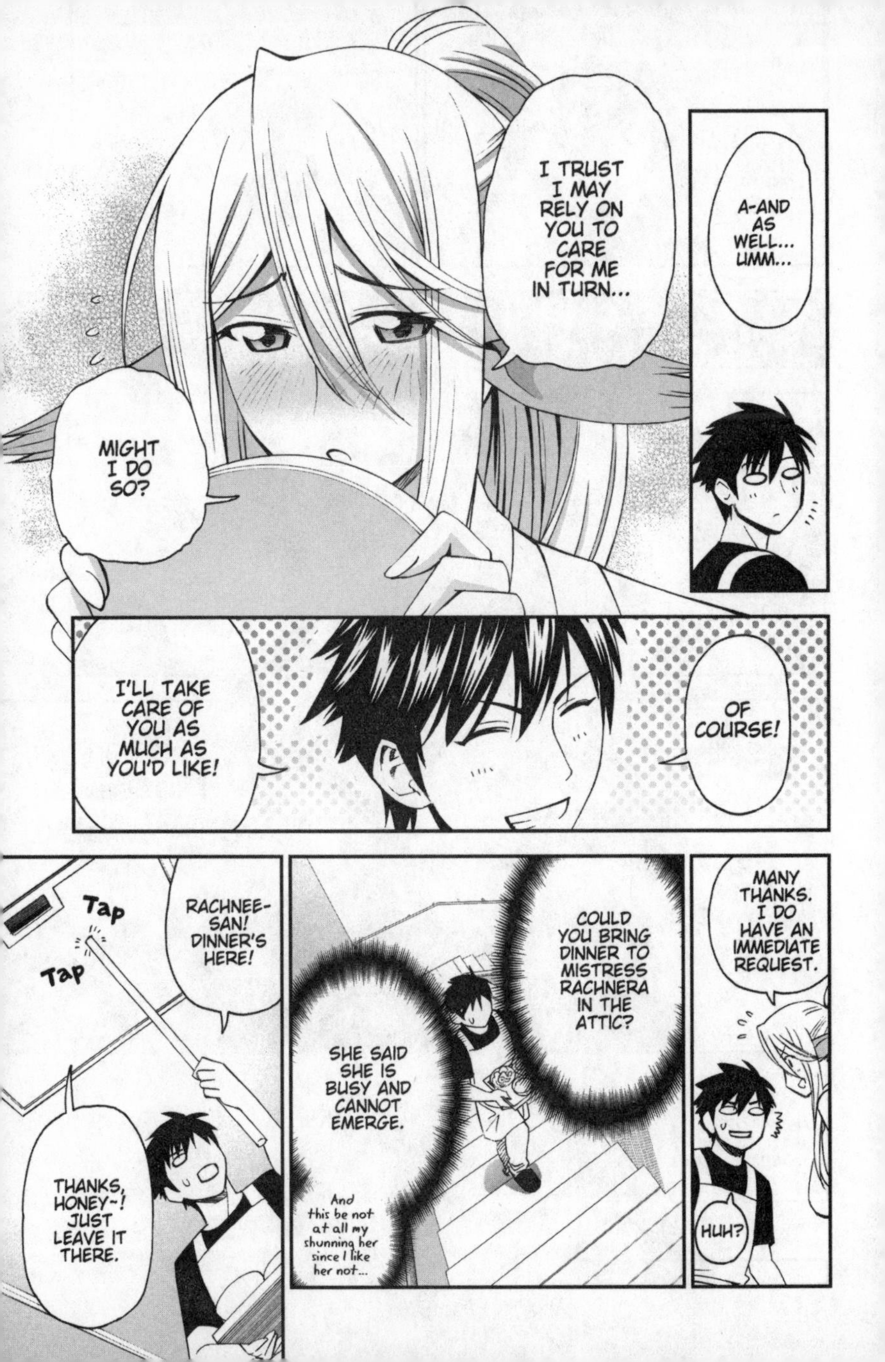
A-AND AS WELL... UMM...
I TRUST I MAY RELY ON YOU TO CARE FOR ME IN TURN...
MIGHT I DO SO?
OF COURSE!
I'LL TAKE CARE OF YOU AS MUCH AS YOU'D LIKE!
MANY THANKS. I DO HAVE AN IMMEDIATE REQUEST.
HUH?
COULD YOU BRING DINNER TO MISTRESS RACHNERA IN THE ATTIC?
SHE SAID SHE IS BUSY AND CANNOT EMERGE.
And this be not at all my shunning her since I like her not...
Tap
Tap
RACHNEE-SAN! DINNER'S HERE!
THANKS, HONEY~! JUST LEAVE IT THERE.

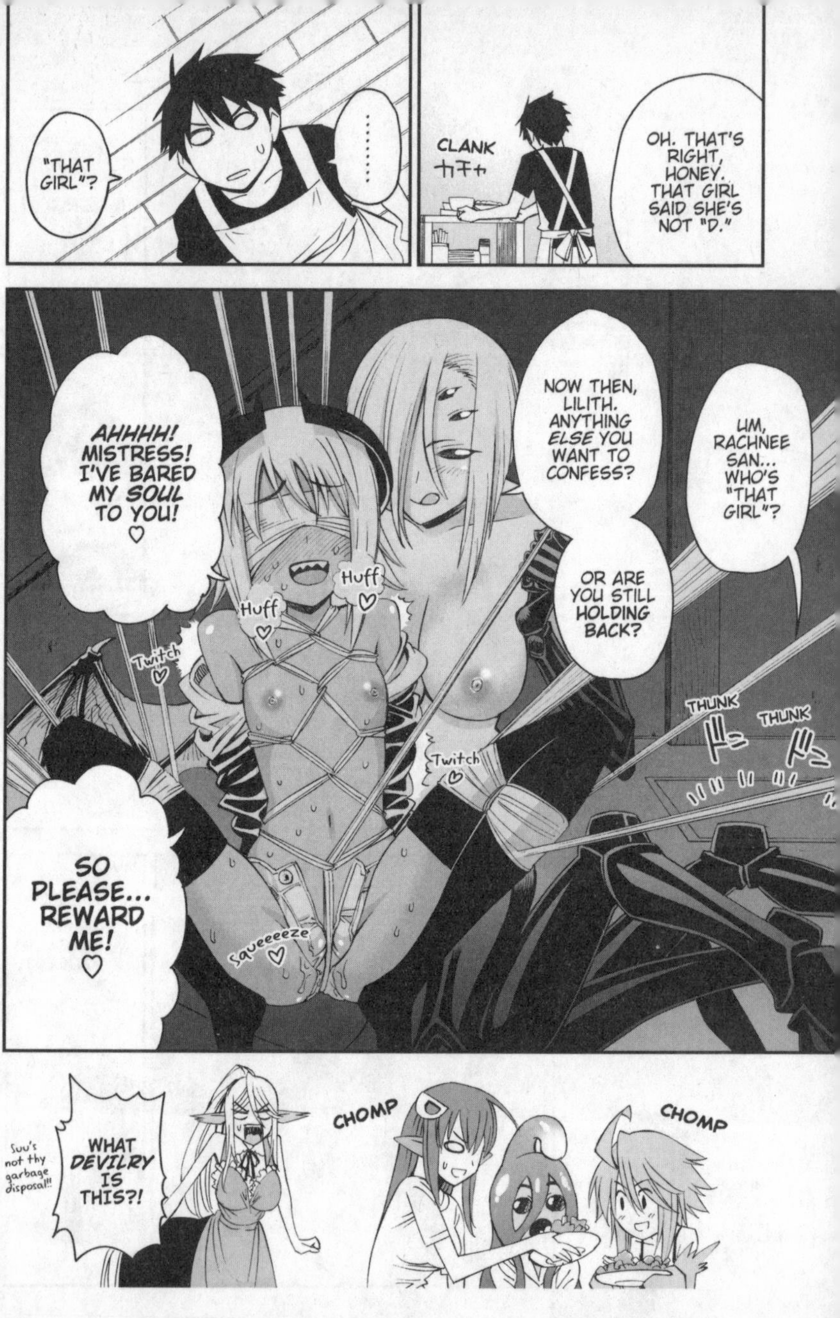
OH. THAT'S RIGHT, HONEY. THAT GIRL SAID SHE'S NOT "D."
CLANK
カチャ
......
"THAT GIRL"?
UM, RACHNEE SAN... WHO'S "THAT GIRL"?
NOW THEN, LILITH. ANYTHING ELSE YOU WANT TO CONFESS?
OR ARE YOU STILL HOLDING BACK?
THUNK
THUNK
AHHHH! MISTRESS! I'VE BARED MY SOUL TO YOU! ♡
Huff ♡
Huff ♡
Twitch ♡
Twitch ♡
SO PLEASE... REWARD ME! ♡
Squeeeeze ♡
CHOMP
CHOMP
WHAT DEVILRY IS THIS?!
Suu's not thy garbage disposal!!

Monster Musume

Everyday Life with Monster Girls

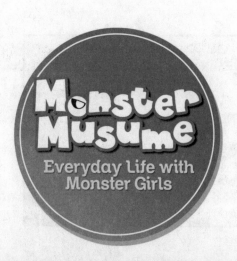

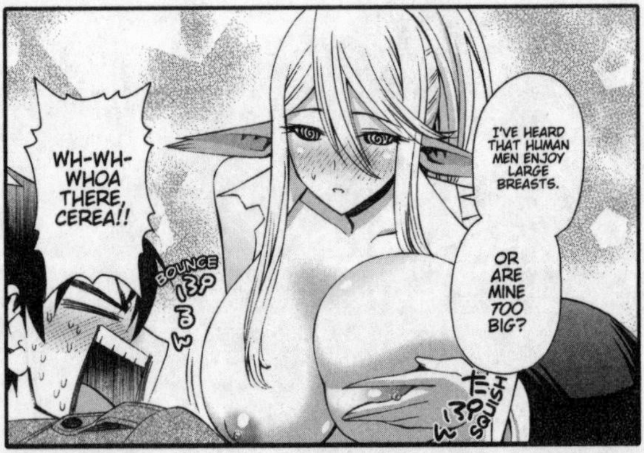
I'VE HEARD THAT HUMAN MEN ENJOY LARGE BREASTS.
OR ARE MINE TOO BIG?
SQUISH
WH-WH-WHOA THERE, CEREA!!
BOUNCE

Chapter 22

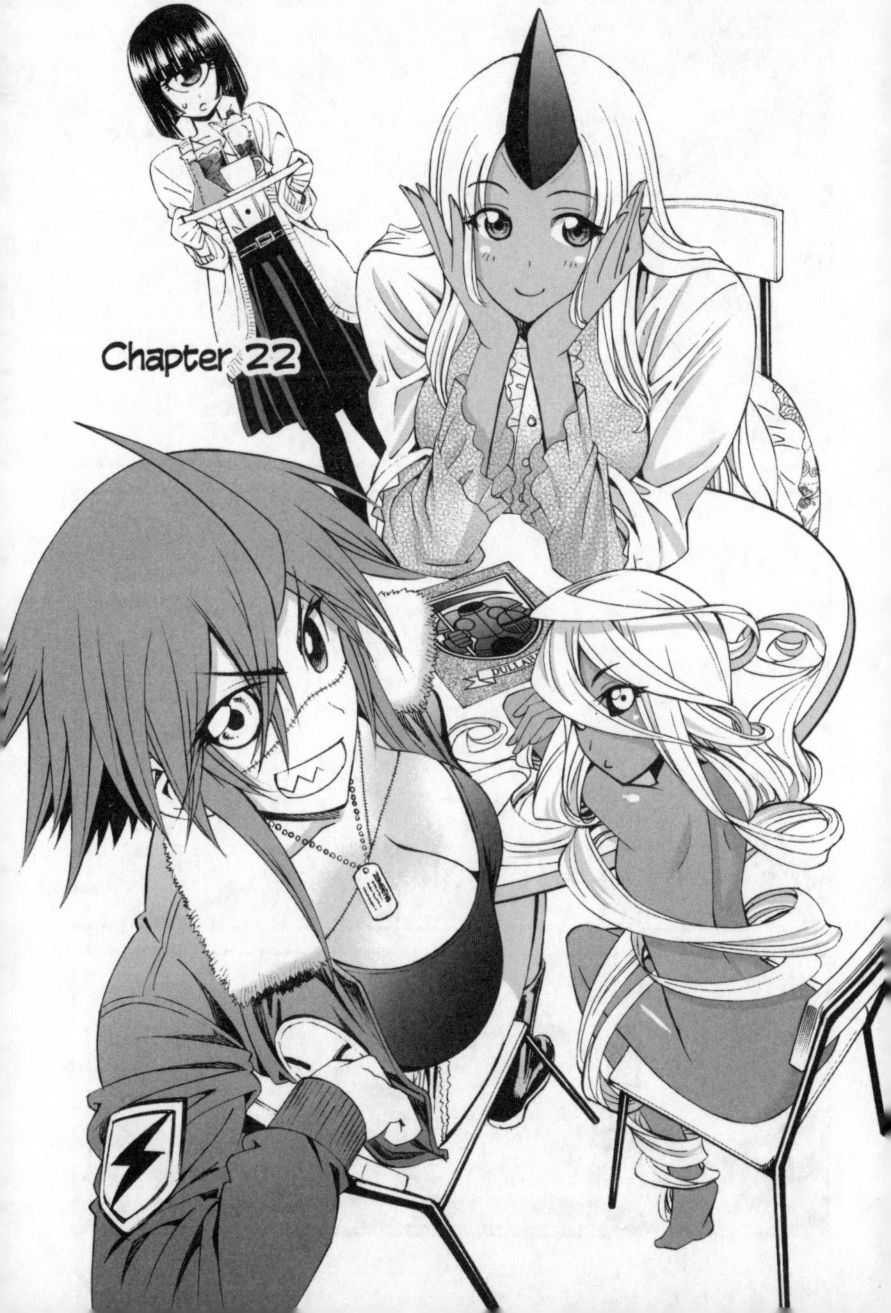

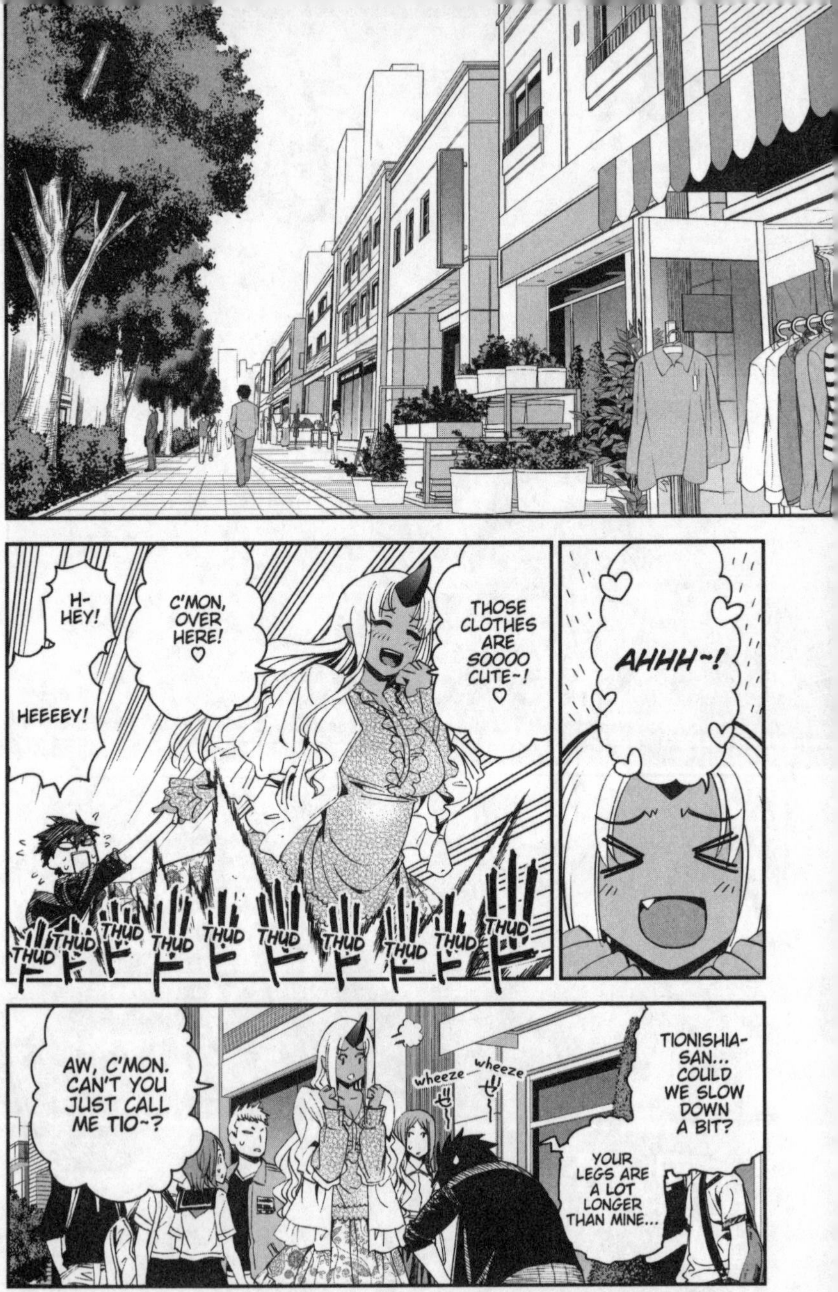
AHHH~!
THOSE CLOTHES ARE SOOOO CUTE~! ♡
C'MON, OVER HERE! ♡
H-HEY!
HEEEEY!
THUD THUD THUD THUD THUD THUD THUD THUD THUD THUD
TIONISHIA-SAN... COULD WE SLOW DOWN A BIT?
YOUR LEGS ARE A LOT LONGER THAN MINE...
wheeze wheeze
AW, C'MON. CAN'T YOU JUST CALL ME TIO~?

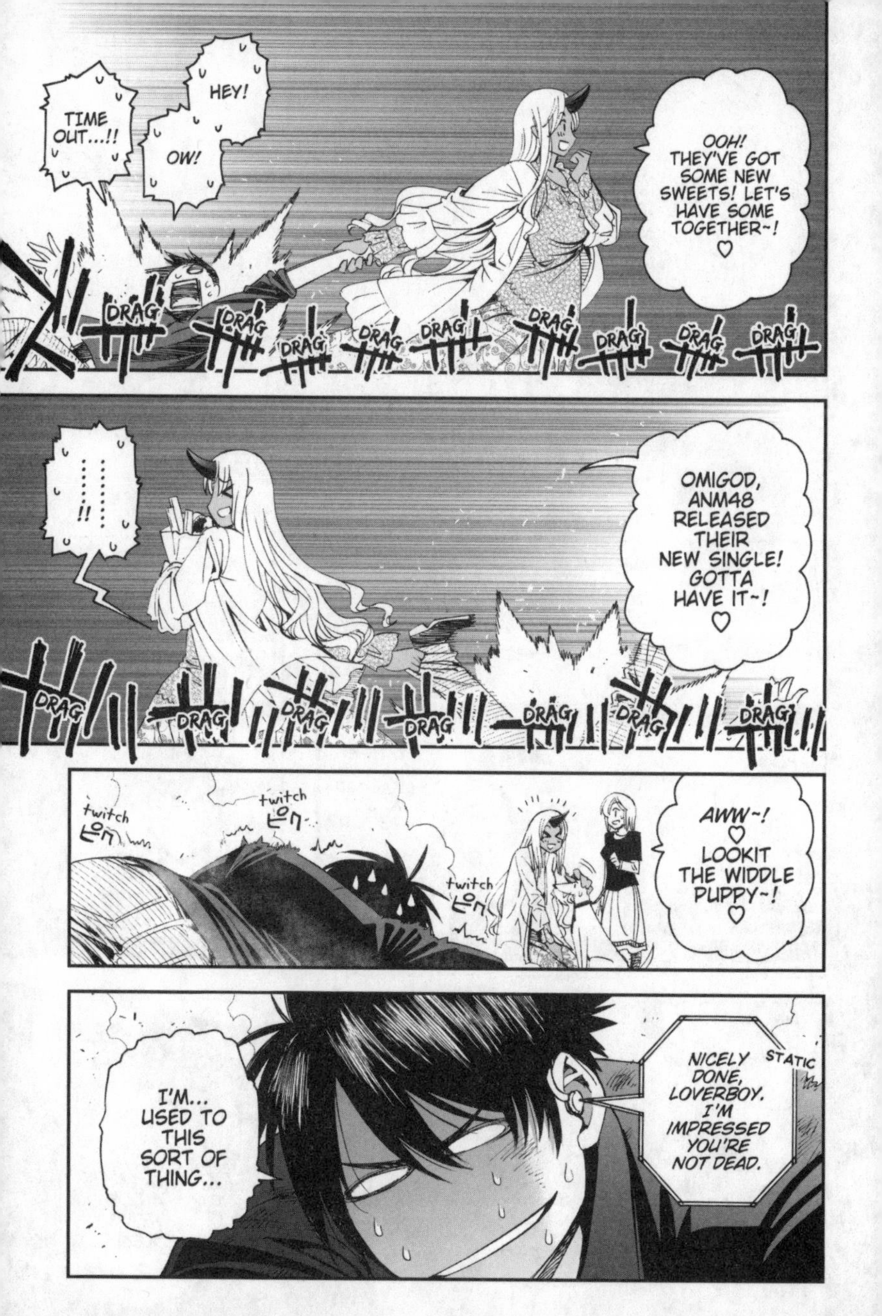
OOH! THEY'VE GOT SOME NEW SWEETS! LET'S HAVE SOME TOGETHER~! ♡
HEY!
OW!
TIME OUT...!!
DRAG DRAG DRAG DRAG DRAG DRAG DRAG DRAG DRAG
OMIGOD, ANM48 RELEASED THEIR NEW SINGLE! GOTTA HAVE IT~! ♡
......!!
DRAG DRAG DRAG DRAG DRAG DRAG DRAG
AWW~! ♡ LOOKIT THE WIDDLE PUPPY~! ♡
twitch ピク
twitch ピク
twitch ピク
STATIC
NICELY DONE, LOVERBOY. I'M IMPRESSED YOU'RE NOT DEAD.
I'M... USED TO THIS SORT OF THING...

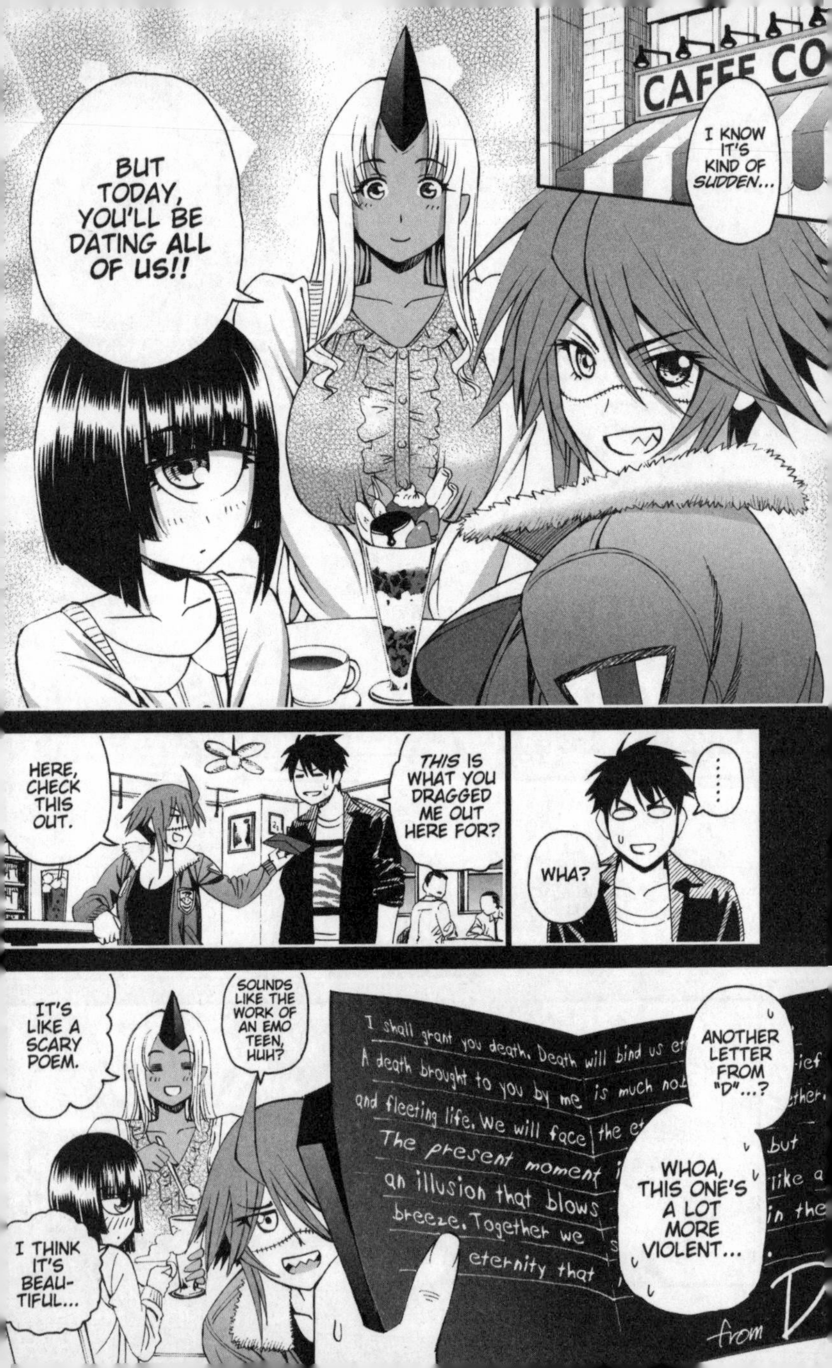
CAFFE CO
I KNOW IT'S KIND OF SUDDEN...
BUT TODAY, YOU'LL BE DATING ALL OF US!!
......
WHA?
THIS IS WHAT YOU DRAGGED ME OUT HERE FOR?
HERE, CHECK THIS OUT.
ANOTHER LETTER FROM "D"...?
WHOA, THIS ONE'S A LOT MORE VIOLENT...
I shall grant you death. Death will bind us et
A death brought to you by me is much no
and fleeting life. We will face the e
The present moment
an illusion that blows
breeze. Together we
eternity that
from D
SOUNDS LIKE THE WORK OF AN EMO TEEN, HUH?
IT'S LIKE A SCARY POEM.
I THINK IT'S BEAUTIFUL...

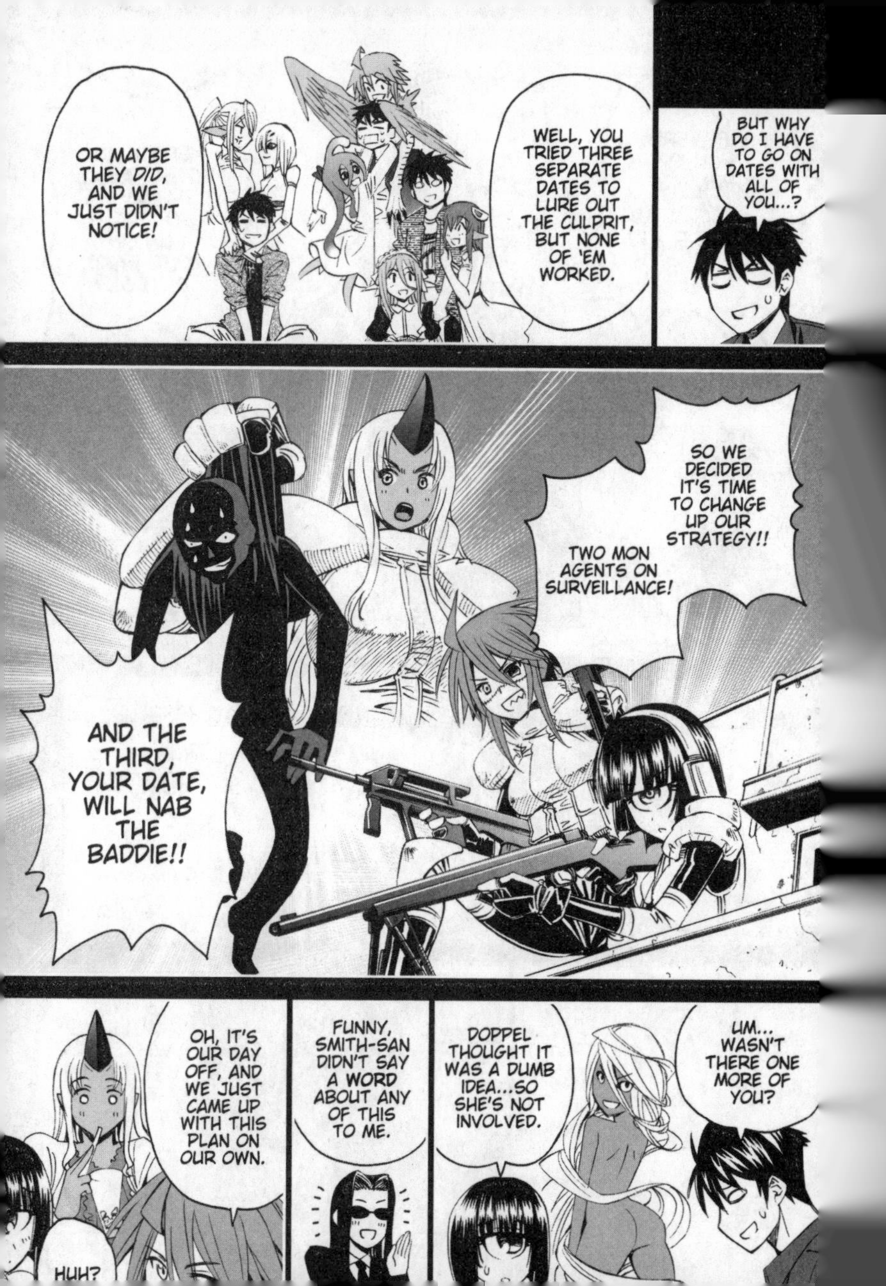
BUT WHY DO I HAVE TO GO ON DATES WITH ALL OF YOU...?
WELL, YOU TRIED THREE SEPARATE DATES TO LURE OUT THE CULPRIT, BUT NONE OF 'EM WORKED.
OR MAYBE THEY *DID*, AND WE JUST DIDN'T NOTICE!
SO WE DECIDED IT'S TIME TO CHANGE UP OUR STRATEGY!!
TWO MON AGENTS ON SURVEILLANCE!
AND THE THIRD, YOUR DATE, WILL NAB THE BADDIE!!
UM... WASN'T THERE ONE MORE OF YOU?
DOPPEL THOUGHT IT WAS A DUMB IDEA...SO SHE'S NOT INVOLVED.
FUNNY, SMITH-SAN DIDN'T SAY A WORD ABOUT ANY OF THIS TO ME.
OH, IT'S OUR DAY OFF, AND WE JUST CAME UP WITH THIS PLAN ON OUR OWN.
HUH?

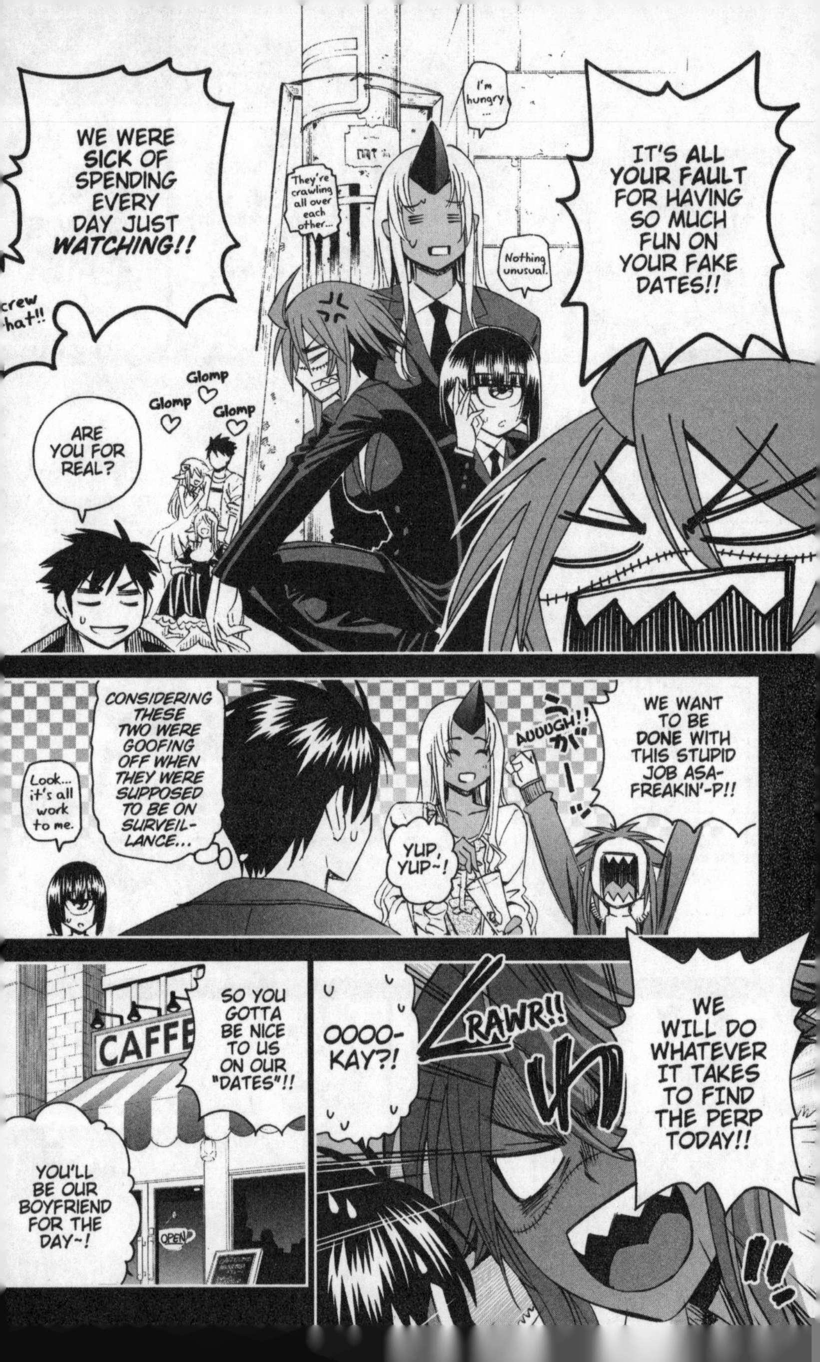
IT'S ALL YOUR FAULT FOR HAVING SO MUCH FUN ON YOUR FAKE DATES!!
I'm hungry...
Nothing unusual.
They're crawling all over each other...
WE WERE SICK OF SPENDING EVERY DAY JUST WATCHING!!
Glomp
Glomp
Glomp
ARE YOU FOR REAL?
WE WANT TO BE DONE WITH THIS STUPID JOB ASA-FREAKIN'-P!!
AUUUGH!!
YUP, YUP~!
CONSIDERING THESE TWO WERE GOOFING OFF WHEN THEY WERE SUPPOSED TO BE ON SURVEIL-LANCE...
Look... it's all work to me.
WE WILL DO WHATEVER IT TAKES TO FIND THE PERP TODAY!!
RAWR!!
OOOO-KAY?!
SO YOU GOTTA BE NICE TO US ON OUR "DATES"!!
CAFFE
YOU'LL BE OUR BOYFRIEND FOR THE DAY~!
OPEN

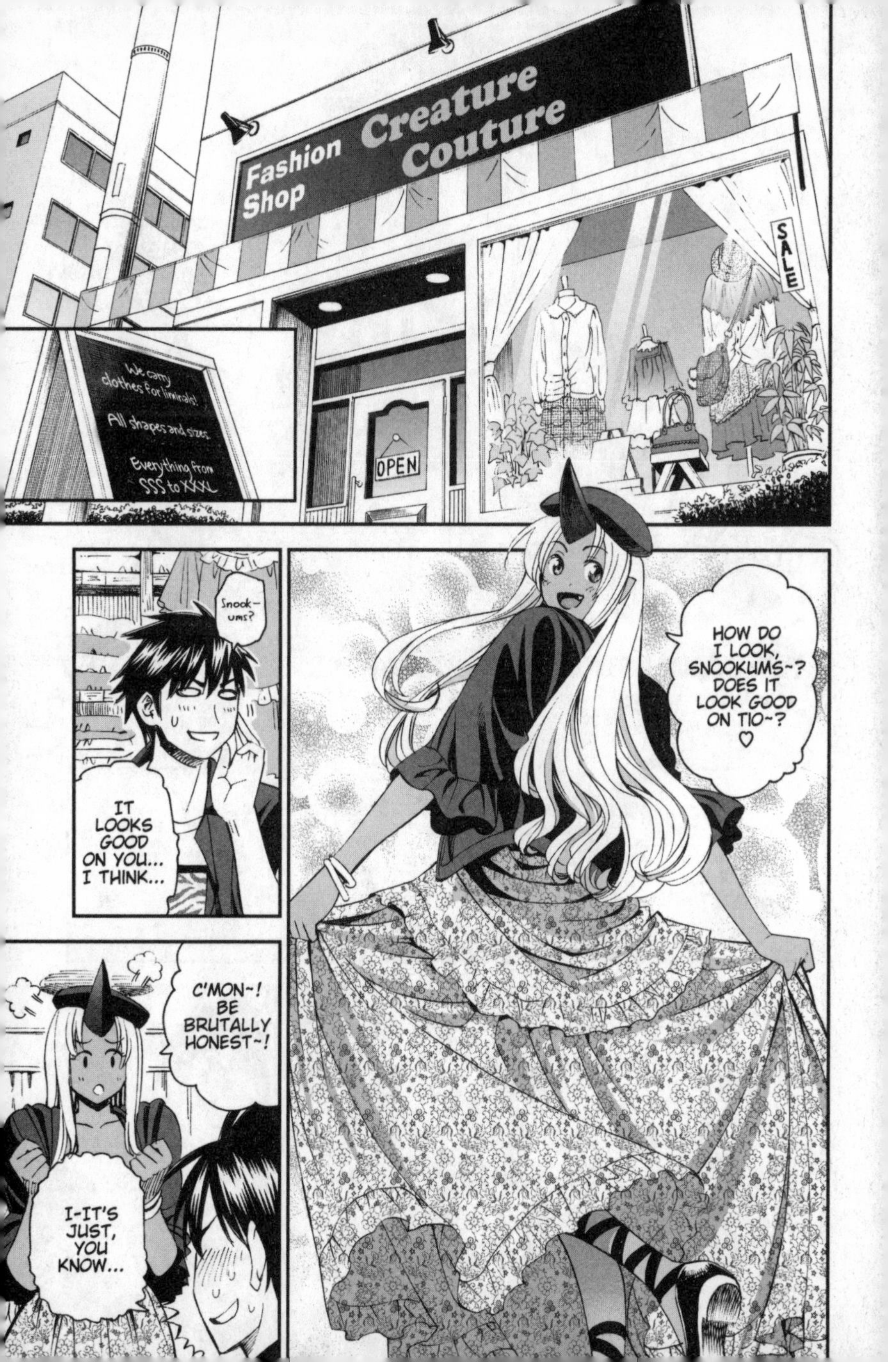

Fashion Shop Creature Couture
SALE
OPEN
We carry clothes for liminals! All shapes and sizes. Everything from SSS to XXXL
HOW DO I LOOK, SNOOKUMS~? DOES IT LOOK GOOD ON TIO~? ♡
Snook-ums?
IT LOOKS GOOD ON YOU... I THINK...
C'MON~! BE BRUTALLY HONEST~!
I-IT'S JUST, YOU KNOW...

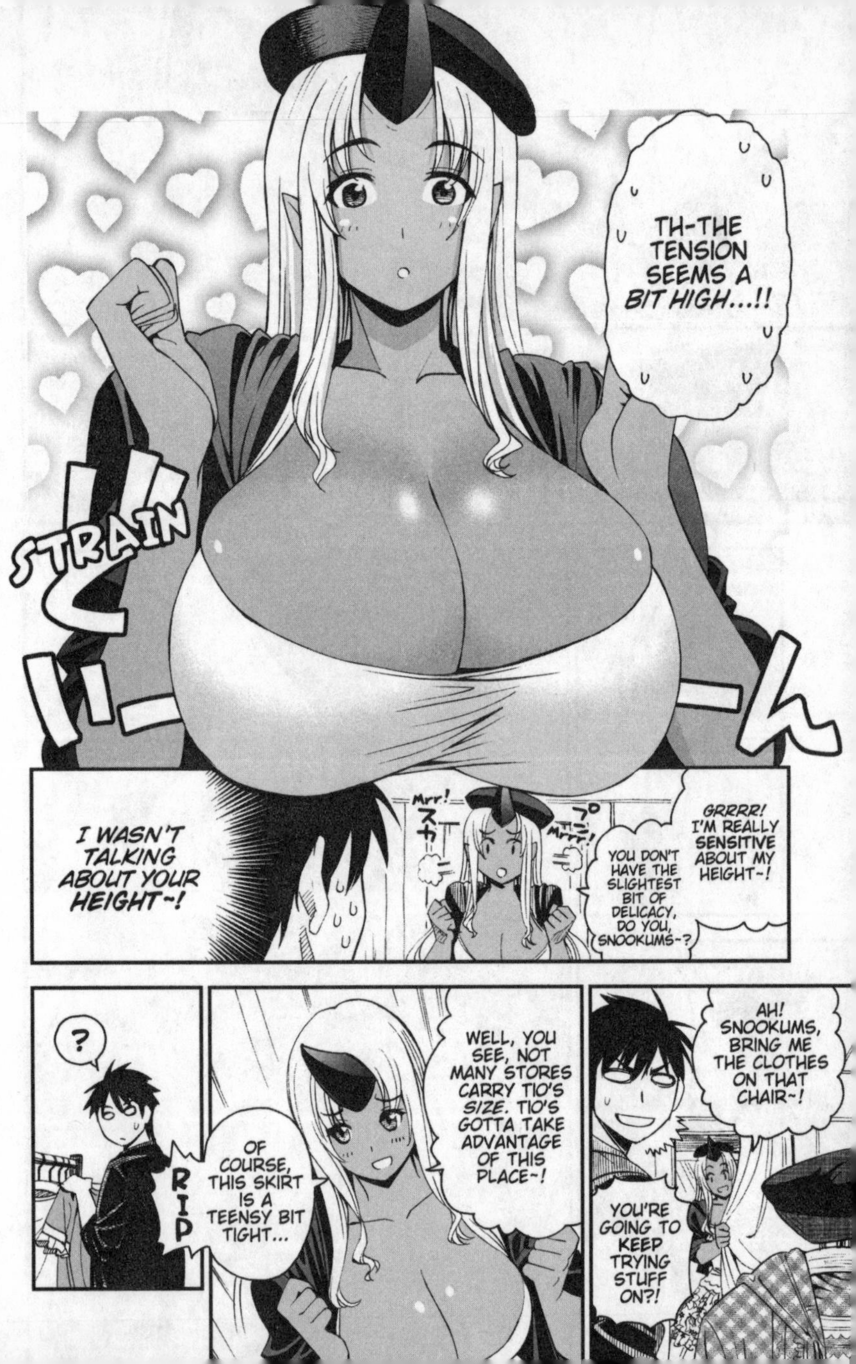
TH-THE TENSION SEEMS A BIT HIGH...!!
STRAIN
GRRRR! I'M REALLY SENSITIVE ABOUT MY HEIGHT~!
YOU DON'T HAVE THE SLIGHTEST BIT OF DELICACY, DO YOU, SNOOKUMS~?
Mrrr!
Mrr!
I WASN'T TALKING ABOUT YOUR HEIGHT~!
AH! SNOOKUMS, BRING ME THE CLOTHES ON THAT CHAIR~!
YOU'RE GOING TO KEEP TRYING STUFF ON?!
WELL, YOU SEE, NOT MANY STORES CARRY TIO'S SIZE. TIO'S GOTTA TAKE ADVANTAGE OF THIS PLACE~!
OF COURSE, THIS SKIRT IS A TEENSY BIT TIGHT...
RIP
?

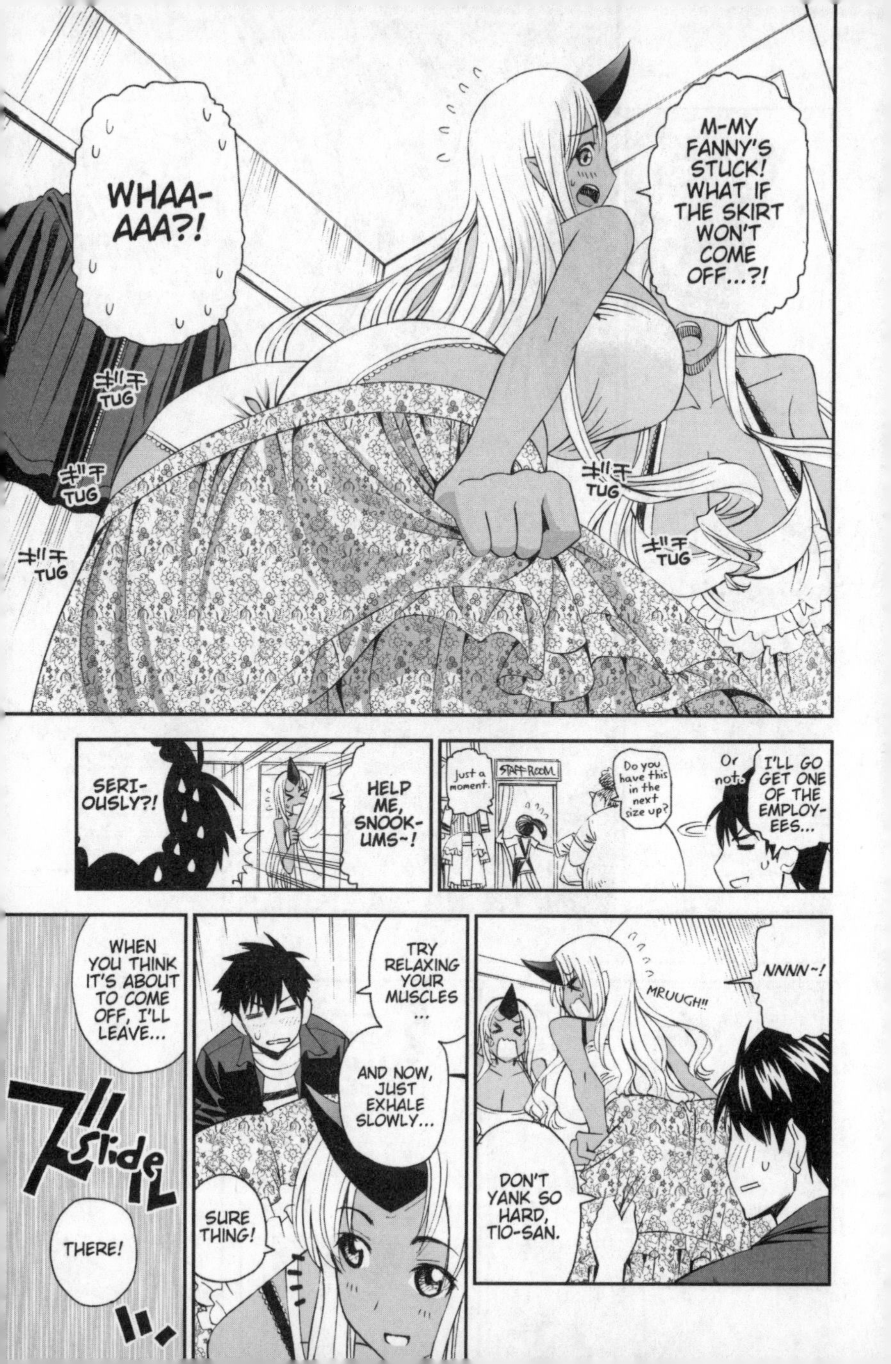
M-MY FANNY'S STUCK! WHAT IF THE SKIRT WON'T COME OFF...?!
WHAAA-AAA?!
TUG
TUG
TUG
TUG
I'LL GO GET ONE OF THE EMPLOYEES...
Or not.
Do you have this in the next size up?
STAFF ROOM
Just a moment.
HELP ME, SNOOKUMS~!
SERIOUSLY?!
NNNN~!
MRUUGH!!
DON'T YANK SO HARD, TIO-SAN.
TRY RELAXING YOUR MUSCLES...
AND NOW, JUST EXHALE SLOWLY...
SURE THING!
WHEN YOU THINK IT'S ABOUT TO COME OFF, I'LL LEAVE...
slide
THERE!

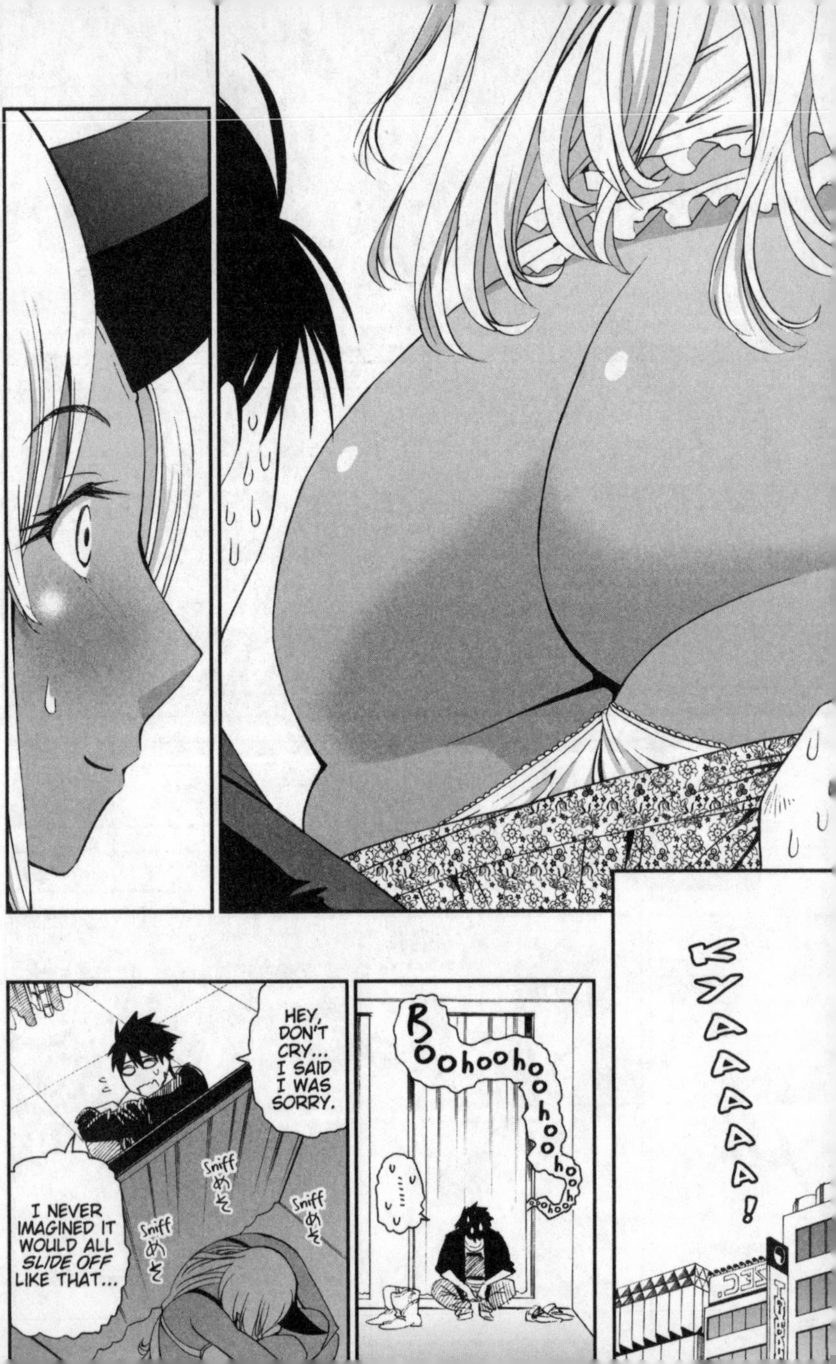
KYAAAAAA!
Boohoohoohoohoohoohooh
......
HEY, DON'T CRY... I SAID I WAS SORRY.
Sniff めそ
Sniff めそ
Sniff めそ
I NEVER IMAGINED IT WOULD ALL *SLIDE OFF* LIKE THAT...

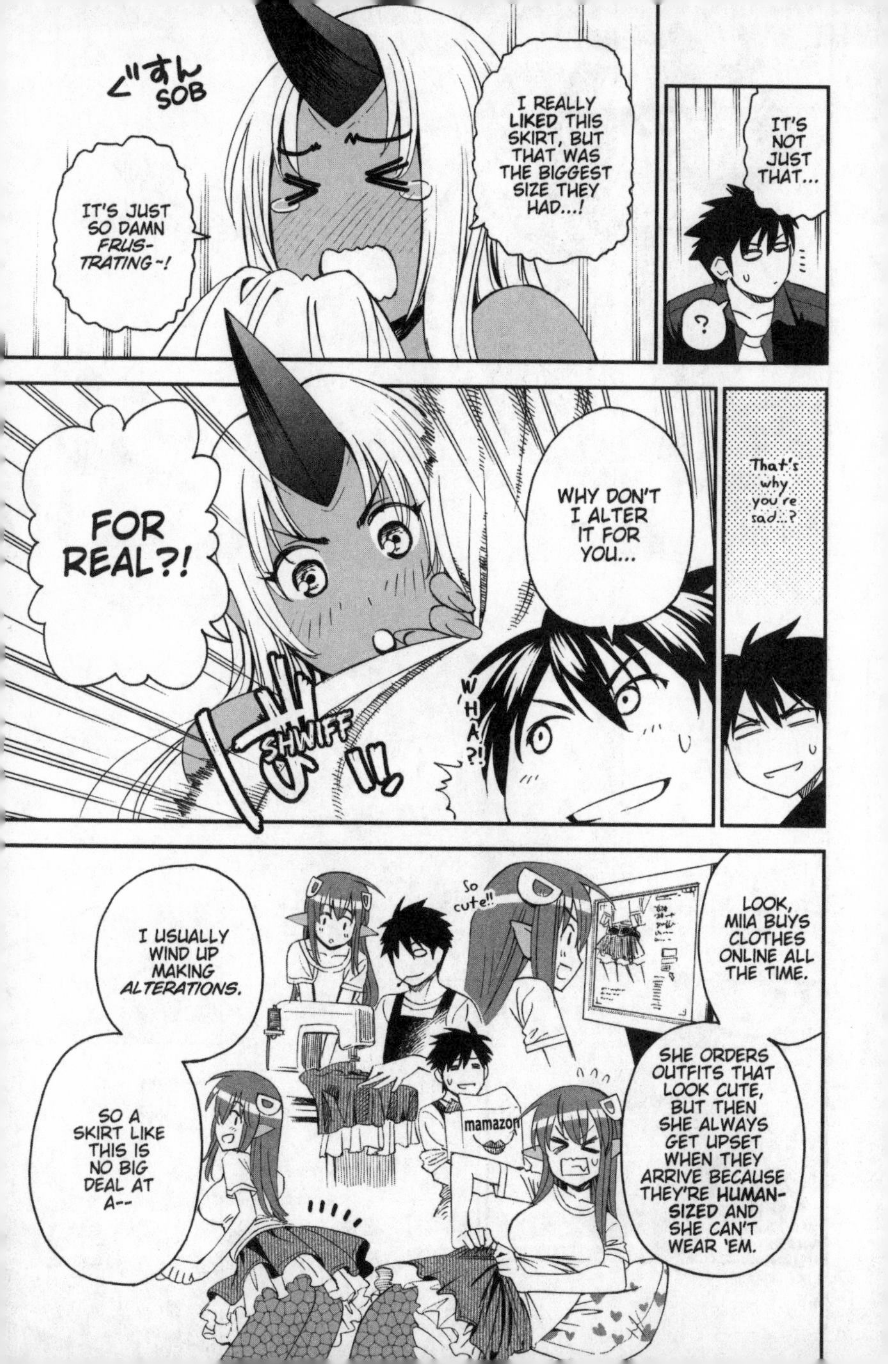
IT'S NOT JUST THAT...
?
I REALLY LIKED THIS SKIRT, BUT THAT WAS THE BIGGEST SIZE THEY HAD...!
ぐすん SOB
IT'S JUST SO DAMN FRUS-TRATING~!
That's why you're sad...?
WHY DON'T I ALTER IT FOR YOU...
FOR REAL?!
SHWIFF
WHA?!
LOOK, MIIA BUYS CLOTHES ONLINE ALL THE TIME.
So cute!!
SHE ORDERS OUTFITS THAT LOOK CUTE, BUT THEN SHE ALWAYS GET UPSET WHEN THEY ARRIVE BECAUSE THEY'RE HUMAN-SIZED AND SHE CAN'T WEAR 'EM.
mamazon
I USUALLY WIND UP MAKING ALTERATIONS.
SO A SKIRT LIKE THIS IS NO BIG DEAL AT A--

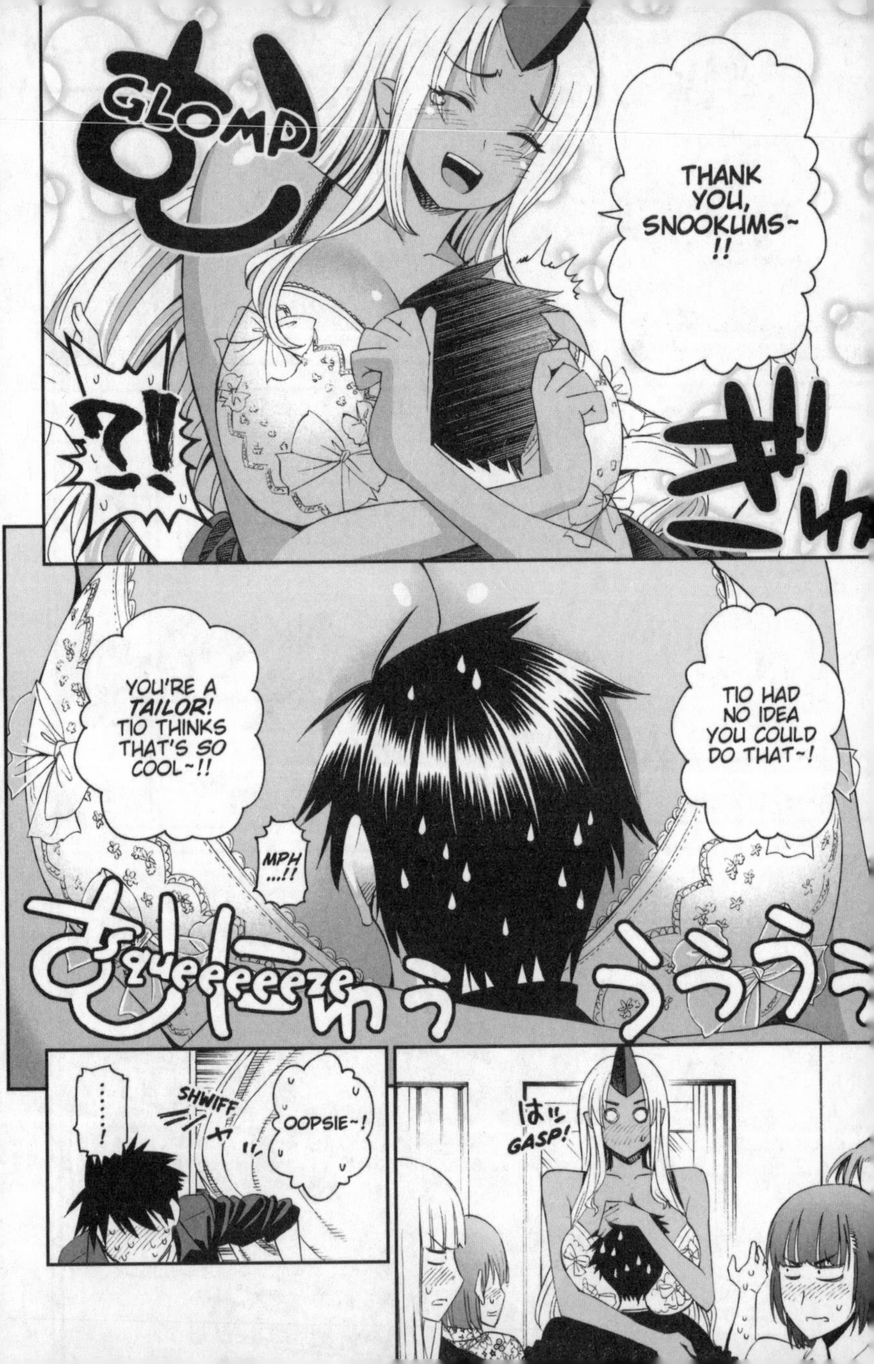

THANK YOU, SNOOKUMS~!!
GLOMP
TIO HAD NO IDEA YOU COULD DO THAT~!
YOU'RE A TAILOR! TIO THINKS THAT'S SO COOL~!!
MPH ...!!
squeeeeeeze
GASP!
OOPSIE~!
SHWIFF
......!

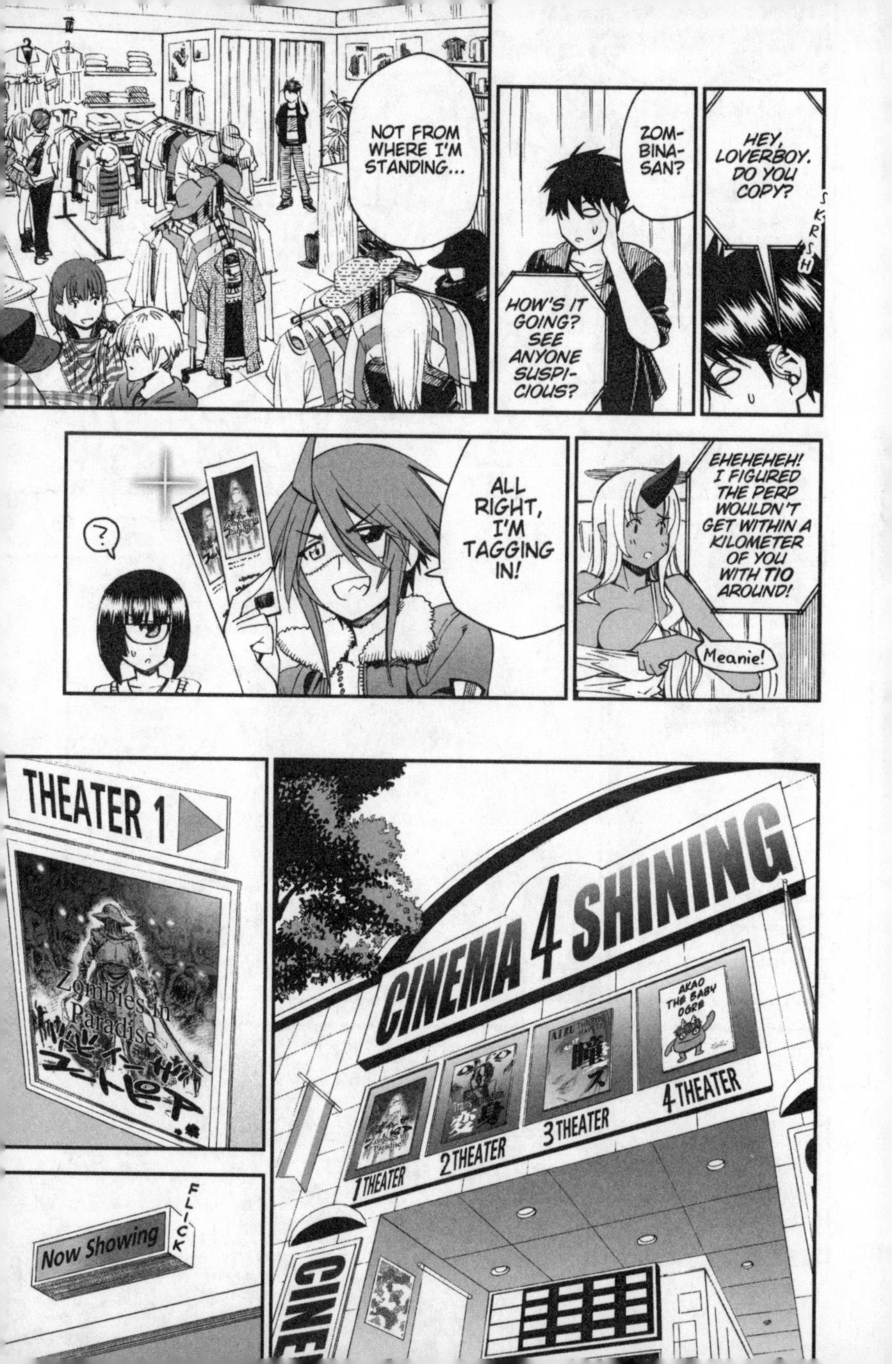
HEY, LOVERBOY. DO YOU COPY?
SKRSH
ZOM-BINA-SAN?
HOW'S IT GOING? SEE ANYONE SUSPICIOUS?
NOT FROM WHERE I'M STANDING...
EHEHEHEH! I FIGURED THE PERP WOULDN'T GET WITHIN A KILOMETER OF YOU WITH TIO AROUND!
Meanie!
ALL RIGHT, I'M TAGGING IN!
?
CINEMA 4 SHINING
AKAO THE BABY OGRE
4 THEATER
3 THEATER
2 THEATER
1 THEATER
Zombies in Paradise
THEATER 1
Zombies in Paradise
Now Showing
FLICK

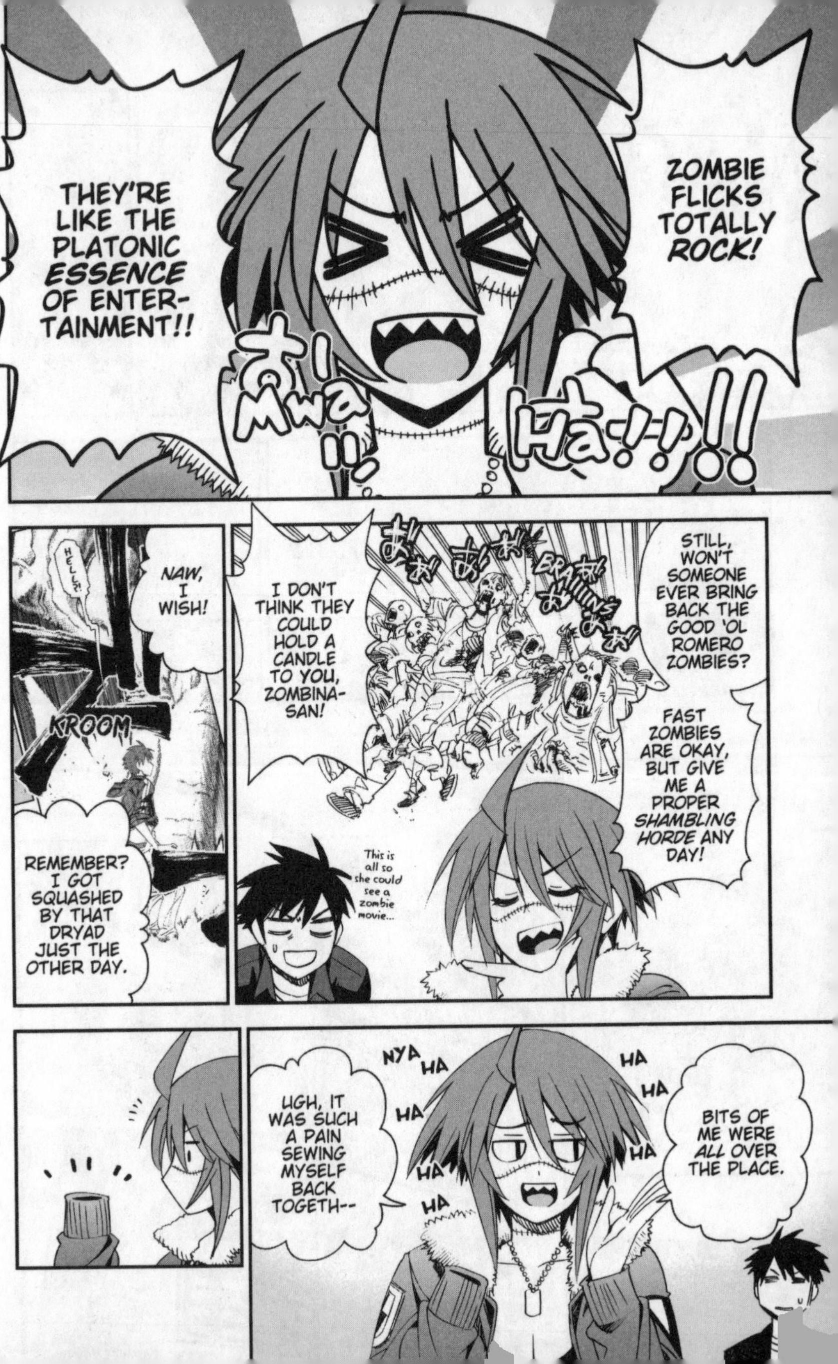
ZOMBIE FLICKS TOTALLY *ROCK!*
THEY'RE LIKE THE PLATONIC *ESSENCE* OF ENTER-TAINMENT!!
MWA
HA!!
STILL, WON'T SOMEONE EVER BRING BACK THE GOOD 'OL ROMERO ZOMBIES?
FAST ZOMBIES ARE OKAY, BUT GIVE ME A PROPER *SHAMBLING HORDE* ANY DAY!
BRAAIIINS
I DON'T THINK THEY COULD HOLD A CANDLE TO YOU, ZOMBINA-SAN!
This is all so she could see a zombie movie...
NAW, I WISH!
HELL?!
KROOM
REMEMBER? I GOT SQUASHED BY THAT DRYAD JUST THE OTHER DAY.
BITS OF ME WERE *ALL* OVER THE PLACE.
NYA HA HA HA HA HA HA
UGH, IT WAS SUCH A PAIN SEWING MYSELF BACK TOGETH--

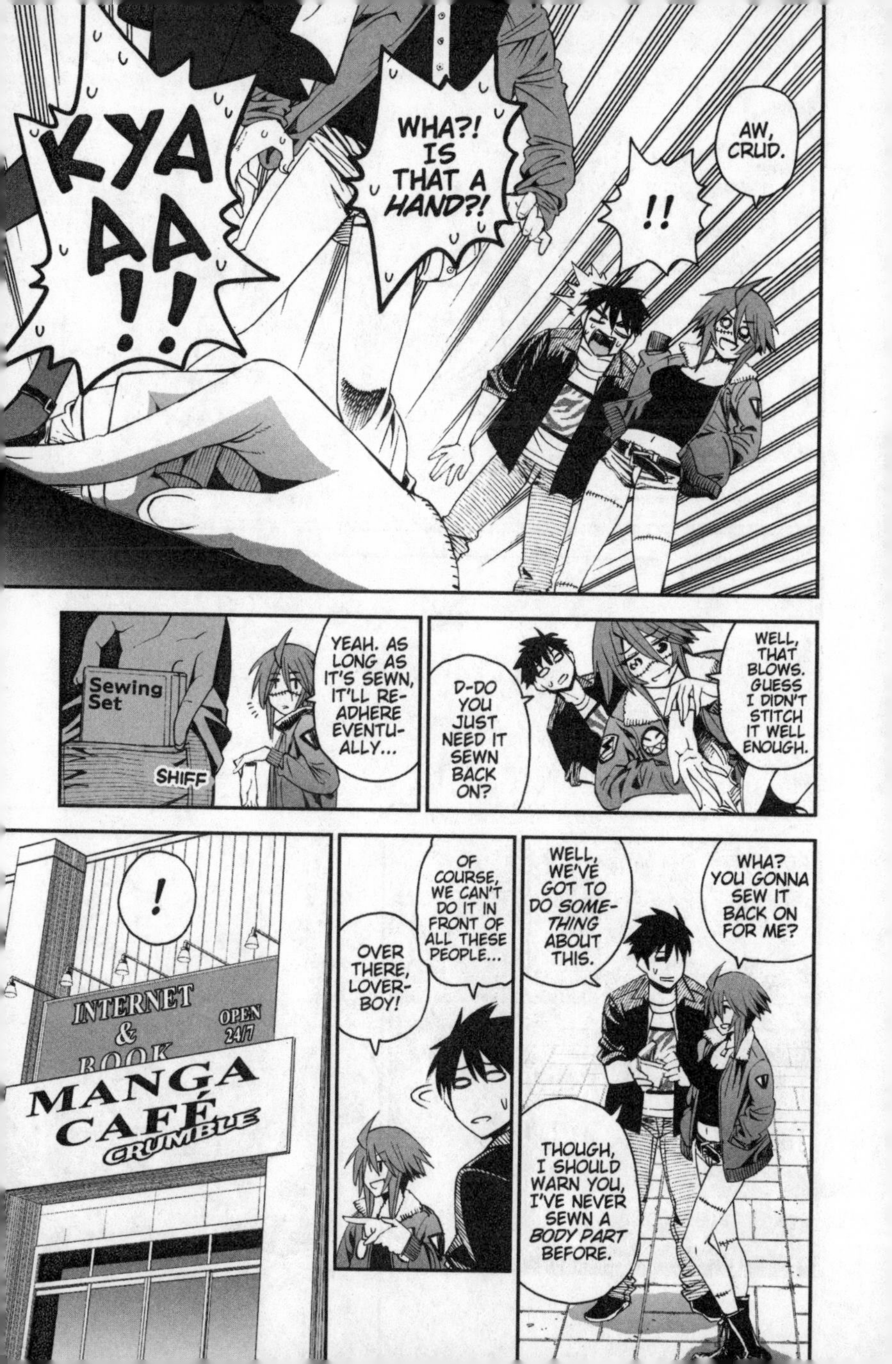
AW, CRUD.
!!
WHA?! IS THAT A *HAND?!*
KYAAA!!
WELL, THAT BLOWS. GUESS I DIDN'T STITCH IT WELL ENOUGH.
D-DO YOU JUST NEED IT SEWN BACK ON?
YEAH. AS LONG AS IT'S SEWN, IT'LL READHERE EVENTUALLY...
Sewing Set
SHIFF
WHA? YOU GONNA SEW IT BACK ON FOR ME?
WELL, WE'VE GOT TO DO *SOMETHING* ABOUT THIS.
THOUGH, I SHOULD WARN YOU, I'VE NEVER SEWN A *BODY PART* BEFORE.
OF COURSE, WE CAN'T DO IT IN FRONT OF ALL THESE PEOPLE...
OVER THERE, LOVER-BOY!
!
INTERNET & BOOK
OPEN 24/7
MANGA CAFÉ
CRUMBLE

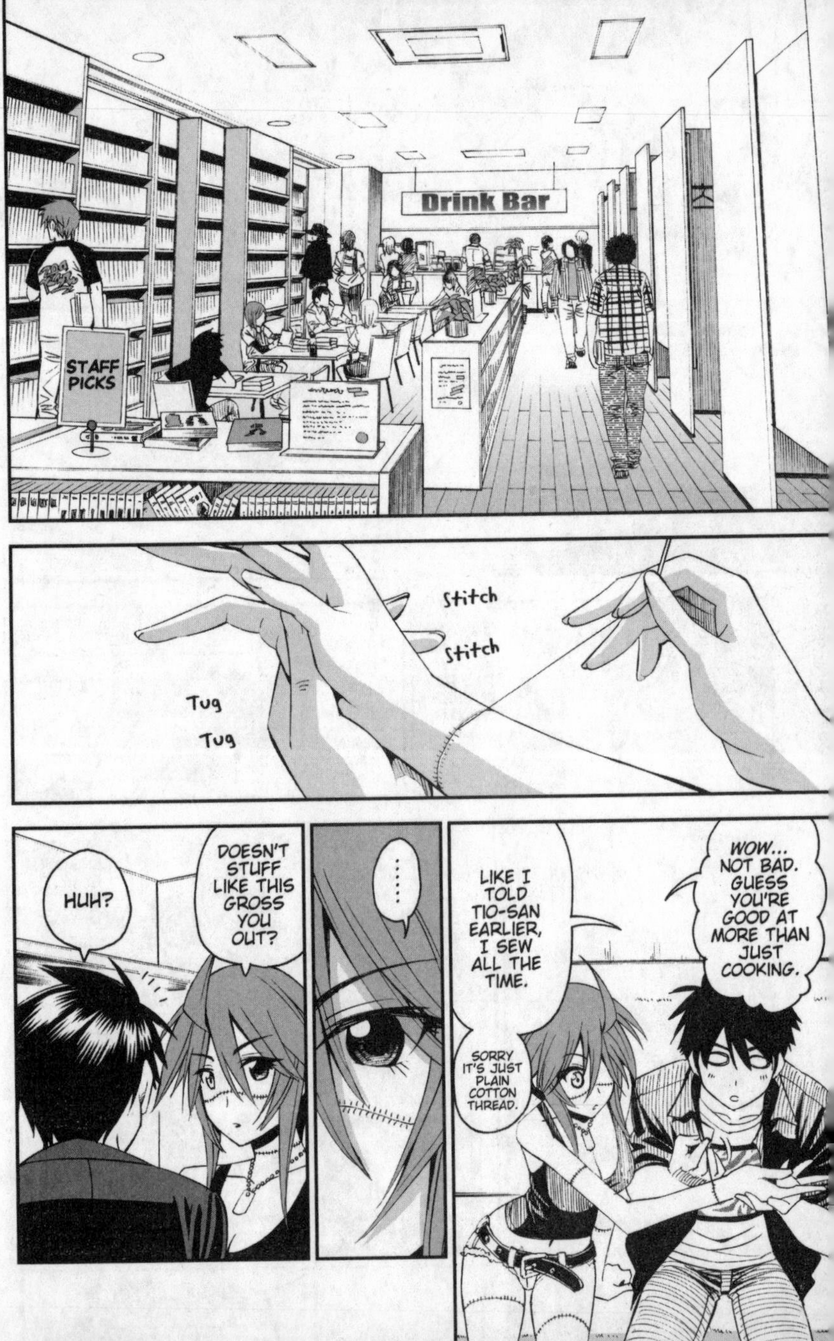
Drink Bar
STAFF PICKS
Stitch
Stitch
Tug
Tug
WOW... NOT BAD. GUESS YOU'RE GOOD AT MORE THAN JUST COOKING.
LIKE I TOLD TIO-SAN EARLIER, I SEW ALL THE TIME.
SORRY IT'S JUST PLAIN COTTON THREAD.
......
DOESN'T STUFF LIKE THIS GROSS YOU OUT?
HUH?

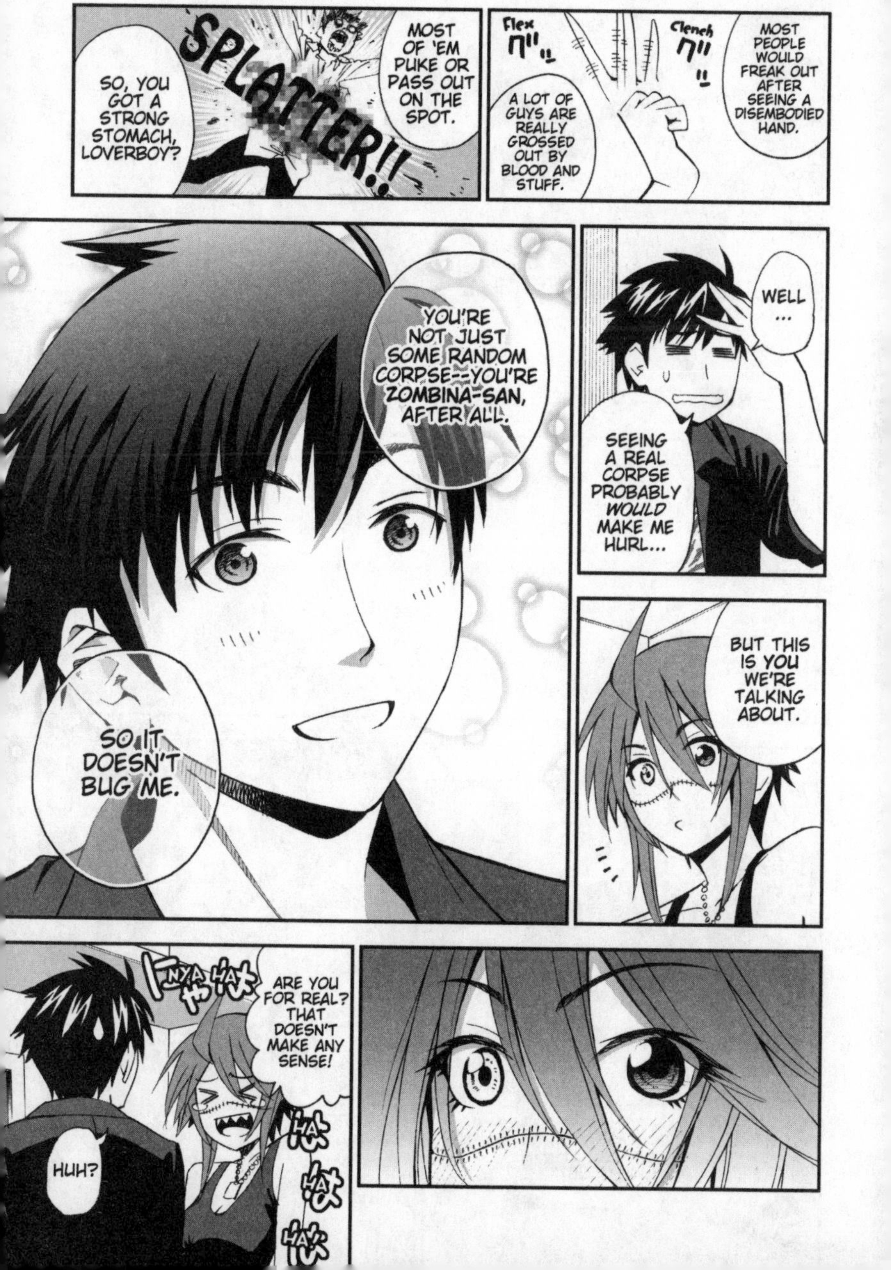
MOST PEOPLE WOULD FREAK OUT AFTER SEEING A DISEMBODIED HAND.
Clench
Flex
A LOT OF GUYS ARE REALLY GROSSED OUT BY BLOOD AND STUFF.
MOST OF 'EM PUKE OR PASS OUT ON THE SPOT.
SPLATTER!!
SO, YOU GOT A STRONG STOMACH, LOVERBOY?
WELL ...
SEEING A REAL CORPSE PROBABLY *WOULD* MAKE ME HURL...
BUT THIS IS YOU WE'RE TALKING ABOUT.
YOU'RE NOT JUST SOME RANDOM CORPSE--YOU'RE ZOMBINA-SAN, AFTER ALL.
SO IT DOESN'T BUG ME.
NYA HA
ARE YOU FOR REAL? THAT DOESN'T MAKE ANY SENSE!
HA
HA
HA
HUH?

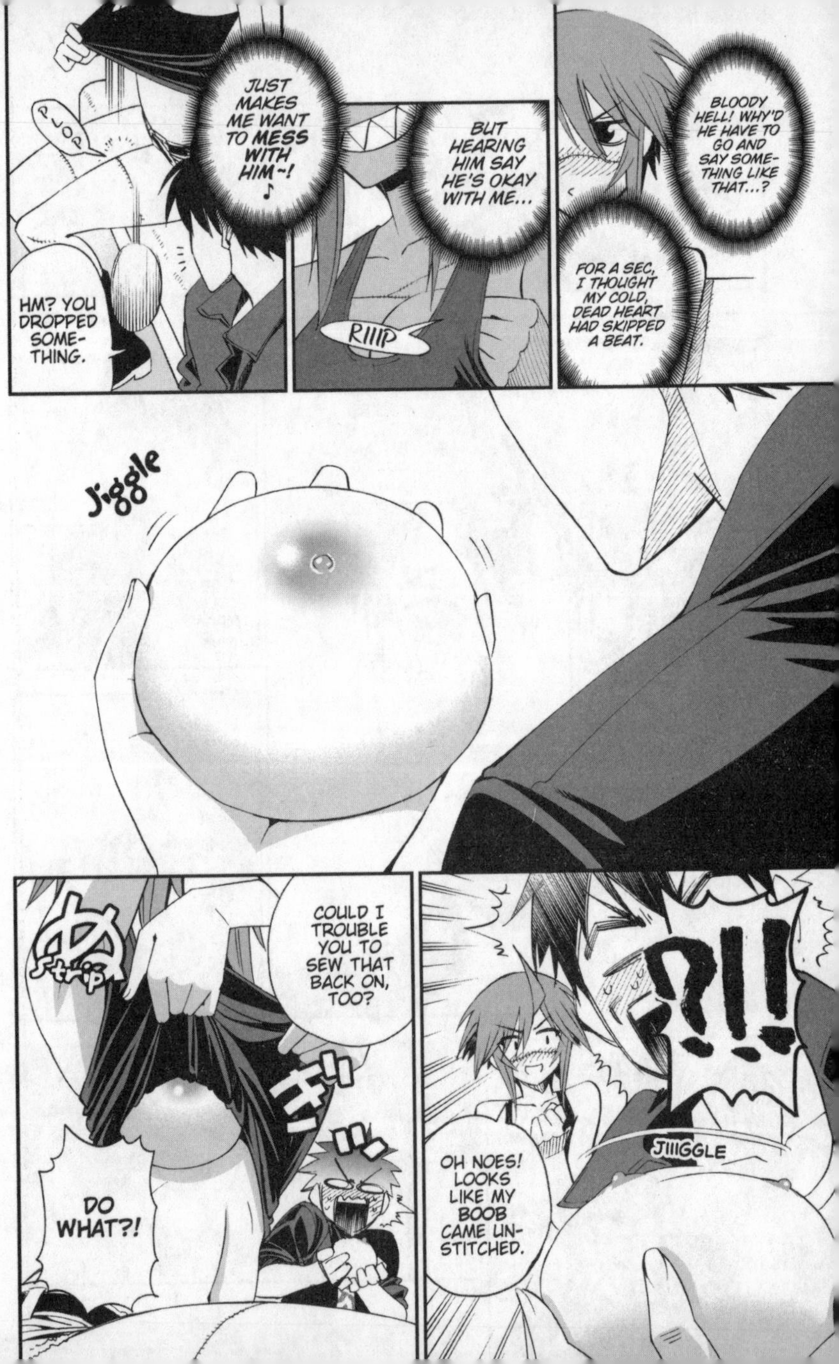
BLOODY HELL! WHY'D HE HAVE TO GO AND SAY SOME-THING LIKE THAT...?
FOR A SEC, I THOUGHT MY COLD, DEAD HEART HAD SKIPPED A BEAT.
BUT HEARING HIM SAY HE'S OKAY WITH ME...
RIIIP
JUST MAKES ME WANT TO MESS WITH HIM~! ♪
PLOP
HM? YOU DROPPED SOME-THING.
Jiggle
?!!
JIIIGGLE
OH NOES! LOOKS LIKE MY BOOB CAME UN-STITCHED.
strip
COULD I TROUBLE YOU TO SEW THAT BACK ON, TOO?
DO WHAT?!

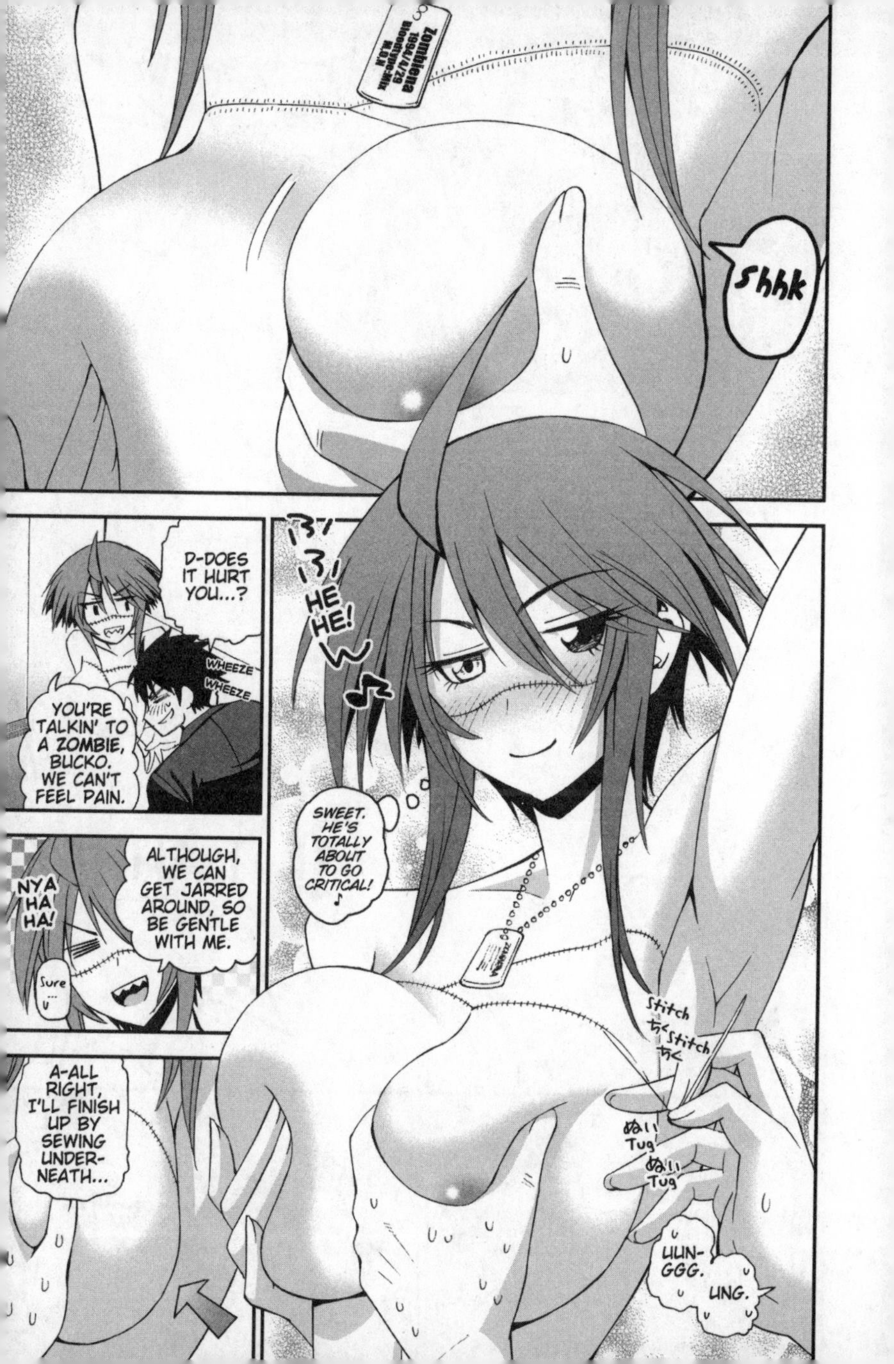
Zombiena
1994/4/29
bloodtype-Mix
M.O.N
Shhk
HE HE!
SWEET. HE'S TOTALLY ABOUT TO GO CRITICAL! ♪
Stitch
Stitch
Tug
Tug
UUN-GGG.
UNG.
D-DOES IT HURT YOU...?
WHEEZE
WHEEZE
YOU'RE TALKIN' TO A ZOMBIE, BUCKO. WE CAN'T FEEL PAIN.
ALTHOUGH, WE CAN GET JARRED AROUND, SO BE GENTLE WITH ME.
NYA HA HA!
Sure...
A-ALL RIGHT, I'LL FINISH UP BY SEWING UNDER-NEATH...

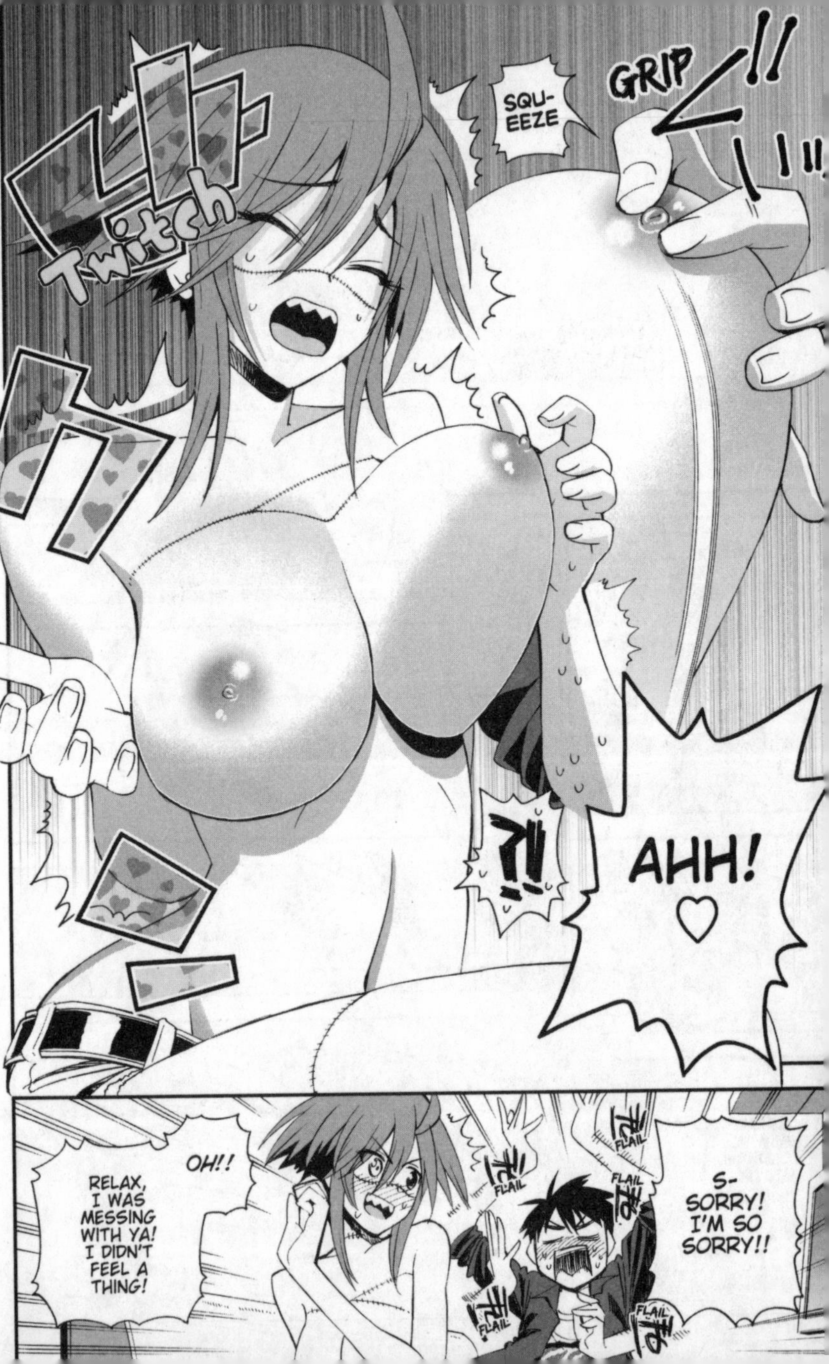
GRIP
SQU-EEZE
Twitch
?!!
AHH! ♥
S-SORRY! I'M SO SORRY!!
FLAIL
FLAIL
FLAIL
FLAIL
FLAIL
OH!!
RELAX, I WAS MESSING WITH YA! I DIDN'T FEEL A THING!

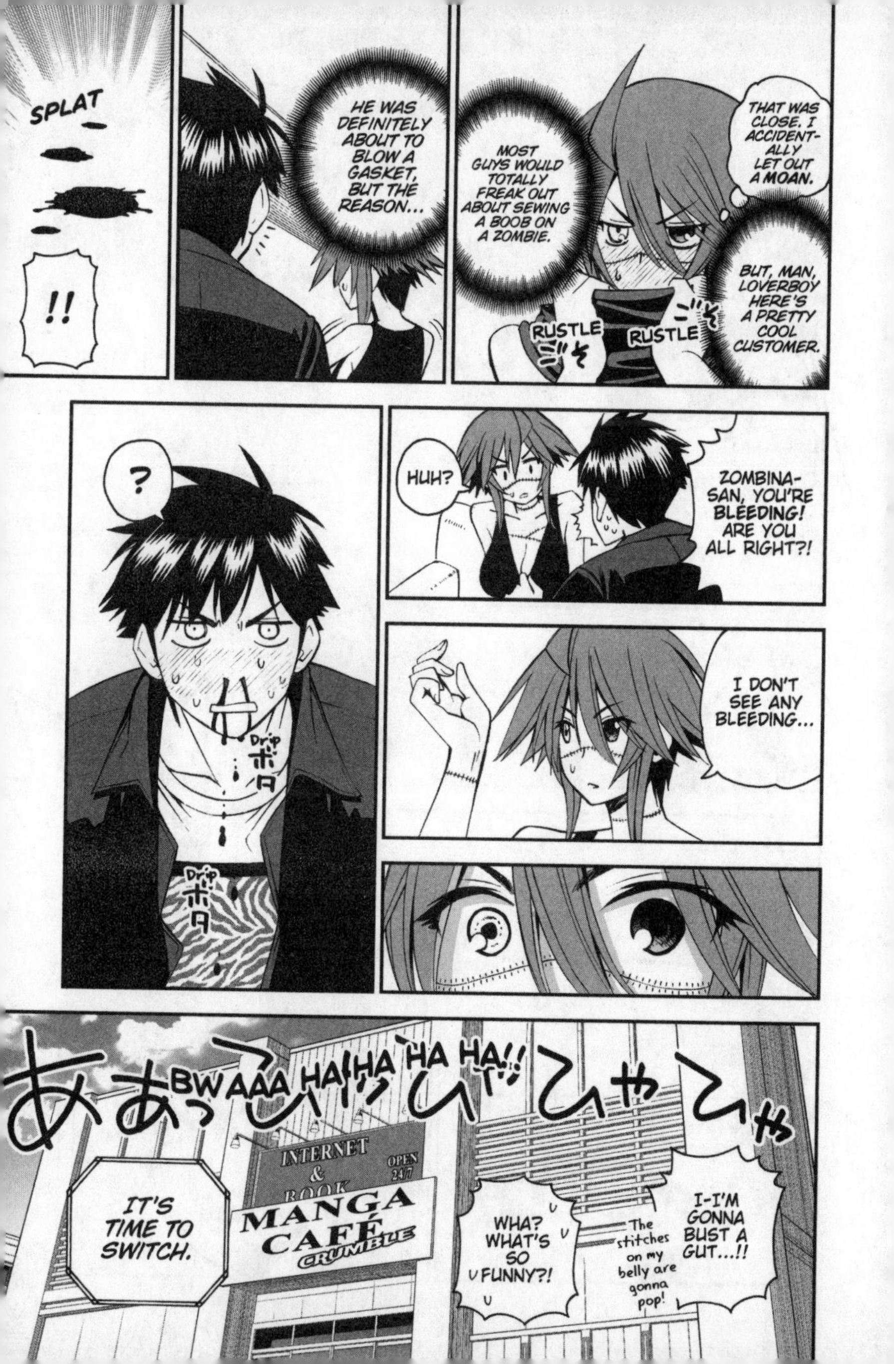
THAT WAS CLOSE. I ACCIDENTALLY LET OUT A MOAN.
MOST GUYS WOULD TOTALLY FREAK OUT ABOUT SEWING A BOOB ON A ZOMBIE.
BUT, MAN, LOVERBOY HERE'S A PRETTY COOL CUSTOMER.
RUSTLE
RUSTLE
HE WAS DEFINITELY ABOUT TO BLOW A GASKET, BUT THE REASON...
SPLAT
!!
ZOMBINA-SAN, YOU'RE BLEEDING! ARE YOU ALL RIGHT?!
HUH?
I DON'T SEE ANY BLEEDING...
?
Drip
Drip
BWAAA HA HA HA HA!!
I-I'M GONNA BUST A GUT...!!
The stitches on my belly are gonna pop!
WHA? WHAT'S SO FUNNY?!
INTERNET & BOOK
OPEN 24/7
MANGA CAFÉ CRUMBLE
IT'S TIME TO SWITCH.

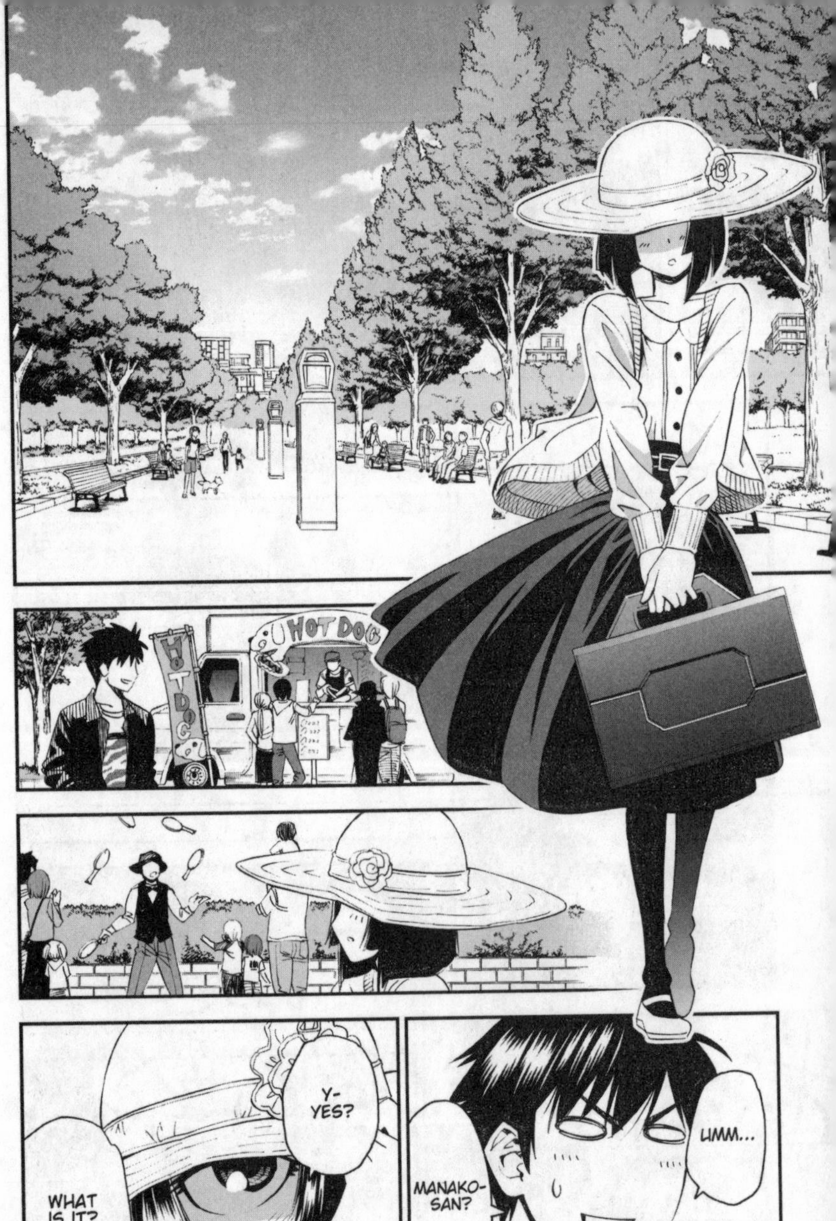
HOT DOG
HOT DOG
UMM...
MANAKO-SAN?
Y-YES?
WHAT IS IT?

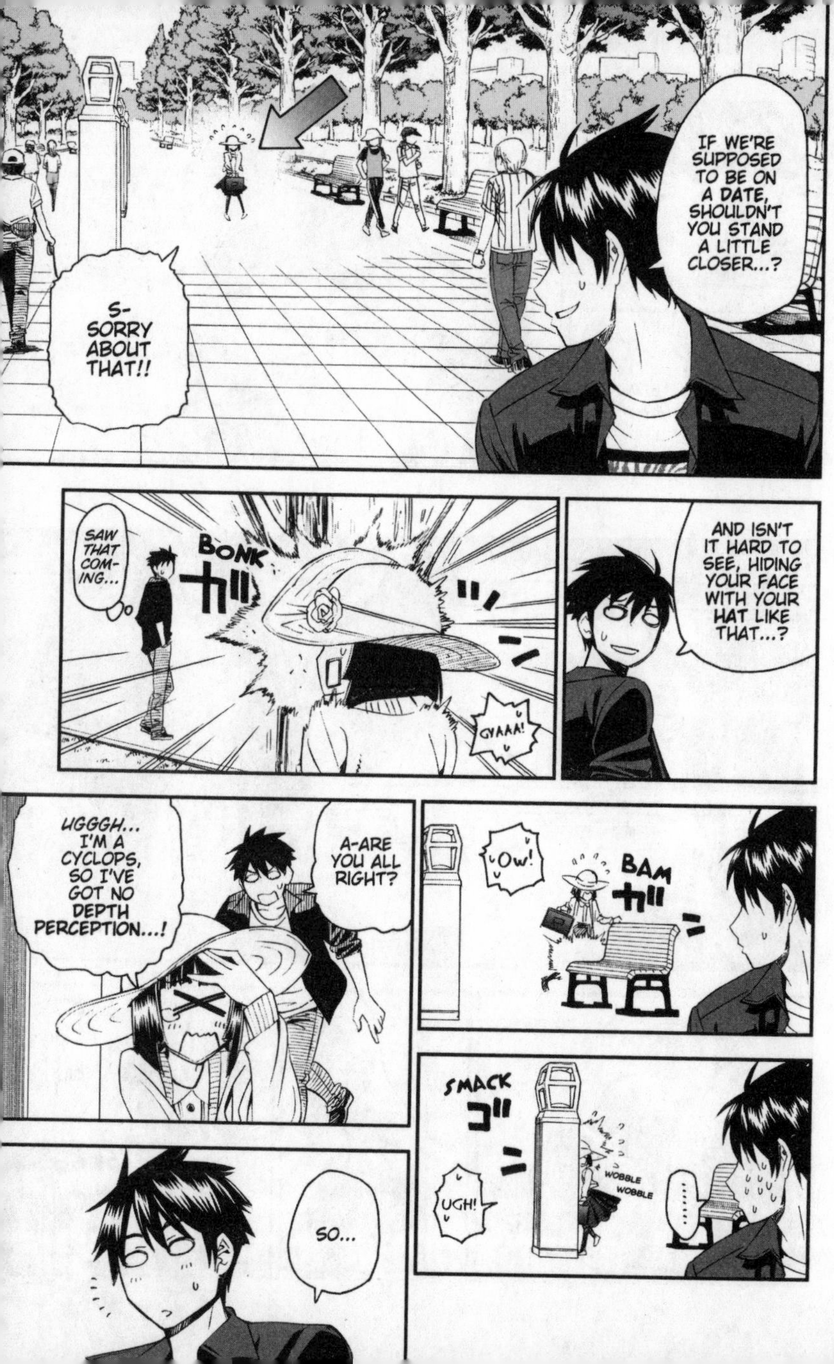
IF WE'RE SUPPOSED TO BE ON A DATE, SHOULDN'T YOU STAND A LITTLE CLOSER...?
S-SORRY ABOUT THAT!!
AND ISN'T IT HARD TO SEE, HIDING YOUR FACE WITH YOUR HAT LIKE THAT...?
BONK
ガッ
GYAAA!
SAW THAT COMING...
BAM
ガッ
OW!
SMACK
ゴッ
UGH!
WOBBLE WOBBLE
......
A-ARE YOU ALL RIGHT?
UGGGH... I'M A CYCLOPS, SO I'VE GOT NO DEPTH PERCEPTION...!
SO...

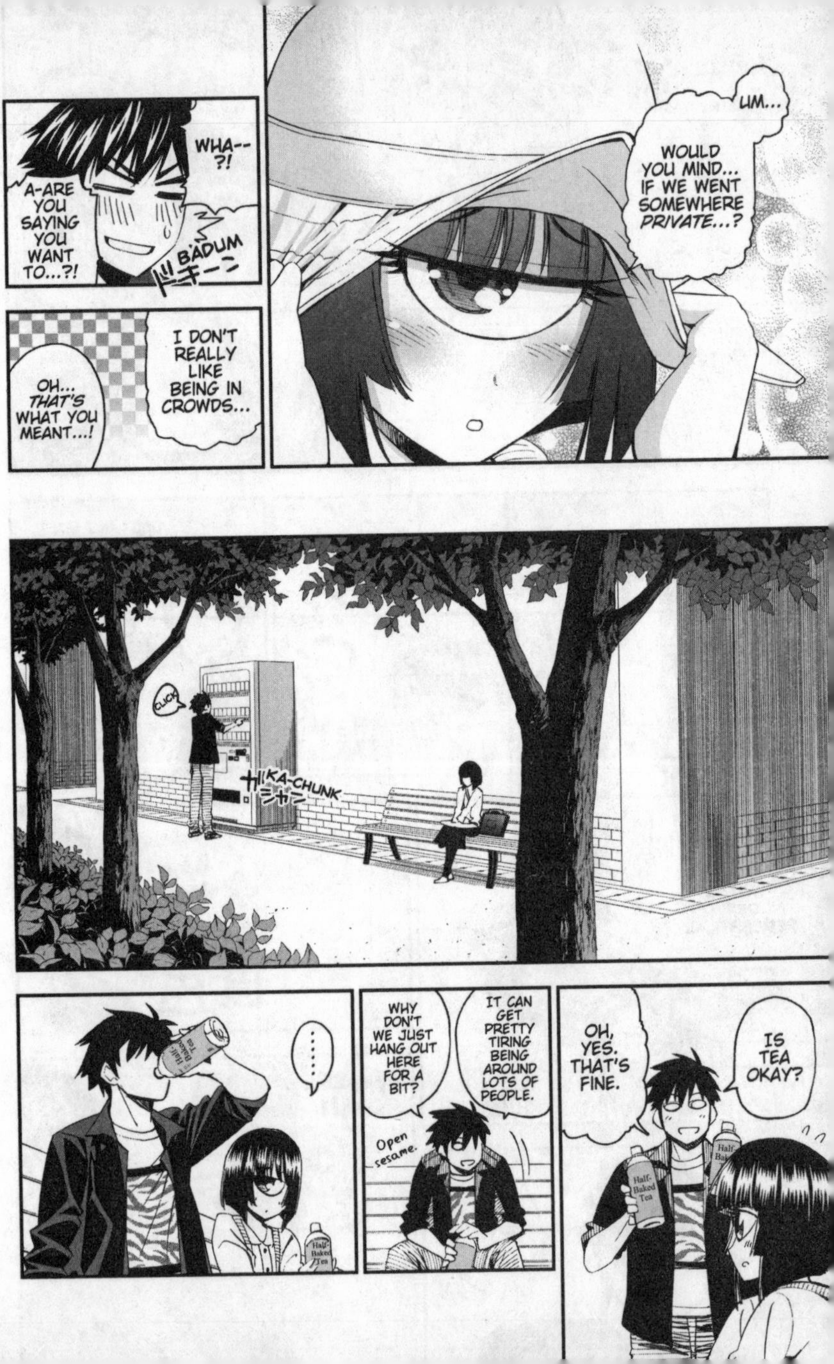
UM...
WOULD YOU MIND... IF WE WENT SOMEWHERE PRIVATE...?
WHA--?!
A-ARE YOU SAYING YOU WANT TO...?!
BADUM ドキーン
I DON'T REALLY LIKE BEING IN CROWDS...
OH... THAT'S WHAT YOU MEANT...!
CLICK
KA-CHUNK ガシャン
IS TEA OKAY?
OH, YES. THAT'S FINE.
Half-Baked Tea
IT CAN GET PRETTY TIRING BEING AROUND LOTS OF PEOPLE.
WHY DON'T WE JUST HANG OUT HERE FOR A BIT?
Open sesame.
......
Half-Baked Tea

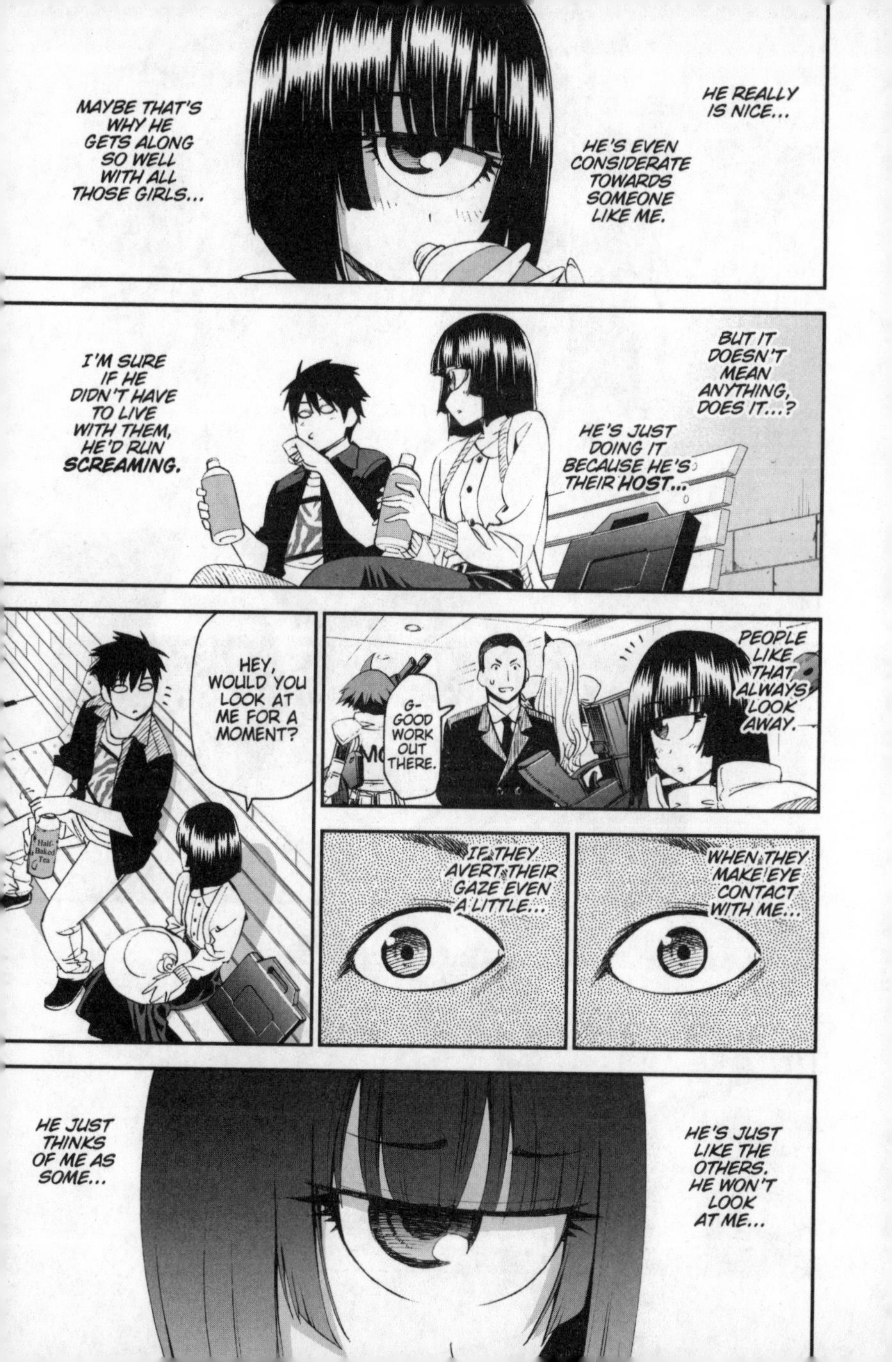
HE REALLY IS NICE...
HE'S EVEN CONSIDERATE TOWARDS SOMEONE LIKE ME.
MAYBE THAT'S WHY HE GETS ALONG SO WELL WITH ALL THOSE GIRLS...
BUT IT DOESN'T MEAN ANYTHING, DOES IT...?
HE'S JUST DOING IT BECAUSE HE'S THEIR HOST...
I'M SURE IF HE DIDN'T HAVE TO LIVE WITH THEM, HE'D RUN SCREAMING.
PEOPLE LIKE THAT ALWAYS LOOK AWAY.
G-GOOD WORK OUT THERE.
WHEN THEY MAKE EYE CONTACT WITH ME...
IF THEY AVERT THEIR GAZE EVEN A LITTLE...
HEY, WOULD YOU LOOK AT ME FOR A MOMENT?
Half-Baked Tea
HE'S JUST LIKE THE OTHERS. HE WON'T LOOK AT ME...
HE JUST THINKS OF ME AS SOME...

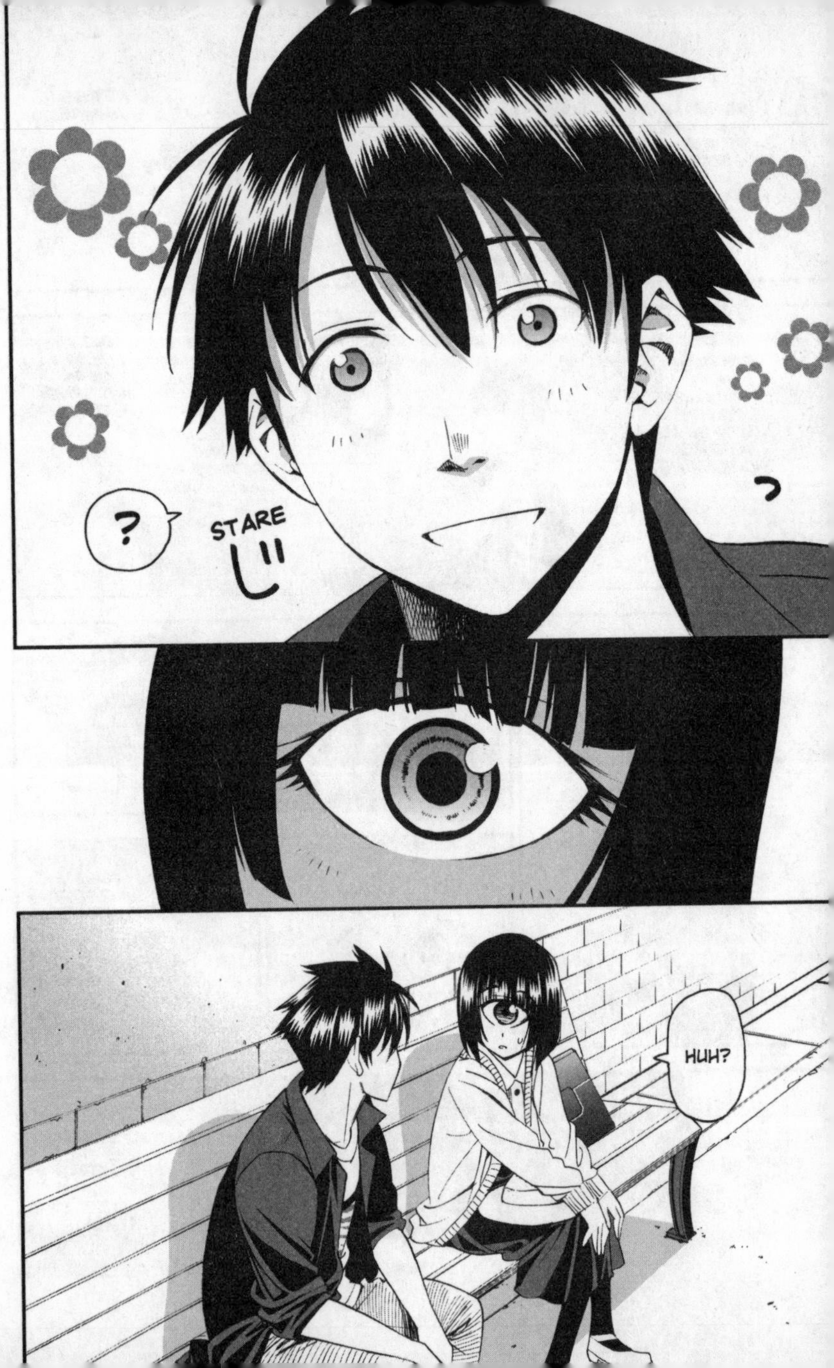
STARE
じい
?
HUH?

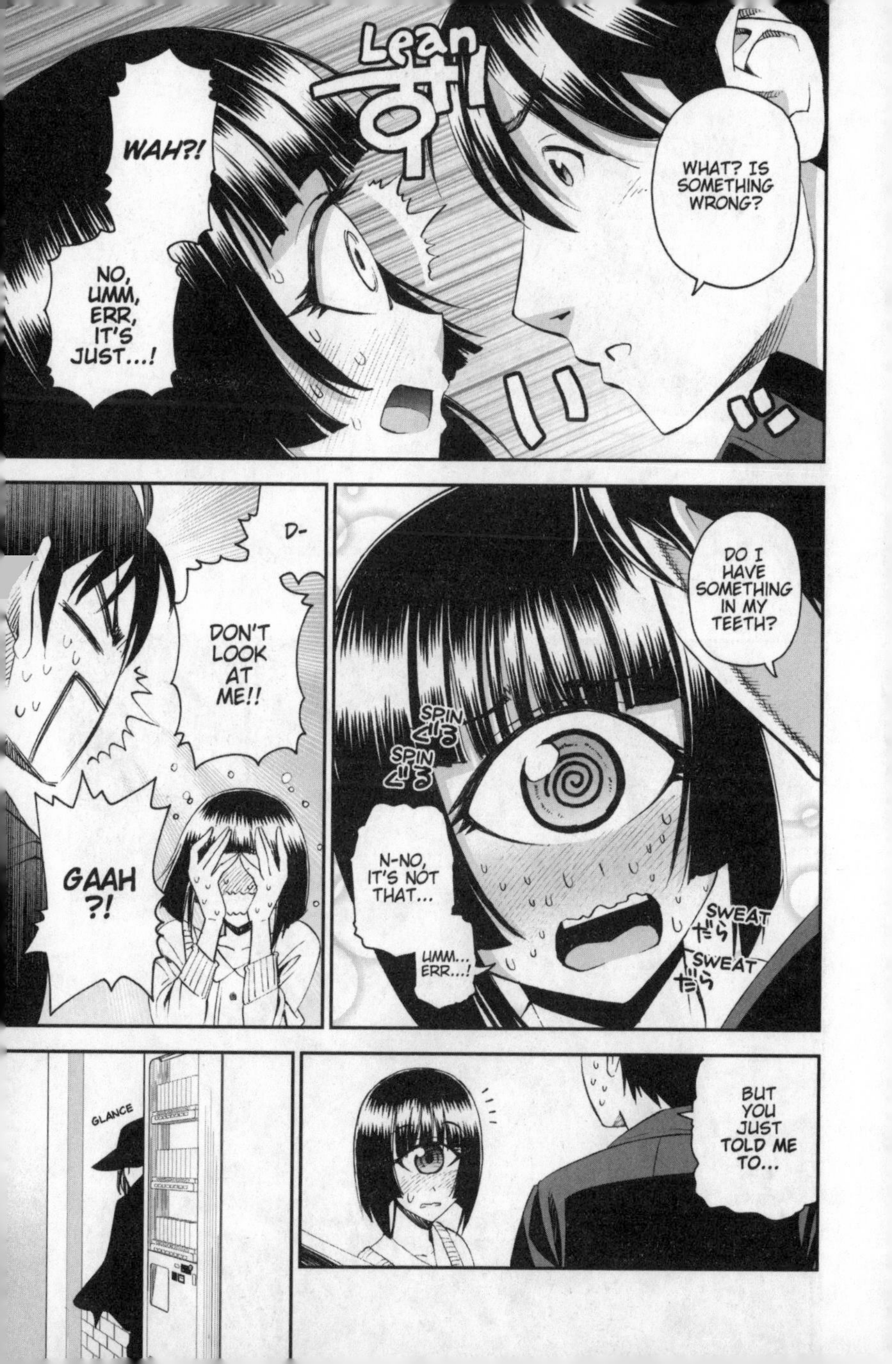

Lean
すっ
WHAT? IS SOMETHING WRONG?
WAH?!
NO, UMM, ERR, IT'S JUST...!
DO I HAVE SOMETHING IN MY TEETH?
SPIN ぐる
SPIN ぐる
N-NO, IT'S NOT THAT...
SWEAT だら
SWEAT だら
UMM... ERR...!
D- DON'T LOOK AT ME!!
GAAH ?!
BUT YOU JUST TOLD ME TO...
GLANCE

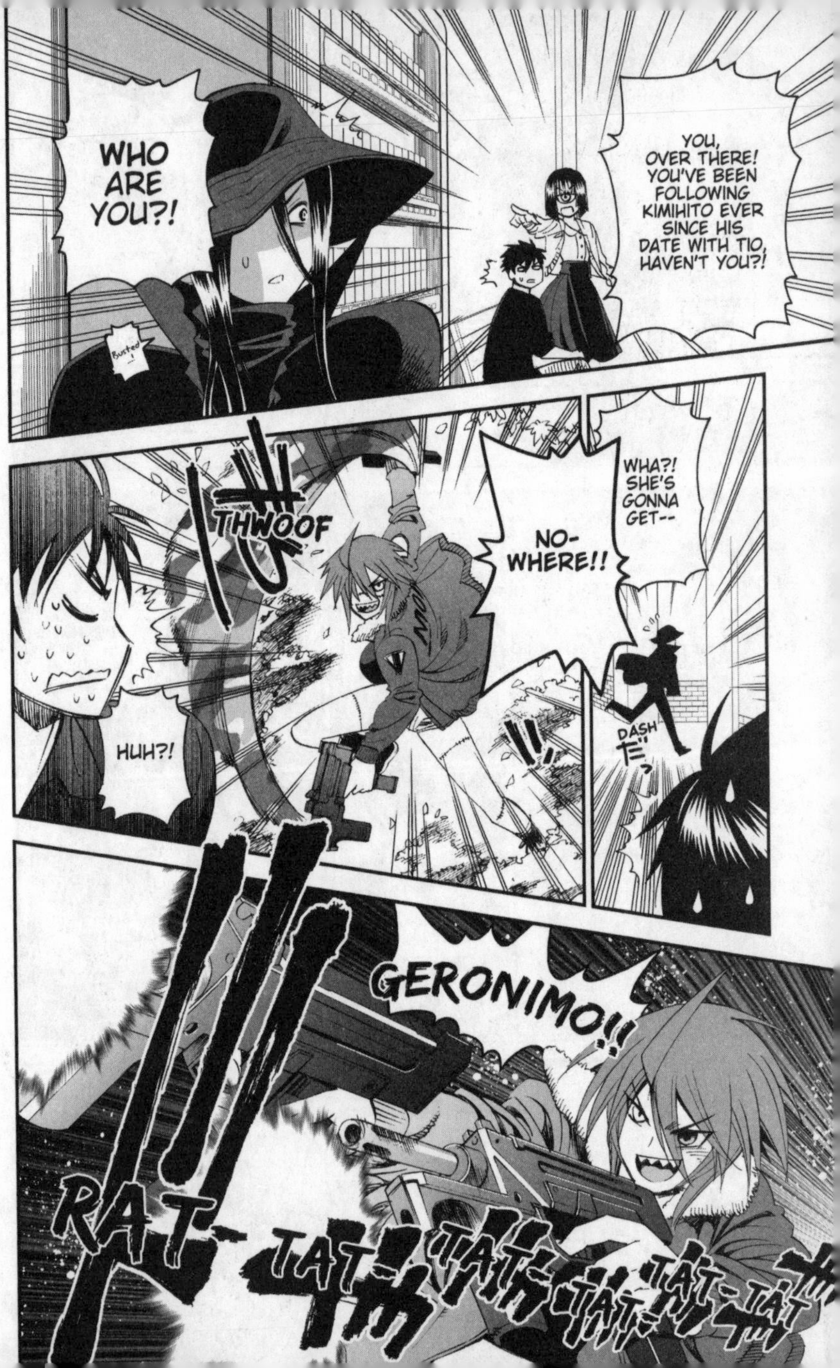
YOU, OVER THERE! YOU'VE BEEN FOLLOWING KIMIHITO EVER SINCE HIS DATE WITH TIO, HAVEN'T YOU?!
WHO ARE YOU?!
Busted...!
WHA?! SHE'S GONNA GET--
NO-WHERE!!
DASH
THWOOF
HUH?!
GERONIMO!!
RAT-TAT-TAT-TAT-TAT-TAT

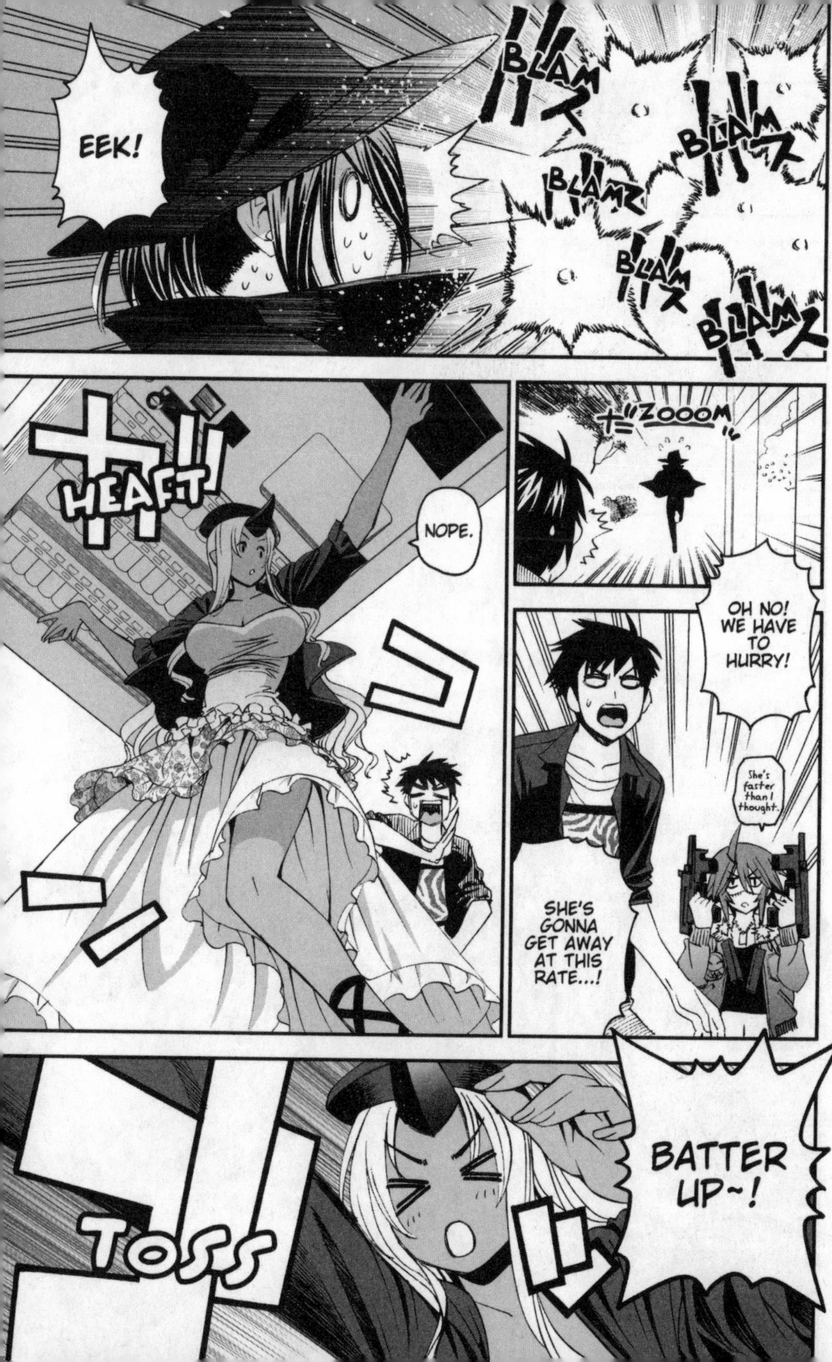
BLAM
BLAM
BLAM
BLAM
BLAM
EEK!
ZOOOM
OH NO! WE HAVE TO HURRY!
She's faster than I thought.
SHE'S GONNA GET AWAY AT THIS RATE...!
NOPE.
HEAFT
BATTER UP~!
TOSS

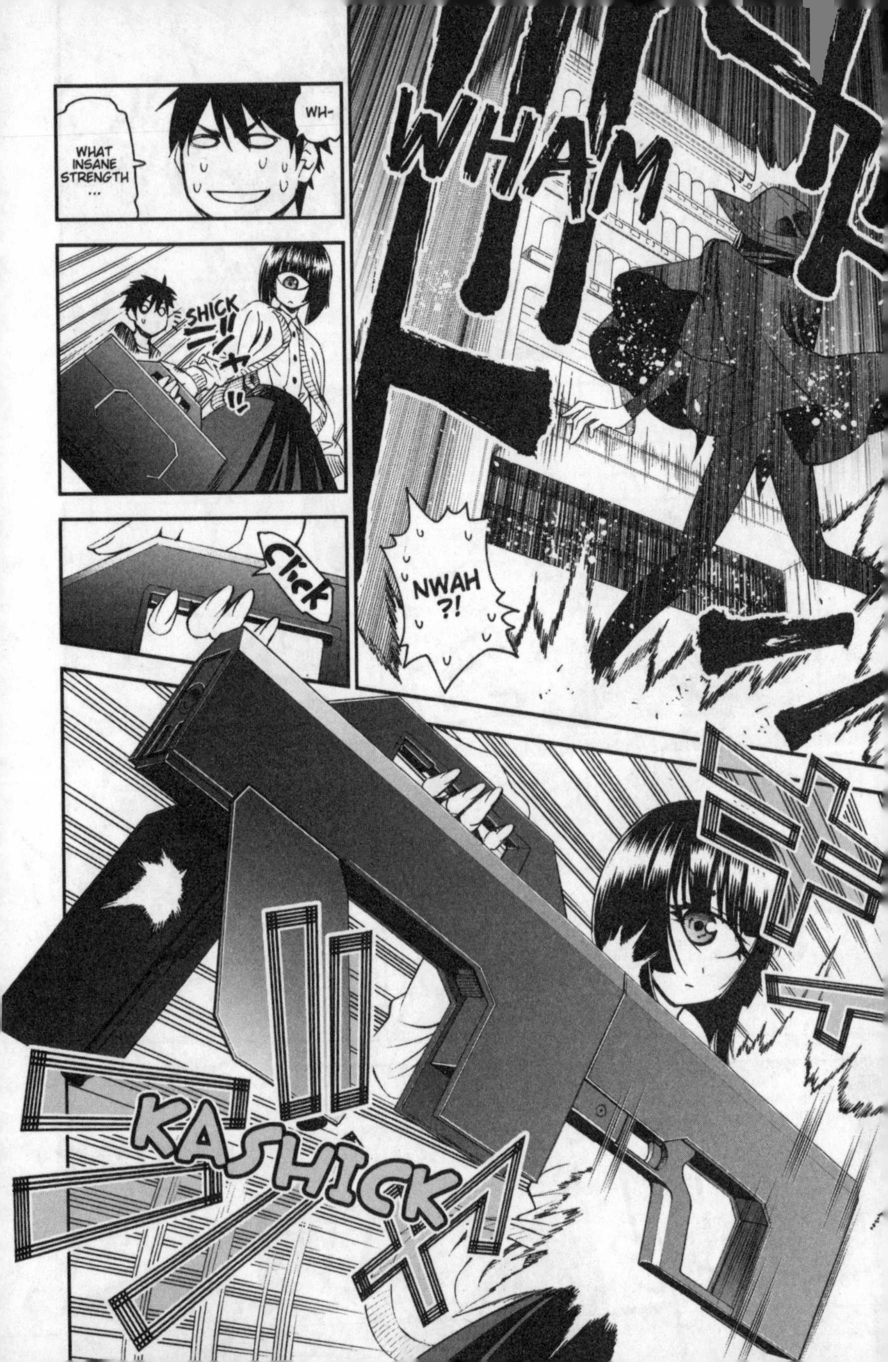
WHAM
NWAH ?!
WH-
WHAT INSANE STRENGTH ...
SHICK
Click
KASHICK

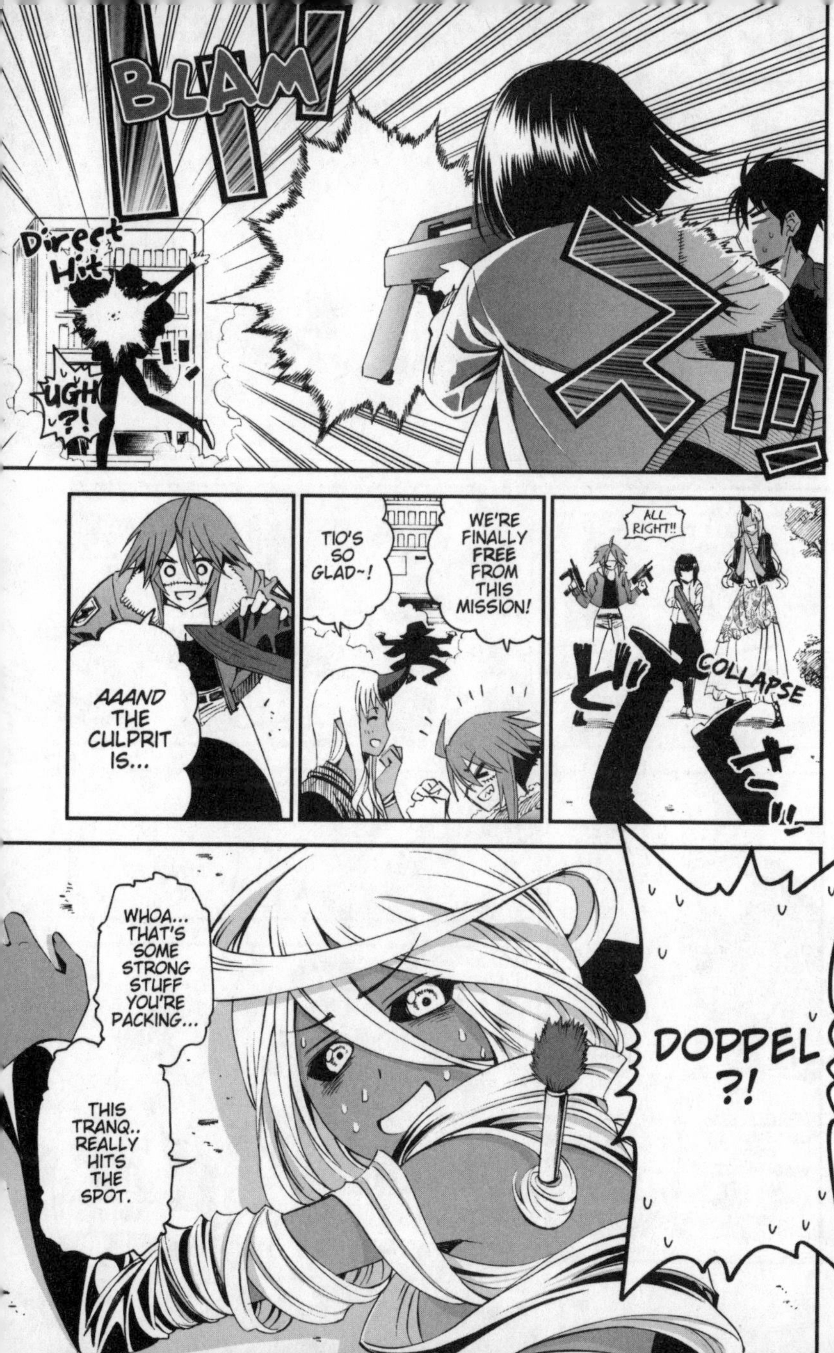
BLAM
Direct Hit
UGH?!
ALL RIGHT!!
COLLAPSE
WE'RE FINALLY FREE FROM THIS MISSION!
TIO'S SO GLAD~!
AAAND THE CULPRIT IS...
DOPPEL?!
WHOA... THAT'S SOME STRONG STUFF YOU'RE PACKING...
THIS TRANQ.. REALLY HITS THE SPOT.

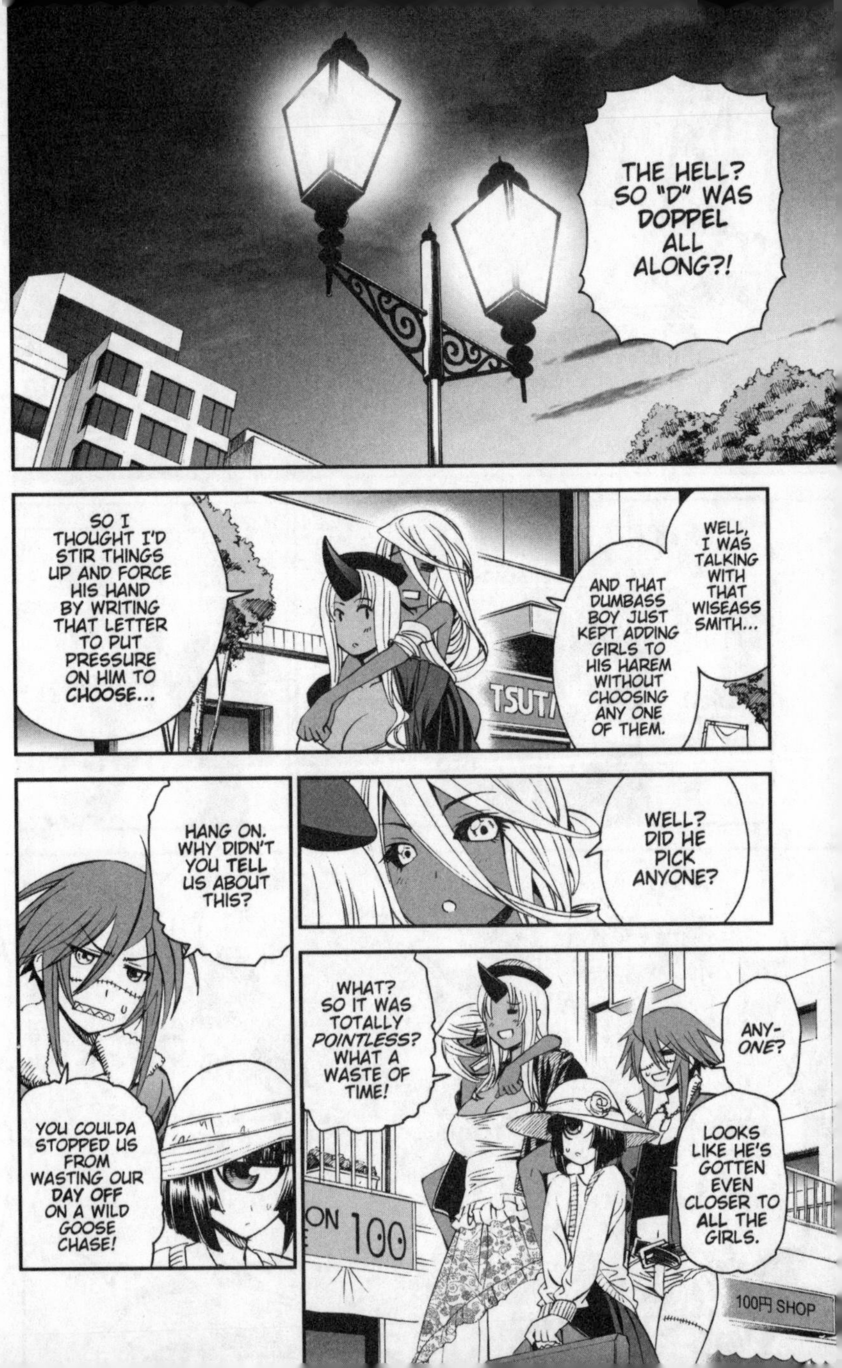
THE HELL? SO "D" WAS DOPPEL ALL ALONG?!
WELL, I WAS TALKING WITH THAT WISEASS SMITH...
AND THAT DUMBASS BOY JUST KEPT ADDING GIRLS TO HIS HAREM WITHOUT CHOOSING ANY ONE OF THEM.
SO I THOUGHT I'D STIR THINGS UP AND FORCE HIS HAND BY WRITING THAT LETTER TO PUT PRESSURE ON HIM TO CHOOSE...
WELL? DID HE PICK ANYONE?
ANY-*ONE*?
LOOKS LIKE HE'S GOTTEN EVEN CLOSER TO ALL THE GIRLS.
WHAT? SO IT WAS TOTALLY *POINTLESS*? WHAT A WASTE OF TIME!
ON 100
100円 SHOP
HANG ON. WHY DIDN'T YOU TELL US ABOUT THIS?
YOU COULDA STOPPED US FROM WASTING OUR DAY OFF ON A WILD GOOSE CHASE!

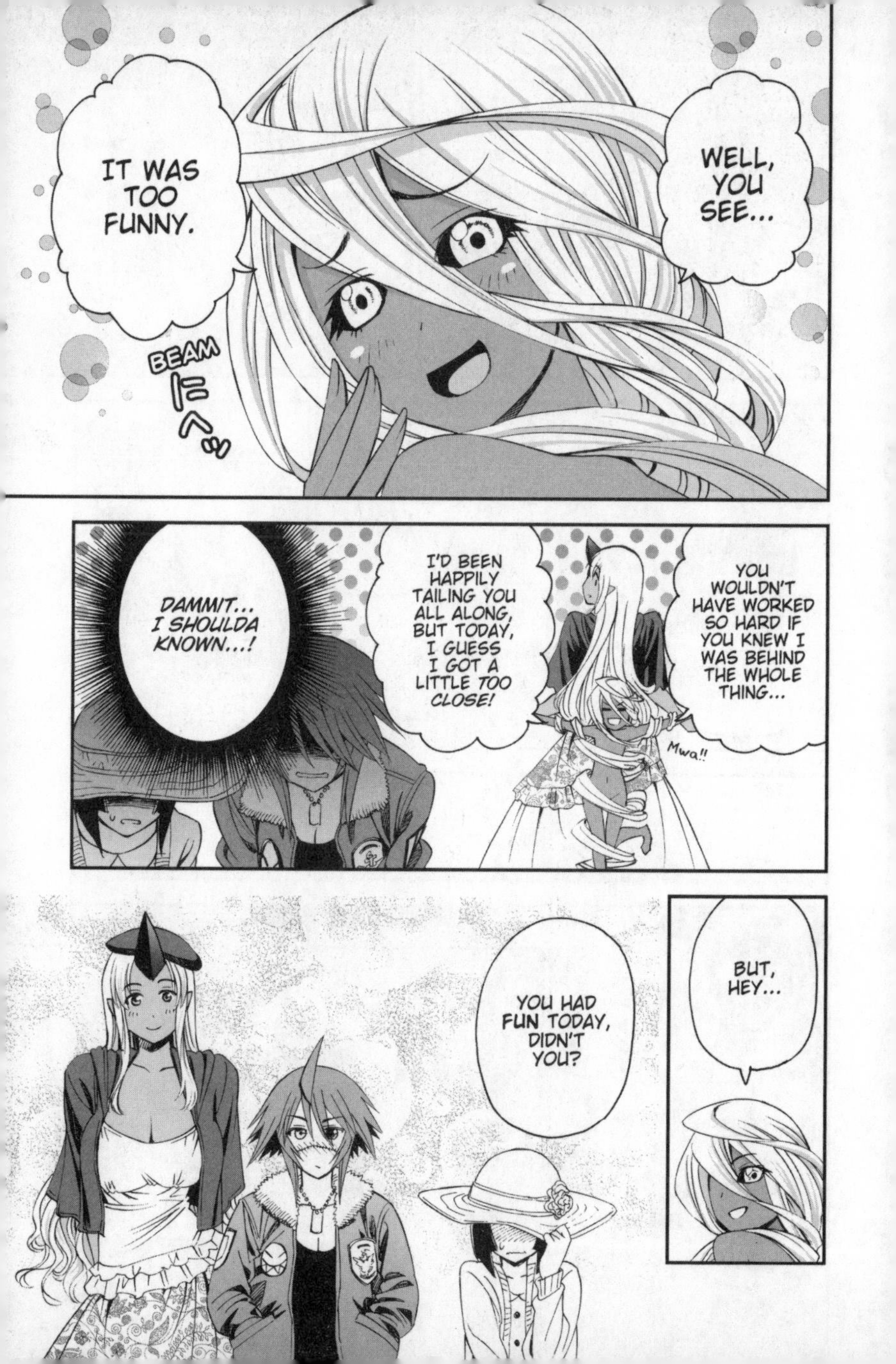
WELL, YOU SEE...
IT WAS TOO FUNNY.
BEAM
にへッ
YOU WOULDN'T HAVE WORKED SO HARD IF YOU KNEW I WAS BEHIND THE WHOLE THING...
Mwa!!
I'D BEEN HAPPILY TAILING YOU ALL ALONG, BUT TODAY, I GUESS I GOT A LITTLE *TOO* CLOSE!
DAMMIT... I SHOULDA KNOWN...!
BUT, HEY...
YOU HAD FUN TODAY, DIDN'T YOU?

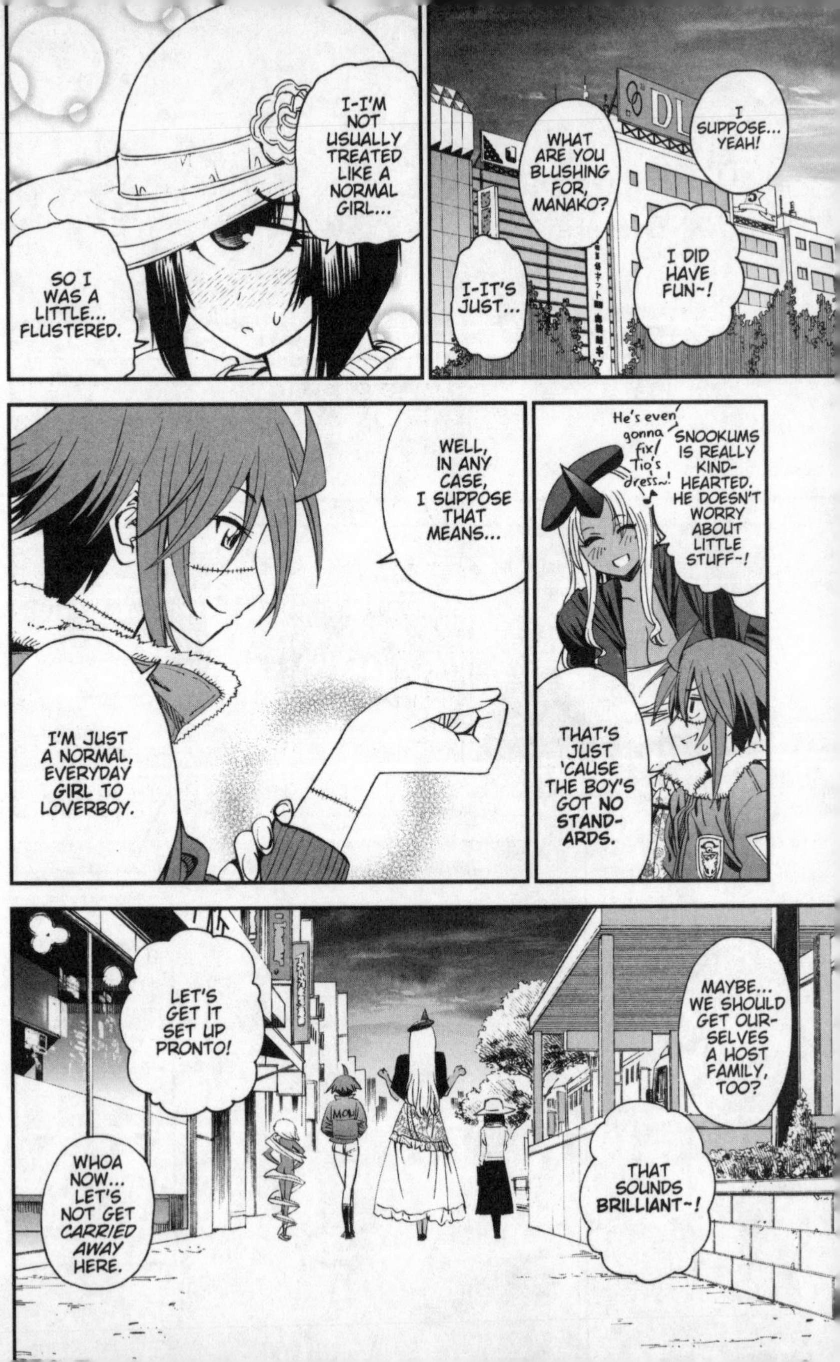
I SUPPOSE... YEAH!
I DID HAVE FUN~!
WHAT ARE YOU BLUSHING FOR, MANAKO?
I-IT'S JUST...
I-I'M NOT USUALLY TREATED LIKE A NORMAL GIRL...
SO I WAS A LITTLE... FLUSTERED.
SNOOKUMS IS REALLY KIND-HEARTED. HE DOESN'T WORRY ABOUT LITTLE STUFF~!
He's even gonna fix Tio's dress~!
THAT'S JUST 'CAUSE THE BOY'S GOT NO STANDARDS.
WELL, IN ANY CASE, I SUPPOSE THAT MEANS...
I'M JUST A NORMAL, EVERYDAY GIRL TO LOVERBOY.
MAYBE... WE SHOULD GET OURSELVES A HOST FAMILY, TOO?
THAT SOUNDS BRILLIANT~!
LET'S GET IT SET UP PRONTO!
WHOA NOW... LET'S NOT GET CARRIED AWAY HERE.

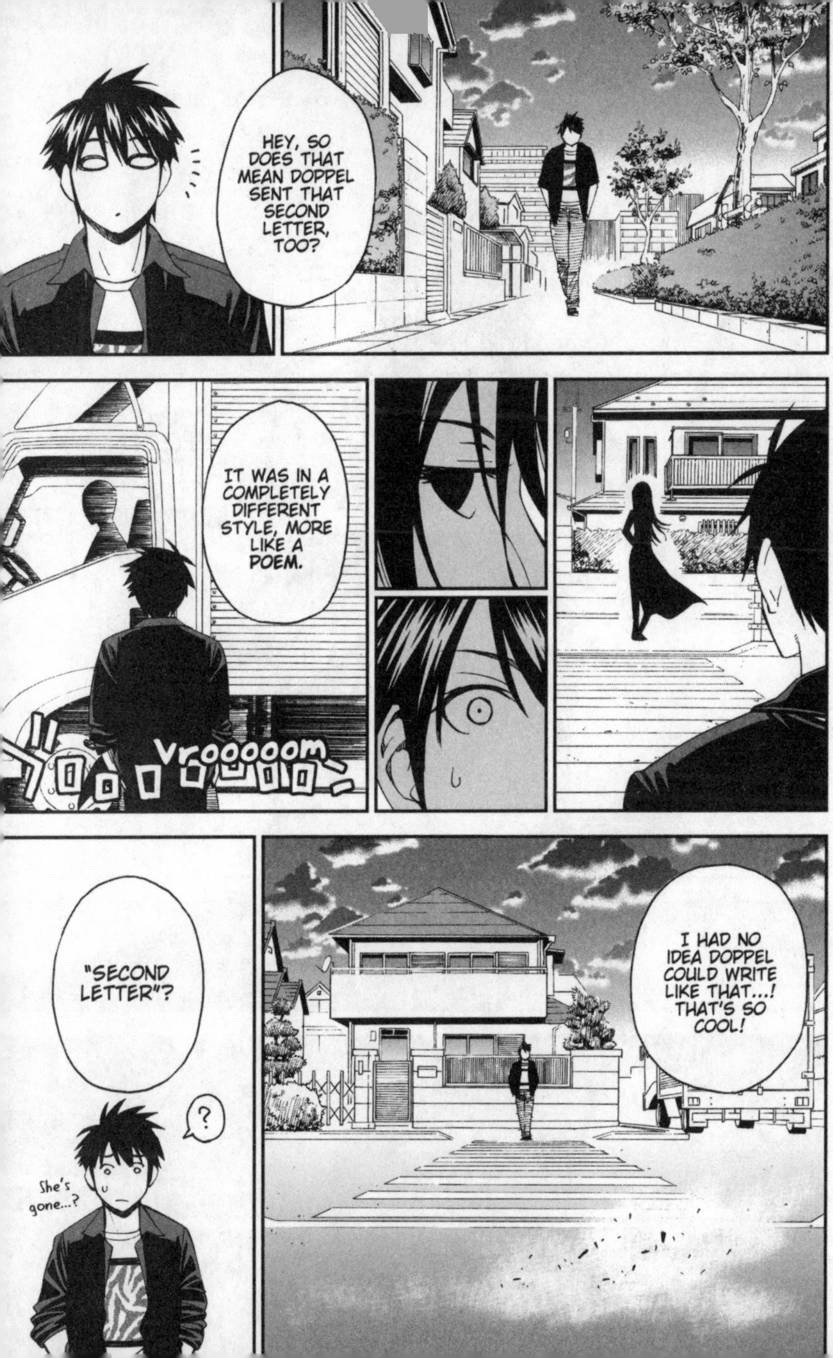
HEY, SO DOES THAT MEAN DOPPEL SENT THAT SECOND LETTER, TOO?
IT WAS IN A COMPLETELY DIFFERENT STYLE, MORE LIKE A POEM.
vroooooom
I HAD NO IDEA DOPPEL COULD WRITE LIKE THAT...! THAT'S SO COOL!
"SECOND LETTER"?
?
She's gone...?

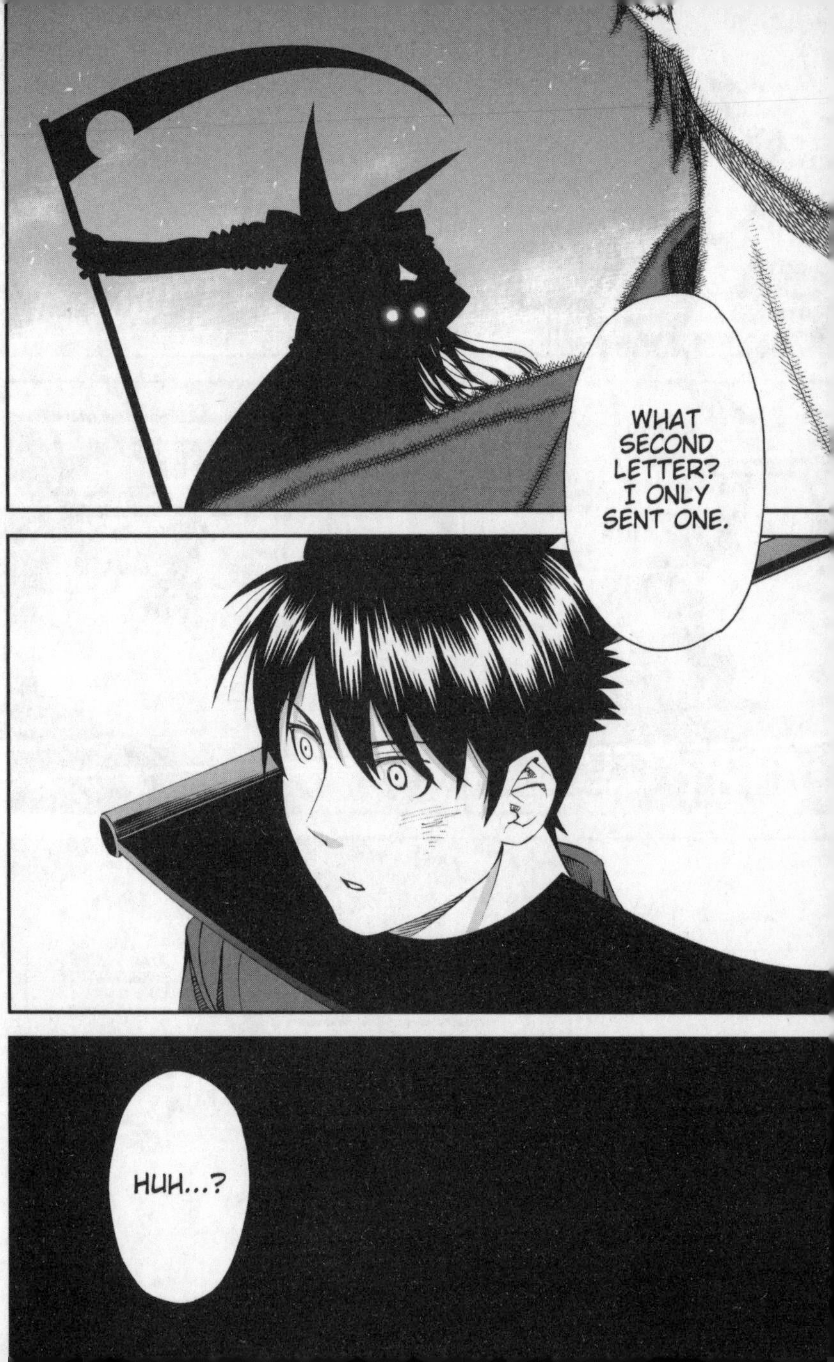
WHAT SECOND LETTER? I ONLY SENT ONE.
HUH...?

Monster Musume

Everyday Life with Monster Girls

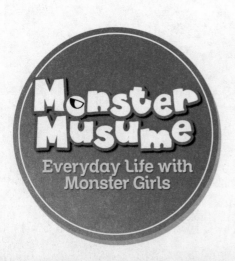

Polt's Kobold Konfessions

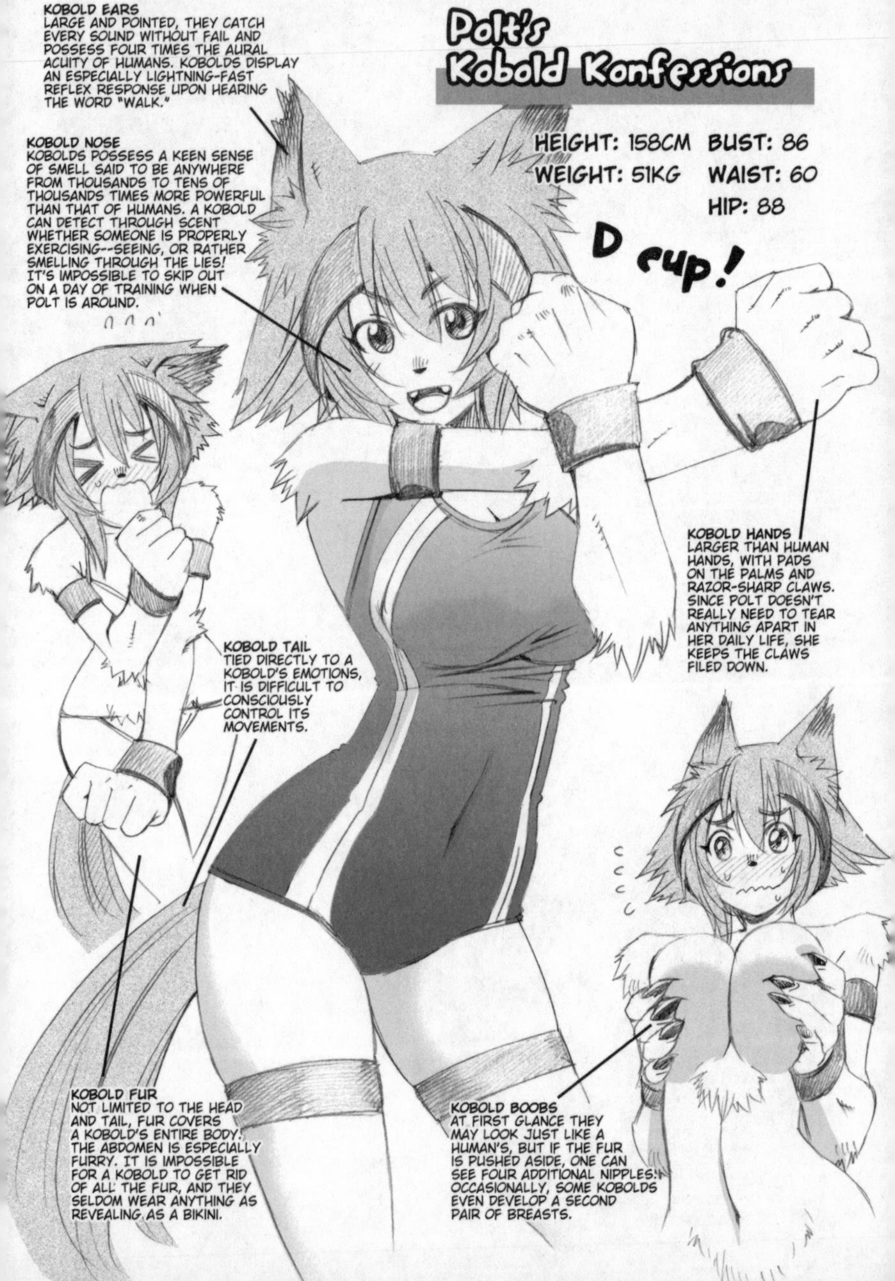
HEIGHT: 158CM BUST: 86
WEIGHT: 51KG WAIST: 60
HIP: 88
D cup!
KOBOLD EARS
LARGE AND POINTED, THEY CATCH EVERY SOUND WITHOUT FAIL AND POSSESS FOUR TIMES THE AURAL ACUITY OF HUMANS. KOBOLDS DISPLAY AN ESPECIALLY LIGHTNING-FAST REFLEX RESPONSE UPON HEARING THE WORD "WALK."
KOBOLD NOSE
KOBOLDS POSSESS A KEEN SENSE OF SMELL SAID TO BE ANYWHERE FROM THOUSANDS TO TENS OF THOUSANDS TIMES MORE POWERFUL THAN THAT OF HUMANS. A KOBOLD CAN DETECT THROUGH SCENT WHETHER SOMEONE IS PROPERLY EXERCISING--SEEING, OR RATHER SMELLING THROUGH THE LIES! IT'S IMPOSSIBLE TO SKIP OUT ON A DAY OF TRAINING WHEN POLT IS AROUND.
KOBOLD HANDS
LARGER THAN HUMAN HANDS, WITH PADS ON THE PALMS AND RAZOR-SHARP CLAWS. SINCE POLT DOESN'T REALLY NEED TO TEAR ANYTHING APART IN HER DAILY LIFE, SHE KEEPS THE CLAWS FILED DOWN.
KOBOLD TAIL
TIED DIRECTLY TO A KOBOLD'S EMOTIONS, IT IS DIFFICULT TO CONSCIOUSLY CONTROL ITS MOVEMENTS.
KOBOLD FUR
NOT LIMITED TO THE HEAD AND TAIL, FUR COVERS A KOBOLD'S ENTIRE BODY. THE ABDOMEN IS ESPECIALLY FURRY. IT IS IMPOSSIBLE FOR A KOBOLD TO GET RID OF ALL THE FUR, AND THEY SELDOM WEAR ANYTHING AS REVEALING AS A BIKINI.
KOBOLD BOOBS
AT FIRST GLANCE THEY MAY LOOK JUST LIKE A HUMAN'S, BUT IF THE FUR IS PUSHED ASIDE, ONE CAN SEE FOUR ADDITIONAL NIPPLES. OCCASIONALLY, SOME KOBOLDS EVEN DEVELOP A SECOND PAIR OF BREASTS.

Discover Drago the Dragonet

HEIGHT: 163CM BUST: 90

WEIGHT: 55KG WAIST: 59

HIP: 85

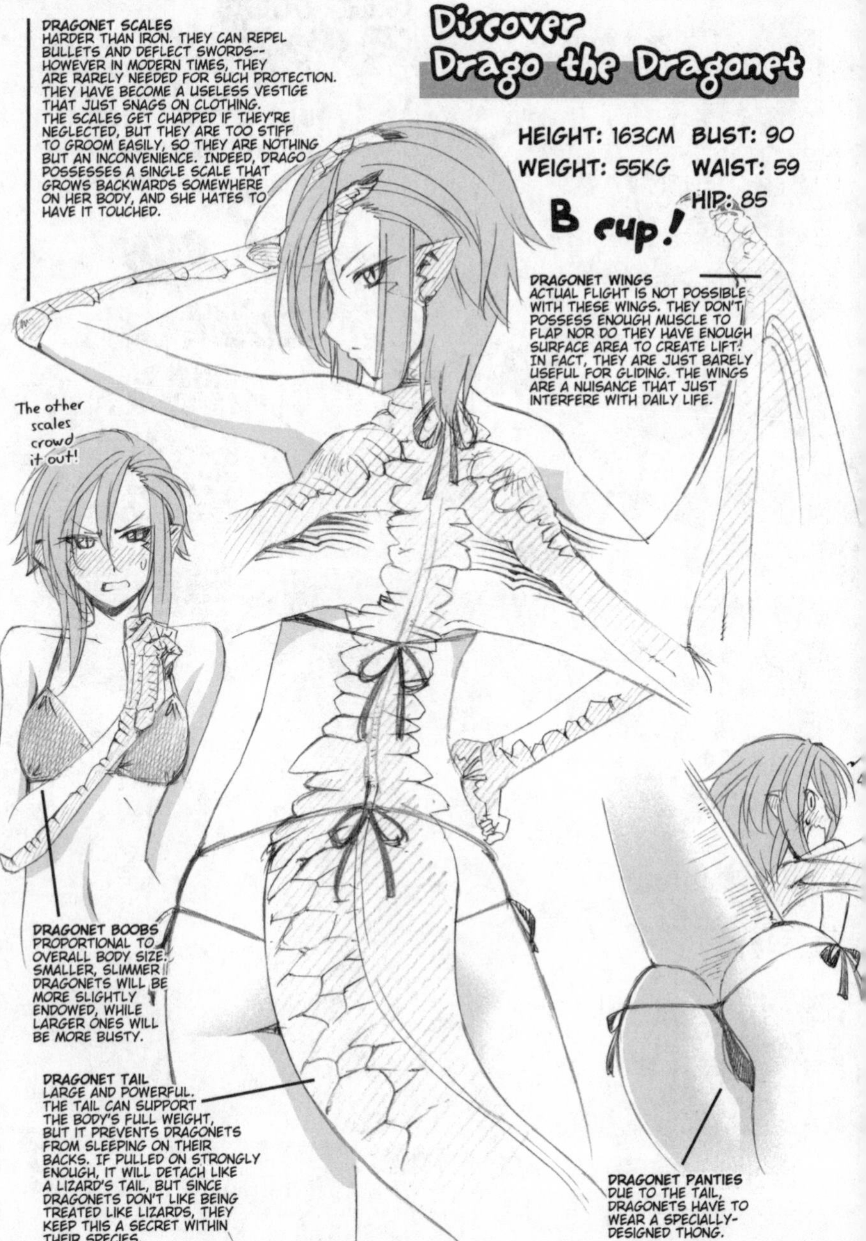

B cup!
DRAGONET SCALES
HARDER THAN IRON. THEY CAN REPEL BULLETS AND DEFLECT SWORDS--HOWEVER IN MODERN TIMES, THEY ARE RARELY NEEDED FOR SUCH PROTECTION. THEY HAVE BECOME A USELESS VESTIGE THAT JUST SNAGS ON CLOTHING. THE SCALES GET CHAPPED IF THEY'RE NEGLECTED, BUT THEY ARE TOO STIFF TO GROOM EASILY, SO THEY ARE NOTHING BUT AN INCONVENIENCE. INDEED, DRAGO POSSESSES A SINGLE SCALE THAT GROWS BACKWARDS SOMEWHERE ON HER BODY, AND SHE HATES TO HAVE IT TOUCHED.
DRAGONET WINGS
ACTUAL FLIGHT IS NOT POSSIBLE WITH THESE WINGS. THEY DON'T POSSESS ENOUGH MUSCLE TO FLAP NOR DO THEY HAVE ENOUGH SURFACE AREA TO CREATE LIFT. IN FACT, THEY ARE JUST BARELY USEFUL FOR GLIDING. THE WINGS ARE A NUISANCE THAT JUST INTERFERE WITH DAILY LIFE.
The other scales crowd it out!
DRAGONET BOOBS
PROPORTIONAL TO OVERALL BODY SIZE. SMALLER, SLIMMER DRAGONETS WILL BE MORE SLIGHTLY ENDOWED, WHILE LARGER ONES WILL BE MORE BUSTY.
DRAGONET TAIL
LARGE AND POWERFUL. THE TAIL CAN SUPPORT THE BODY'S FULL WEIGHT, BUT IT PREVENTS DRAGONETS FROM SLEEPING ON THEIR BACKS. IF PULLED ON STRONGLY ENOUGH, IT WILL DETACH LIKE A LIZARD'S TAIL, BUT SINCE DRAGONETS DON'T LIKE BEING TREATED LIKE LIZARDS, THEY KEEP THIS A SECRET WITHIN THEIR SPECIES.
DRAGONET PANTIES
DUE TO THE TAIL, DRAGONETS HAVE TO WEAR A SPECIALLY-DESIGNED THONG.

Concerning Kii the Dryad

HEIGHT: ??CM BUST: ?
WEIGHT: ??KG WAIST: ??
HIP: ??

? cup

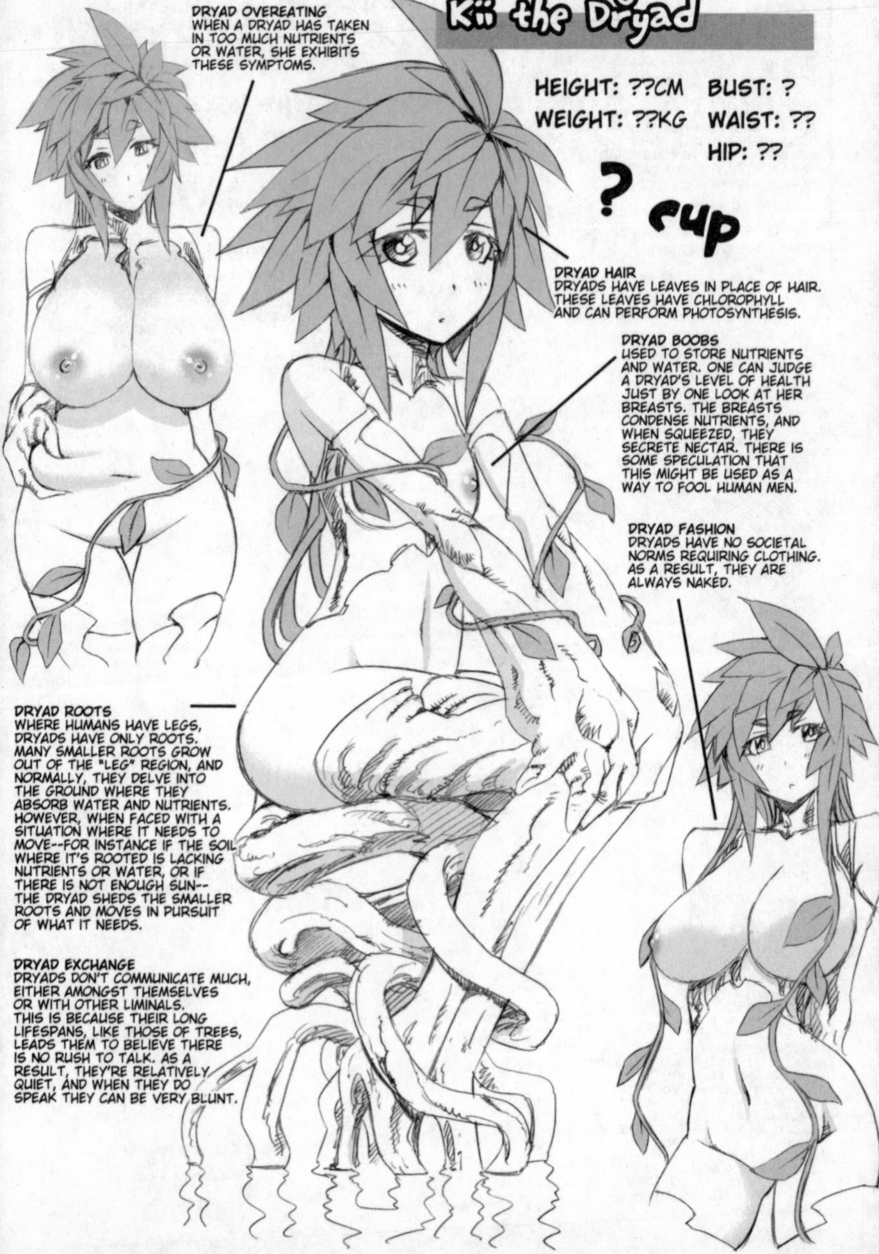

DRYAD OVEREATING
WHEN A DRYAD HAS TAKEN IN TOO MUCH NUTRIENTS OR WATER, SHE EXHIBITS THESE SYMPTOMS.

DRYAD HAIR
DRYADS HAVE LEAVES IN PLACE OF HAIR. THESE LEAVES HAVE CHLOROPHYLL AND CAN PERFORM PHOTOSYNTHESIS.

DRYAD BOOBS
USED TO STORE NUTRIENTS AND WATER. ONE CAN JUDGE A DRYAD'S LEVEL OF HEALTH JUST BY ONE LOOK AT HER BREASTS. THE BREASTS CONDENSE NUTRIENTS, AND WHEN SQUEEZED, THEY SECRETE NECTAR. THERE IS SOME SPECULATION THAT THIS MIGHT BE USED AS A WAY TO FOOL HUMAN MEN.

DRYAD FASHION
DRYADS HAVE NO SOCIETAL NORMS REQUIRING CLOTHING. AS A RESULT, THEY ARE ALWAYS NAKED.

DRYAD ROOTS
WHERE HUMANS HAVE LEGS, DRYADS HAVE ONLY ROOTS. MANY SMALLER ROOTS GROW OUT OF THE "LEG" REGION, AND NORMALLY, THEY DELVE INTO THE GROUND WHERE THEY ABSORB WATER AND NUTRIENTS. HOWEVER, WHEN FACED WITH A SITUATION WHERE IT NEEDS TO MOVE--FOR INSTANCE IF THE SOIL WHERE IT'S ROOTED IS LACKING NUTRIENTS OR WATER, OR IF THERE IS NOT ENOUGH SUN--THE DRYAD SHEDS THE SMALLER ROOTS AND MOVES IN PURSUIT OF WHAT IT NEEDS.

DRYAD EXCHANGE
DRYADS DON'T COMMUNICATE MUCH, EITHER AMONGST THEMSELVES OR WITH OTHER LIMINALS. THIS IS BECAUSE THEIR LONG LIFESPANS, LIKE THOSE OF TREES, LEADS THEM TO BELIEVE THERE IS NO RUSH TO TALK. AS A RESULT, THEY'RE RELATIVELY QUIET, AND WHEN THEY DO SPEAK THEY CAN BE VERY BLUNT.

Learn about Lilith the Devil

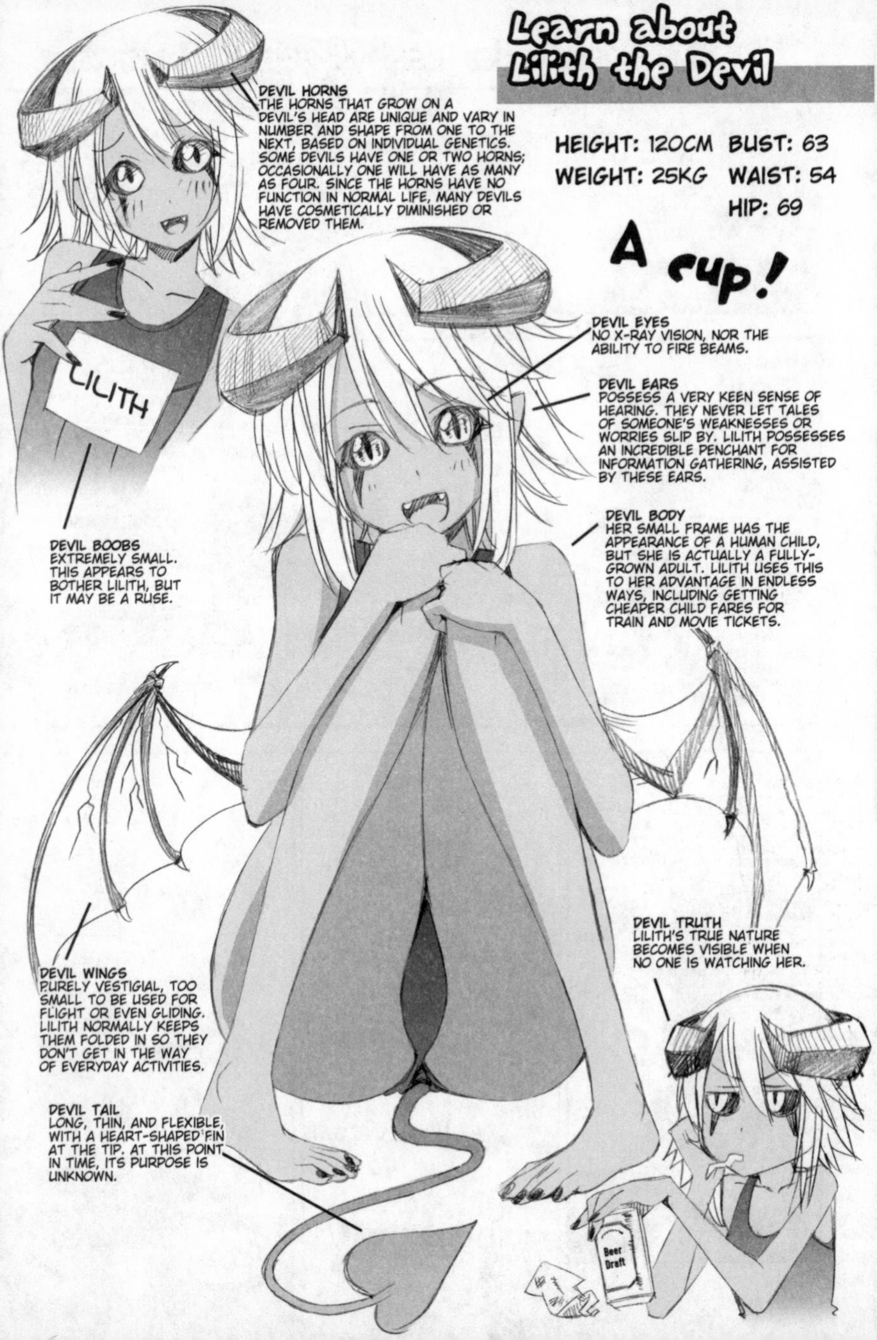
HEIGHT: 120CM BUST: 63
WEIGHT: 25KG WAIST: 54
HIP: 69
A cup!
DEVIL HORNS
THE HORNS THAT GROW ON A DEVIL'S HEAD ARE UNIQUE AND VARY IN NUMBER AND SHAPE FROM ONE TO THE NEXT, BASED ON INDIVIDUAL GENETICS. SOME DEVILS HAVE ONE OR TWO HORNS; OCCASIONALLY ONE WILL HAVE AS MANY AS FOUR. SINCE THE HORNS HAVE NO FUNCTION IN NORMAL LIFE, MANY DEVILS HAVE COSMETICALLY DIMINISHED OR REMOVED THEM.
LILITH
DEVIL EYES
NO X-RAY VISION, NOR THE ABILITY TO FIRE BEAMS.
DEVIL EARS
POSSESS A VERY KEEN SENSE OF HEARING. THEY NEVER LET TALES OF SOMEONE'S WEAKNESSES OR WORRIES SLIP BY. LILITH POSSESSES AN INCREDIBLE PENCHANT FOR INFORMATION GATHERING, ASSISTED BY THESE EARS.
DEVIL BODY
HER SMALL FRAME HAS THE APPEARANCE OF A HUMAN CHILD, BUT SHE IS ACTUALLY A FULLY-GROWN ADULT. LILITH USES THIS TO HER ADVANTAGE IN ENDLESS WAYS, INCLUDING GETTING CHEAPER CHILD FARES FOR TRAIN AND MOVIE TICKETS.
DEVIL BOOBS
EXTREMELY SMALL. THIS APPEARS TO BOTHER LILITH, BUT IT MAY BE A RUSE.
DEVIL TRUTH
LILITH'S TRUE NATURE BECOMES VISIBLE WHEN NO ONE IS WATCHING HER.
DEVIL WINGS
PURELY VESTIGIAL, TOO SMALL TO BE USED FOR FLIGHT OR EVEN GLIDING. LILITH NORMALLY KEEPS THEM FOLDED IN SO THEY DON'T GET IN THE WAY OF EVERYDAY ACTIVITIES.
DEVIL TAIL
LONG, THIN, AND FLEXIBLE, WITH A HEART-SHAPED FIN AT THE TIP. AT THIS POINT IN TIME, ITS PURPOSE IS UNKNOWN.
Beer Draft

The Penalty for Unaccompanied Excursions

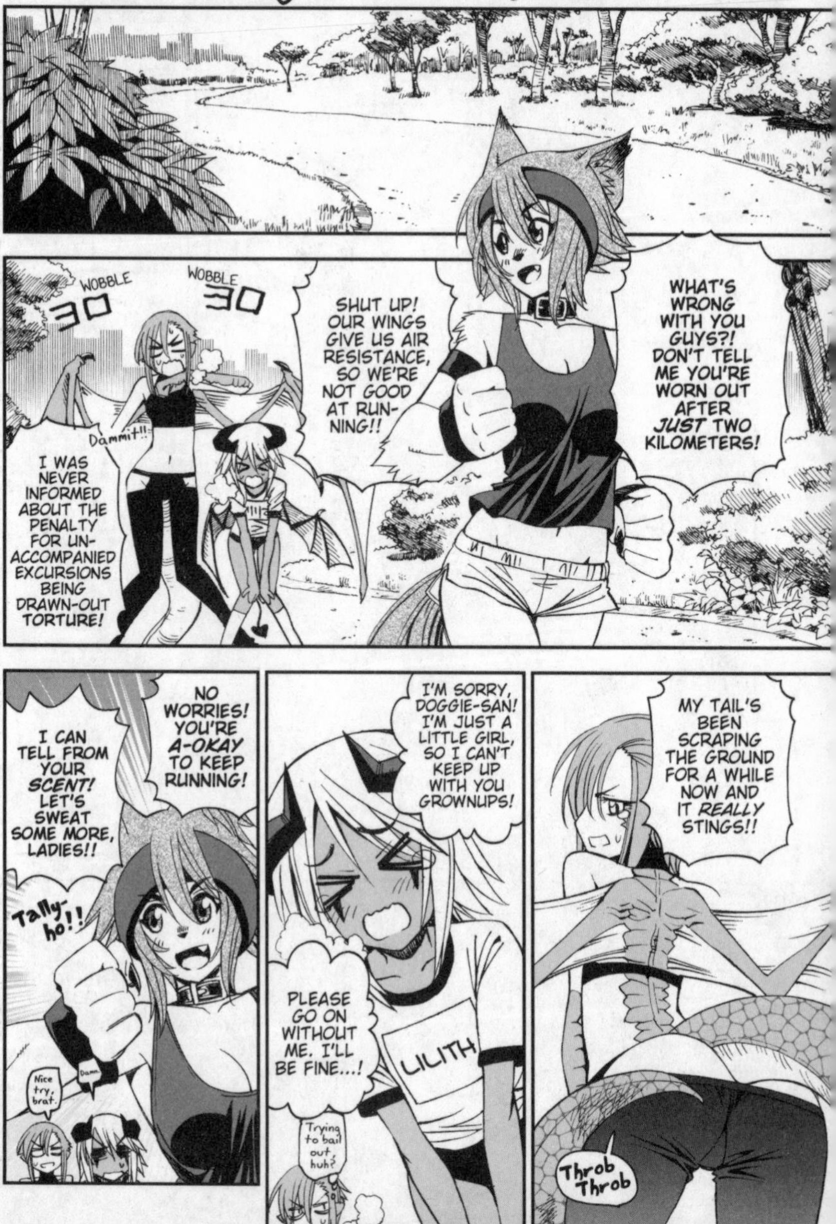
WHAT'S WRONG WITH YOU GUYS?! DON'T TELL ME YOU'RE WORN OUT AFTER *JUST* TWO KILOMETERS!
SHUT UP! OUR WINGS GIVE US AIR RESISTANCE, SO WE'RE NOT GOOD AT RUN-NING!!
WOBBLE
WOBBLE
Dammit!!
I WAS NEVER INFORMED ABOUT THE PENALTY FOR UN-ACCOMPANIED EXCURSIONS BEING DRAWN-OUT TORTURE!
MY TAIL'S BEEN SCRAPING THE GROUND FOR A WHILE NOW AND IT *REALLY* STINGS!!
Throb Throb
I'M SORRY, DOGGIE-SAN! I'M JUST A LITTLE GIRL, SO I CAN'T KEEP UP WITH YOU GROWNUPS!
PLEASE GO ON WITHOUT ME. I'LL BE FINE...!
LILITH
Trying to bail out, huh?
NO WORRIES! YOU'RE *A-OKAY* TO KEEP RUNNING!
I CAN TELL FROM YOUR *SCENT*! LET'S SWEAT SOME MORE, LADIES!!
Tally-ho!!
Damn...
Nice try, brat.

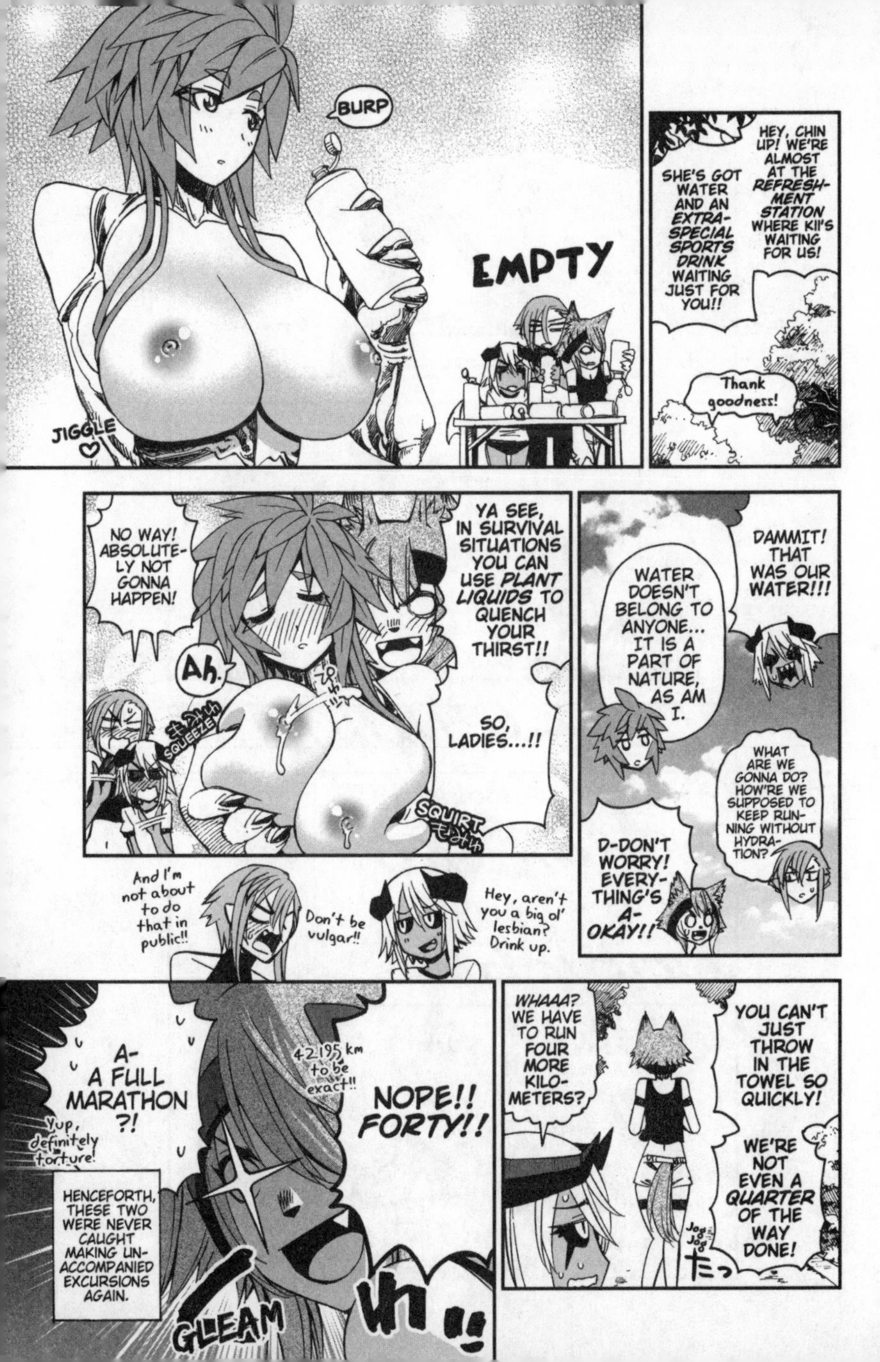
HEY, CHIN UP! WE'RE ALMOST AT THE *REFRESHMENT STATION* WHERE KII'S WAITING FOR US!
SHE'S GOT WATER AND AN *EXTRA-SPECIAL SPORTS DRINK* WAITING JUST FOR YOU!!
Thank goodness!
BURP
EMPTY
JIGGLE ♡
DAMMIT! THAT WAS OUR WATER!!!
WATER DOESN'T BELONG TO ANYONE... IT IS A PART OF NATURE, AS AM I.
WHAT ARE WE GONNA DO? HOW'RE WE SUPPOSED TO KEEP RUNNING WITHOUT HYDRATION?
D-DON'T WORRY! EVERYTHING'S A-OKAY!!
YA SEE, IN SURVIVAL SITUATIONS YOU CAN USE *PLANT LIQUIDS* TO QUENCH YOUR THIRST!!
NO WAY! ABSOLUTELY NOT GONNA HAPPEN!
Ah.
SQUEEZE
SO, LADIES...!!
SQUIRT
Hey, aren't you a big ol' lesbian? Drink up.
Don't be vulgar!!
And I'm not about to do that in public!!
WHAAA? WE HAVE TO RUN FOUR MORE KILOMETERS?
YOU CAN'T JUST THROW IN THE TOWEL SO QUICKLY!
WE'RE NOT EVEN A *QUARTER* OF THE WAY DONE!
Jog Jog
A- A FULL MARATHON ?!
42.195 km to be exact!!
NOPE!! *FORTY!!*
Yup, definitely torture!
HENCEFORTH, THESE TWO WERE NEVER CAUGHT MAKING UNACCOMPANIED EXCURSIONS AGAIN.
GLEAM

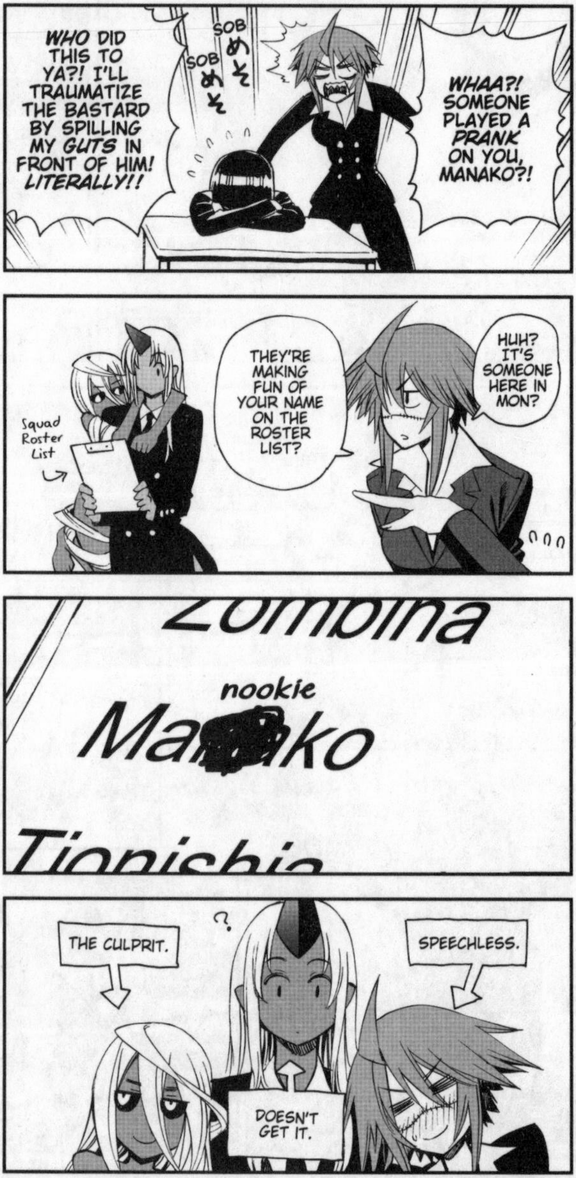
WHAA?! SOMEONE PLAYED A PRANK ON YOU, MANAKO?!
SOB めそ
SOB めそ
WHO DID THIS TO YA?! I'LL TRAUMATIZE THE BASTARD BY SPILLING MY GUTS IN FRONT OF HIM! LITERALLY!!
HUH? IT'S SOMEONE HERE IN MON?
THEY'RE MAKING FUN OF YOUR NAME ON THE ROSTER LIST?
Squad Roster List
Zombina
nookie
Ma[redacted]ko
Tionishia
SPEECHLESS.
THE CULPRIT.
DOESN'T GET IT.

Diagram! (Manako's) FOLDING RIFLE

A PROTOTYPE MADE TO MEET THE GROWING NEED FOR A CONVENIENT, PORTABLE, HIGH-FIREPOWER GUN TO BE USED IN RESPONSE TO ANY LIMINAL-RELATED CASE THAT MIGHT ARISE UNEXPECTEDLY.

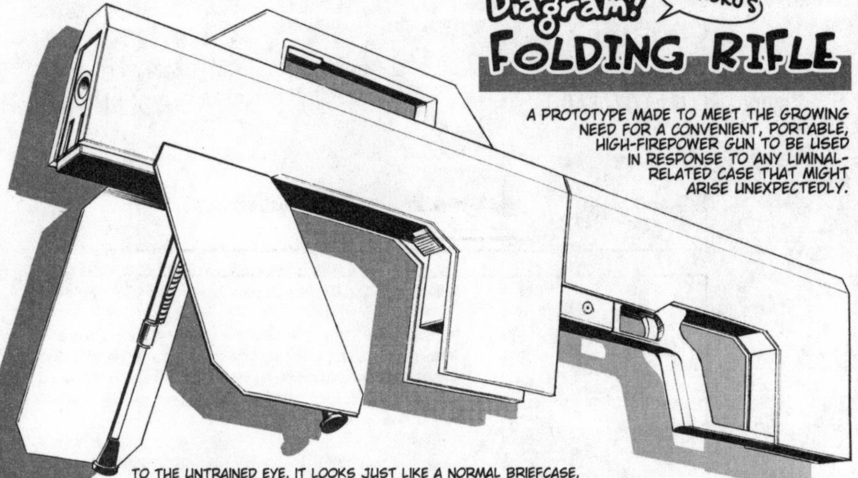

TO THE UNTRAINED EYE, IT LOOKS JUST LIKE A NORMAL BRIEFCASE, BUT AT THE PRESS OF A SWITCH, IT TRANSFORMS QUICKLY INTO A SNIPER RIFLE.

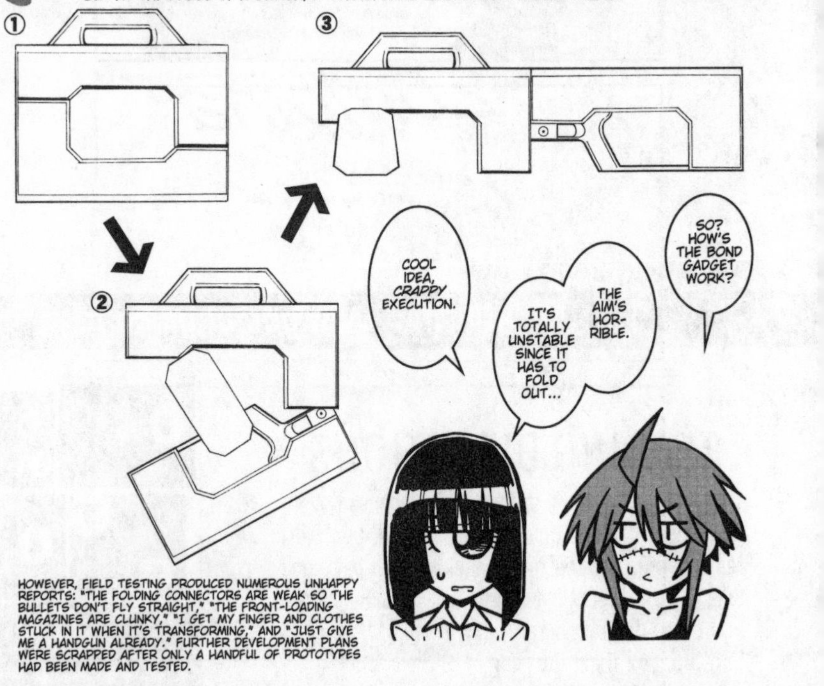
①
②
③
SO? HOW'S THE BOND GADGET WORK?
THE AIM'S HORRIBLE.
IT'S TOTALLY UNSTABLE SINCE IT HAS TO FOLD OUT...
COOL IDEA, CRAPPY EXECUTION.

HOWEVER, FIELD TESTING PRODUCED NUMEROUS UNHAPPY REPORTS: "THE FOLDING CONNECTORS ARE WEAK SO THE BULLETS DON'T FLY STRAIGHT," "THE FRONT-LOADING MAGAZINES ARE CLUNKY," "I GET MY FINGER AND CLOTHES STUCK IN IT WHEN IT'S TRANSFORMING," AND "JUST GIVE ME A HANDGUN ALREADY." FURTHER DEVELOPMENT PLANS WERE SCRAPPED AFTER ONLY A HANDFUL OF PROTOTYPES HAD BEEN MADE AND TESTED.

SEVEN SEAS ENTERTAINMENT PRESENTS

Monster Musume

story and art by **OKAYADO**

VOLUME 5

TRANSLATION
Ryan Peterson

ADAPTATION
Shanti Whitesides

LETTERING AND LAYOUT
Ma. Victoria Robado

LOGO DESIGN
Courtney Williams

COVER DESIGN
Nicky Lim

PROOFREADER
Janet Houck
Lee Otter

MANAGING EDITOR
Adam Arnold

PUBLISHER
Jason DeAngelis

MONSTER MUSUME NO IRU NICHIJO VOLUME 5

Originally published in Japan in 2014 by TOKUMA SHOTEN PUBLISHING CO., LTD., Tokyo. English translation rights arranged with TOKUMA SHOTEN PUBLISHING CO., LTD., Tokyo, through TOHAN CORPORATION, Tokyo.

ISBN: 978-1-626921-06-1

Printed in Canada

First Printing: November 2014

10 9 8 7 6 5 4 3 2 1

FOLLOW US ONLINE: ***www.gomanga.com***

READING DIRECTIONS

This book reads from ***right to left***, Japanese style. If this is your first time reading manga, you start reading from the top right panel on each page and take it from there. If you get lost, just follow the numbered diagram here. It may seem backwards at first, but you'll get the hang of it! Have fun!!

1
2
3
4
5
6
7
8
9

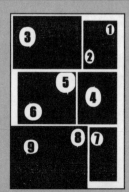